More on Nolo.com

...s companion page at:

www.nolo.com/back-of-book/PUBL.html

When there's an important change to the law affecting this book, we'll post updates. You'll also find articles and other related materials.

More Resources from Nolo.com

Legal Forms, Books, & Software
Hundreds of do-it-yourself products—all written in plain English, approved, and updated by our in-house legal editors.

Legal Articles
Get informed with thousands of free articles on everyday legal topics. Our articles are accurate, up to date, and reader friendly.

Find a Lawyer
Want to talk to a lawyer? Use Nolo to find a lawyer who can help you with your case.

NOLO
LAW for ALL

9th Edition

The
Public Domain

Find and Use Free Content for Your Website, Book, App, Music, Video, Art, and More

Stephen Fishman, J.D.

Ninth Edition	JUNE 2020
Editor	ELIZABETH GJELTEN
Book Design	SUSAN PUTNEY
Proofreading	IRENE BARNARD
Index	JULIE SHAWVAN
Printing	BANG PRINTING

ISSN: 2326-5965 (print)
ISSN: 2328-9325 (online)
ISBN: 978-1-4133-2756-4 (pbk)
ISBN: 978-1-4133-2757-1 (ebook)

This book covers only United States law, unless it specifically states otherwise.

Please note

We know that accurate, plain-English legal information can help you solve many of your own legal problems. But this text is not a substitute for personalized advice from a knowledgeable lawyer. If you want the help of a trained professional—and we'll always point out situations in which we think that's a good idea—consult an attorney licensed to practice in your state.

Acknowledgments

Many thanks to all the folks at Nolo for their outstanding work, including Marcia Stewart, Susan Putney, Richard Stim, Elizabeth Gjelten, Irene Barnard, and Bob Wells.

Thanks also to the following people who generously contributed advice and/or information:

- Professor Emmy Werner
- Roger A. Sayles
- Eric Eldred, and
- Lynn Nagrani and all the other people at the Public Domain Information Project.

Finally, special thanks to Stanley Jacobsen, without whose indefatigable research assistance this book would never have been completed.

About the Author

Stephen Fishman is a Washington-based attorney and author of 20 books (many available at Nolo.com) and hundreds of articles, all focused on making the law understandable to nonlawyers. Among his books are the bestsellers, *The Copyright Handbook* and *Working for Yourself*. His website is: www.fishmanlawandtaxfiles.com.

Table of Contents

Your Map to the Public Domain Treasure Trove 1

1 Introduction to the Public Domain 3

What Is the Public Domain? 4

Dealing With Public Domain Gray Areas 12

What If Someone Challenges Your Public Domain Claim? 15

Documenting Your Use of Public Domain Materials 17

2 The Use and Abuse of Copyright 19

What Copyright Protects 20

The Looting of the Public Domain 26

3 Writings 33

What Can You Do With Public Domain Writings? 34

Determining Copyright Status of Written Works 38

Is the Work Eligible for Copyright Protection? 39

Has the Work Been Published? 59

Has the Work's Copyright Expired? 62

Is the Work in the Public Domain Due to Lack of a Copyright Notice? 63

Does a Copyright Trap Apply? 63

Misuse of Copyright Notices 74

Sources of Public Domain Writings 78

4 Music 79

The Difference Between Music and Sound Recordings 81

What Can You Do With Public Domain Sheet Music? 82

Has the Sheet Music Been Published? 86

Has the Copyright in the Music Expired? 93

Is the Music in the Public Domain Due to Lack of a Copyright Notice?..........93

Is It a Derivative Work?...94

Is It an Arrangement or Adaptation?...95

Is the Music a Collective Work? 106

Does the Music Have Public Domain Elements?..109

Sources of Public Domain Sheet Music..111

Sound Recordings...112

5   Art 119

Part I: Original Works of Art..121

What Good Is Public Domain Art?...121

Deciding If Original Art Is in the Public Domain..124

Has the Art Been Published? 125

Has the Copyright in the Art Expired?...129

Is the Art in the Public Domain Due to Lack of a Copyright Notice? 129

Is the Artwork Eligible for Copyright Protection?......................................130

Do You Intend to Use the Art in Advertising or on Merchandise?................138

Is the Art Protected by a Design Patent?..139

Sources of Original Art..140

Part II: Art Reproductions...140

Is the Original Work of Art in the Public Domain?.....................................141

Has the Reproduction Been Published?..141

Has the Copyright in the Reproduction Expired? 142

Is the Reproduction in the Public Domain Due to Lack
of a Copyright Notice?...142

Does the Reproduction Lack Originality?..142

Is the Reproduction Dedicated to the Public Domain?................................147

Will You Use the Reproduction in Advertising or on Merchandise?..............147

Are Elements of the Reproduction in the Public Domain?...........................148

Sources of Art Reproductions...148

6 Photography 149

What Good Are Public Domain Photographs? 150

Deciding Whether Photographs Are in the Public Domain 150

Sources of Public Domain Photographs 161

7 Movies and Television 163

Part I: Films 165

What Good Are Public Domain Films? 165

Has the Film Been Published? 166

Has the Copyright Expired? 168

Is the Film in the Public Domain Due to Lack of a Copyright Notice? 176

Is the Film Protected by Copyright? 176

Does the Film Contain Copyrighted Visual Art? 178

Do You Plan to Use the Film for Advertising or Other
    Commercial Purposes? 179

Part II: Television Programs 179

Has the Television Program's Copyright Expired? 180

Is the Television Program in the Public Domain Due to Lack
    of a Copyright Notice? 182

Is It a U.S. Government TV Program? 182

Video Dedicated to the Public Domain 182

Does the Program Contain Copyrighted Visual Art? 183

Will You Be Using Public Domain TV Programs for Advertising
    or Other Commercial Purposes? 183

Sources of Public Domain Films and TV Programs 184

8 Computer Software 185

Is the Software Dedicated to the Public Domain? 186

Was the Software Created by the U.S. Government? 190

Has the Copyright in the Software Expired? 191

Is the Software in the Public Domain Due to Lack of a Copyright Notice? 193

Sources of Public Domain Software 193

9 Architecture 195

What Good Is Public Domain Architecture? 196

Architectural Plans 197

Constructed Buildings 202

10 Maps 207

Has Copyright in the Map Expired? 208

Is the Map in the Public Domain Due to Lack of a Copyright Notice? 208

Was the Map Created by the U.S. Government? 209

Is the Map Eligible for Copyright Protection? 210

Are Elements of the Map in the Public Domain? 210

Sources of Public Domain Maps 212

11 Choreography 213

Deciding If Choreography Is in the Public Domain 214

Sources of Public Domain Choreography 217

12 Databases and Collections 219

Part I: Databases 221

Is the Work a Database? 222

Does the Database Lack Creativity? 225

Was the Database Created by the U.S. Government? 228

Has the Copyright in the Database Expired? 230

Is the Database in the Public Domain for Lack of a Copyright Notice? 231

Is the Database Protected by Means Other Than Copyright? 231

Part II: Collections of Public Domain Works 235

Are the Collected Materials in the Public Domain? 235

Does the Collection Lack Minimal Creativity? 238

Is It a De Minimis Collection? 239

Is It a U.S. Government Collection? 239

Has the Collection's Copyright Expired? 239

Is the Collection in the Public Domain for Lack of a Copyright Notice? 240

Is the Collection Protected by Means Other Than Copyright? 240

13 Titles 241

Titles of Copyrighted Works 242

Titles of Public Domain Works 246

Using Disclaimers to Avoid Public Confusion 248

Titles Used on Merchandise and Other Products 249

The First Amendment and Titles 249

14 Public Domain Elements in Copyright Writings 251

Ideas 252

Facts 256

Unprotected Elements in Works of Fiction 261

Unprotected Elements in Works of Fact 265

15 Copyrights Restored From Public Domain 271

The GATT Agreement 272

What Works Were Restored? 273

What Works Were Not Restored? 276

Who Owns Restored Works? 278

Copyright Infringement of Restored Works 278

16 The Public Domain Outside the United States 283

Introduction 284

Copyright Duration in Other Countries 287

The Rule of the Shorter Term 294

Researching Foreign Copyright Laws 297

17 The Internet and the Public Domain 299

Two Preliminary Rules 300

Internet Content in the Public Domain 301

Potential Problems Using Public Domain Materials on the Internet 307

Hyperlinks and the Public Domain 312

Copyright and the Internet's Global Dimension 313

18   Copyright Protection: How Long Does It Last? 315

Works First Published in the United States 316

Copyright Term for Unpublished Works 324

Works First Published Outside the United States 327

Sound Recordings 331

19   Copyright Notice Requirements 335

Copyright Notices and the Public Domain 336

Does the Work Lack a Valid Notice? 338

Is a Copyright Notice Required? 342

Is the Omission of a Valid Notice Excused? 347

What If You Make a Mistake? 352

20   Traps for the Unwary 355

Should You Worry About Trademark or Publicity Problems? 356

The Right of Publicity 357

Trademarks 362

21   Researching Copyright Office Records 371

Researching Copyright Renewal Records for Works Published
Before 1964 372

Researching Copyright Registration Records 387

22   What If a Work Is Not in the Public Domain? 389

Find Another Public Domain Work 390

Obtain Permission to Use the Work 390

Use the Work Without Permission on the Grounds of Fair Use 393

Index 405

Your Map to the Public Domain Treasure Trove

Are you a screenwriter looking for material to adapt; a theater company looking for plays to perform for free; a filmmaker looking for copyright-free footage; a publisher looking for royalty-free titles; a musician looking for inexpensive sheet music that you can freely reproduce; or the creator of a website looking for free material of all types? Then this book is for you.

There's a vast public domain treasure trove free for the taking—books, movies videos, artwork, photos, software, and more—but there's one catch. You have to know how to recognize it and find it.

That's where this book comes in. Part manual, and part map, this book explains the rules that surround the public domain. And using the materials in this book you'll be able to identify—with a little effort—creative works that you can use without permission. If you can find just one public domain work using this book, then it will have paid for itself.

How do you go about it? Start by reading Chapter 1 which provides a good introduction to the public domain and how to use it. Then review Chapter 2, which provides a useful overview of copyright law and the ways many creative people are using public domain materials (and how to avoid legal problems).

Next, read the chapter covering the particular type of work you're interested in. Separate chapters cover:

- writings of all types (Chapter 3)
- music (Chapter 4)
- art (Chapter 5)
- photography (Chapter 6)
- film and television (Chapter 7)
- computer software (Chapter 8)
- architecture (Chapter 9)
- maps (Chapter 10)
- choreography (Chapter 11)
- databases and collections (Chapter 12), and
- titles (Chapter 13).

You'll see that some legal rules are common to all types of creative works. These issues are dealt with in separate chapters. They include:

- works first published abroad (Chapter 15)
- how long copyright protection lasts (Chapter 18)

- where and how copyright notices must appear (Chapter 19), and
- legal problems involving trademarks and the right of publicity (Chapter 20).

It also may be necessary for you to research U.S. Copyright Office records to determine whether many works are in the public domain, particularly those published less than 95 years ago but before 1964. Chapter 21 explains how to do this research.

You should always keep in mind that all the chapters listed above deal only with the public domain in the United States. Many works that are in the public domain in the United States are still protected by copyright outside the United States and vice versa. The public domain outside the United States is covered in Chapter 16.

If you determine that the work you want to use is not in the public domain, you might still be able to use it without permission because of a legal exception to copyright law called "fair use." See Chapter 22 for a detailed discussion of your alternatives when a work is not in the public domain.

Get Updates and More on Nolo.com

When there are important changes to the information in this book, we'll post updates online, on a page dedicated to this book:

www.nolo.com/back-of-book/PUBL.html

You'll find other useful information there, too, including blogs and podcasts on intellectual property issues.

Introduction to the Public Domain

What Is the Public Domain? 4

    Copyright and the Public Domain 4

    What Is in the Public Domain? 5

    How Can You Use the Public Domain? 6

    Why Have a Public Domain? 6

    How Do You Know If a Work Is in the Public Domain? 10

    How Do You Find Public Domain Materials? 11

    Are Public Domain Works Always Free? 11

Dealing With Public Domain Gray Areas 12

    What Is the Likelihood of Discovery? 13

    How Valuable Is the Material? 14

What If Someone Challenges Your Public Domain Claim? 15

    Handling the Claim Yourself 15

    Hiring a Lawyer Experienced in Copyright Law 16

Documenting Your Use of Public Domain Materials 17

Are you a musician wanting to perform or record a song written by someone else? A documentary filmmaker who wants to include newsreels or combat footage? An author or website developer looking for photos or artwork to include in your latest project? A screenwriter hoping to adapt a novel or a play? If your answer to any of these questions is "yes," you could be in luck. The content you need may be free for the taking. It may lie in a land of creative riches known as the public domain. You just have to know how to recognize and find it. This book is a type of treasure map that shows you how.

What Is the Public Domain?

As used in this book, the words "public domain" mean creative works that for one reason or another are not protected by copyright law and are usually—but not always—free for all to use. There are literally billions of creative works—including books, artwork, photos, songs, movies, and more—in the public domain. All of these works, no matter what form they take, are called "works of authorship" or, more simply, "works."

Copyright and the Public Domain

To safely use public domain works, you must first know a little about copyright law, which is a federal law that protects all kinds of works of authorship including books, magazines, newspapers, and other writings, music, art and sculpture, photography, films and videos, choreography, architecture, computer software, and maps.

The owner of a work protected by copyright is given a bundle of exclusive rights, including:

- reproduction rights—that is, the right to make copies of a protected work
- distribution rights—that is, the right to sell or otherwise distribute copies to the public
- the right to create adaptations (also known as "derivative works")—that is, the right to prepare new works based on the protected work, and
- performance and display rights— that is, the right to perform a protected work in public, such as a stageplay, or display a work in public.

If someone wrongfully uses material covered by a copyright, the owner can sue to obtain compensation for any losses suffered. In this sense, a copyright is a type of property—it belongs to its owner, and the courts can be asked to punish anyone who uses it without permission.

However, copyright protection does not last forever, and some works are not entitled to any copyright protection at all. When a work enters the public domain for any reason, the rights listed above do not apply. In other words, the work can be freely copied, distributed, adapted, or performed or displayed in public without asking anyone's permission or paying a fee. For example, you don't need to obtain permission to copy and distribute a play by Shakespeare, adapt it into a movie, create an app based upon it, or perform it in public. That is because Shakespeare's plays were first published so long ago that copyright law does not protect them.

"Public domain" means what it says—public domain works belong to the public as a whole. Anyone is free to use them any way they wish. No one can ever obtain copyright protection for public domain material. Once a work enters the public domain it usually stays there forever. (See Chapter 2 for a more detailed discussion of copyright law.)

What Is in the Public Domain?

A work of authorship may be in the public domain for a variety of reasons. For example:

- the work was published before there was a copyright law
- the work's copyright protection expired
- copyright protection was lost or never acquired for some reason
- the copyright owner dedicated the work to the public domain, or
- the work was never entitled to copyright protection.

A vast treasure trove of creative works are in the public domain for one or more of these reasons. They include many great classics of world art and literature, such as the works of Shakespeare, Dickens, Bach, and Beethoven. But the public domain does not just include dusty old books and other works published hundreds of years ago.

All works published in the United States more than 95 years ago are in the public domain. But there are also millions of works published as recently as 1963 that are in the U.S. public domain. Indeed, copyright experts estimate that 85% of all the works of authorship published in the United States before 1964 are in the public domain. In addition, millions of more recent works have been dedicated to the public domain by their creators, often through the use of a Creative Commons CC0 license (www. creativecommons.org—see Chapter 17 for a detailed discussion of such licenses). Indeed, creators are dedicating new works to the public domain every day.

But the public domain does not end there. Even works published today with full copyright protection contain elements that are unprotected and, thus, in the public domain. This includes, for example, the facts and ideas contained in a work of nonfiction. Other newly published works are denied copyright protection completely, including U.S. government works and many blank forms.

How Can You Use the Public Domain?

The only limit on how you can use public domain materials is your own imagination. For example:

- Web and app developers can use the public domain as a free source of content, including writings, photography, artwork, and music
- creative writers can adapt public domain works into new works—for example, create screenplays based on public domain novels, stories, and plays
- musicians can perform and record public domain music without paying permission fees
- publishers can freely republish public domain works
- artists can freely copy public domain artworks
- filmmakers can freely use public domain footage, and
- librarians can copy public domain works for their collections.

Why Have a Public Domain?

At first glance, the concept of the public domain may seem unfair to creative people. After all, once a work enters the public domain, the author or his or her heirs can no longer collect royalties from sales of copies or otherwise profit from it. Why should this be?

The reason we have copyright laws is to encourage authors to create new works and thereby promote the progress of human knowledge. The encouragement takes the form of an economic incentive—authors are given a monopoly over the use of their works. By selling or licensing their rights they can earn a livelihood and create even more works. However, enriching authors is not the primary goal of copyright law. The primary goal is to foster the creation of new works that will one day enter the public domain where they can be freely used to enrich everyone's lives.

New Works Birthed From the Public Domain

New works are constantly being created from public domain materials, either directly or indirectly. Nothing is wholly original. Instead, "everything is a remix," copying, combining, and transforming preexisting works and ideas. There is even a blog and video series about this (see https://everythingisaremix.info).

Here are just a few examples of new works created from the public domain:

- the Broadway play *Natasha, Pierre & the Great Comet of 1812*, by Dave Malloy, an electro-pop adaptation of a section of the 1869 novel *War and Peace* by Leo Tolstoy

- the Disney film *Frozen*, based on the Hans Christian Andersen story *The Ice Queen*
- the YouTube multimedia series *The Misselthwaite Archives*, based on the 1911 novel *The Secret Garden* by Frances Hodgson Burnett
- the educational app *Heuristic Shakespeare—The Tempest*, based on the play by William Shakespeare
- the computer game Sherlock Holmes and The Hound of the Baskervilles, based on Arthur Conan Doyle's 1902 novel
- the interactive online 3D world Ever, Jane, where players act out scenes from novels by Jane Austen (www.everjane.com)
- the real-time day-by-day republication on Twitter (https://mobile.twitter.com/samuelpepys) of Samuel Pepys's famed London diaries from the 1660s, first published in 1825
- the book *LOL Cat Bible*, which translates the Old and New Testaments of the Bible into "cat speak"
- *Color Your Own Italian Renaissance*— an adult coloring book published by Dover Masterworks containing outlines of 30 Renaissance masterpieces by DaVinci, Raphael, Michelangelo, and others; and
- a website called *The Public Domain Review* (http://publicdomainreview.org) that collects and makes freely available for download public domain materials of all types and has commissioned well-known scholars and authors to write long-form essays about them.

As these examples show, the only limit on how you can use the public domain is your own imagination.

Our Intellectual Commons

Towns and cities of the 18th and 19th centuries often had a place called a commons: a centrally located unfenced area of grassland that was free for all to use. The public domain is, in essence, our intellectual and artistic commons. This commons benefits us all in a variety of ways:

- **Low-cost or free editions of public domain materials are available.** When a work enters the public domain, it often becomes available to the public in many free or low-cost editions. This is possible because copyright owners do not get royalty payments. Also, anyone can publish a public domain work, so competitive pressures keep prices lower.

- **The public domain promotes artistic freedom.** When a work is protected by copyright, the owner has the legal right to restrict how it is used. Some copyright owners rigidly control new performances and other uses of well-known works. However, when a work enters the public domain, such control ends. Thus, public domain works can be used in new ways, given new interpretations and new meanings. For example, the plays

Transformation of *The Secret Garden*

Back in 1911, Frances Hodgson Burnett wrote a novel called *The Secret Garden*. It tells the story of Mary Lennox, a lonely girl sent to live with her uncle Archibald in Yorkshire after her parents died from a cholera epidemic in India. The novel became a children's classic, beloved by millions. Its U.S. copyright expired on January 1, 1987. Its copyright in most of the rest of the world expired in 1995, at which point anyone was free to use the novel without obtaining permission from the former copyright owner or paying any permission fees (which would be substantial for such a well-known novel). *The Secret Garden* has since been transformed in a variety of ways—here are just a few examples:

- a made-for-TV adaptation, *The Secret Garden*, starring Gennie James and Derek Jacobi (1987)
- a musical, *The Secret Garden*, music by Lucy Simon, book & lyrics by Marsha Norman (1991)
- a film adaptation, *The Secret Garden*, starring Maggie Smith (1993)
- two sequels based on Burnett's characters, *Return to the Secret Garden* (1999) and *Back to the Secret Garden* (2001)

- a cookbook, *The Secret Garden Cookbook: Recipes Inspired by Frances Hodgson Burnett's the Secret Garden*, by Amy Cotler and others (1999)
- an electronic book version, *The Secret Garden* (1996)
- a BBC Playhouse Video, *The Secret Garden* (1988)
- two audiobooks, *The Secret Garden* read by Johanna Ward, and *The Secret Garden* read by Josephine Bailey (2003)
- a multimedia Web series adaptation of *The Secret Garden* titled *The Misselthwaite Archives* (released on YouTube in 2015), and
- a steampunk-inspired video adaptation of *The Secret Garden* produced by Amazon (2017).

If the original novel, *The Secret Garden*, were not in the public domain, it's unlikely that many of these projects could have been undertaken because the permission fees would have been too great or the copyright owners would not grant permission at any price. This is another example of how the public domain enriches us all.

of Shakespeare have been altered, performed, and filmed in every way imaginable, from modern dress to in the nude. Since Shakespeare's plays are all in the public domain, no one can object.

- **Scholars and others may freely use public domain materials.** Scholars, researchers, historians, biographers, and others can freely quote and use public domain materials. This enriches their works and makes some projects possible that might otherwise be blocked by the copyright owners of important materials, often the descendants of famous people.

The Public Domain Can Save You Money

On a more mundane level, the public domain can save you money. Copyright owners generally charge a fee for permission to use their works. Such permission fees can range from $100 or less to copy a photo or a few pages from a book to millions of dollars to adapt a work into a movie or play.

Copyright permission fees are unnecessary when a work is in the public domain (although this doesn't mean that public domain works are always free). For example, to use a well-known Irving Berlin song such as "Blue Skies" in a television commercial, you might have to pay Berlin's heirs—the copyright owners of his songs—as much as $250,000. But you can use one of Berlin's many songs that have

already entered the public domain—such as "Alexander's Ragtime Band"—for free.

But you don't have to be a rich television or movie producer to take advantage of the public domain. Here are real-life examples of some projects by ordinary people that were made possible only because public domain materials were available:

- Leslie, a composer, set to music dozens of public domain poems by Emily Dickinson. Had the poems still been under copyright, her project would probably have been financially impossible, because permission fees to adapt the works of famous authors are often enormous.
- Mary Beth wanted to create an old-fashioned illustrated reading book for homeschooled children, but she was daunted by how much the copyright holder wanted to charge for illustrations from schoolbooks discarded in the 1940s (but still under copyright). She used public domain illustration instead and saved the permission fee. Her book is now selling like hotcakes to others who homeschool their children.
- Harvey invented a new kind of computer music playback system, but he couldn't market it because the electronic media royalty on copy-righted songs is around $2,000 per song. So instead he found a bunch of public domain songs and paid no royalties at all.

- A local senior center wanted to put on a copyrighted musical, but the permission fee would have cost more than the gate receipts. They used public domain music instead and got to keep all the money.
- Professional musician Kimiko Ishizaka started a Kickstarter project to create studio-quality recordings of Bach's *Goldberg Variations*. The project was funded at nearly double its original goal; as a result, all 30 variations performed by Ishizaka are now available for free download at www.opengoldbergvariations.org.

How Do You Know If a Work Is in the Public Domain?

The public domain has been aptly compared to "a vast national park without … a guide for the lost traveler, and without clearly defined roads or even borders." (Krasilovsky, "Observations on the Public Domain," *Bulletin,* Copyright Society of USA.) This is because it can often be difficult to know whether a work is in the public domain.

Public domain materials don't look any different than works still protected by copyright. The fact that a work contains a copyright notice—the © followed by the publication date and copyright owner's name—does not necessarily mean it really is protected by copyright law; people often place notices on works that are actually in the public domain (see Chapter 2). The absence of a copyright notice also does not necessarily mean a work is in the public domain.

Public Domain Mark

There is no official government-approved marking that can be placed on a work to show that it is in the public domain. However, the organization Creative Commons has created an unofficial Public Domain Mark that can be used for this purpose:

The Public Domain Mark operates as a tag or a label to communicate that a work is no longer restricted by copyright and can be freely used by others. Creative Commons recommends that the mark only be used on works that are free of known copyright around the world. These will typically be very old works whose copyright has expired throughout the world. For more information, visit https://creativecommons.org/share-your-work/public-domain/pdm.

There is no list or database of all the works that are in the public domain. It would be impossible to create one because so much material is in the public domain. Moreover, the U.S. Copyright Office, the federal agency that registers copyrights, will not tell you if a work is in the public domain. It's a waste of your time even to ask them.

You have to determine whether a work is in the public domain yourself by understanding and applying some basic copyright rules. Sometimes this is easy; sometimes it can be very difficult. This book is designed to walk you through the process. If this task is too daunting, you can hire an attorney or copyright expert to help you.

How Do You Find Public Domain Materials?

In the past, public domain materials were primarily available in libraries, archives, museums, and private collections. It was necessary to go to their physical locations to access such materials. These are still good sources of public domain works. However, digital copies of millions of public domain works have been created and made freely available for download on the Internet. This includes public

domain books, photos, maps, films, sheet music, and many other works. Indeed, digital copies of most of the world's public domain published books are freely available on the Google Books website (www.books.google.com) and the Internet Archive (www.archive.org). As a result, public domain works are more accessible than they have ever been.

Are Public Domain Works Always Free?

The fact that a work is in the public domain does not necessarily mean that it is freely available for your use. Even though a work is in the public domain, the physical substance in which it is embodied—whether it be on paper, canvas, clay, film, or videotape—is usually still owned by somebody. The owner could be a library, archive, museum, private collector, or nearly anyone else.

The owner enjoys all the rights of any personal property owner. This means the owner may restrict or even deny public access to the work or charge for access or the right to make copies. This is usually not a problem for written works, which can be found in bookstores, libraries, and archives, but it is a problem for other types of works.

For example, museums and individual collectors usually control access to valuable works of art that are in the public domain. They often own all available photographs of such works. Getting permission to use such photographs or to take new ones can be difficult and expensive.

You may also have to pay fees to obtain access to and make use of public domain photographs, film, and music from collectors, private archives, and other sources. For example, the stock photo agency Getty Images (www.gettyimages.com) has a vast library of public domain images it licenses to the public for a fee. In return for paying for such licenses, Getty provides purchasers with specialized image search tools and research support and will indemnify purchasers against any legal claims arising from their use of the images.

Dealing With Public Domain Gray Areas

Following the step-by-step procedures in this book will help you determine whether a particular work you want to use is in the public domain. But often the answer will not be clear; the law can often be foggy. There may be questions about a particular work that are unanswerable. The law may not be clear or definitive on whether copyright or some other legal protection covers a particular work. Or someone may simply think that they own a copyright in a work when they really don't. Throughout this book we highlight these uncertainties with an icon that looks like this:

GRAY AREA

These public domain foggy areas are far more common than you might think. For example, problems may arise when someone makes a copy of a public domain work and changes it in some way. It can be hard to determine for certain whether or not the changes merit new copyright protection. If you apply the rules outlined in later chapters, you might decide that the work should not be protected. But the person who created the original work may not agree.

When faced with foggy areas, how should you proceed? If you think it's likely the work is in the public domain should you go ahead and use it, even if there is no definitive answer? Or should you treat the work as copyrighted and ask permission to use it? Should you consult a lawyer?

No book can tell you what to do in every real-world situation. However, we can show you when it is more or less likely someone will complain or even sue you if you treat a work as in the public domain.

Whenever you see a fog icon in the text, you should first answer the following threshold question: Are you going to use the material to directly compete with someone's business? If so, you should consult an attorney, because these types of uses invite lawsuits.

People and companies often get so upset about competitive uses that they file lawsuits even where the material involved is not especially valuable. For example, a company that published cookbooks and cooking magazines filed a copyright infringement lawsuit when a competitor copied and republished several yogurt recipes contained in a cookbook called *Discover Dannon— 50 Fabulous Recipes With Yogurt*. The suit was ultimately lost. *Publications Int'l .Ltd. v. Meredith Corp.*, 88 F.3d 473 (7th Cir. 1996).

If you do not intend to use the work to compete with someone's business, it might be relatively safe for you to treat it as being in the public domain. However, you should carefully consider the following two factors before deciding on what to do:

- the likelihood your use will be discovered, and
- the economic value of the material.

The smaller the chance of discovery, the more willing you should be to use materials whose public domain status is uncertain. Likewise, the lower the economic value of the materials, the safer it is for you to treat them as being in the public domain.

What Is the Likelihood of Discovery?

No one can complain about your using a work unless they know about it. People get in trouble using works they believe are in the public domain when they publish the work or otherwise make it available to the general public—for example, by placing it on the Internet. Here is a recent example:

EXAMPLE: Texas resident Peter Veeck placed a copy of the Denison, Texas, municipal code on his webpage. Veeck assumed the code was in the public domain because it was a government statute. However, it turned out that a private company called the Southern Building Code Congress International (SBCCI) had written the code. The company creates and sells model codes to local governments. SBCCI claimed that it owned the copyright in the code and demanded that Veeck remove it from his website. When he refused, SBCCI sued him for copyright infringement. Whether the private companies that create and sell these private codes can claim copyright in them is a public domain gray area (Veeck ultimately prevailed; see Chapter 3). However, it's likely that SBCCI would never have discovered that Veeck copied the code had he not placed it on the Internet, which is, of course, accessible to anyone with computer access.

The chances of discovery are virtually nil if you use a work for your personal use or make it available to only a restricted group of people. In the example above, SBCCI would never have discovered that Peter Veeck copied its code if he only used it for himself or a small group of friends. Similarly, there is little risk of discovery if a piano teacher photocopies an arrangement of a musical work that may not be in the public domain; or if a choir director makes copies of a choral work for a local church chorus; or a teacher makes a few copies of a chapter from a book for a class.

Of course, people who use public domain materials do frequently want to publish them, place them on the Internet, or make them as widely available as possible. This doesn't necessarily mean that they can't use the material. But, if there are questions over the public domain status of a work, you should consider the economic value of the work.

How Valuable Is the Material?

If an individual or a company feels that you have cheated them out of a substantial permission or licensing fee, there is a good chance you'll receive a complaint or be sued if your use is discovered.

Examples of materials that were deemed valuable enough for someone to sue include:

- the famous children's novel *Bambi: A Life in the Woods*
- a published collection of about 150 works of classical music by such famous composers as Beethoven, Bach, Bartok, and Brahms
- a collection of thousands of copies of legal decisions by U.S. courts
- a database containing over 90 million residential and business phone numbers that cost millions of dollars to compile
- a published book listing used car prices
- 150 photographs of public domain paintings by such masters as Rembrandt and da Vinci
- Martin Luther King's "I Have a Dream" speech, and
- a *New Yorker* magazine cartoon by Saul Steinberg.

On the other hand, complaints or lawsuits are far less likely where the work you want to use has little economic value. Many—probably most—public domain works fall into this category. It's often not worth the time and trouble to complain about works that are not worth much. And it certainly makes no financial sense to hire a lawyer and file a lawsuit over such a work. The damages that can be obtained if such a lawsuit is successful are just not large enough to justify the expense involved.

Even if someone does complain in these cases, you can probably resolve the complaint if you stop using the work or pay a nominal permission fee. Examples of public domain works that often have little economic value include old postcards, articles and books by obscure authors, artwork by unknown artists, and sheet music for long-forgotten popular songs. One way to tell if a gray-area work is valuable is to determine whether anyone is selling either the original or copies to the public. If not, the materials probably have little or no value.

What If Someone Challenges Your Public Domain Claim?

Sometimes, a person or company will claim that materials you have used are not in the public domain and that they, in fact, own the copyright in them.

Often in these cases you'll receive a letter from an attorney asking that you "cease and desist" from any further uses of the materials. You can find numerous examples of cease and desist letters at the Lumen website (https://lumendatabase. org). You should respond immediately that you have received the letter and are investigating the claims. Don't ignore such a letter. This will only make it more likely that you will be sued and help make you look like a "bad guy" to a judge or jury.

Handling the Claim Yourself

You may be able to handle the claim yourself. This is particularly likely where the material isn't very valuable. If it is clear that the materials involved are in the public domain, you may be able to get the other side to drop its complaint by showing your documentation and explaining why the material is in fact in the public domain. Some people don't understand what public domain means, so you may have to explain this too.

If you have made a mistake and the materials are not in the public domain or they inhabit a gray area, you may be able to resolve the matter by offering to pay a small permission or licensing fee or stop using or distributing the work.

Obviously, you should seek to settle the complaint if the work you are using turns out to be protected by copyright. But, even if you think the claim is not valid, it may be cheaper and easier to settle than to fight.

EXAMPLE: Eric Eldred, a Massachusetts-based technical analyst, digitally scanned and placed on his website copies of dozens of public domain works, including books by Nathaniel Hawthorne, Oliver Wendell Holmes, William Dean Howells, and Joseph Conrad. In one case, however, a museum's publishing department claimed that excerpts from a book on canoeing he placed on his site were not in the public domain and that it owned the copyright in the work. The museum asked him to remove the material from his website. Eldred was certain the material was in the public domain; nevertheless he agreed to the museum's demand. He says that "I decided to remove the book just because these public institutions complained that I was stealing their income."

Hiring a Lawyer Experienced in Copyright Law

You should contact an attorney knowledgeable in copyright law if:

- you believe the claim is not valid and don't want to agree to the other side's demands, or
- the materials involved are highly valuable and any permission or licensing fee would be substantial, or
- the other side insists that you stop using the materials, but this would be impossible or very expensive for you to do—for example, you have used them in a book or film you've already distributed to the public.

Where can you find a lawyer experienced in copyright law? Asking for a referral to an intellectual property attorney from someone you trust can be a good way to find legal help. Whether you want to hire an attorney (for example, in response to a cease and desist letter) or simply want a brief consultation, try these excellent and free resources:

- **Nolo's Lawyer Directory.** Nolo has an easy-to-use online directory of lawyers, organized by location and area of expertise, such as intellectual property law. You can find the directory and its comprehensive profiles at www.nolo.com/lawyers.
- **Lawyers.com.** At Lawyers.com, you'll find a user-friendly search tool that allows you to tailor results by area

of law and geography. You can also search for attorneys by name. Attorney profiles prominently display contact information, list topics of expertise, and show ratings—by both clients and other legal professionals.

- **Martindale.com.** Martindale.com offers an advanced search option that allows you to sort not only by practice area and location, but also by criteria like law school. Whether you look for lawyers by name or expertise, you'll find listings with detailed background information, peer and client ratings, and even profile visibility.

Lawyer Organizations That Help Artists

Looking for free or low-cost legal advice, such as with a copyright or intellectual property issue? Check out these nonprofit lawyer organizations:

- Volunteer Lawyers for the Arts (https://vlany.org)
- California Lawyers for the Arts (https://calawyersforthearts.org), and
- Lawyers for the Creative Arts (https://law-arts.org).

You can find a state-by-state directory of such nonprofits at the Digital Media Law Project website (www.dmlp.org/legal-guide/nonprofit-legal-assistance-organizations-state).

There are also several nonprofit lawyer organizations that provide artists of all sorts (visual artists as well as filmmakers, photographers, writers, and others) with legal help for free or for a small fee. See "Lawyer Organizations That Help Artists," above, for more information.

Documenting Your Use of Public Domain Materials

It is important to document your research into the public domain status of every work you plan to use, unless you plan to use it purely for your own private enjoyment. Any work that will be shown to the public in any way should be documented. This is because it is not uncommon for people and companies to make false claims of copyright ownership in public domain materials. Such people could threaten to sue you if they discover you've copied or otherwise used materials they claim to own. Also, if you need to obtain insurance for your project against libel, slander, or other errors or omissions, your documentation can help convince an insurer or broadcaster that they will not face any copyright problems.

You should create a permanent file for each work of authorship you plan to use. In the file you should include a completed checklist and worksheet, along with a narrative description of your research, if you feel it is necessary. You should also take the following steps:

- Keep the original work or a copy— for example, photographs, articles, sheet music. If this is not possible because the material is too big— for example, an entire book or can of film—you should attempt to keep a copy of the work in storage somewhere and make a notation in the worksheet where it is stored.
- If the work is in the public domain because the copyright has expired, include a photocopy of the work's copyright notice showing the date the work was published (also include a copy of the title page, if any).
- If the work is in the public domain because it's a U.S. government work, include a copy of the title page or other page showing it was created by or for the government.
- If the work has been dedicated to the public domain, include a copy of the public domain dedication.
- If you've conducted a copyright renewal search or had the U.S. Copyright Office or private search firm conduct one for you, keep a copy of the results.
- If you've sent email to anyone to confirm that material is in the public domain, print it out along with the responses you've received and keep the copies in your file.
- Keep any postal correspondence in this file as well.

The Use and Abuse of Copyright

What Copyright Protects 20

    Copyright Law: A Short History 20

    What Is Copyright? 22

    What Can Be Protected by Copyright? 22

    Three Requirements for Copyright Protection 22

    How Is a Copyright Created and Protected? 24

    Limitations on Copyright Protection 25

The Looting of the Public Domain 26

    Spurious Copyright Claims in Public Domain Materials 26

    Use of Contracts to Restrict the Public Domain 28

    Legislative Shrinking of the Public Domain 31

The legitimate use of copyright law protects the authors of creative works and allows them to profit from their work. Below we describe the general protections that copyright law provides. We also outline how people and companies unscrupulously abuse the public domain and claim copyright protection where none exists.

What Copyright Protects

The copyright law gives creators or owners of creative works the legal right to control how the works are used. This section provides an overview of the copyright law and introduces some important concepts that will appear again and again in later chapters.

RESOURCE

For a detailed discussion of copyright law, refer to *The Copyright Handbook: What Every Writer Needs to Know,* by Stephen Fishman (Nolo).

Copyright Law: A Short History

The U.S. Constitution gives Congress the power to protect works of authorship by enacting copyright laws. But it is up to Congress to actually write the copyright laws and decide on the details of what should be protected and for how long. The first federal copyright law was enacted in 1790. The federal copyright laws have been amended many times since then. The last major revision occurred in 1976 when an entirely new copyright law called the Copyright Act of 1976 (18 U.S.C. § 101 and following) was passed by Congress. This Act took effect in 1978. However, many of the basic copyright rules in effect under the law in existence before 1978 still apply to works that were published before that year. Time and again throughout this book you'll see that copyright rules differ for works published before and after 1978.

Like most laws, the copyright law is not perfectly crafted. Some of its provisions are ambiguous, poorly written, or simply don't cover every situation that arises in real life. When people get into disputes with each other about how to apply or interpret the copyright laws, it's ultimately up to the federal courts to resolve them. Their decisions on how to interpret and apply the copyright laws are legally binding on the public and other courts, and in effect, become part of the law itself.

Unfortunately, the courts don't always agree on how to interpret the copyright laws. Moreover, there are some questions about the copyright laws that have yet to be addressed by the courts. As a result, there are a number of important copyright issues for which we currently have no clear answers.

Finally, there is a federal agency called the United States Copyright Office, which

Other Laws Protecting Works of Authorship

Copyright is by far the most important law that protects works of authorship. However, in some situations other laws also give power to creators or owners of works of authorship to control how their works are used. These laws may prevent you from using some materials that are not protected by copyright. They include:

- **The right of publicity:** A patchwork of state laws protects against the unauthorized use of a person's name or image for advertising or other commercial purposes (see Chapter 20).
- **Trademark laws:** Brand names such as Nike and McDonald's, as well as logos, slogans, and other devices that identify and distinguish products and services are protected under federal and state trademark laws (see Chapter 20).
- **Patent laws:** Federal laws that protect inventions—everything from new types of mousetraps to satellites. This book does not cover inventions. However, a special type of patent called a design patent may be used to protect a new, original ornamental design embodied in a manufactured object. The design can be a surface ornament such as a pattern on a beer mug or consist of the shape of the article itself such as the shape of a Rolls-Royce automobile or silverware set (see Chapter 5).
- **Trade secrecy laws:** State and federal trade secret laws protect some business information. An example of a trade secret would be a confidential marketing plan for the introduction of a new software product or the secret recipe for a brand of salsa. The extent of trade secret protection depends on whether the information gives the business an advantage over competitors, is kept secret, and is not known by competitors (see Chapter 14).

is in charge of registering copyrights and helps advise Congress on copyright matters. The Copyright Office is part of the Library of Congress, not the judiciary. Although it has made public its views on many copyright issues, the Copyright Office's views on copyright matters are not binding on the public or the courts. The courts do, however, usually give them some weight. So in considering questions of copyright law that have not been settled by the courts, it helps to know the Copyright Office position in deciding whether to use a particular work. The Copyright Office does not decide whether a particular work is in the public domain. This is ultimately up to the courts to determine.

State Copyright Laws

Before 1978, the United States had a two-tier copyright system: published works were protected by the federal copyright law (provided they met the requirements discussed below), while unpublished works were protected by state copyright laws, also called common law copyright. These state laws were enforced by state courts and were completely separate from the federal copyright that protected published works throughout the United States. However, in 1978 this system was abandoned. Federal copyright law now protects both published and unpublished works. As a result, common law copyright has little application today. But, it might apply in some cases to protect works that have never been written down or otherwise preserved (see Chapter 14).

What Is Copyright?

As explained in Chapter 1, a copyright is a legal tool that provides the creator of a work of authorship the right to control how the work is used, including the exclusive right to reproduce, distribute, adapt, display, and perform the work. For example, the author of a book or musical composition has the exclusive right to publish it.

What Can Be Protected by Copyright?

Copyright protects works of authorship. A work of authorship is any creative work created by a human being that can be communicated to other humans, either directly or with the aid of a device such as a film projector. Works of authorship include, but are not limited to:

- writings of all types
- musical works, including song lyrics
- plays
- photographs
- databases
- maps
- artworks, sculpture, and graphics
- movies and videos
- computer software
- sound recordings
- pantomimes and choreographic works, and
- architectural drawings and blueprints and the design of actual buildings.

These are the types of works we deal with in this book.

Three Requirements for Copyright Protection

Not all works of authorship are entitled to copyright protection. A work is protected only to the extent it satisfies the following three fundamental requirements. If only part of a work meets these requirements, only that part will be protected.

Requirement 1—Fixation

The most basic requirement that a work of authorship must meet to qualify for copyright protection is that it must be fixed in a "tangible medium of expression." The copyright law is not picky about how a work is fixed; any medium from which it can be read back or heard, either directly or with the aid of a machine, will suffice. In other words, a work will be protected if it is written on a piece of paper, painted on canvas, saved on a computer disk or in the cloud, filmed or recorded with an iPhone or camera, or preserved by any other means.

The federal copyright law does not protect works that have not been fixed in some way. For example, it doesn't protect something someone says but never writes down or otherwise preserves. However, as mentioned in "State Copyright Laws" above, state law might be used to protect such unfixed works (see Chapter 14).

Requirement 2—Originality

A work fixed in a tangible form is protected by copyright only if it is original. If only part of a work is original, only that part will be protected. But a work need not be novel—that is, new to the world—to be protected. For copyright purposes, a work is original if it—or at least a part of it—owes its origin to the author. A work's quality, ingenuity, aesthetic merit, or uniqueness is not considered. In short, the copyright law does not distinguish between the Great American Novel and a letter from a six-year-old to her Aunt Sally; both are entitled to copyright protection to the extent they were not copied by the author—whether consciously or unconsciously—from other works. So long as its author independently created a work, it is protected even if other similar works already exist.

The originality requirement has extremely important ramifications for the public domain. Because of this requirement, someone who merely makes an exact copy of a public domain work is not entitled to receive a copyright on the reproduction. Something new must be added for the work to be copyrighted. And it is only the new material that is protected, not the unchanged public domain material.

EXAMPLE: Actress Emma Thompson created a screenplay from the classic public domain novel *Sense and Sensibility*, by Jane Austen. In doing so, she added a good deal of new material, including some scenes and dialog that were not in the novel. She also organized the work into cinematic scenes, cut material that did not fit into a two-hour movie, added camera directions, and so forth. Only this new material was protected by copyright. All the material Thompson copied from Austen's novel remains in the public domain.

Requirement 3—Minimal Creativity

Finally, a minimal amount of creativity over and above the independent creation requirement (Requirement 2, above) is necessary for copyright protection. Works completely lacking in creativity are denied copyright protection even if they have been independently created. However, the amount of creativity required is very slight. A work need not be novel, unique, ingenious, or even any good to be sufficiently creative. All that's required is that the work be the product of a very minimal creative spark. Most works of authorship—including catalog copy, emails, and thirdrate poetry—make the grade.

But there are some types of works that are usually deemed by judges to contain no creativity at all. For example, a mere listing of ingredients or contents, such as in a recipe, is considered to be completely lacking in creativity and cannot be protected by copyright (but explanatory material or other original expression in a recipe or other list can be protected). Telephone directory white pages have also been deemed by judges to lack even minimal creativity. Other listings of data may also completely lack creativity (see Chapter 12).

Like the originality requirement, the creativity requirement works to prevent someone who makes an exact copy of a public domain work—for example, a photocopy of a public domain drawing—from receiving copyright protection. Other types of exact copies of public domain works—for example, photographs of public domain paintings—may also fail the minimal creativity requirement (see Chapter 5).

Moreover, certain types of changes made to public domain works, even though original, are not copyrightable because they are not minimally creative. For example, transposing a public domain musical composition from one key to another is not minimally creative and such a transposition is not protected by copyright (see Chapter 4).

How Is a Copyright Created and Protected?

How a copyright is created and protected differs for works published before and after 1978. Before 1978, state copyright law automatically protected unpublished works that were original and minimally creative the moment they were created. Then, when such a work was published with a valid copyright notice it automatically obtained protection under the federal copyright law and its state law protection ended.

Starting in 1978 this all changed. The federal copyright law was amended to protect all unpublished works as well as published materials. Unpublished works created before 1978 automatically lost their state law protection and acquired a federal copyright. Copyright protection for all works created after 1978 begins the instant a work meets the three requirements set forth in the previous section—that is, the moment an original and minimally creative work is fixed in a tangible medium of expression. There is no waiting period and it is not necessary to register with the Copyright Office. Copyright protects both drafts and completed works, and both published and unpublished works.

Copyright Notices

Before March 1, 1989 all published works had to contain a copyright notice (the © symbol or the word "Copyright" or abbreviation "Copr." followed by the publication date and copyright owner's name) to be protected by copyright. Works published before March 1, 1989 without a valid copyright notice are now in the public domain unless the failure to include a proper notice was excused (see Chapter 19).

Although use of copyright notices has been optional since 1989, they still are usually placed on published works. Indeed, their use is often abused.

It's important to understand that neither the Copyright Office nor anyone else polices or regulates the use of copyright notices. It is not necessary to obtain government permission to place a notice on a work. People often place copyright notices on public domain works they copy and/or resell to the public. As discussed later in this chapter, the penalties for placing a notice on a public domain work are very small.

Registration

Both published and unpublished works of authorship may be registered with the U.S. Copyright Office in Washington, DC. This involves sending the Copyright Office one or two copies of the work along with a registration form and fee. Technically, registration is not mandatory. It is not required to establish a copyright. But a work must be registered before its owner can file a lawsuit for copyright infringement. Even so, many works have never been registered. These unregistered works can still be protected by copyright. Their owners can register at any time and file copyright infringement lawsuits.

Limitations on Copyright Protection

The purpose of copyright is to encourage intellectual and artistic creation. Paradoxically, giving authors too much copyright protection could inhibit rather than enhance creative growth. To avoid this, some important limitations on copyright protection have been developed.

Copyrights Only Last for a Limited Time

The single most significant limitation on copyright protection is that copyright protection lasts for only a limited time. Just how long a copyright lasts depends on when it was created or published. When a work's copyright expires it enters the public domain, where it can be used freely by everyone (see Chapter 18).

Ideas and Facts Are Not Protected

Copyright only protects the particular way an author expresses facts and ideas. Copyright does not protect the facts or ideas themselves; facts and ideas are free for anyone to use. To give an author a monopoly over the facts and ideas contained in his or her work would hinder intellectual and artistic progress, not encourage it. For example, imagine how scientific progress would have suffered if Charles Darwin could have prevented anyone else from writing about evolution after he published *The Origin of Species* (see Chapter 14).

Fair Use

To foster the advancement of the arts and sciences there must be a free flow of information and ideas. If no one could quote from a protected work without the author's permission—which could be withheld or given only upon payment of a permission fee—the free flow of ideas would be stopped dead. To avoid this, a special "fair use" exception to copyright protection was created. An author is free to copy from a protected work for purposes such as criticism, news reporting, teaching, or research, so long as the value of the copyrighted work is not diminished (see Chapter 22).

Certain Works Are Ineligible for Copyright Protection

Finally, certain types of works are ineligible for copyright protection, even if they satisfy the fixation, originality, and creativity requirements discussed above. Most significant among these are works created by U.S. government employees (see Chapter 3).

The Looting of the Public Domain

The public domain contains a lot of very valuable material. Indeed, with the rise of the Internet and new technologies, the market value of some public domain works has grown enormously in recent years. So, there is money to be made from selling copies of public domain works. And, in the best American tradition, money is being made. Unfortunately, some of the business practices used by people and companies selling copies of public domain works are illegal, unethical, or antithetical to the fundamental purposes of the public domain.

Spurious Copyright Claims in Public Domain Materials

Out of ignorance, greed, or a combination of the two, people and companies who sell copies of public domain works often claim copyright in the copies and place copyright notices on them. You can find copyright notices and various warning statements on copies of works that have been in the public domain for centuries, such as the music of Bach or Shakespeare's plays. For example, the Arden Shakespeare edition of Shakespeare's *King Henry IV, Part II,* contains the legend "No part of this book may be reprinted, reproduced or utilized in any form or by any electronic, mechanical or other means … without permission in writing from the publishers."

Ordinarily, a copy of a public domain work is itself in the public domain. Something new must be added to the original work for a valid copyright claim to arise. For example, if you add notes or new illustrations to a public domain book, the new material would be copyrighted. But the original text remains in the public domain.

By claiming copyright in public domain materials, these unscrupulous people try to intimidate the public into paying permission fees or royalties for works that should be free for all to use. This practice is tantamount to someone fencing off a portion of a national park and charging the public a fee for admission.

Is it illegal to claim copyright in a public domain work? Yes, it is, but the penalties for violations are laughably small. Claiming copyright in public domain works is a federal crime, but the maximum penalty for engaging in this sort of criminal conduct is a fine of $2,500. 17 U.S.C. Section 506(c). Moreover, violators are rarely prosecuted.

In effect, the federal government encourages spurious copyright claims. The potential economic rewards for making such claims are great, while the possibility of getting caught and paying a price is small.

However, people are fighting back against spurious copyright claims and are beginning to win some important victories. For example, a successful class action lawsuit was brought against the music publisher Warner/Chappell Music, Inc., that claimed it was the copyright owner to the song "Happy Birthday" and collected over $2 million per year in permission fees for the use of the song in films, television, and recordings. The plaintiffs established that the song was in the public domain and Warner/Chappell agreed to pay $14 million in damages. *Good Morning to You Productions Corp. v. Warner/Chappell Music, Inc.*, No. CV 13-04460-GHK (C.D. Cal. March 14, 2016).

In another significant victory, a court held that all the Sherlock Holmes stories except for ten published after 1923 were in the public domain. The plaintiffs in the case were allowed to publish a collection of new stories containing the Sherlock Holmes character without obtaining permission from the Conan Doyle estate. They also were awarded $30,000 in attorneys' fees by the court. *Klinger v. Conan Doyle Estate, Ltd.*, 755 F.3d 496 (7th Cir. 2014).

This book will help you recognize when copyright claims are, in fact, spurious.

Oregon Backs Down When Spurious Copyright Claim Is Challenged

Many state governments make spurious claims of copyright ownership in their state laws. One state that did so was Oregon. The state's Legislative Counsel even sent out cease and desist letters to websites such as Public.Resource.Org and Justia.com that posted copies of Oregon's laws without seeking permission. The letters demanded that the websites pay for a license to post the copies of Oregon's state statutes or remove them. Fortunately, Public Resource, a nonprofit that makes available free copies of laws and court opinions, did not take the threat lying down. It sent back to the Oregon Legislative Counsel letters explaining why the statutes were in the public domain and could be freely posted. The Oregon legislature eventually held a hearing on the matter in which members of Public Resource and others testified. Ultimately the Oregon legislature unanimously agreed to stop claiming copyright ownership in the state's laws.

Use of Contracts to Restrict the Public Domain

Just as pernicious as spurious copyright claims is the widespread use of contracts to restrict how the public can use public domain materials. These contracts are commonly called licenses.

A person or company that sells copies of public domain works or allows the public to make copies of public domain works in its possession has every legal right to charge a fee for the copies or access. However, in addition to doing this, many owners of public domain works require users to sign license agreements restricting how the works can be used.

Such licenses take many forms. Some are preprinted form contracts you are required to sign, while others are negotiated agreements tailored to particular individuals or institutions. If the public domain materials are distributed online or on physical media, the license will often be a click-wrap license—that is, a license that appears on a computer screen when the user attempts to access the materials. The user must accept the license by clicking on a button—usually marked with the word "accept"—before he or she can access the materials.

Some book publishers even attempt to impose license-like restriction on how you may use public domain materials. For example, Dover Publications, the largest publisher of public domain clip-art in book form, typically includes the following statement in its clip-art collections:

> You may use the designs and illustrations for graphics and crafts applications, free and without special permission, provided that you include no more than ten in the same publication or project.

Licenses are commonly used in electronic books, even where the book is merely a republication of a public domain work. For example, a publisher who created an e-book version of the public domain novel *Middlemarch,* by George Eliot, included a license agreement in the book, the terms of which permitted readers to copy only ten text sections into their computer's clipboard memory every ten days, and to print no more than ten pages of the novel each day.

License Restrictions

Among other things, these license agreements impose restrictions on how the licensee (the person obtaining or accessing a copy of the work) can use the work. Typically, the licensee is barred from making more than a specific number of copies or reselling them to the public. The licensee may even be barred from creating new works from the public domain materials or displaying or performing them in public.

If the licensee violates the restrictive terms contained in a license, the licenser (person who owns the copies of the public domain materials) can't sue for copyright infringement because the materials are in the public domain—they have no copyright protection. Instead, the licenser threatens or actually does sue the licensee for violating the license. This is a suit under state law for breach of contract.

In effect, people who use such licenses are trying to use contracts to obtain the same exclusive rights that are provided under copyright law, rights they can't get because the work is in the public domain.

Are License Restrictions Legal?

Many copyright experts believe that licenses imposing copyright-like restriction on how the public may use public domain materials should be legally unenforceable. This is because the federal copyright law preempts (overrides) state contract law and prevents people from using contracts to create their own private copyrights. Moreover, there are sound policy reasons for holding such license restrictions unenforceable—their widespread use diminishes the public's access to the public domain.

However, almost all courts have ignored the experts and enforced these licenses. In the first and most important court decision on this issue, the court held that a license restricting the use of public domain materials was enforceable. The case involved a CD-ROM containing 95 million business telephone listings. The listings were all in the public domain (see Chapter 12), but the CD-ROM contained a click-wrap license agreement requiring users to agree to certain restrictions before they could access the information. For example, the license barred purchasers of the CD-ROM from copying, adapting, or modifying the listings. When Matthew Zeidenberg copied the listings and placed them on his website, the company that owned the CD-ROM successfully sued him for violating the license. The court held that the license restrictions were enforceable even though the listings were in the public domain. *ProCD v. Zeidenberg*, 86 F.3d 1447 (7th Cir. 1996).

Since the *ProCD* case was decided, a majority of courts have gone along with its reasoning and enforced license restrictions on public domain materials. This has led to even more widespread use of licenses.

Fighting for the Public Domain

While Congress has acted to shrink the public domain, and the business community has exploited it, a grassroots movement to preserve it has sprouted. Librarians, legal scholars, historians, artists, musicians, archivists, website creators, and many others have grown increasingly alarmed at the attacks on the public domain. Numerous organizations and groups have begun to help educate the public about the public domain's importance, agitate for its preservation, and encourage copyright owners to dedicate their works to the public. Because of this new consciousness of the public domain's importance, Congress will never again be able to remove millions of works from the public domain or extend the term of copyright without a fight. Among these organizations are:

- The Creative Commons (https://creative commons.org)
- The Internet Archive (www.archive.org)
- The Electronic Frontier Foundation (www.eff.org)
- Public Knowledge (www.public knowledge.org)
- Communia: The European Thematic Network on the Digital Public Domain (http://communia-project.eu)
- The Berkman Klein Center for Internet and Society at Harvard Law School (https://cyber.law.harvard.edu), and
- The Center for the Study of the Public Domain (www.law.duke.edu/cspd).

What Should You Do About Licenses?

When it comes to such restrictive license agreements, the best advice is to avoid them like the plague. A license (or any other contract) is enforceable only against a person who signs it or otherwise agrees to it. People who don't agree to it are not legally bound by it.

You may have to work harder to find public domain materials not subject to license agreements. For example, instead of quickly and easily obtaining a public domain photo from a stock photo agency that uses licenses, you'll have to dig through an archive or local historical society that will let you make copies without signing a license.

However, in some cases it may be impossible to obtain public domain materials you need without agreeing to a license. Always read any agreement carefully and try to negotiate with the licenser to limit the restrictions as much as possible so that you'll be able to live with the license.

Legislative Shrinking of the Public Domain

As if widespread spurious copyright claims and use of restrictive licenses weren't bad enough, Congress got into the act as well. Egged on by huge corporate copyright owners such as the Hollywood film studios, Congress passed a series of laws dramatically reducing the public domain. Millions of foreign works that used to be in the public domain in the United States had their copyrights restored (see Chapter 15). Millions more domestic works had their copyrights extended (see Chapter 18). Because of these laws, no published works entered the public domain due to copyright expiration for 20 years—from 1998 through 2018. Fortunately, this legislative freezing of the public domain has ended and new works began to enter the public domain due to copyright expiration in 2019.

Writings

What Can You Do With Public Domain Writings? 34

    Republishing Public Domain Writings 35

    Quoting From Public Domain Writings 35

    Copying Public Domain Writings 36

    Performing Public Domain Writings in Public 38

    Creating New Works From Public Domain Writings 38

Determining Copyright Status of Written Works 38

Is the Work Eligible for Copyright Protection? 39

    Copies of Public Domain Works 42

    U.S. Government Works 42

    Laws and Court Decisions 51

    Words, Names, Slogans, and Other Short Phrases 54

    Blank Forms 55

    Information That Is Common Property 57

    Food and Drink Recipes 57

    Works Dedicated to the Public Domain 58

Has the Work Been Published? 59

    Has the Work Been Distributed to the General Public? 59

    Has the Work Been Performed or Displayed, But Not Distributed? 60

    Has the Work Received Only Limited Distribution? 60

    Date and Country of Publication 61

Has the Work's Copyright Expired? 62

Is the Work in the Public Domain Due to Lack of a Copyright Notice? 63

Does a Copyright Trap Apply? 63

    Is the Work a Derivative Work? 64

    Is the Work a Compilation? 73

Misuse of Copyright Notices 74

Sources of Public Domain Writings 78

This chapter will help you determine if a published or unpublished written work is in the public domain, including all types of fiction and nonfiction books, plays, screenplays, poetry, magazines, newspapers, pamphlets, letters, diaries, advertising copy, and any other work that consists primarily of written words.

! **CAUTION**
It is possible for a work to be in the public domain in the United States but protected by copyright in another country, and vice versa. This chapter only covers the public domain in the United States. If you want to know whether a work is in the public domain in a country other than the United States, see Chapter 16.

What Can You Do With Public Domain Writings?

Billions of written works are in the public domain, ranging from literary masterpieces such as Shakespeare's plays to the most trivial and mundane cliches written for old advertising copy. You can use these public domain works in any way you desire, limited only by your imagination. Below are some common ways people use writings in the public domain.

In addition, e-book versions of hundreds of thousands of public domain books have been published on Amazon.com. Some are free, others are available at low cost. Apps such as Free Books also provide access to electronic versions of thousands of public domain works.

Jane Austen + Zombies = Bestseller

If you think the public domain just consists of a bunch of worthless old stuff no one cares about, think again. People with the imagination and skill to repurpose public domain materials can make big money. Consider Jane Austen's public domain novel *Pride and Prejudice*. After looking at a list of public domain book titles, editor Jason Rekulak came up with the idea of creating a mash-up called *Pride and Prejudice and Zombies*. He turned over the idea to writer Seth Grahame-Smith, who kept about 85% of the novel's original text while adding zombie and ninja horror elements to the story. The 2009 book became a massive bestseller, with over 750,000 copies in print. It was later adapted into a film, video game, and graphic novel. The work's success spawned many other mash-ups combining public domain works with modern horror themes such as *Sense and Sensibility and Sea Monsters*, *Android Karenina*, and *Mansfield Park and Mummies*.

Republishing Public Domain Writings

When a written work enters the public domain, anyone is free to republish it without obtaining permission from the former copyright owner. Nor is it necessary to pay the author, or more likely his or her heirs, a royalty. This makes it possible to publish cheap editions of works in the public domain. For example, when *This Side of Paradise*, the first novel by the famed Jazz Age novelist F. Scott Fitzgerald, entered the public domain in 1996, publishers printed numerous new editions, some available for just a few dollars each.

Classic public domain writings, usually works of fiction, drama, and poetry, are constantly being republished. You can find many in the literature section of any bookstore.

Quoting From Public Domain Writings

A major advantage to using works in the public domain is that you do not need permission to quote from them. When a work is protected by copyright, you often need to obtain permission from the copyright owner to quote from it. Payment may be demanded for such permission. There are no standard fees for such permissions. They may range from a few dollars to hundreds or thousands of dollars, depending on the work involved and what is done with it. For example, the *Wall Street Journal* charges over $500 to reprint an entire article in a book with a 10,000-copy print run and $192 to reprint up to five paragraphs.

In some cases, permission to quote may be unavailable at any price. This is what happened when author Ian Hamilton attempted to write an unauthorized biography of the notoriously reclusive novelist J.D. Salinger. Hamilton wanted to quote from some of Salinger's personal letters. Salinger not only denied permission, he successfully sued Hamilton for copyright infringement when he attempted to use the quotations without permission.

There are also many cases where the heirs of famous people have refused to permit biographers and historians to use copyrighted materials. For example, the late poet Sylvia Plath's family and executor have refused to allow serious literary biographers to quote from Plath's copyrighted works because they didn't like the content of the biographies.

In some circumstances, authors may quote from a copyrighted work without permission. The legal concept of "fair use" allows authors to use small portions of another writer's work without permission for some purposes, including scholarship, education, and news reporting.

But applying the rules of fair use can be difficult and confusing. And simply claiming "fair use" does not mean that the author or the author's heirs won't sue you anyway. (For a detailed discussion of fair use, see Chapter 22.) By contrast, when a work enters the public domain, the rules are simple and clear: You may quote freely from a public domain work, using as much or as little as you want, for whatever purpose. You do not need to obtain permission or pay for the use.

Copying Public Domain Writings

Commercial copy shops such as FedEx Office may require that you obtain written permission from the copyright holder before allowing you to photocopy a copyrighted work. For example, FedEx Office's copying policy—explained in the FAQs that appear only when you click "Start Print Order" on its website (www.fedex.com)—requires you to warrant that you have permission to copy any documents.

Plagiarism, Attribution, and the Public Domain

If you copy from a public domain writing, do you have to credit the author? The U.S. Supreme Court has answered "No," holding that there is no legal requirement to provide any attribution when public domain works are copied and placed into new works. *Dastar Corp. v. 20th Century Fox Film Corp.*, 539 U.S. 23 (2003). (See Chapter 20 for a detailed discussion of *Dastar*.) However, just because there is no legal requirement to give credit to the creators of public domain works, that doesn't mean you need not do it. There is still something called plagiarism.

Plagiarism occurs when people pose as the originator of words they did not write, ideas they did not conceive, or facts they did not discover. Although you cannot be sued for plagiarizing a public domain work, the process can result in professional penalties.

For example, in the case of college professors and journalists, it may result in termination; in the case of well-known historians, it can result in public humiliation.

To avoid charges of plagiarism, authors of scholarly works (histories, biographies, legal and scientific works, and the like) always give proper credit to the sources of their ideas and facts, as well as any words they borrow. This is so even if the work borrowed from is in the public domain. Authors of less serious works—for example, how-to books—often attribute direct quotations, though do not always give credit for ideas and facts they borrow. It is neither customary nor necessary for authors of works of fancy, such as novels and plays, to credit the sources of their inspiration—regardless of the source—but they should give proper attribution to direct quotations.

No such permission is needed when a work is in the public domain. You may freely photocopy any public domain writing and use the copies in any way you wish. However, before asking a copy shop to photocopy a public domain work, you should ask what proof they need that the work you want copied is not protected by copyright.

You are also free to make digital copies of public domain writings and place them on the Internet or email them to colleagues, friends, or coworkers. Copies of millions of classic public domain works have been posted on the Internet at websites such as the Internet Archive (www.archive.org) and many others.

Plays in the Public Domain

Public domain works are in constant use in the theater world. Public domain plays are often staged, and new plays and musicals are created from public domain works. In New York City alone, these were some of the public domain plays being performed during the 2019–2020 season:

- *An Enemy of the People*, an 1882 play by Henrik Ibsen
- *Timon of Athens*, by William Shakespeare
- *Medea*, by Euripides, and
- *Hamlet*, by William Shakespeare.

At the same time, the following plays and musicals adapted from public domain works graced the New York stage:

- *Drunk Shakespeare*, based on various plays by William Shakespeare
- *Alice in Wonderland*, a musical based on the 1865 novel by Lewis Carroll
- *Cyrano*, a musical based on the 1897 play by Edmund Rostand
- *Frankenstein*, a musical based on the 1818 novel by Mary Shelley
- *Romeo and Bernadette*, an adaptation of *Romeo and Juliet* by William Shakespeare
- *A Christmas Carol*, based on the 1843 novel by Charles Dickens
- *Chekhov/Tolstoy: Love Stories*, short plays adapted from short stories by Leo Tolstoy and Anton Chekhov
- *Aladdin*, a musical based on a Middle Eastern folk tale published in *The Book of One Thousand and One Nights* in 1717
- *The Phantom of the Opera*, a musical based on the 1910 novel by Gaston Leroux
- *The Inheritance*, based on the 1910 novel *Howard's End*, by E.M. Forster, and
- *Wicked*, by Joe Mantello, a musical based on the 1900 novel *The Wonderful Wizard of Oz*, by L. Frank Baum.

Performing Public Domain Writings in Public

You ordinarily need to obtain permission to perform a copyrighted play or other dramatic work in public. Permission fees to perform well-known plays by Eugene O'Neill, Arthur Miller, Neil Simon, and other famous authors run into the many thousands of dollars. In contrast, public domain plays can be performed for free. This includes, for example, the complete works of Shakespeare. There is yet another advantage to performing a public domain play or other dramatic work: Neither the author nor his or her heirs have any control over the performance. You can cut, rewrite, or otherwise alter the play in any way you wish.

Creating New Works From Public Domain Writings

Perhaps most important of all, anyone is free to create a new work based upon a public domain writing—for example, create a screenplay or stage play based on a public domain novel or short story. Such works are called derivative works. Classic public domain works such as the novels of Jane Austen or Charles Dickens are recycled over and over again in new movies, plays, and other derivative works.

Authors may also create new stories using characters from public domain novels and other literary works. One outstanding example is the 2019 novel *Marley*, by Jon Clinch, which uses the characters from Charles Dickens's classic tale *A Christmas Carol*. Clinch's novel fleshes out the backstory of Jacob Marley and Ebenezer Scrooge in brilliant and surprising ways (Marley was involved in the slave trade). Examples of the many different types of derivative works that can be created from public domain writings are listed later in this chapter.

In contrast, if a work is protected by copyright, you must obtain permission to create a derivative work from it. Such permission usually doesn't come free, if it is given at all.

Determining Copyright Status of Written Works

There are three main ways a written work enters the public domain. If it is not in the public domain one way, it could be in another. To know for sure whether a work is in the public domain or protected by copyright you need to look at each of these pathways:

- Many works are not eligible for copyright protection and automatically enter the public domain the moment they are created.

- A work may enter the public domain because its copyright has expired or they were created before there was a copyright law. Millions of works fall into this category, including most of the best-known public domain works, such as Shakespeare's plays and Dickens's novels.
- A work may enter the public domain because it was published before 1989 without a valid copyright notice. However, it can be difficult to tell for sure which works published without notices really are in the public domain. Determining public domain status from the first two pathways is like driving on a highway, but this pathway is more like struggling along an overgrown jungle trail.

Also, if you determine that a work is not in the public domain, this does not necessarily mean you can't use it. Many elements in copyrighted works are in the public domain even though the work as a whole is not—this includes the facts and ideas contained in a written work. See Chapter 14 for a detailed discussion of public domain elements in copyrighted writings.

In addition, in some situations it is legally permissible to quote from copyrighted writings without permission, on the grounds of fair use. The fair use privilege is covered in detail in Chapter 22.

 RESOURCE

What if the work is not in the public domain? If you find that the work you want to use is not in the public domain, you may be able to use it anyway under a legal exception called "fair use" (see Chapter 22). If you do not qualify for this exception, you will need to obtain permission to use the work. For a detailed discussion of how to obtain copyright permissions refer to *Getting Permission: Using & Licensing Copyright-Protected Materials Online & Off*, by Richard Stim (Nolo).

Is the Work Eligible for Copyright Protection?

Copyright law never protects certain works, regardless of when they were created and whether or not they have been published. These works are ordinarily free for the taking by anyone. Such works include:

- republications or reprinting of works in the public domain
- works by U.S. government employees and officers
- laws and court decisions
- individual words, names, slogans, and short phrases
- many blank forms
- information that is common property, such as standard calendars
- food and drink recipes, and
- works dedicated to the public domain —that is, works whose authors have voluntarily relinquished their copyright protection.

Attention Screenwriters: Free Ideas

Want to write a screenplay, but short on ideas? Adapt an already published novel by somebody else. Getting permission to create a screenplay from a novel by Stephen King, James Patterson, or John Grisham may cost millions of dollars. But there are tens of thousands of novels and other literary works by far better writers that are in the public domain and available for free. The following chart lists just a few classic novels that are in the public domain and that can be freely adapted into a screenplay. Many of them have already been filmed, but this doesn't mean they can't be filmed again. For example, William Shakespeare's *Romeo and Juliet* has been adapted for the movies 44 times since 1900, according to the Internet movie database at www.imdb.com.

This list represents an infinitesimal fraction of all the written works that are in the public domain, but may give you an idea of just how rich the public domain treasure trove is.

Author	Title	Publication Date
Adams, Henry	Democracy	1880
Alcott, Louisa May	Little Women	1868
Anderson, Sherwood	Winesburg, Ohio	1919
Austen, Jane	Pride and Prejudice	1813
Austen, Jane	Emma	1816
Austen, Jane	Sense and Sensibility	1811
Beerbohm, Max	Zuleika Dobson	1911
Bennett, Arnold	The Old Wives' Tale	1908
Brontë, Charlotte	Jane Eyre	1847
Brontë, Emily	Wuthering Heights	1847
Carroll, Lewis	Alice's Adventures in Wonderland	1865
Carroll, Lewis	Through the Looking Glass	1871
Christie, Agatha	The Mysterious Affair at Styles	1920
Cleland, John	Fanny Hill	1749
Collins, Wilkie	The Woman in White	1860
Conrad, Joseph	Lord Jim	1900
Conrad, Joseph	Nostromo	1904
Cooper, James Fenimore	The Last of the Mohicans	1826
Dickens, Charles	Bleak House	1853
Dickens, Charles	Great Expectations	1861
Doyle, Sir Arthur Conan	The Principal Works in Fiction	1913
Dreiser, Theodore	Sister Carrie	1900

Attention Screenwriters: Free Ideas (continued)

Author	Title	Publication Date
Eliot, George	*Middlemarch*	1871–72
Fielding, Henry	*Tom Jones*	1749
Fitzgerald, F. Scott	*This Side of Paradise*	1920
Forster, E.M.	*Howard's End*	1910
Galsworthy, John	*The Man of Property*	1906
Goldsmith, Oliver	*The Vicar of Wakefield*	1766
Haggard, H. Rider	*She*	1887
Hardy, Thomas	*The Mayor of Casterbridge*	1886
Hughes, Thomas	*Tom Brown's Schooldays*	1857
Irving, Washington	*The Sketch Book*	1820
James, Henry	*Portrait of a Lady*	1881
Joyce, James	*Dubliners*	1914
Kipling, Rudyard	*The Jungle Book*	1894
Lawrence, D.H.	*Sons and Lovers*	1913
Lewis, Sinclair	*Babbitt*	1922
London, Jack	*The Call of the Wild*	1903
Maugham, W. Somerset	*Of Human Bondage*	1915
Melville, Herman	*Moby Dick*	1851
Melville, Herman	*Billy Budd*	1924
Poe, Edgar Allan	*The Complete Works*	1902
Scott, Sir Walter	*Ivanhoe*	1819
Shelley, Mary	*Frankenstein*	1818
Sterne, Laurence	*Tristram Shandy*	1760–67
Stowe, Harriet Beecher	*Uncle Tom's Cabin*	1852
Swift, Jonathan	*Gulliver's Travels*	1726
Tarkington, Booth	*Alice Adams*	1921
Thackeray, William Makepeace	*Vanity Fair*	1847–48
Trollope, Anthony	*The Way We Live Now*	1875
Twain, Mark	*The Adventures of Tom Sawyer*	1876
Twain, Mark	*The Adventures of Huckleberry Finn*	1885
Wells, H.G.	*The Time Machine*	1895
Wharton, Edith	*The Age of Innocence*	1920
Wodehouse, P.G.	*My Man Jeeves*	1919

TIP

Here's a shortcut: If the work you're interested in doesn't fall into any of the categories listed above, it is not in the public domain if it was published after 1988. However, even though such a work is not in the public domain as a whole, it will usually contain elements that are in the public domain, such as facts or ideas. Refer to Chapter 14 to read about these.

Copies of Public Domain Works

Works that are simply copied from other works are not protected by copyright. If the original work is in the public domain, the copy will be as well. For example, a newly published copy of Mark Twain's novel *The Adventures of Tom Sawyer* (whose copyright expired long ago) is as much in the public domain as the original published version. You are free, in most cases, to make actual copies of every page of a reprint or use it in any other way you want. U.S. copyright law does not protect typefaces, so even if a publisher uses a new typeface for a new edition of a public domain work, you are still free to photocopy the text (see Chapter 5).

However, some publishers who reprint public domain works add new material, for example, a new introduction, explanatory notes, photos, or illustrations. This new material would be entitled to copyright protection, but the original public domain work would still remain in the public domain. For example, if new illustrations were added to a new edition of *The Adventures of Tom Sawyer*, you couldn't copy the illustrations without permission, but you would still be free to copy the novel itself—that is, Mark Twain's words.

Publishers and others who add new material to reprints of public domain works typically include copyright notices in the reprints. Although legally permissible, such notices may mislead or confuse people into thinking that the original works themselves are protected by copyright when actually they are in the public domain.

U.S. Government Works

All written works by the U.S. (federal) government are in the public domain. This is true whether the work is published or unpublished.

A work is a U.S. government work if it was prepared by an officer or employee of the federal government as part of that person's official duties. "Officers" include all elected and appointed officials of all branches of the U.S. government—for example, the president, members of Congress, cabinet members, and judges, as well as lower-level U.S. government officials and members of the federal bureaucracy.

As you might imagine, there are a massive number of U.S. government works in the public domain. Just a few examples of public domain U.S. government works include:

- most, but not all work published by the U.S. Government Printing Office (www.gpo.gov)
- all IRS publications, forms, rulings, and other IRS documents (www.irs.gov)
- official speeches, letters, and other documents by the president, Congress, and other federal government officers and employees, and
- published and unpublished documents by the U.S. Copyright Office, Patent and Trademark Office, and other federal agencies.

A portal to the websites of all federal agencies can be found at www.usa.gov.

However, not everything created by U.S. government officers or employees is automatically in the public domain. Works created outside official government duties are eligible for copyright protection. Moreover, private contractors working for the U.S. government may obtain copyright protection for some works they create.

U.S. government agencies may, but are not required to, place notices in their works stating that they are in the public domain. The form of such notices varies; one example is provided below:

This is a work of the U.S. government and is not subject to copyright protection in the United States. Foreign copyrights may apply.

If you find a notice like this, the work is in the public domain. However, absence of such a notice doesn't necessarily mean the work is not public domain. You'll need to do more investigation to see if one of the exceptions noted below applies.

Works Created Outside of Official Duties

Only works created by U.S. government employees or officers as part of their official duties are in the public domain. In other words, the work must be created as part of the job of the employee or officer. For example, a personal letter written by former president Nixon or General Douglas MacArthur would not be in the public domain, because such a letter would not have been created as part of their official duties. Similarly, a court held that certain speeches written by Admiral Hyman Rickover (the father of the nuclear Navy) were his private property and entitled to copyright protection. The speeches in question did not concern his Navy duties and were created and delivered on his free time. *Public Affairs Assocs., Inc. v. Rickover*, 268 F.Supp. 444 (D.D.C. 1967).

Copyrighted Works Containing U.S. Government Materials

U.S. government writings are frequently included within copyrighted works published by the private sector. For example, a work on U.S. population trends could include material from the U.S. Census Bureau; a biography of Franklin Roosevelt could include lengthy quotations from his official speeches and letters. Including such U.S. government materials within another work does not take them out of the public domain.

If a privately published work consists mostly of U.S. government materials, the copyright notice must identify those portions of the work that are not government materials and are thus protected by copyright. This enables you to tell which portions of the work are in the public domain. For example, a work on U.S. population that consists primarily of six appendixes containing U.S. Census Bureau documents could contain a copyright notice like this: "Copyright © by Joe James 2020. No protection is claimed in works of the United States government as set forth in Appendixes 1-6."

By Linda Allison, copyright © Nolo 2020

Nor would a book or article written by a government employee outside of his or her duties be in the public domain even if it involved government activities. Memoirs written by public officials or employees after they leave office are not in the public domain, even if they discuss what they did when they were in the government. *Harper & Row Publishers v. Nation Enterprises*, 723 F.2d 195 (2d Cir. 1983).

The fact that a government employee or officer occasionally uses a government office, secretary, or other government facility to help create a work does not mean that the work was created as part of the employee's duties. Government employees sometimes use such facilities to create works that are not within their job duties. Such a work would not be in the public domain (but the employee might be subject to discipline for misusing federal facilities). For example, the speeches by Admiral Hyman Rickover mentioned above were found not to be in the public domain even though the administrative assistant at his Navy office had typed the final drafts.

Nor is a work in the public domain simply because it is printed by the U.S. government. Such a work could be copyrighted, for example, if an independent contractor created it for the government (see below).

The Three Levels of Government

You need to know what level of government a document or other work comes from before you can know whether it's in the public domain. There are three basic levels of government in the United States.

- The U.S. (or federal) government, which is headquartered in Washington, DC, and includes the Executive Branch, Congress, the Supreme Court and other federal courts, and federal agencies such as the IRS, Department of Defense, and Copyright Office.
- The 50 state governments, headquartered in the 50 state capitals, including the state governors, legislatures, state courts, and state agencies such as your state's motor vehicle agency.
- The thousands of city, county, and other local governments located throughout the United States. This includes local mayors, city councils, and local government agencies such as your local planning department or school district.

Only works by employees or officers of the U.S. government are automatically in the public domain. State and local governments can claim copyright in works they create, subject to one exception for government edicts, discussed below.

It is usually not difficult to tell what level of government a written work emanates from. If the work has been published, the cover or title page will usually indicate what government agency wrote the work. If the work is an unpublished letter, memo, or other item, the stationery on which it is written will usually show where it comes from. However, if you're not sure whether the work was created by a U.S. government agency, contact them and ask.

Works by Independent Contractors

The U.S. government often hires independent contractors to help create written works of all kinds. Works created for the federal government by independent contractors—meaning people who are neither U.S. government officers nor employees—can be protected by copyright. It all depends on what the government decides at the time the independent contractor is hired. If the government wants the work to be in the public domain, it can require the independent contractor to sign a work-made-for-hire agreement. In this event, the U.S. government, not the contractor who actually wrote the work, would be considered the author of the work for copyright purposes. The work would be in the public domain.

On the other hand, if the U.S. government does not require the contractor to sign a work for hire agreement, the work would be protected by copyright. The copyright could be owned either (1) by the contractor who created it, or (2) by the U.S. government if it required the contractor to assign his or her copyright to it. In most cases, the government does not take steps to assert full ownership of works created by independent contractors, and the copyright in such works ends up being held by the contractor.

If the contractor gets copyright ownership, the U.S. government gets a license to use the work. The U.S. government's license is a nonexclusive, irrevocable, worldwide license to use, modify, reproduce, release, perform, display, or disclose the work. The United States may use the work for government-related purposes without restrictions. It also may permit people outside the government to use, modify, reproduce, release, perform, display, or disclose the work on its behalf. The government's license includes the right to distribute copies of the work to the public for government purposes—for example, on government websites. This means that, even if a contractor holds a copyright in a work created for the government, you could use it if you get the government's permission to do so on its behalf. Of course, you could also get permission from the contractor. Finally, you could use it

without obtaining permission if your use constitutes a fair use. (See Chapter 22.)

When a contractor obtains ownership of a work created under a contract with a U.S. government civilian agency or NASA, federal regulations require the contractor to place a copyright notice on it acknowledging U.S. government sponsorship (including the contract number). The notice must be on the work when it is delivered to the government, published, or deposited for registration with the U.S. Copyright Office. (Federal Acquisition Regulation (FAR) 52.227-14 (www.acquisition.gov/far).) Here's a suggested format for such a notice:

COPYRIGHT STATUS: This work, authored by _____ employees, was funded in whole or in part by _____ under U.S. government contract _____, and is, therefore, subject to the following license: The government is granted for itself and others acting on its behalf a paid-up, nonexclusive, irrevocable worldwide license in this work to reproduce, prepare derivative works, distribute copies to the public, and perform it publicly and display it publicly, by or on behalf of the government. All other rights are reserved by the copyright owner.

It is possible, however, for published works to lack a copyright notice and for unpublished works to not have any notices or warning statements. For this reason, always look for other signs that a work was created by contractors. For example, contractors and/or their company will usually be given credit on the title page or somewhere else in the document, or the contractors' company may be referred to in the work in some way that makes it clear that independent contractors created it.

If you suspect independent contractors have created a work, it is a good idea to call, write, or email the government agency involved to ask if the work is in the public domain or if you need permission from the government agency or the contractor to use it.

Works by State and Local Government Employees

The rule that U.S. government works are in the public domain does not apply to works by state and local government employees; those works may be protected by copyright. For example, a state tax pamphlet or booklet on air pollution or water conservation published by a city or county may be protected. However, there is one exception: State and local government laws and court decisions are in the public domain.

Not all state and local governments claim copyright in their publications, but many do. Some may claim copyright in some publications, but not in others. For a comprehensive guide to the copyright policies of the 50 states, refer to *The State Copyright Resource Center* at Harvard University at http://copyright.lib.harvard.edu/states. This outstanding resource contains summaries of the copyright policies of all 50 states, as well as links to the relevant state legislation and case law. It also ranks the states according to an "openness score."

You can tell that copyright is claimed if you find a copyright notice (a © symbol or the word "Copyright" followed by a publication date and copyright owner's name) on a work in the name of the state or local government entity. However, the absence of a copyright notice doesn't necessarily mean copyright isn't being claimed, because use of a copyright notice is not mandatory for works published after March 1, 1989 (see Chapter 19). If you're not sure whether copyright is claimed in a particular state or local publication or unpublished document, call, write, or email the agency involved and ask them.

The District of Columbia and Puerto Rico are treated the same as states for these purposes.

Public Domain Does Not Mean Public Access

The fact that U.S. government written works are in the public domain—that is, not protected by copyright—does not mean they are always accessible to the public. Millions of government documents are classified for national security reasons and are not made available to the general public. This includes, for example, most works created by employees of the Central Intelligence Agency, FBI, and State Department. Many other documents are not publicly available for reasons of privacy—for example, tax records kept by the IRS and health records maintained by the National Institutes of Health. Eventually, many classified documents do become publicly available.

For example, the National Security Agency has declassified thousands of documents created by the VENONA Project. VENONA was the code name used for the U.S. Signals Intelligence effort to collect and decrypt the text of secret Soviet spy agency messages in the 1940s. These messages provided extraordinary insight into Soviet attempts to infiltrate the highest levels of the U.S. government. The National Security Agency has placed copies of many of these decrypts on its website. Because U.S. government employees created them, they are in the public domain and may be freely copied.

Members of the public may obtain copies of many U.S. government documents through the Freedom of Information Act, a federal law that requires federal agencies to make certain types of records publicly available. A few examples of the wide variety of records that citizens have obtained under the Freedom of Information Act include: reports on silicone breast implants from the Food and Drug Administration; statistics on boycotts from the Department of Commerce; and records on the assassination of former President Kennedy from the FBI and the CIA.

However, not every government document can be obtained under the Freedom of Information Act. The government won't release documents if doing so would violate privacy or security rules.

A comprehensive set of weblinks on the FOIA is at www.llsdc.org/freedom-of-information-act-resources. Useful guides to the Freedom of Information Act can also be found at the following organizations' websites:

- the United States Justice Department at (www.foia.gov)
- the Reporters Committee for Freedom of the Press at (www.rcfp.org/federal-open-government-guide), and
- the National Security Archive at (https://nsarchive2.gwu.edu//nsa/foia/guide.html.)

Foreign Government Works

Subject to one exception for government edicts, materials prepared by any foreign government with which the United States has copyright relations (see Chapter 15) are entitled to claim copyright protection in the United States. Also included in this category are works prepared by the United Nations and any of its agencies such as UNESCO, and the Organization of American States.

Not all foreign governments claim copyright in their official publications, but many do—for example, the United Kingdom and Canada have something called Crown Copyright, which protects most government publications. You must research the law of the country involved to know if it claims copyright in its publications (see Chapter 16).

Quasi-Governmental Organizations

Some organizations that you might think are U.S. government agencies really aren't. Instead, they are quasi-governmental organizations or independent corporations established under U.S. government auspices. Such organizations are allowed to claim a copyright in their publications and other works. These include, for example:

- the Smithsonian Institution, which is an "independent trust instrumentality" of the United States
- the U.S. Postal Service, which became an independent corporation in 1970, and
- the Corporation for Public Broadcasting, which is a private nonprofit corporation established and partly funded by Congress.

Organizations such as these normally place copyright notices on their published works, Web pages, and other copyrighted materials. But, if you're not sure whether an organization whose material you want to use is a U.S. government agency or a quasi-government organization, contact them and ask.

Certain Technical Data

The U.S. Department of Commerce runs something called the Standard Reference Data Program. This program creates publications and databases of technical data regarding metals, chemicals, industrial fluids and materials, and similar items for technical problem-solving, research, and development by scientists and engineers. The Commerce Department is allowed to claim a copyright in such standard reference data. 15 U.S.C. Section 290(e).

Anticounterfeiting Rules

Although federal government documents are ordinarily in the public domain, federal anticounterfeiting laws may prevent you from freely copying some of them. These laws apply to such documents as negotiable bonds and passports.

To prevent counterfeiting, federal law requires that some materials can only be photocopied in black and white, single-sided, and must be reduced to 75% or enlarged to 150% of their original size. The requirements cover:

- treasury notes
- gold certificates
- Internal Revenue stamps
- postage stamps, and
- government, bank, or corporation bonds and securities. 18 U.S.C. Section 504.

Some other documents can only be copied in black and white, including:

- passports
- U.S., state, or foreign government identification cards
- driver's licenses
- Social Security cards
- birth certificates
- immigration papers, and
- certificates of U.S. citizenship.

In addition, U.S. government securities, notes, and other obligations may not be used in advertisements. 18 U.S.C. Section 475.

Paper currency may be reproduced in black and white if reduced to at least 75% or enlarged to at least 150% of its original size. Currency may also be reproduced in color if the reproduction is:

- one-sided
- reduced to at least 75% or enlarged to at least 150% of the bill's original size, and

---

The Smithsonian Exception

As mentioned above, the Smithsonian Institution is not considered part of the federal government. However, the Smithsonian does receive some funding from the U.S. government, and the U.S. government pays some of the people who work there. The Smithsonian regards works created by employees paid by the government to be in the public domain. But the Smithsonian does claim copyright in all works created by employees it pays itself (such workers are called trust fund employees). The Smithsonian also ordinarily acquires copyright ownership on works created on its behalf by outside independent contractors.

Unless a Smithsonian Institution publication or other document specifically states that it is in the public domain, the only way you can determine for sure if it is in the public domain is to contact the Institution and ask.

- all negatives, plates, digitized storage medium, graphic files, and any other thing used to make the reproduction that contain an image of the currency are destroyed and/or deleted or erased after their final use. 31 C.F.R. Section 411.

Laws and Court Decisions

For our political and legal system to function properly, we must all have free access to official legal documents such as judicial opinions, legislation, public ordinances, administrative rulings, and similar items. For this reason, all such works are in the public domain. This rule applies to all levels of government—local, state, and federal, and even includes foreign government laws and legal rulings. Thus, all laws, from the United Nations Charter to your local zoning regulations, are in the public domain.

Privately Published Laws and Decisions

Federal and state judges frequently issue written opinions when they decide court cases. These opinions are a vital resource for understanding how the courts interpret the laws passed by Congress and the state legislatures.

In the United States, most of the opinions by the federal and state courts are collected and published by private legal publishers, as are most of the laws passed by the Congress and state legislatures. These publishers cannot claim copyright in the text of the decisions and laws themselves, but they are entitled to a copyright in some material they create and add to these publications.

For example, editors at legal publishing companies typically write summaries of the court decisions they publish. These summaries (called headnotes) are copyrighted, but the legal opinions themselves are in the public domain.

Other elements typically added to court rulings by legal publishers have been found by courts not to be protected by copyright. These elements include the names of the lawyers, parties, and court; the date of decision; and the procedural history of the case. *Matthew Bender v. West Publishing Corp.*, 158 F.3d 674 (2d Cir. 1998). One federal court found that brief descriptive titles and chapter and article headings added to a collection of government statutes were not protected by copyright. *State of Georgia v. Harrison Co.*, 548 F.Supp. 110 (N.D. Ga. 1982). And at least one federal appellate court ruled that unique page numbering systems used in legal publications do not merit copyright protection. *Matthew Bender v. West Publishing Corp.*, 158 F.3d 693 (2d Cir. 1998).

> **CAUTION**
> **Individual court decisions appear to be fair game so long as they are stripped of the copyright-protected material added by the private legal publisher.** But copying an entire published volume of legal opinions produced by a private legal publisher (or a substantial portion of it) and reproducing the opinions in the same order they appeared in the volume could violate the publisher's compilation copyright in the volume as a whole. Consult a copyright attorney before attempting to do such copying.

State Copyright Claims

Despite the rule that state laws are in the public domain, many states assert copyright claims in their statutes. Some states, such as Virginia, claim copyright on the historical notes, editorial notes, format, and captions included in the official published version of their state statutes. However, no copyright is claimed in the text of the statutes themselves. While the practice has not yet been challenged, it is likely that, according to current copyright law, the format and captions are not protected by copyright. But the copyright claim for the notes might be valid. Notes are not laws, and states are entitled to claim copyright in works created by their employees (other than laws and court rulings). This was an issue the U. S. Supreme Court was considering as this book went to press (the case is *Georgia v. Public.Resource.Org, Inc.*).

However, several states—including Nebraska, Michigan, and Mississippi—assert extraordinarily broad claims in the texts of their statutes themselves, something clearly not permitted under the law. Nevada and Pennsylvania claim copyright in all state publications. Only Illinois specifically disclaims all copyright claims in all its laws. 25 Ill. Comp. Stat. Ann. Section 135/5.04.

Many states also attempt to place copyright-like restrictions on the public's use of state laws posted on websites. For example, Oregon claimed copyright in its laws and demanded that nonprofit websites pay for a license to post them. However, the state backed down on its claims when the organization Public.Resource.Org began to reproduce the Oregon state statues on its website. Many states also claim copyright protection for regulations—that is, rules adopted by state agencies that interpret and enforce state laws.

Such state copyright claims would almost certainly not apply to your copying of state laws and regulations for your personal use, but the state might take action if you published or otherwise tried to commercially exploit them, for example, by publishing them in a book or on a website.

You can find summaries of the copyright policies of the states toward their statutes, as well as links to the relevant state legislation and case law, at the website of The State Copyright Resource Center at Harvard University at http://copyright.lib.harvard.edu/states.

Digital Copies of Court Decisions

Legal opinions are digitally copied and reproduced on both commercial and nonprofit websites. Some compilers of such online collections assert no copyright claims in the legal materials. For example, Google, Inc., has made thousands of legal decisions available at its Google Scholar website (http://scholar.google.com) without making any copyright claims. However, others do assert copyright claims and include copyright notices on the digital copies of legal decisions, and they may require users to agree to license restrictions on how they may use the digital copies. The best advice is to avoid websites that impose such restrictions. If you can't find what you want on a website that does not make copyright claims, you can always go to a law library and copy the cases in the printed bound volumes, instead of using digital copies. Published books are not subject to license restrictions.

Copyrighted Model Codes

Creating a local building code, planning ordinance, or similarly complex legislation is a time-consuming and difficult task. To make this drafting process easier, private publishers have written what are called model codes. Instead of writing their own codes from scratch, many governments license and use the models.

For decades, publishers of such model codes have claimed copyright in their creations. Local laws, codes, and ordinances based on such codes often contain copyright notices in the publisher's name or some other indication that copyright is claimed by the publisher. In a significant victory for public domain proponents, a federal appellate court found that model codes enter the public domain when they are enacted into law by local governments and the wording of the model code is actually included in a statute or other law. *Veeck v. Southern Building Code Congress Int'l, Inc.,* 293 F.3d 791 (5th Cir. 2002).

However, model codes that have not been included in state and local laws are still protected by copyright. Additionally, some state and local statues incorporate all or part of a model code by reference, instead of including the actual wording of the code in the law itself. The user must go to the website of the model code publisher to read the language incorporated by reference into law. Model code publishers are asserting copyright claims over their codes in these cases. One organization fighting these claims is Public.Resource. Org (https://publicresource.org).

However, you are on very safe ground if you copy a government statute, ordinance, or regulation itself, even if it is word-for-word the same as a model code.

Quasi-Official Legal Documents

Some types of privately created works are adopted by, or receive official approval from, government agencies. Such documents, in effect, obtain a quasi-official status, but courts have ruled that they do not enter the public domain. The rationale for this is that such documents are not themselves official laws. Rather, the law requires that citizens consult or use these privately published documents to fulfill their obligations. For example:

- The American Medical Association created and published a medical procedure coding system that was adopted by the federal Health Care Financing Administration for use in completing Medicare and Medicaid claim forms. The system was ruled to be protected by copyright. *Practice Management Information Corp. v. The American Medical Association*, 121 F.3d 516 (9th Cir. 1997).
- The insurance regulations of several states required that the used car prices listed in the *Red Book*—a privately published used car price guide—be used as a standard for insurance payments. It was ruled not in the public domain. *CCC Information Services v. Maclean Hunter Market Reports*, 44 F.3d 61 (2d Cir. 1994).

- A tentative map for a residential subdivision prepared by a private developer was approved by the town council and therefore had legal effect, but it did not enter the public domain. *Del Madera Properties v. Rhodes & Gardner, Inc.*, 637 F.Supp. 262 (N.D. Cal. 1985).

Words, Names, Slogans, and Other Short Phrases

Individual words are never protected by copyright, even if a particular person invents them. For example, the word "newspeak," invented by George Orwell for his novel *1984,* is in the public domain. If individual words were copyrighted, people would be discouraged from using them, and the growth of our language would be greatly retarded. As explained by the U.S. Supreme Court, "words are the common property of the human race and are as little susceptible of private appropriation as air or sunlight." *Holmes v. Hurst*, 174 U.S. 82 (1899).

Names, whether of individuals, products, or business organizations or groups, are likewise not protected by copyright. Titles also are not copyrightable (see Chapter 13).

Ordinarily, slogans and other short phrases are not protected by copyright— for example, the phrases "Gift Check," "Priority Message," and "Contents Require

Immediate Attention" used in a direct mail advertising campaign were held to be in the public domain. *Magic Mktg. v. Mailing Servs. of Pittsburgh*, 634 F.Supp. 769 (W.D. Pa. 1986). Likewise, short lists of numbers used to identify various types of screws— for example, "402-10-202-10"—were too brief to qualify for copyright protection. *Southco Inc. v. Kanebridge Corporation*, 390 F.3d 276 (2004). The U.S. Copyright Office has also refused to register a "tweet"—a 280-character message sent on Twitter.com—on the grounds that it was an unprotectable short phrase.

However, courts have made exceptions in the cases of some highly creative and well-known literary phrases. For example, courts have held that the following phrases are copyrightable:

- "E.T. phone home" from the movie *E.T.—The Extra-Terrestrial. Universal City Studios v. Kamar Indus., Inc.*, 217 U.S.P.Q. 1162 (S.D. Tex. 1982).
- "When there is no room in hell ... the dead will walk the earth" from the movie *Night of the Living Dead. Dawn Assocs. v. Links*, 203 U.S.P.Q. 831 (N.D. Ill. 1978).
- "Look!... Up in the sky!... It's a bird!... It's a plane!... It's Superman!" from a trailer for the *Superman* television show. *DC Comics v. Crazy Eddie*, 204 U.S.P.Q. 1177 (S.D.N.Y. 1977).

Courts are particularly likely to rule that such phrases are copyright protected when they are used for commercial purposes in, for example, an advertisement.

> **CAUTION**
>
> **Any of the items discussed in this section could have protection under state and federal trademark laws if they are used in connection with the sale of a product or service.** Using a person's name to help sell a product or service could also violate the person's right to publicity. (See Chapter 20 for a detailed discussion.)

Blank Forms

Blank forms designed solely to record information are in the public domain. The U.S. Copyright Office will not register them. 37 C.F.R. Section 202.1(c). According to the Copyright Office, this includes such items as time cards, graph paper, account books, standard bank checks that don't contain illustrations, scorecards, address books, diaries, report forms, and order forms.

Forms such as these typically consist only of simple arrangements of horizontal and vertical lines with perhaps a few short headings. The headings are so obvious that their selection cannot be said to be even minimally creative. Some examples are a baseball scorecard with columns headed "innings" and lines headed "players" or a travel diary with headings for "cities," "hotels," and "restaurants." Below is an example of an account book ledger design the Supreme Court held was not entitled to copyright protection in *Baker v. Seldon*, 101 U.S. 99 (1879):

However, courts generally find more elaborate and creative forms can obtain copyright protection, even if they consist primarily of blank spaces to be filled in. For example, a court held that the following baseball pitching statistics form was copyrightable:

This form, the first of its kind, lists four items of information about each day's games—the teams, the starting pitchers, the game time, and the betting odds—and then lists nine items of information about each pitcher's past performance, grouped into three categories. The court held that the selection of this particular combination of baseball statistical categories required enough creativity to merit copyright protection. *Kregos v. Associated Press*, 937 F.2d 700 (2d Cir. 1991).

Forms that contain substantial text—for example, forms that contain detailed instructions, and insurance policies, contracts, and other legal forms—are protected by copyright. However, where there are only a few ways to express the facts and ideas contained in such forms, a legal rule called the merger doctrine might severely limit protection (see Chapter 14).

For example, one court held that insurance bond forms and indemnity agreements were entitled to copyright protection. But the court said that because the forms contained standard language that would have to be included in any form designed to accomplish the same purpose, only verbatim copying of the exact wording would constitute copyright infringement. *Continental Casualty Co. v. Beardsley*, 253 F.2d 702 (2d Cir. 1958).

Even if an individual form is in the public domain, a work consisting of multiple forms could be protected by copyright as a compilation. In this event, copyright protection extends only to the compiler's selection and arrangement of all the forms as a group. (See Chapter 12 for detailed discussion of compilations.)

GRAY AREA

In many cases it may be difficult to tell for sure whether a blank form is in the public domain, or whether it contains enough information to be copyrighted. See Chapter 1 for a detailed discussion of how to deal with such public domain gray areas.

Information That Is Common Property

According to the U.S. Copyright Office, works consisting of information that is common property are in the public domain. Examples of such works include standard calendars, height and weight charts, tape measures and rulers, schedules of sporting events, and lists or tables taken from public documents or other common sources. 37 C.F.R. Section 202.1(d).

However, new material added to such works is protectable. Although a standard calendar is not protected by copyright, photos, illustrations, or quotations added to a calendar can be protected. But copyright protection only extends to this new material, not to the standard calendar itself.

Food and Drink Recipes

A mere listing of ingredients for a recipe is not copyrightable. However, if a cookbook author spices up his or her recipes with explanatory material, such material is protectable. One court has suggested that this could include advice on wines to go with the meal, hints on place settings and appropriate music, or tales of a recipe's historical or ethnic origin. *Publications Int'l Ltd. v. Meredith Corp.*, 88 F.3d 473 (7th Cir. 1996). Photographs or drawings included in a cookbook would also be copyrightable unless taken from other public domain sources. A how-to video of a chef implementing a recipe would also be protectable as a video, but this would not protect the recipe's list of ingredients.

Keep in mind, however, that it is only the individual bare-bones recipes that are in the public domain. A collection of numerous recipes can be protected as a compilation. But in this event the copyright only extends to the selection and arrangements of all the recipes as a whole. The individual recipes are still not protected. (See Chapter 12 for a detailed discussion of compilations.)

Moreover, to be protectable, the compilation must be original and minimally creative. Most cookbooks would likely fail this test. For example, "beginning a cookbook with an illustrated cover, following it with an introduction by a third-party, a narrative by the author, lists of appliances and ingredients ... instructions about preparing common ingredients, and a list of recipes" was insufficient to be a protectable compilation. Thus comedian Jerry Seinfeld's wife did not commit copyright infringement when she included similar elements in a cookbook of her own. *LaPine v. Seinfeld*, No. 08 Civ. 128. (S.D.N.Y. 2009).

Copyright never protects a procedure, discovery, or system itself, only the way an author expresses it. For example, if someone writes a book describing how to grow an organic garden using minimal water, the words in the book are protected, but the gardening procedure is not. Anyone can read the book and use the procedure it describes. Likewise, anyone can read a cookbook and use a recipe it describes—that is, create a dish based on the recipe.

Works Dedicated to the Public Domain

Authors need not enjoy copyright protection if they don't want it. Instead, they may dedicate their work to the public domain. This means they give up all their rights in the work forever and anyone may use the work without asking their permission.

There is no prescribed formula for dedicating a work to the public domain. The author or other copyright owner simply has to make clear his or her intentions. For example, stating "This work is dedicated to the public domain" on a book or article's title page would be sufficient. It's not even necessary to make the dedication in writing. It could be done orally, but it's always best to write something down to avoid possible misunderstandings.

Be careful, however, where an author sends mixed messages—for example, by stating that the work is in the public domain but restricting how the public may use it with the statement: "This work is public domain but may not be posted online without my permission." When a work is dedicated to the public domain, the author may not restrict how it is used. A statement like this leaves it unclear whether the author really intended to dedicate the work to the public domain. It's wise to seek clarification from the author or ask permission for the restricted use.

Similarly the use of the phrase "copyright free" by the author need not mean the work is dedicated to the public domain. The words "copyright free" are often used to describe works (particularly photos and clip-art) that are under copyright, copies of which are sold to the public for a set fee rather than under a royalty arrangement.

One way to dedicate a work to the public domain is by using a Creative Commons CC0 license (see Chapter 17 for a detailed discussion of such licenses). You can search for such material online by using the Creative Commons search engine at http://search.creativecommons.org.

Has the Work Been Published?

If a work can be protected by copyright, as discussed above, you must decide whether it has been published for copyright purposes. Being published for copyright purposes has a specific legal meaning. The answer to this question is vitally important, because it is used to determine whether the work is in the public domain because its copyright has expired or because it lacks a valid copyright notice.

Has the Work Been Distributed to the General Public?

A written work is published for copyright purposes when the copyright owner, or someone acting on the owner's behalf, makes it available to the *general* public. In other words, any interested member of the public may obtain a copy. *Burke v. National Broadcasting Co.*, 598 F.2d 688 (9th Cir. 1979).

The copies do not necessarily have to be sold for publication to occur; they can also be leased or rented, loaned, or even given away. For example, they can be handed out to the public for free on a street corner or left in a public place for anyone to take. Nor is it necessary for large numbers of copies to be distributed. So long as the work has been made freely available to the general public, it makes no difference if just one copy has been sold or distributed. *Gottsberger v. Aldine Book Publishing Co.*, 33 F. 381 (C.C.D. Mass. 1887).

Obviously, if a work is printed and copies are offered for sale to the general public in brick-and-mortar bookstores, online or through mail order, or by any other means of public distribution, a publication has occurred. The same holds true for magazines, newspapers, and all other written works made available to the public at large.

However, a publication does not occur simply because an author signed a publishing contract or delivered a manuscript to a publisher, magazine, or newspaper editor. Copies of the work must actually have been printed and distributed, or at least sent to retail dealers for distribution. *Press Publishing Co. v. Monroe*, 73 F. 196 (2d Cir. 1896).

Dedicating Works to the Public Domain Through the Creative Commons

The Creative Commons, a nonprofit organization designed to foster the public domain, has established a program to help copyright owners dedicate their works to the public domain. See Chapter 17 for a detailed discussion.

To be published, a work doesn't necessarily have to be disseminated to the public through normal distribution channels like, for example, bookstores, magazine and newspaper racks, subscriptions, or mail order. Other, nontraditional means of distribution can also constitute a publication. For example, courts have ruled that publication occurred in the following situations:

- Copies of several speeches by Admiral Hyman Rickover (the father of the nuclear Navy) were made freely available to the press. *Public Affairs Associates v. Rickover*, 268 F.Supp. 444 (D.D.C. 1967)
- About 200 copies of a manuscript were mimeographed and mailed to various persons interested in the subject matter with a letter saying they should pass the work on to others after they read it. *White v. Kimmell*, 193 F.2d 744 (9th Cir. 1952).

Has the Work Been Performed or Displayed, But Not Distributed?

For a publication to occur for copyright purposes it is crucial that *copies* of the work be made available to the general public. For this reason, merely performing or displaying a work in public is not considered a publication. For example, performing a play in public is not a publication. Copies of the play must be made available to the general public, not just to the actors. *Ferris v. Frohman*, 223 U.S. 424 (1912).

Similarly, delivering a public lecture, speech, or sermon is not a publication. This is so regardless of the size of the audience that hears the speaker. For example, courts have held that Martin Luther King's "I Have a Dream" speech was not published when it was delivered before over 200,000 people at the Lincoln Memorial and broadcast live on television and radio to millions. *Estate of Martin Luther King Jr., Inc. v. CBS Inc.*, 194 F.3d 1211 (11th Cir. 1999).

Publicly displaying a manuscript, letter, or similar item in, for example, a library or museum exhibit also does not constitute a publication.

Has the Work Received Only Limited Distribution?

A publication occurs for copyright purposes only when copies are made available to the *general* public—that is, to anyone who wants a copy. In contrast, publication does not occur where copies are limited to a selected group of people for a limited purpose without the right of further distribution, reproduction, or sale. *Academy of Motion Picture Arts & Sciences v. Creative House Promotions*, 944 F.2d 1446 (9th Cir. 1991).

For example, publication would not occur where:

- an author distributes a small number of copies of a manuscript to colleagues or friends for comment and criticism with the understanding that the work may not be duplicated or circulated
- an author or publisher sends a limited number of copies of a work to reviewers so they can write reviews
- a playwright makes copies of a play available to the actors who will perform it
- a teacher distributes texts at a seminar for use only by attendees at the seminar, or
- a company produces an in-house newsletter for its employees who are expressly prohibited from reproducing it or disseminating it outside the company.

Date and Country of Publication

If you determine that the work you're interested in has been published, you should also determine the year of publication and the country where it was first published. Both these factors will affect how long the U.S. copyright in the work lasts (see Chapter 18).

Date of Publication

You only need to know the year, not the exact date, a work was first published. You can usually determine the publication date from the work itself. The vast majority of published written works have copyright notices. The date in the notice is the year date of publication—for example, © 1966 by Scrivener & Sons. (See Chapter 19 for a detailed discussion of copyright notices.)

However, if the work lacks a copyright notice, but you have determined that it was published, you'll have to look elsewhere for clues about when the work was published. It may contain a date of publication somewhere else—for example, on the title page. If not, try the following:

Check the Library of Congress Card Catalog. You can do this in person at the Library in Washington, DC, or online through the Library's website (https://catalog.loc.gov). The Library's catalog contains the publication dates for millions of written works in the Library's collection.

Check Copyright Office Records. If the work was registered with the U.S. Copyright Office, checking Copyright Office registration records will reveal when it was first published. These records can be researched online (see Chapter 21). However, not all published works are registered with the Copyright Office, so there may be no record for it.

Check Reference Works. There are hundreds of reference works that may be able to tell you when a written work was published. For example, in the realm of literature these include such works as *Contemporary Authors, Contemporary Literary Criticism,* and various books in the *Dictionary of Literary Biography* Series, all published by Gale. These and many other similar reference works are searchable online through local or university libraries. Ask your local librarian for assistance.

Research the Author. Researching the author of the work may reveal when the work was published. For well-known authors, biographies or critical studies may have detailed publication histories of their works.

Use the Internet. Many helpful reference works and much information about authors and their works are available on the Internet. Do a search using the author's name, the name of the work involved, and the publisher. There may be a website devoted to the author or even to the particular work, or an online reference (such as Wikipedia) with detailed information about the work.

Contact the Publisher. Contact the work's publisher and ask them to tell you when the work was first published.

Country of Publication

Unfortunately, a work's country of publication is not listed in the copyright notice. However, books, magazines, newspapers, and other written works typically say where they were published or printed. You can often find this information on the title page or the same page as the copyright notice. If you can't find the country of publication from the work itself, try using the resources listed above—they will ordinarily provide the country of publication as well as the publication date.

Has the Work's Copyright Expired?

Copyright protection does not last forever. When it ends the work enters the public domain. Indeed, the greatest single body of public domain materials is made up of works for which U.S. copyright has expired. Works published in the United States as recently as 1963 could be in the public domain because their copyright expired. Moreover, the copyright for millions of unpublished works expired on Jan. 1, 2003. Because determining the expiration date of a copyright is complex, we have devoted an entire chapter to it. Once you have determined whether the work has been published, you should refer to Chapter 18 for a detailed discussion of copyright duration to determine if copyright protection has expired.

➡️ **SKIP AHEAD**
If a work was published after 1963, its copyright has not expired and you need not read Chapter 18 unless you want to know when the work's copyright will eventually expire.

Is the Work in the Public Domain Due to Lack of a Copyright Notice?

Some works have entered the public domain because they lack a proper copyright notice. They must be published works and they must have been published before 1989, because in that year copyright notices became optional. Examine the work carefully to determine if it has a notice. A copyright notice on a written work must contain three elements:

- the familiar © symbol, the word "Copyright," or the abbreviation "Copr."
- the publication year date, and
- the name of copyright owner.

For example, a proper copyright notice will often look like this:

© 1945 Ralph Cramden

You can usually find the notice on the page immediately following the title page of a book or on the title page itself. Copyright notices for magazines, newspapers, journals, and other periodicals are usually found on the title page, the first page of text, or under the title heading. The notice may also appear in a magazine's masthead.

If you're interested in a work that has been published as part of a larger work— for example, an article published in a magazine or newspaper—it's sufficient that the larger work has a notice. For example, a notice in the name of a magazine will cover all the articles in the magazine.

However, if the work has no notice or the notice lacks one of the three elements described above—copyright symbol © or word Copyright, publication date, copyright owner's name—it could be in the public domain. Read Chapter 19 for detailed guidance on how to determine whether a published work is in the public domain because it lacks a valid copyright notice.

Does a Copyright Trap Apply?

The copyright law contains some traps for the unwary that might lead you to believe that a work is in the public domain when parts of it might be protected by copyright. This can be so even if you think the work is in the public domain because it's ineligible for copyright protection, its copyright has expired, or it was published before 1989 without a valid copyright notice. If the work is a derivative work or collective work, it may still contain copyrighted elements. Conversely, even if the work as a whole is protected by copyright, substantial portions of it may be in the public domain if it is a derivative or compilation. It's important that you understand what these traps are so you can avoid them.

Is the Work a Derivative Work?

When a work enters the public domain you are free to use it any way you want. You can simply republish the work in its original form. For example, Shakespeare's plays have been republished over and over again through the centuries. On the other hand, you can also transform or adapt a public domain work to create a new and different work. Such a work is called a derivative work.

A derivative work is a work that is based upon or adapted from a preexisting work. A good example of a derivative work is a screenplay based on a written work, like the many films and TV programs based on Dickens's tale *A Christmas Carol*. To create such a work, the screenwriter must take a novel's words, characters, and structure, then add his or her own new expression to it. The screenwriter must organize the material into cinematic scenes, add dialog and camera directions, and delete prose descriptions and other material that can't

be filmed. The result is a new work of authorship that can be separately protected by copyright: a screenplay that is clearly different from the novel, yet clearly based upon, or derived from it.

Of course, all works are derivative to some extent. Authorship is more often than not a process of translation and recombination of previously existing ideas, facts, and other elements. Rarely, if ever, does an author create a work that is entirely new. For example, writers of fiction often draw bits and pieces of their characters and plots from other fictional works they have read. The same is true of writers of factual works. However, a work is derivative for copyright purposes only if its author has taken a substantial amount of a previously existing work's expression—that is, the author's original words and the structure and organization of the material.

How much is substantial? Enough so that the average intended reader of the work would conclude that it had been adapted from or based upon the previously existing expression. There is no precise numerical formula that can be applied here. You must use your common sense. This is what judges and juries do when they are called upon to decide whether one work infringes upon another.

The right to create derivative works is one of the exclusive rights a copyright owner has. So long as a work is under copyright, permission must be obtained from the copyright owner to create a derivative work from it. However, once a work enters the public domain anyone can create a derivative work from it without permission and can obtain copyright protection for the material added to create the new work.

An uncountable number of derivative works have been created from public domain works. This creates a real trap for the unwary because a work you might think is in the public domain could be a derivative work that is entitled to some copyright protection. Before you conclude that any work is in the public domain you must make sure that it is not a protected derivative work. This is usually not difficult.

Types of Derivative Works

There are many different ways a public domain written work may be adapted or transformed into a derivative work protected, at least in part, by copyright law. The following list shows the various types of derivative works that can be created from writings. It lists what preexisting material the derivative work author takes and what new material he or she adds to create the derivative work.

Editorial Revisions and Elaborations

Preexisting material taken: The entire text of any preexisting work.

New material added: Editorial revisions and/or other new material such as new illustrations and photographs.

EXAMPLE: An economist takes Adam Smith's classic public domain work on economics, *The Wealth of Nations*, and updates and revises it to reflect current economic thinking. He adds several new chapters and revises the other chapters in light of recent developments. The new edition is a derivative work based on, but not designed to take the place of, the original edition.

Fictionalizations

Preexisting material taken: A substantial portion of the protected material contained in a factual work (biography, history, etc.).

New material added: Editing, reorganization, new dialog, descriptions, and other new material needed to transform the preexisting nonfiction work into a novel, play, screenplay, or other work of fiction.

EXAMPLE: Art takes General Ulysses S. Grant's memoirs (whose copyright expired long ago) and transforms them into a stage play. To do so, he deletes prose descriptions, adds new dialog, organizes the work into scenes and acts, and adds new scenes and incidents that weren't in the memoirs. But he also retains as much of Grant's expression—his words—as possible. The play is a derivative work based on the nonfiction memoirs.

Dramatizations

Preexisting material taken: All or a substantial part of the material in a fictional work not meant to be performed in public—that is, a short story, novel, or poem.

New material added: Editing, reorganization, new dialog, and other new material needed to transform the work into a work that can be performed in public—for instance, a stage play or screenplay.

> EXAMPLE: Leslie takes Charles Dickens's public domain novel *Great Expectations* and transforms it into a screenplay.

Translations Into a New Medium

Preexisting material taken: All or a substantial portion of the text of a written work in one medium—for example, a published book.

New material added: Transfer of the work into a new medium.

> EXAMPLE: Audio Books hires an actor to make a recording of the novel *Vanity Fair*, by Thackeray, and markets the tape as an audio book. The recording is a derivative work based on the written public domain novel.

Translations Into a New Language

Preexisting material taken: All the material contained in a preexisting work.

New material added: Translation of the work into a new version in another language.

> EXAMPLE: Mark Twain's public domain novel *The Adventures of Tom Sawyer* is translated into French. To do so, the translator takes Twain's expression (the words contained in the novel) and replaces them with French words. The resulting translation is a derivative work based on the original English-language novel.

Abridgments and Condensations

Preexisting material taken: A substantial portion of a work's protectable material.

New material added: Editing and other revisions that transform the work into a new, shorter version.

> EXAMPLE: Reader's Digest condensed books creates an abridged version of Herman Melville's public domain novel *Moby Dick*.

Annotations

Preexisting material taken: All or a substantial portion of a work's protected material.

New material added: Notes and/or other materials that clarify the meaning of the preexisting text.

> EXAMPLE: The annotated version of Lewis Carroll's work *Alice in Wonderland* is a derivative work prepared from the original public domain version of the book.

Extent of Copyright Protection for Derivative Works

Whenever a derivative work is created from a public domain work, only the new material added by the author of the derivative work is entitled to copyright protection. The original work remains in the public domain, as do those portions of the original work that are used in the new derivative work, since they come entirely from the original public domain material.

Thus, in all the examples of derivative works listed above, only the *new* material added is protected by copyright. For example, the author of a screenplay based on Dickens's public domain novel *Great Expectations* is entitled to copyright protection only for the new material she adds to create the screenplay—for example, new dialog or scenes. Anyone may create his or her own screenplay of *Great Expectations*. Such a person may copy freely from the public domain novel, but may not copy without permission any new elements present in the prior screenplay.

Changes Not Entitled to Copyright Protection

To create a derivative work, an author must make more than merely trivial or minuscule changes to the original work. Changes that are unoriginal or completely uncreative do not merit copyright protection. To be protectable, a derivative work must differ from the preexisting work in some meaningful way.

Examples of changes to preexisting written works that courts have held do *not* merit copyright protection include the following:

- Forty thousand changes to a book, consisting "almost entirely of elimination and addition of punctuation, changes of spelling of certain words, elimination and addition of quotation marks and correction of typographical errors." *Grove Press, Inc. v. Collectors Publication, Inc.*, 264 F.Supp. 603 (C.D. Cal. 1967).

- Translating a list of 850 single words and 45 short phrases from Arabic into English and then transliterating the Arabic words into Roman letters with phonetic spellings. *Signo Trading Int'l, Ltd. v. Gordon*, 535 F.Supp. 362 (N.D. Cal. 1981).

- Changing the language of a public domain form for the sale of merchandise from a sales contract to a service contract, a change requiring only a few minor wording changes. *Donald v. Uarco Business Forms*, 478 F.2d 764 (8th Cir. 1973).

- Making minor wording changes to the well-known Cajun sayings "We *gon* pass a good time, *cher*," and "You *gotta* suck *da* head on *dem der* crawfish." *Emanation, Inc. v. Zomba Recording, Inc.*, 72 Fed.App'x. 187 (5th Cir. 2003).

Works such as these receive no copyright protection at all if the original is in the public domain. For example, if a publisher merely corrects punctuation and spelling errors in a public domain work and republishes it, you are free to copy the entire republished work.

GRAY AREA

In some cases it may be difficult to tell for certain whether the changes someone has made to a public domain work are significant enough to merit copyright protection. See Chapter 1 for detailed guidance on how to deal with such public domain gray areas.

Scholarly Editions

Scholarly or "definitive" editions of famous public domain writings are constantly being published. These include, for example, new editions of the works of Mark Twain, Shakespeare, Thomas Hardy, D.H. Lawrence, and many others. Copyright is frequently claimed in these new editions because they contain copyright notices.

New editions of public domain works can be copyrighted derivative works if they contain annotations or substantial editorial revisions or additions. However, copyright protection extends only to the new material added to the original public domain work. For example, if a publisher adds a preface and explanatory notes to a new edition of

Charles Dickens's *Great Expectations*, the additions are copyrighted. But Dickens's words remain in the public domain.

What about changes to the public domain text itself—can these be copyrighted? Changes that consist only of correcting misspellings and typographical errors or standardizing punctuation are not copyrightable because they are not sufficiently original or creative. However, some scholarly editions of classic public domain works add new material. If this has never been published before, it is copyrightable. For example, a new edition of D.H. Lawrence's 1915 novel, *The Rainbow,* contains previously unpublished material from Lawrence's manuscript. This new material is protected by copyright. In this case, Lawrence's heirs own the new material, since Lawrence originally wrote it. The editors or their publisher would own new material created by the editors of the new edition.

New editions that don't include any unpublished material may also be copyrightable—for example, where an editor prepares a "definitive" edition of a public domain work from multiple prior editions. *Matthew Bender v. West Publishing Corp.,* 158 F.3d 674, n. 14 (2d Cir. 1998). This would be true, for example, where prior editions of a public domain work contain many differences in content and the editor must pick and choose among all the differences to devise what the editor views as a "definitive" version of the work. The editor's selection of which portions of the work to include in his or her "definitive" edition would be copyrightable. But, again, the actual words contained in the work would remain in the public domain.

If copyright is claimed in a new edition of a public domain work, it will ordinarily contain a copyright notice. Sometimes the notice will indicate the elements of the work where copyright is claimed. Unfortunately, this is not always the case. Explanatory notes may also reveal what changes or additions have been made to the original text. Checking Copyright Office registration records for the work may also be helpful (see Chapter 21).

> **EXAMPLE:** A new "definitive" edition of Mark Twain's classic novel *The Adventures of Huckleberry Finn* was published in 1996. This edition contained substantial new material from Twain's handwritten manuscript, which had been lost for decades. The new material was copyrighted, even though the original published version of the novel entered the public domain in 1942. (See Chapter 18 for a detailed discussion of this issue.)
>
> The new edition contained an excellent copyright notice that made clear that copyright was only being claimed in the previously unpublished material and in an introduction, foreword, and afterword written by the editors of the work. The notice says:
>
> Previously unpublished text, foreword, and afterword copyright © by The Mark Twain Foundation
>
> Introduction copyright © by Justin Kaplan
>
> In addition, the new edition contained extensive editorial notes that allow the reader to determine what material was added and what was taken from the original version of the novel. By referring to these notes, one can avoid using any of the copyrighted material.

The easy way to avoid problems is to avoid using new editions of public domain works in which copyright is claimed. Use an older edition or one that doesn't include a copyright notice. Although, technically speaking, use of copyright notices is optional on works published since 1989 (see Chapter 19), in practice they are almost universally used in books, magazines, and other written publications in which copyright is claimed. Absence of a notice strongly indicates that no copyright is being claimed in the publication. This is particularly likely to be true where a public domain work is republished.

Digital Copies of Public Domain Writings

Millions of public domain works and documents have been digitized and made available to the public on the Internet (see "Mass Book Digitization Projects," below). Such public domain works include

U.S. government works, laws and court decisions, and works whose copyright has expired.

For decades, the Copyright Office's policy has been that "digitization of ... a preexisting copyrightable work does not result in a new work of authorship. The digitized version is a copy of the preexisting work and would be protected as such, but no new work of authorship is created. A novel may be digitized and stored in an electronic medium. Protection depends on the status of copyright in the novel; digitization does not add any new authorship." *Copyright Office Policy Decision on Copyrightability of Digitized Typefaces,* 53 Federal Register 189 (Sept. 29, 1988).

The courts have agreed with the Copyright Office's view—for example, a court held that an e-book version of a printed book was not copyrightable because transferring the print version to e-book format involved "nothing more than rote copying." *Peter Mayer Publishers, Inc. v. Shilovskaya*, 11 F.Supp.3d 421 (S.D.N.Y. 2014).

Thus, an exact digital copy of a preexisting work is copyrighted only if the preexisting work is protected. If the preexisting work is in the public domain, the digital copy is too. This is because an exact digital copy of a written work does not require any originality or even minimal creativity —two of the requirements for copyright protection. A digital copy of a text is no more a copyrightable work of authorship than a photocopy of a page of text.

Nevertheless, the people and companies who create digital versions of public domain texts often include copyright notices on them. They apparently are claiming the digital copies are protectable derivative works. Such claims are spurious. To enjoy such protection, something new must be added to the text. For example, if you find a copyright notice on a webpage containing a copy of a public domain text, there could be a compilation copyright in the collection and arrangement of all the components of the website or in other new elements of the website, such as photos or custom-made html code, but the copied public domain text itself is not copyrighted.

Microfilms of Public Domain Works

In order to save space, many public domain written works have been microfilmed and the original copies discarded by libraries and archives. This is particularly common for public domain newspapers and magazines. It's not unusual to find copyright notices on such microfilm editions of public domain works, usually in the name of the company that created the microfilm. However, a microfilm—that is, a photograph—of a public domain text is not copyrightable because no creativity is required to take such a photo. Indeed, a microfilm of a text should be no more copyrightable than a photocopy. The creation of such copies is a purely mechanical act that does not result in any copyrightable authorship.

Where a number of public domain works are collected together in a single microfilm edition, there may be a limited copyright in the selection and arrangement of the entire work, but not in the individual microfilms themselves (see Chapter 12).

When Derivative Work Is Public Domain but Original Is Not

It's possible for a derivative work to enter the public domain while the original work, upon which it is based, is still protected by copyright. This can happen, for example, if the derivative work was published before 1964 and its copyright was not renewed on time 28 years after its publication, but the original work was renewed on time. (See Chapter 18 for an explanation of timely renewal.) It could also happen if the derivative work was published before March 1, 1989 without a valid copyright notice while the original work had a valid notice. (See Chapter 19 for more on this issue.)

If the derivative work enters the public domain does this mean the original work automatically becomes public domain too? The answer is no. The original work remains copyrighted, as do those portions of the original included within the derivative work. All that enters the public domain are the new elements that the creator of the derivative work added to the original work.

EXAMPLE: George Bernard Shaw's 1913 play, *Pygmalion*, was turned into a movie (starring Leslie Howard and Wendy Hiller) in 1938. The copyright in the movie, a derivative work based upon the play, was not renewed in 1966 and therefore entered the public domain in 1967 (see Chapter 7). However, the copyright on the play was renewed on time by Shaw in 1941 and remained under copyright through 1988. The court held that the fact that the movie was in the public domain had no effect on the copyright status of the original play. It was still entitled to a full term of copyright protection. In addition, those portions of the play (dialog, story) that were used to make the derivative film were also still protected by copyright through 1988. *Russell v. Price*, 612 F.2d 1123 (9th Cir. 1979).

Because the original work is still protected by copyright, the derivative work may not be used without permission from the owner of the original work. This is because by using the derivative work one ordinarily must also use those portions of the original work included within it. This meant that the film *Pygmalion* could not be distributed without permission from Shaw's estate (the holder of the copyright in the play *Pygmalion*). Distributing the film without such permission violated the copyright in the original play. (But after 1988, the play entered the public domain and both the movie and the play could be distributed without such permission.)

The only exception to the permission requirement in this situation would be where only the new public domain elements added to create the derivative work are used.

> **EXAMPLE:** Assume that a student edition of Tennessee Williams's plays was published in 1960. The work contained copious notes and annotations created by the editors. The student edition was a derivative work—an annotation. The notes and annotations were protected by copyright as were the plays themselves. However, the student edition's copyright was not renewed in 1988 and the work entered the public domain (see Chapter 18). Williams's plays are still protected by copyright, but the notes and annotations are in the public domain. You can freely copy these notes from the student edition, but you cannot use the plays themselves without permission from Williams's estate.

Avoiding Problems With Derivative Works

Unless you're careful, you could end up using a work you think is in the public domain that is really a protected derivative work. Here's a real-life example:

In 1912 the Senate Commerce Committee conducted extensive hearings on the *Titanic* disaster at which many of the survivors testified. The lengthy reports of these hearings were published by the Government Printing Office. The report,

a U.S. government work, was in the public domain. Some 86 years later, Pocket Books published a one-volume version of this report. You might think this work was also in the public domain, but you'd be wrong. It is a protected derivative work.

This is because the Pocket Books version was not an exact copy of the report. Rather, a reporter from the *New York Times*, Tom Kuntz, edited the multivolume report into a single 570-page volume and added an introduction and a number of public domain photographs. This made the work an editorial revision—one type of protected derivative work. The new expression Kuntz added to the original public domain report is protected by copyright—that is, his selection and editing of the material to include in the book and his introduction. None of the individual words, sentences, or paragraphs is protected, but the work as a whole is. You can copy selected portions of the book, but you can't copy the *entire* book without permission. To do would violate Kuntz's copyright in his selection and editing.

This is why you should always examine a published work carefully for a copyright notice, even if you think it should be in the public domain. If it contains a notice, it may be a derivative work. If you look at the copyright notice included in the Pocket Books edition of *The Titanic Disaster Hearings*, you'd find it states "Introduction and compilation copyright © 1998 by Tom

Kuntz." This makes it quite clear what portions of the work are copyrighted.

You can avoid having to ask permission to use a derivative work based on a public domain work by using only those portions of the work copied from the original work. But this is not always possible. For example, it would not be possible to use any portion of an English translation of a foreign-language public domain work, since the entire translation is protected.

Another option is to find and use the original work—for example, although a 1995 English translation of Homer's *Iliad* is copyrighted, the original Greek version is in the public domain. Or, you can use an earlier derivative work that is in the public domain. For example, a translation of *The Iliad* published in 1920 is in the public domain (because the copyright has expired) and may be copied freely.

Is the Work a Compilation?

Besides derivative works described in the previous section, there is yet another way an author can create a copyrightable work from public domain materials. This is by creating a compilation.

A compilation is a work created by selecting, organizing, and arranging previously existing material in such a way that the resulting work as a whole constitutes an original work of authorship.

Compilations differ from derivative works because the author of a compilation makes no changes in the preexisting material and need not add any new material of his or her own. Moreover, protectable compilations can be created solely from material that is in the public domain.

Fact Compilations (Databases)

One basic type of protectable compilation is a fact compilation or database. This type of compilation is created by selecting and arranging facts or other items that are not works of authorship and are therefore in the public domain. These types of compilations are discussed in detail in Chapter 12.

Collective Works

Selecting preexisting materials that are separate and independent works of authorship into one whole work may also create a compilation. Such compilations are called collective works. Many written works are collective works.

> **EXAMPLE:** Elliot compiles an anthology of the 25 best American short stories published during the 1990s. Each story is a separate and independent work that was protected by copyright the moment it was created. However, Elliot has created a new protectable collective work by selecting and arranging the stories into a collective whole, that is, a collection of the best short stories of the 1990s.

Other examples of collective works include newspapers, magazines, and other periodicals in which separately protectable articles are combined into a collective whole, encyclopedias consisting of independently protectable articles on various topics, and collections of the various writings by a single author. Collective works are discussed in detail in Chapter 12.

Misuse of Copyright Notices

Public domain works are constantly being used to create new derivative works and collective works. If public domain writings are used to create a new derivative work or collective work, the work is entitled to contain a copyright notice when it is published.

The best practice when this is done is for the publisher to indicate in the notice what elements of the public domain work are copyrighted. For example, the copyright notice for an English translation of Caesar's *Gallic Wars* states: "Translation copyright © by 1985 by Anne Wiseman, Illustrations copyright © 1985 by Barry Cunliffe."

However, there is no legal requirement that the copyright notice explicitly state what elements of the work are copyrighted. The notice only need state the name of the copyright owner of the derivative or collective work and the date it was published. In fact, many publishers don't bother

to make clear what portion of the work the notice covers. Thus, for example, the copyright notice for *The Oxford Anthology of English Literature* states simply "Copyright © 1973 by Oxford University Press, Inc."

Though legal, a notice such as this is extremely misleading. A reader unfamiliar with the niceties of copyright law might believe that the notice means that Oxford University Press holds the copyright to the entire work. In fact, it means no such thing. *The Oxford Anthology of English Literature* consists of a collection of literary works that are almost all in the public domain because their copyrights have expired, such as poems by Wordsworth and Keats, a novella by Joseph Conrad, and a portion of a work by Thomas Carlyle. Despite what the copyright notice says, Oxford University Press does not own a copyright in these works. It only holds a copyright in the new material added to these works to create the anthology—that is, to the selection of the materials included in the anthology and to introductions and notes written for the anthology by its editors. The literary works themselves are in the public domain and may be copied freely.

An even worse example is the reprinting of the *Mueller Report* by the *Washington Post*. The copyright notice for this work states "Copyright © 2019 by WP Company LLC."

Mass Book Digitization Projects

Several projects are underway with the goal of digitizing and making freely available to the public every public domain book in existence, as well as other public domain and copyrighted materials. These include:

Library of Congress Digitization Projects

Since 1994 the Library of Congress has made digitized versions of collection materials available online, such as photographs, manuscripts, maps, sound recordings, motion pictures, and books, as well as "born digital" materials such as websites. Its digital collections are focused primarily on the Library's unique and rare collections. Major initiatives include: American Memory, which has more than nine million items online related to U.S. history and culture and organized into more than 100 thematic collections; Historic American Newspapers, which provides access to 900,000 U.S. newspapers published between 1836 and 1922; World Culture and Resources, which presents bilingual digital collections from various media from different regions and countries from around the world; Prints and Photographs, which contains over 1.2 million digitized images; and many others. See https://loc.gov/collections.

In addition, the World Digital Library, a joint venture of the Library of Congress and UNESCO, makes available high-quality digital items representing each UNESCO member's cultural heritage. See www.wdl.org/en.

National Archives and Records Administration (NARA)

Via the National Archives Catalog, NARA plans to digitize and make fully available online its vast collection of hard-copy historical U.S. government documents, gathered from NARA's two Washington, DC, facilities and 14 regional archives, as well as the 13 presidential libraries under NARA operation. The National Archives Catalog provides access to more than 126,500 digitized historical documents, photographs, and images. See www.archives.gov/research/catalog.

In addition, NARA's Electronic Records Archives ("ERA") preserves and provides access to U.S. government records born digitally; that is, those documents that exist only in electronic format. See www.archives.gov/era.

Mass Book Digitization Projects (continued)

Internet Archive

The Internet Archive is a nonprofit organization that offers permanent access for researchers, historians, scholars, people with disabilities, and the general public to historical collections that exist in digital format. Although the Internet Archive is primarily known for its vast collection of Internet websites and other "born digital" content, it also contains digitized versions of over 10 million books. The Internet Archive provides specialized services for adaptive reading and information access for the blind and other persons with disabilities. See https://archive.org.

Project Gutenberg

Billing itself as the first producer of free electronic books, U.S.-based Project Gutenberg is a private-sector project offering over 53,000 public domain texts, including literature and reference materials to the general public through e-book downloads to portable devices. It has partners in various countries, including Australia, Canada, the United Kingdom, and France, through which over 100,000 free e-books are available. See www.gutenberg.org/wiki/Main_Page.

Google Book Search

Launched in 2004, the Google Book Search ("GBS") project has scanned more than 25 million books from more than 100 countries in over 400 languages. As originally conceived, the project aimed to create a digital card catalog of the world's books, and make such books searchable. GBS provides full access to over a million public domain titles, and titles for which it has secured permission from applicable rights holders.

For other copyrighted works for which it has no agreement, GBS supplies only a short three-line "snippet" based on a user's search query. See https://books.google.com.

California Digital Library

Founded by the University of California in 1997, the California Digital Library (CDL) has digitized 3.6 million books, and serves as a repository for over 600 million Web files. Projects within CDL include the Online Archive of California, an archive of primary source materials related to California history; and UC Shared Images, a database of arts and humanities images designed for educators. CDL is composed of numerous contributing partners and project members, including Google Books and the Internet Archive. See https://cdlib.org.

Mass Book Digitization Projects (continued)

HathiTrust Digital Library

The HathiTrust is a group of 57 libraries, including the Library of Congress, whose goal is to "contribute to the common good" by providing a shared platform for making digital collections available to users. The initial focus of the trust was on preserving and providing access to digitized books and journals in collaboration with Google, the Internet Archive, Microsoft, and in-house digitization initiatives. Currently over eight million books have been digitized. See www.hathitrust.org.

Digital Public Library of America

The Digital Public Library of America (DPLA) went online in mid-2013. It was created by Harvard University's Berkman Center for Internet & Society, with financial support from various funders. The DPLA aggregates metadata records for millions of photographs, manuscripts, books, sounds, moving images, and more from hundreds of libraries, archives, and museums around the United States. Each record links to the original object on the content provider's website. Many of the items are in the public domain. Digital copies of some objects are available for download, based on the content provider and the individual rights status of the object. See https://dp.la.

Officially titled *Report on the Investigation into Russian Interference in the 2016 Presidential Election*, the *Mueller Report* is the official report documenting the findings and conclusions of Special Counsel Robert Mueller's investigation into Russian efforts to interfere in the 2016 United States presidential election. It is in the public domain because it was prepared by United States government employees. The *Washington Post's* copyright notice applies only to an introduction, biographical notes, and timeline prepared by the newspaper's editors and added to its edition of the report.

To add insult to injury, the *Washington Post* also includes the following statement after the misleading copyright notice: "All rights reserved, including the right to reproduce this book or portions thereof in any form whatsoever." This statement has absolutely no legal effect and appears to be included by the publisher in an effort to intimidate readers into not copying or otherwise using the report. In fact, anyone is free to reproduce the *Mueller Report* without the *Washington Post's* permission. It's only the introduction and other new material that can't be used.

Remember, anyone can place a copyright notice on any written work. You don't need permission from the U.S. Copyright Office or anyone else to do so. The fact that a work has a notice doesn't mean that all or part of it isn't in the public domain.

When you find a copyright notice on a work that contains public domain material, you need to investigate carefully to figure out what new authorship has been added to the preexisting public domain materials. Only this new authorship is entitled to copyright protection, no matter what the copyright notice says. If you can't tell from the work itself what new material has been added, you could try checking Copyright Office registration records (see Chapter 21) or comparing it with earlier versions of the same work.

Sources of Public Domain Writings

Below are some useful websites for locating public domain writings and libraries that contain public domain works:

- Google Book Search (https://books.google.com)
- Library of Congress (https://catalog.loc.gov)
- LibriVox audio recordings of public domain books (https://librivox.org)
- Project Gutenberg (www.gutenberg.org)
- Project Bartleby (www.bartleby.com/index.html)
- The Universal Digital Library (http://ulib.isri.cmu.edu)
- The Internet Archive (https://archive.org)
- U.S. Government Publishing Office (www.gpo.gov)
- Digital Book Index (www.digitalbookindex.org)
- The Online Books Page (http://onlinebooks.library.upenn.edu), and
- Wikisource (https://en.wikisource.org/wiki/Main_Page).

Music

The Difference Between Music and Sound Recordings 81

What Can You Do With Public Domain Sheet Music? 82

    Publicly Performing Sheet Music 82

    Recording Sheet Music 82

    Reproducing Sheet Music 84

    Using Sheet Music in Audiovisual Works 84

    Using Sheet Music in Digital Works 85

    Adapting Sheet Music 85

Has the Sheet Music Been Published? 86

    Sheet Music Is Not Published by Public Performance 87

    Music Not Published by Pre-1978 Recordings 87

    Determining Whether Sheet Music Is Published 88

    How to Determine the Year a Musical Work Was Published 89

    Determining the Country in Which Music Was Published 91

Has the Copyright in the Music Expired? 93

Is the Music in the Public Domain Due to Lack of a Copyright Notice? 93

Is It a Derivative Work? 94

    No Permission Needed Where Preexisting Work Is in Public Domain 94

    Only New Material Is Copyrightable 95

Is It an Arrangement or Adaptation? 95

    Avoiding Problems With Arrangements 96

    Using Arrangements for Which Copyright Is Claimed 97

    Which Arrangements Are Copyrightable? 100

Is the Music a Collective Work? 106

    Minimal Creativity Required 107

    Small Collections Not Protected 108

    How Much of a Collective Work Can You Copy? 108

Does the Music Have Public Domain Elements?...109

    Music Copied From Public Domain Sources..109

    Ideas...110

    Simple Melodies..110

    Song Titles...111

    Musical Forms 111

    Information That Is Common Property...111

Sources of Public Domain Sheet Music..111

Sound Recordings 112

    Sound Recordings Made Before Feb. 15, 1972...113

    Sound Recordings Made or Published After Feb. 15, 1972 115

    U.S. Government Sound Recordings...116

This chapter deals with two forms of music: sheet music and sound recordings. Few sound recordings are in the public domain, but this is scheduled to change starting in 2022. In the meantime, vast amounts of sheet music and musical scores are in the public domain. This sheet music—and the lyrics published along with it—represents one of the richest parts of the creative treasure trove that is the public domain. Most of the sheet music for the greatest classical music ever written is in the public domain, as is the sheet music for many popular and traditional songs.

CAUTION
Many works that are in the public domain in the United States are still protected by copyright abroad, and vice versa. This chapter covers only the public domain in the United States. For a detailed discussion of the public domain outside the United States, see Chapter 16.

The Difference Between Music and Sound Recordings

Musical compositions—such as pop songs, classical symphonies, or operas—are protected by copyright. Protection begins once the composer creates and fixes the composition in some tangible form, traditionally by writing it down using musical notation, commonly in the form of sheet music. However, a composition can also be fixed by recording it on tape or any other recording medium.

Since copyright expires after a number of years, vast numbers of musical compositions, from one or two pages of sheet music to full-length musical scores, are in the public domain. (See Chapter 18 for details on when copyrights expire.)

Before the advent of recording devices, in the late 19th century, copyright protection for sheet music and musical scores was all that was necessary to protect the rights of composers, since it was not possible to save their music for later replay. But with the advent of recording devices, a second form of music copyright—called "sound recording" copyright—was created to protect recorded performances. Sound recording copyright only protects the way a musical composition is performed and recorded. There can be many sound recordings of a composition, but there is only one underlying musical copyright for the song. For example, there are hundreds of recordings of the song "Yesterday," each with its own sound recording copyright. However, there is only one musical composition copyright for the song.

Very few sound recordings are currently in the public domain. But, due to recent changes to the federal copyright law, recordings will begin to enter the public domain for the first time starting in 2022. For a detailed discussion, read "Sound Recordings," below.

Because of this reality, most of this chapter concerns sheet music, not musical recordings.

What Can You Do With Public Domain Sheet Music?

When sheet music is in the public domain, it is freely available to be performed in public, recorded, copied and distributed, and used to create new types of musical works. All of this can be done without asking permission or paying permission fees to composers, music publishing companies, or anyone who previously controlled the copyright on a piece of music.

Publicly Performing Sheet Music

You might be surprised to learn that copyrighted sheet music cannot be freely performed in public. With some exceptions noted below (nonprofit or religious performances), permission from the copyright owner—typically, a music publisher—is needed to perform sheet music at a place open to the public or where a substantial number of people outside the normal circle of a family and social acquaintances are gathered. This includes, for example, performing sheet music live over the radio or on television, performing a song in a nightclub or concert hall, webcasting a performance, playing sheet music during a football game halftime, or playing live music at a dancing school.

The permission fees for these types of public performances are called performance royalties. Almost all music publishers, composers, and songwriters belong to performance rights societies. These companies offer license agreements allowing music to be publicly performed in return for a fee. The best known of these societies are ASCAP and BMI. The fees charged vary according to the nature of the use—they may range from a few hundred dollars at bars or dancing schools to many thousands of dollars to perform music in a large concert hall or on television.

No performance royalties need be paid when sheet music is in the public domain. It can be publicly performed at any place, for any reason, for free.

Recording Sheet Music

Permission must also be obtained to record a copyrighted song or other musical composition on an audio recording such as a compact disc. The fees for this permission are called mechanical royalties.

Nonprofit or Religious Musical Performances Are Permitted

It is legal to publicly perform copyrighted music without obtaining permission from the copyright owner in the following situations. This includes performing sheet music or playing a musical recording before a live audience.

- **Religious services.** No permission is needed to use music at a house of worship. This exemption applies to both religious and nonreligious music so long as it is performed in the course of religious services. However, permission is required to broadcast music performed at a religious service and to copy sheet music used for religious purposes.

- **Free shows.** No permission is needed if sheet music or a musical recording is played before a live audience, performers are not paid, and admission is not charged.

- **Shows for charitable or educational purposes.** No permission is needed if sheet music is used or a music recording is played before a live audience, so long as the performers are not paid, the net proceeds are used exclusively for education, charitable, or religious purposes, and the music publisher is notified and given more than 10 days to object. If the publisher objects, permission must be obtained.

- **Agricultural fairs.** Permission is also not required to perform sheet music or play a musical recording for a live audience at nonprofit agricultural or horticultural fairs.

- **Fraternal and veterans events.** Permission is not required when nonprofit veterans' organizations like the American Legion or fraternal groups like the Elks or Shriners perform sheet music or play musical recordings, provided that the general public is not invited and the net profits are used exclusively for charity.

- **Sorority and fraternity events.** Permission is not required to perform music or play music recordings at college fraternity and sorority social functions, provided that the purpose is solely to raise funds for charity. 17 U.S.C. Section 110.

Mechanical royalty rates for physical recordings are 9.1 cents per copy for songs under five minutes. For example, if you wanted to make 10,000 compact discs of a copyrighted three-minute song, you'd have to pay $910 in mechanical royalties to the music publisher. The rates for on-demand streaming are about 6 cents per 100 on-demand streams. For details, see www.royaltyexchange.com.

From Public Domain to Public Domain

Musician Dave Alvin and his brother used to collect old blues, folk, rhythm & blues, and country recordings, including many long-out-of-print reissue albums on obscure labels. When looking for material for a solo album, Alvin decided to use many of these public domain songs. The result is *Public Domain*, a recording released by Oakland's Hightone Records. Among the songs recorded by Alvin were "Shenandoah," "Walk Right In," "Short Life of Trouble," "What Did the Deep Sea Say," "Engine 143," "Delia," and "The Murder of the Lawson Family." Because the songs were in the public domain, Hightone Records didn't have to pay any mechanical royalties to use them.

Public Domain, **Dave Alvin,** Ⓟ ©
copyright Hightone Records

In contrast, public domain music can be recorded for free. Of course, tens of thousands of recordings of public domain classical music have been made. But classical music is not the only public domain music that is recorded. For example, performers such as Peter, Paul, and Mary, Pete Seeger, and Joan Baez have made fortunes recording public domain folk songs, like "John Henry" and "Down by the Riverside."

Reproducing Sheet Music

Permission is also required to republish copyrighted sheet music or lyrics in a book or magazine, on a website, to photocopy them, or to reproduce lyrics on album liner notes. The fees for this vary widely. Of course, if sheet music and lyrics are in the public domain, you may reproduce them in any way you want for free. No permission is necessary from anybody.

Using Sheet Music in Audiovisual Works

Permission is also required to play copyrighted sheet music or lyrics in a movie, television show, commercial, or video. These types of permissions are called synchronization licenses or videogram licenses, depending on the use. These are the most expensive permissions of all. For example, you may have to pay as much as $250,000 to use a famous Gershwin song in a television commercial. Fees for using copyrighted music in a movie can range from just a few thousand dollars to $25,000 or more.

Again, public domain sheet music may be performed in an audiovisual work without paying these permission fees.

Teaching From the Public Domain

Fred, a piano teacher based in Northern California, has photocopied the sheet music for hundreds of public domain piano pieces. These range from the works of classical composers such as Chopin to folk and traditional songs. He found the sheet music in used bookstores, flea markets, and in newly published collections of public domain music. He keeps his public domain music collection in a large filing cabinet and from time to time makes photocopies of various pieces to give to his students. Because the music is in the public domain, he may photocopy it freely for any purpose.

Using Sheet Music in Digital Works

You have to pay for permission as well if you want to record and include copyrighted sheet music in a digital product such as a computer or video game. Royalty rates for such uses vary. To use a song in a video game, you may have to pay a royalty of 0.5% to 1% of the retail price of the game. Royalties for multimedia uses are typically between five and 15 cents per unit.

Of course, you may make your own recording of public domain sheet music and include it on a digital product without having to pay any permission fees.

Adapting Sheet Music

If you want to borrow or adapt a melody or lyric from a copyrighted song and use it in a new song of your own, you must obtain permission from the music publisher. In the case of well-known works, permission may not be available at any price. Permission must also be obtained to create and publish or perform an entirely new arrangement of a copyrighted work.

Once a song or other musical composition enters the public domain, you may adapt it in any way you wish. Thousands of the greatest melodies ever written by the greatest musical geniuses are free for the taking.

Classical composers have been borrowing from each other for centuries. For example, there is a long tradition in classical music of creating variations— taking a theme or melody from another composer and adapting it into a new work.

Beethoven, Hayden, Schubert, Chopin, Brahms, Tchaikovsky, and many other classical composers all created variations. Classical composers have also drawn heavily from folk music—for example, Brahms's *Hungarian Dances* and Liszt's *Hungarian Rhapsodies* are based on ancient Hungarian gypsy tunes, while many of Bach's melodies are based on traditional airs. Even popular music has found its way into classical works. For example, Charles Ives's Fourth Symphony quotes such famous public domain songs as "Yankee Doodle" and "Turkey in the Straw." The Center for the History of Music Theory and Literature, at Indiana University's School of Music, has compiled an extraordinary bibliography listing hundreds of examples of composers who have borrowed from preexisting works. It can be found on the Internet at www.chmtl.indiana.edu/borrowing.

But classical composers aren't the only ones who borrow. Many popular song-writers have created hits by adapting public domain music, including:

- "Besame Mucho" (1944), based on the "Nightingale" aria from *Goyescas,* by Enrique Granados
- "A Fifth of Beethoven" (1976), based on Beethoven's Fifth Symphony
- "Good Night Sweetheart" (1931), based on themes from Schubert's Symphony in C and the Liszt *Preludes*
- "Love Me Tender" (1956), based on "Aura Lee," by George Poulton; and

- "The Lion Sleeps Tonight" (also called "Wimoweh") (1962), based on a traditional African song.

Public domain music is also constantly being adapted for movies, television, commercials, elevator music, and many other uses.

RESOURCE

What if the work is not in the public domain? If you find that the work you want to use is not in the public domain, you may be able to use it anyway under a legal exception called "fair use" (see Chapter 22). If you do not qualify for this exception, you will need to obtain permission to use the work. For a detailed discussion of how to obtain copyright permissions refer to *Getting Permission: Using & Licensing Copyright-Protected Materials Online & Off,* by Richard Stim (Nolo).

Has the Sheet Music Been Published?

The first question you need to answer to determine whether sheet music is in the public domain is whether or not it has been published. This will determine how long the copyright in the work lasts and whether it had to contain a copyright notice when it was published.

Sheet music is published for copyright purposes when the copyright owner—or someone acting on behalf of the copyright owner—makes one or more copies of the music available to the *general* public. In other words, any interested member of the public may obtain a copy. *Burke v. National Broadcasting Co.*, 598 F.2d 688 (9th Cir. 1979).

If sheet music is printed and the copies offered for sale to the general public in music stores, bookstores, through mail order, or by any other means of public distribution, publication has occurred. But to be published a work doesn't necessarily have to be disseminated to the public through normal distribution channels such as music stores. Nontraditional means of distribution can also constitute a publication—for example, where a songwriter/performer sold copies of his songs to audiences or sold them to the public through a website.

Moreover, the copies don't necessarily have to be offered for sale for a publication to occur: They can also be leased or rented, loaned, or even given away—for example, where copies of a symphony or choral work are rented to orchestras and choruses. Nor is it necessary for large numbers of copies to be distributed. So long as the work has been made available to the general public, it makes no difference if just one copy has been sold or distributed. *Gottsberger v. Aldine Book Publishing Co.*, 33 Fed. 381 (C.C.D. Mass. 1887).

Sheet Music Is Not Published by Public Performance

For a publication to occur for copyright purposes it is crucial that *copies* of the work be made available to the general public. For this reason, merely performing music in public is not a publication. This is so whether the music is performed before a live audience or a performance is broadcast to the public by radio or television. Copies of the sheet music must be made available to the general public for publication to occur. *Ferris v. Frohman*, 223 U.S. 424 (1912).

Music Not Published by Pre-1978 Recordings

Prior to 1978, a song or other musical work was published for copyright purposes only when copies of the sheet music were publicly distributed. Distribution of sound recordings made before 1978 does not constitute a publication of the music on the recording.

> **EXAMPLE:** Imagine that the song "Do Wa Wa" was written in 1958 and recorded by the Baddelles in 1959. The recording was publicly distributed throughout 1959 by Stim Records, Inc. However, the sheet music for the song was never copied and publicly distributed. As a result, the song was not published for copyright purposes, even though thousands of people bought the recording.

This rule was changed beginning January 1, 1978. So sound recordings made and distributed after that date *do* result in publication of the music on the recording.

> **EXAMPLE:** The song "What the Gnu Knew" was written in 1944, and recorded in that year and then again in 1950, 1962, 1968, and 1979. The sheet music for the song was never copied and distributed. However, the song was published when the 1979 recording was publicly distributed.

Determining Whether Sheet Music Is Published

There are a number of ways to determine whether sheet music has been published.

Examine a Copy

If you have a copy of the sheet music, examine it carefully. You can be virtually certain that sheet music has been published if it has been professionally printed and contains a copyright notice; the familiar © symbol followed by the date of publication and copyright owner's name—for example, © 1945 by Good Music, Inc. The copyright notice normally was printed on the first page or on the title page (or the cover, in the case of sheet music for a single song).

> ! **CAUTION**
>
> **If the copy of the music you're examining isn't the original edition or a facsimile of the original,** the publication date in the notice may not be the date the original version of the music was published.

If the sheet music lacks a copyright notice, it could still have been published. Look for telltale signs of publication. For example:

- **Is the name of a music publisher listed on the work?** This almost certainly means the sheet music has been published unless, for some reason, copies of the work were printed but never distributed to the public.
- **Does the sheet music contain a selling price?** This almost certainly means it was offered for sale to the public.

Check Music References

If you're still not sure whether the work is published, you will need to do some research. There are many music reference works that you can consult to determine whether a work has been published. Most of these also give the date of publication that can be used to determine whether the copyright in the work has expired.

Check Music Stores

Try visiting or calling a music store that carries sheet music to see if they sell copies of the piece. If they do, the work has been published.

Check Copyright Office Records

You can also check the U.S. Copyright Office's records to see if the sheet music has been registered. When a work is registered, the applicant must indicate on the registration application whether the work has been published. However, not all published music is registered, so the Copyright Office may have no record for it. (See Chapter 21 for a detailed discussion of how to search Copyright Office records.)

Check Library Catalogs

Also, check the card catalog of the Library of Congress in Washington, DC. You can do this through the Library's website at www.loc.gov. If a work is listed in the catalog as published, you can safely assume it has been published. However, contrary to popular belief, the Library of Congress does not contain copies of all works published in the United States. A work may be published but not be in the Library's card catalog.

How to Determine the Year a Musical Work Was Published

It's not enough to determine that a musical work was published at some time. To determine whether the copyright has expired, you must find out the year it was originally published. (The exact date isn't necessary, just the year.) There are several ways to determine this.

Examine the Copyright Notice

If you have access to the sheet music, simply look at the publication date in the copyright notice. This will usually be on the first page or the title page.

Note carefully, however, that unless the sheet music you're examining is the original published version or a copy of it, it's quite possible that the date in the notice is not the date the music was first published. When public domain music is republished, you'll often find copyright notices containing recent publication dates. For example, one edition of several Chopin piano works contains a 1987 copyright notice. Of course, Chopin's music was not originally published in 1987. In these cases, the music publisher is claiming copyright protection for a new arrangement or edition of the work or a compilation copyright for the selection and grouping of the work in a sheet music collection.

The publication date in copyright notices such as these only represents the year the arrangement or collection was published, not the year the original version of the work was published. Therefore, this date is useless for determining whether the copyright in the original version of the work has expired. You will usually need to do a little more research to determine the original publication date of a work.

Use Music Reference Works

There are many music reference works you can consult to determine whether a work has been published—that is, if it's not listed as published you can assume it's unpublished. You can also use these works to help determine when a work has been published.

These references include the following:

Biographical Dictionaries of Music. There are several biographical musical dictionaries that alphabetically list the names of composers and give the dates of publication for many of their best-known works. Of course, you must know the name of the composer of a song to efficiently use such a work. Such works include:

- *Baker's Biographical Dictionary of Musicians* (G. Schirmer)
- *The Da Capo Companion to 20th Century Popular Music*, by Phil Hardy and Dave Laing (Da Capo Press)
- *The Harvard Biographical Dictionary of Music*, Don Michael Randel (Editor) (Harvard University Press Reference Library), and

- *The Oxford Dictionary of Music*, Michael Kennedy and Joyce Bourne (Editors) (Oxford University Press).

Musical Biographies. Hundreds of biographies of well-known composers have been written. These will generally list the composers' works (at least the well-known ones) and often provide publication dates.

Song Lists. These works list songs alphabetically or by composer and give the date of publication:

- *The Book of World-Famous Music*, by James J. Fuld (Dover Publications). A stunning work of scholarship, this book gives the complete publication history for nearly 1,000 well-known works, popular, folk, and classical.
- *The Da Capo Catalog of Classical Music Compositions*, by Jerzy Chwialkowski (Da Capo Press). This work lists all the known works created by 132 of the best-known classical composers. However, it usually gives the dates such works were created, not the dates they were first published. This limits its usefulness for the researcher. However, it does include the publication date for every George Gershwin song.
- *The Great Song Thesaurus*, by Roger Lax and Frederick Smith (Oxford University Press). This work lists thousands of popular songs starting in 1226. If a work is listed here, you can be certain it was published sometime. However, note carefully that the dates provided in this book

are not always the dates the works were actually published, but rather the dates they became popular (which could be some time after initial publication).

- *The Oxford Companion to Popular Music*, by Peter Gammond (Oxford University Press), lists thousands of popular songs. When a © is included with a date, this is the date the work was first published.

- *Who Wrote That Song?* by Dick Jacobs and Harriet Jacobs (Writer's Digest Books), gives the publication dates for more than 12,500 American popular songs. This is probably the cheapest and best resource if you want to know the publication date of any relatively well-known American popular song.

Guides to Public Domain Music. Several lists have been created that contain hundreds of well-known popular songs in the public domain because their copyright has expired. They include the following:

- *Public Domain Music Song List.* The Public Domain Music website (www.pdinfo.com) has an alphabetical, searchable list of more than 3,000 public domain songs.

- *The Mini-Encyclopedia of Public Domain Songs*, 1998, by Barbara Zimmerman (Bz Rights Stuff Inc.). This book bills itself as "a listing of the best-known songs in the Public Domain in print today." The book contains more than 800 well-known songs.

- *The Lester S. Levy Sheet Music Collection.* An online index of the Lester S. Levy Collection of Sheet Music at Johns Hopkins University containing more than 29,000 pieces of music, focusing on popular American music from 1780 to 1960. Contains digital copies of thousands of public domain songs. See http://levysheetmusic.mse.jhu.edu.

Year-by-Year Musical Bibliographies. There are several musical bibliographies that attempt to list all the sheet music published in a given year. These include the following:

- *Popular Music, 1900-1919*, by Barbara Cohen-Stratyner (Gale). All the songs listed here are in the public domain.

- *Variety Music Cavalcade: Musical-Historical Review 1620- 1969.* (*A Chronology of Vocal and Instrumental Music Popular in the United States*), by Julius Mattfeld (Prentice Hall, 1971). This is a year-by-year list.

Determining the Country in Which Music Was Published

In addition to the year date of publication, you need to know the country in which the sheet music was published. Published sheet music and musical scores usually show the country of publication. You'll normally find it on the title page or the same page as the copyright notice. If not, try using the following resources:

Special Rules for Music First Published Outside the U.S.

Special rules apply to music that was first published outside the United States. Much foreign music that used to be in the public domain had its copyright renewed on Jan. 1, 1996. This included foreign works whose copyrights expired because they were never renewed and works published in countries with which the United States had no copyright relations.

Of particular interest to the classical music world is the fact that all music published in the Soviet Union before 1973 used to be in the public domain in the United States because the two countries had no copyright relations before that year. The copyright in all this music has been restored provided that it is still under copyright in Russia or any of the other nations of the former Soviet Union. This includes, for example, most of the works by the great Soviet composers Prokofiev, Khachaturian, and Shostakovich, as well as early works by Schnittke, Gubaidulina, Shchedrin, Denisov, and others.

ASCAP, the music collective rights agency, has a searchable list posted on its website of many works in its repertory that have had their copyright restored; the URL is: www.ascap.com/restored_works.

See Chapter 15 for a detailed discussion.

Check the Library of Congress Card Catalog. You can do this in person at the Library, in Washington, DC, or online through the Library's website (http://catalog.loc.gov). The Library's catalog contains the publication dates for millions of written works in the Library's collection.

Check Copyright Office Records. If the sheet music was registered with the U.S. Copyright Office, checking Copyright Office registration records will reveal where it was first published. These records can be researched online (see Chapter 21). However, not all published musical works are registered with the Copyright Office, so there may be no record for it.

Check Music Reference Works. Check the music reference works listed in the previous section. These will often provide the country of publication.

Research the Composer. Researching the composer of the work may reveal where the work was published. If the composer is well known, a biography or critical study may have a detailed publication history for his or her works.

Use the Internet. Many helpful reference works and much information about composers and their works are available on the Internet. Do a Web search using the composer's name, the name of the work involved, and the publisher. There may be a website devoted to the composer or even to the particular work, or some online reference with detailed information about the work.

Contact the Publisher. The work's publisher will likely be able to tell you where the work was first published.

Has the Copyright in the Music Expired?

Copyright protection does not last forever. When it ends the work enters the public domain where it remains forever. The greatest single body of public domain music is works for which the U.S. copyright has expired. This includes most classical music and many popular songs by such famed composers as Irving Berlin.

Unfortunately, determining whether a copyright has expired can be somewhat complex. You'll need to determine which of several possible copyright terms apply to the work in question. Sheet music published as recently as 1963 could be in the public domain. On the other hand, music created more than one hundred years ago (and more) could still be protected by copyright.

Copyright terms for all creative works are the same no matter what type of work they are, so they are discussed in detail in one place: Chapter 18. Turn to that chapter to determine whether the copyright in a work you're interested in has expired.

Is the Music in the Public Domain Due to Lack of a Copyright Notice?

SKIP AHEAD

Before reading this section, you should have determined whether the sheet music you want to use has been published for copyright purposes. If the sheet music was never published, it doesn't need a copyright notice. You don't need to read any more of this section. Go on to the next section.

If sheet music was published before 1989 without a valid copyright notice, it could be in the public domain. A copyright notice on a work of sheet music must contain three elements—the familiar © or the word "Copyright" or abbreviation "Copr.," the publication date, and the name of copyright owner—for example: © Buddy Budapest 1945. You can usually find the notice on the title page or first page of sheet music. If the sheet music has been published as part of a collection, it's sufficient that the collection itself has a notice. Each individual piece included in such a collection need not have its own notice (although they often do).

If the work has a notice in the format described above, it will not be in the public domain for lack of a proper copyright. There is no need to read Chapter 19, which explains copyright notice requirements in detail. Go on to the next section.

However, if the work has no notice or the notice lacks one of the three elements described above, it could be in the public domain. Read Chapter 19 for detailed guidance on how to determine whether a published work is in the public domain because it lacks a valid copyright notice.

Is It a Derivative Work?

A derivative work is one that is based on or adapted from one or more preexisting works. A classic example of a derivative work is a movie based on a novel. The movie is a new work based on or adapted from the preexisting novel. Musical works can also be derivative works. Examples include:

- musical arrangements or orchestrations of preexisting works—for example, when unique harmonies are added to a folk song
- musical adaptations in which original melodies and rhythms are reworked —for example, a jazz version of the "Battle Hymn of the Republic"
- adding lyrics to an instrumental work or rewriting or translating the lyric for an existing song
- abridgments of existing musical works—for example, creating a new 30-minute version of a four-hour Wagner opera
- new instrumentation—for example, changing an orchestral work into a form playable on the piano or other

keyboard or changing a piano piece into a work for orchestra (as Ravel did many times), and

- new published editions of sheet music in which the editor adds substantial new copyrightable material.

No Permission Needed Where Preexisting Work Is in Public Domain

When a composer creates a musical work, one of the rights he or she receives through copyright is the exclusive right to create derivative works from it. That is, only the composer or other copyright owner has the right to fashion a new work based on the existing work. However, when musicians obtain permission to record a copyrighted song, they are ordinarily given some latitude to make minor changes. But substantial changes to the structure, such as altering the lyrics or melody, require explicit permission. For example, you would need to obtain permission from Cole Porter's estate to alter the lyrics or melody of the famous 1932 Porter song "Night and Day."

In addition to permission to create your derivative work, you would also need permission to reproduce those portions of the original copyrighted song included in your new work.

Once a work enters the public domain, all the composer's or other copyright owner's exclusive rights come to an end. Anyone can play or record the work and can create a derivative work from the public domain work without obtaining permission. For example, you are free to create new versions of any of Stephen Foster's songs—such as "Beautiful Dreamer," "Oh! Susanna," or "Jeanie With the Light Brown Hair"—since the copyright for these songs expired long ago.

Only New Material Is Copyrightable

When a person creates a derivative work from preexisting public domain music, only the new material added to the old work can be copyrighted by the creator of the derivative work. All the public domain material included in the derivative work remains in the public domain. For example, if you took a portion of a Chopin nocturne and added a lyric to it, the new lyric would be copyrighted, but none of Chopin's music would be. Anyone else would be free to use the same Chopin nocturne, but they could not copy your lyrics without your permission.

Is It an Arrangement or Adaptation?

If you go into the sheet music department of any music store and examine recently published sheet music for the works of such composers as Bach, Beethoven, and Chopin, you'll be surprised to find copyright notices in the music publishers' names. The same is true for many old popular music gems such as the songs of Stephen Foster and traditional songs such as "Greensleeves" that have been around for centuries.

The copyright in the original versions of classic works such as these expired long ago; or, in the case of extremely old works such as the music of J.S. Bach, they were never entitled to copyright protection in the first place. As explained in detail in Chapter 18, all such works are in the public domain. So why are music publishers claiming copyright by placing copyright notices on them?

The publisher's copyright claim may be completely spurious. This would be the case, for example, where a publisher reprints an exact copy of the original sheet music for a work in the public domain and simply adds a copyright notice. A straight reprinting of a public domain work is not entitled to any new copyright protection. Such a reprint may be copied as freely as the original version of the work.

Usually one of two things is happening when music publishers place copyright notices on public domain works:

- the publisher is claiming that its edition of the work is a copyrightable arrangement or adaptation, or
- the work is published as part of a sheet music collection for which the publisher claims a compilation copyright.

Arrangements and adaptations are discussed in this section. Copyright for sheet music compilations is discussed in the next section.

There is hardly a single well-known public domain work for which someone hasn't claimed to have made a new arrangement and claimed a new copyright. For many popular public domain musical works, hundreds of arrangements have been registered with the Copyright Office—for example, more than 300 arrangements for the public domain song "America the Beautiful" have been registered since 1950.

In some cases, these claims are valid and the creator or publisher of the arrangement is entitled to copyright protection for the material added to the original work. However, in many other cases the changes in the new arrangement are not significant enough to merit copyright protection.

GRAY AREA

Unfortunately, it can be difficult to determine which arrangements are protected by copyright and which are not. Refer to Chapter 1 for detailed guidance on how to deal with such public domain gray areas.

Avoiding Problems With Arrangements

Musical arrangements present a hornet's nest of copyright problems. But fortunately there are two simple ways to avoid these problems.

Use the Original Public Domain Song

You completely avoid worries about copyrighted arrangements where you use the original public domain version of the song. This involves either using the original sheet music for the work or a later published edition that is identical to the original. How do you know if a later published edition of a song or other musical work is identical to the original? Often, the sheet music publisher will tell you so somewhere on the work. The absence of a copyright notice in the publisher's name is also a sure sign that the work is not a new arrangement. Publishers almost always add new copyright notices to new arrangements.

You can also tell that the music in a newly published edition is the same as the original public domain music where the edition consists of exact copies of the original sheet music. These copies are in the public domain and can be copied freely—a music publisher doesn't get a new copyright by publishing an exact copy of public domain sheet music. However, the publisher may have a collective work copyright in the work as a whole. Many sheet music collections consist of exact copies of the original sheet music. Before the advent of modern-day computers and printing processes, sheet music printing plates were quite expensive to make. For this reason, most music collections were reprints of the original sheet music using the original plates. But, even today many exact copies of public domain sheet music are being made.

Use Public Domain Arrangements

Many arrangements of public domain songs are also in the public domain because their copyrights have expired. For example, if the publication date in the copyright notice is over 95 years old, the copyright in the arrangement has expired. You can use the arrangement freely.

> EXAMPLE: G. Schirmer, the well-known publisher of classical music, published an edition of a Beethoven sonata. The edition contains a number of editorial comments and new fingerings. Schirmer claimed copyright in the edition and included a copyright notice on the title page. However, the copyright notice reveals that the G. Schirmer edition was published in 1894. Even if the changes Schirmer's editors made to the original public domain version of the sonata were copyrightable, this edition is in the public domain because its copyright expired.

Even if the date in the notice is less than 95 years old, the arrangement could still be in the public domain. All works first published in the United States less than 95 years ago but before 1964 had to be renewed during the 28th year after

publication or they entered the public domain. Thus, even if the arrangement contained material protected by copyright, it will be in the public domain if the copyright was not renewed during the 28th year of publication. You must check U.S. Copyright Office records to see if a renewal was filed (see Chapter 21). If you discover that no renewal was filed, it is in the public domain and you may use the work for any purpose.

> EXAMPLE: The Remick Music Corp. published an arrangement by pianist Eddie Duchin of the well-known popular song "My Buddy," by Gus Kahn and Walter Donaldson. The original version of "My Buddy" was published in 1922 and is therefore in the public domain. The copyright notice for the Duchin arrangement contains a 1935 publication date. The arrangement would only retain its copyright if Remick filed a renewal notice 28 years after it was published, in 1963. Copyright Office records must be checked to determine if the arrangement was renewed.

Using Arrangements for Which Copyright Is Claimed

Unfortunately, it may not always be possible to obtain a copy of the original public domain version of a song or an arrangement that is in the public domain.

The only readily available version of a work in the public domain may be a recently published arrangement for which copyright is claimed. In this situation, you must decide how to deal with the arrangement. You have two options:

- you can treat the copyright claim as valid and seek permission from the music publisher to copy, record, or otherwise use the work, or
- you can determine whether the arrangement is really copyrightable and, if not, treat it as if it is in the public domain.

SKIP AHEAD

If you decide to treat the copyright claim as valid and seek permission from the music publisher to copy, record, or otherwise use the work, there is no need to read the rest of this section. If you want to determine whether the arrangement really has copyright protection, follow the step-by-step approach described below.

RESOURCE

For detailed guidance on how to obtain permission to use copyrighted music, refer to *Getting Permission: Using & Licensing Copyright-Protected Materials Online & Off*, by Richard Stim (Nolo).

Step 1: Determine What Changes Have Been Made

Before you can know whether an arrangement is or is not copyrightable, you must determine exactly what changes have been made to the original public domain work. It can be very difficult to determine just what changes have been made, because an arranger or publisher is not required to explain on the arrangement how it has been altered from the original. If the arrangement has been registered with the Copyright Office, the copyright registration will contain a brief description of how the work was changed. But this is usually too general to be of much help—for example, it may simply say "new arrangement for piano and orchestra."

In many cases the only way to know for sure what changes have been made is to compare the arrangement with the original unaltered version of the work. You'll have to obtain a copy to compare with the new arrangement. Obviously, if you have access to the original public domain version, you can simply use it to copy, adapt, or play rather than bother with the new arrangement. In this event, you can skip the rest of this discussion.

Fortunately, it may be possible to determine what changes have been made in an arrangement without obtaining a copy of the original public domain version of the music—for example:

- You may be intimately familiar with the original version of the music and not need to compare the original with the arrangement to see what changes were made.
- The music publisher may indicate what changes were made. This information is often on the same page as the copyright notice or in a preface or introduction.

The well-known piano music collection *Easy Classics to Moderns,* published by Consolidated Music Publishers, provides a good example of how a publisher may let you know what changes were made to public domain music. It contains a foreword on the title page that says:

> All selections are in their easy original form ... are neither re-arranged or simplified. In very rare cases pieces have been transposed to more suitable keys, but are otherwise unaltered. Marks of phrasing and expression are often editorial additions, especially in music of the Purcell-to-Beethoven period.

Step 2: Determine Whether the Arrangement Is Copyrightable

After you determine what changes the arranger or editor has made to the public domain version of the music, you must decide whether the changes are worthy of copyright protection. Use the guidelines in the next section to decide whether the changes are substantial and copyrightable, or trivial or obvious and therefore uncopyrightable. If you decide the arrangement is clearly not copyrightable, you may elect to treat it as a public domain work. If you decide the changes are copyrightable, you must obtain permission to use the arrangement. However, even if you're certain an arrangement is not copyrightable, a music publisher may disagree with you and complain or even sue you for copying it. Before you do such copying, read Chapter 1 for a detailed discussion of how to weigh the risks involved.

GRAY AREA

In some cases, it will be clear that an arrangement is not copyrightable—for example, where the only change is the transposition of the work from one key to another. In other cases where far more substantial changes have been made, it may be difficult to decide whether they merit copyright protection or not. It may be possible to remove the changes and create your own public domain version of the music (see "Getting Paid for Your Own Arrangements of Public Domain Works," below). But if this is not possible, refer to Chapter 1 for detailed guidance on how to deal with public domain gray areas.

⊘ CAUTION

Beware of collective works. Be careful if the work you want to use is printed in a collection—that is, an edition that contains a number of individual works. Even if an arrangement for a particular piece in such a collection is not copyrightable, the publisher may have a valid collective work copyright in the collection as a whole. That is, a copyright in the manner in which all the individual pieces in the collection were selected and placed.

Which Arrangements Are Copyrightable?

Some arrangements or adaptations of public domain music can obtain copyright protection, many others cannot. Unfortunately, the legal standards in this area are hazy. It is generally accepted, however, that an arrangement, adaptation, or alteration of a public domain musical work must be the result of originality and at least a minimal amount of creativity to obtain a valid copyright.

It is easier to tell when an arrangement is not original than when it is. No originality exists where the changes to a work in the public domain are:

- obvious, routine, or typical
- trivial
- mechanical in nature, or
- dictated solely by musical convention or tradition.

This is so even where substantial effort, skill, or musical training is required to make such changes. For example, "cocktail pianist variations" of a piece that are "standard fare in the music trade by any competent musician" are not copyrightable. *Woods v. Bourne Co.,* 60 F.3d 978 (2d Cir. 1995). Likewise, changes to a public domain work that can be created by music computer software with just the press of a key—for example, transposing a work from one key to another—cannot obtain a valid copyright.

For an arrangement to be copyrightable, "there must be something of substance added making the piece to some extent a new work with the old song embedded in it but from which the new has developed." In other words, the changes must be substantial or great enough so that the arrangement is to some extent a new work. In the case of a popular song, examples of such substantial changes would be such things as "'unusual vocal treatment, additional lyrics of consequence, unusual altered harmonies, novel sequential uses of themes.'" *Woods v. Bourne Co.,* 60 F.3d 978 (2d Cir. 1995.)

One way to determine whether an arranger has exercised the requisite originality and creativity is to ask whether the arranger had to choose among a number of aesthetic choices in creating the arrangement. Without choice, there can be no originality and no copyright protection.

Below are examples of the types of changes that are frequently made to public domain music along with discussions as to whether such changes are copyrightable.

New Editions

Public domain music is often republished in new editions and the publishers of such new editions often claim copyright in them. However, despite what music publishers may claim, new editions of public domain music are not protected by copyright.

As mentioned above, one type of new edition that is clearly not copyrightable is a reproduction of a public domain work—that is, an edition that is simply an exact copy of the original work. Making an exact copy of a piece of sheet music is purely a mechanical act. No new authorship is added in such an edition so there is nothing that can be copyrighted. There is also no copyrightable authorship in a new edition where the changes consist only of a new typeface or different size type. U.S. copyright law does not protect typefaces (see Chapter 5).

Often, editors who assemble a new edition of a public domain work will correct misprints in the original or later editions of the work. Although extremely helpful, such corrections are not "original" in the copyright sense and are definitely not copyrightable.

Copyright Notices Are Not Conclusive

Even if a work contains a copyright notice, it may not actually have copyright protection. Anyone can put a copyright notice on any work. No permission is required from the U.S. Copyright Office or any other government agency. All a copyright notice means is that someone claims that a work is protected by copyright law.

A copyright notice is not necessarily valid, even if the work has been registered with the Copyright Office. A Copyright Office opinion that an arrangement has copyright protection is not binding on you or the courts. In several instances courts have determined that arrangements registered with the Copyright Office were not copyrightable.

For example, a music publisher called Bourne Co. registered with the Copyright Office 16 different arrangements for the song "When the Red, Red, Robin Comes Bob, Bob, Bobbin' Along." When Bourne attempted to enforce its claimed copyright in these arrangements in court, the judge held that they did not merit copyright protection because they were not sufficiently original. *Woods v. Bourne Co.*, 60 F.3d 978 (2d Cir. 1995).

On the other hand, many new editions, particularly of classical music, contain significant editorial comments. These may consist of historical notes, music criticism, or detailed guidance on how the music should be played. Comments such as these are protected by copyright. However, the public domain music they accompany remains in the public domain and may still be copied freely.

Transpositions and Recleffing

Transposition is transferring music from one key to another, note for note—for example, transferring a piece from the key of F to the key of B flat. Public domain musical works are often transposed from their original keys to make them easier to sing or play.

Here is an example of transposing a portion of the public domain song "My Bonnie" from F to B flat:

"My Bonnie" in F

"My Bonnie" in B flat

Since the relationship of all the notes to one another remains the same, and all that is required is the simple act of measuring intervals between the notes, transposition is a purely mechanical act that clearly does not merit copyright protection. The B flat version of "My Bonnie" is as much in the public domain as the F version.

The process of recleffing very old public domain music written in obsolete clefs into the modern bass or treble clefs also does not earn copyright protection. This is also a purely mechanical act.

Keyboard Reductions

In a keyboard reduction, an arranger takes a work written for instruments other than the piano or other keyboards, such as a symphony or opera, and arranges it to be played on the piano or other keyboard instrument. Keyboard reductions may be copyrightable, depending on whether the keyboard arranger exercised significant aesthetic choices in creating the arrangement.

It's likely that most reductions of complex music such as orchestral works and operas are copyrightable. Many aesthetic choices must be made when arranging a piano version of a symphony or opera that originally contained many lines of music intended to be played by different instruments. Obviously, some of the original music will probably have to be left out or simplified, since a pianist with only ten fingers cannot replicate the sound of an entire symphony orchestra. Such a piano arrangement could be written in many different ways and it's likely that no two arrangers would do it in exactly the same way. Reductions or arrangements where the arranger significantly alters the music—for example, adds new melodies or harmonies—can also obtain copyright protection.

On the other hand, some piano reductions are clearly not copyrightable because the music is created in a mechanical way. One example would be a piano reduction of a choral work that consisted merely of writing out for piano the same notes that the chorus sings.

New Harmonies

Adding new harmonies to a public work may result in a copyrightable arrangement if the harmonies are original and not dictated solely by the melody or musical conventions. However, conventional harmonies driven by the melody or dictated by accepted rules of musical composition are not original and are therefore not copyrightable. *Northern Music Corp. v. King Record Distrib. Co.*, 105 F.Supp. 393 (S.D.N.Y. 1952). Of course, music experts could differ as to which harmonies are original and which are not, so determining which arrangements of this type are copyrightable and which are not is difficult.

Fingering Suggestions

Many new editions of public domain music contain fingering suggestions that were not included in the original version of the work. Some fingering suggestions are copyrightable, but many are not.

Often, fingering suggestions are intended to make a piece of music easier to play. These often consist of standard fingerings that have been used for centuries. This type of fingering is not original and should not be copyrightable since it is dictated solely by the need to make the piece playable. No aesthetic choices are involved—that is, the piece doesn't sound any different because of the fingering suggestions.

Obtaining Expert Music Help

If you do not know enough about music to judge whether an arrangement is sufficiently original to merit copyright protection, you'll need to obtain assistance from someone who does. Ideally, this would be a person intimately familiar with the genre of music involved—classical, popular, religious, etc. Only such a person can tell you whether the changes made to create the arrangement are obvious, routine, trivial, mechanical, or dictated by musical conventions. Few lawyers have this level of musical expertise. You would be better off consulting with an experienced musician, music teacher, musicologist, or composer.

Usually, it's not difficult for a person who knows about music to tell the difference between standard fingerings added for playing ease and nonstandard fingerings. The Bach minuet reproduced below is a good example of an instance where a music publisher has added extremely simple, standard fingerings to public domain music.

J.S. Bach

"Minuet" in G Major

On the other hand, some fingering suggestions are not made to make a piece of music easier to play. Instead, they may be suggestions intended to change how a piece sounds when played by accomplished musicians. Choices in fingering or bowing methods can significantly affect how a musical work sounds, particularly in compositions for string instruments. Fingering suggestions such as these may be copyrightable if they are not obvious or dictated by musical conventions.

If you're not sure whether the fingerings merit copyright protection, the safest course is to assume that they are copyrightable. In these cases, you can still use the sheet music if you eliminate the fingerings.

Rhythm

Standard rhythms such as a bossa nova or waltz beat are not copyrightable, but new and original rhythms can be. If you're not sure whether the rhythm is new or standard, it's safest to assume that it is protected by copyright.

Dynamic Markings

Dynamic markings consist of words and symbols composers add to sheet music telling musicians how loud or soft to play the music. Much public domain music was published without any dynamic markings because musicians didn't need them: musicians knew the conventions that dictated how the music should be performed. Later editions often added dynamic markings. Such markings are not copyrightable if they are dictated by musical convention or are copied from earlier editions of the music that are in the public domain.

However, changes in dynamics could be copyrightable if they are not obvious and they significantly alter the sound of the piece. In other words, simply adding the word "fortissimo" to a public domain work does not result in a copyrightable arrangement. But changes in dynamics that alter the very essence of the work could be copyrightable.

It may be difficult to discern with any certainty whether dynamic markings are or are not obvious. In these cases the safest course is to assume that they are copyrightable. However, you can still use the sheet music if you eliminate the markings.

Simplified Versions

Popular public domain music is often republished in simplified versions designed to be easier for novice musicians to play. Music publishers often claim copyright in these simplified arrangements. However, simplified versions are not protected by copyright if the simplifications are trivial, mechanical, or obvious—for example, simplifying the chords or transposing the work to an easier key.

However, a truly radical simplification of a piece could hold a valid copyright. For example, one arranger has taken Chopin's piano masterpiece "Ballade No.1 in G Minor Opus 23," a work comprising 14 pages of difficult-to-play music, and reduced it to a simple one-page work called "Theme From Ballade Opus 23." All that remains of the original work is a simplified version of the famous theme. In effect, the arranger has created a new work using the theme. This work is fully entitled to copyright protection. See *It's Easy to Play Chopin*, arranged by Daniel Scott (Wise Publications 1988).

Getting Paid for Your Own Arrangements of Public Domain Works

If you create your own arrangement of a public domain work that you believe is copyrightable, you are entitled to register it with the Copyright Office and, if it's published, place a copyright notice on it in your name. This entitles you to collect permission fees if your arrangement is performed in public or recorded. Fees for public performances are collected by the music performing rights societies ASCAP, BMI, and SESAC. Fees for recordings are usually collected by the Harry Fox Agency. Typically, these agencies will pay you a royalty for an arrangement of a public domain work equal to 10% to 20% of what they would pay for a completely original song. However, if your changes are very substantial, they may agree to pay more. A musicologist may be retained to compare your arrangement with the original public domain version to see how substantial your changes are.

You must join ASCAP, BMI, or SESAC to collect performance royalties. They all have excellent websites, at www.ascap.com, www.bmi.com, and www.sesac.com. The Harry Fox Agency website is at www.harryfox.com. For a detailed discussion of how to earn money from music, refer to *Music Law: How to Run Your Band's Business*, by Richard Stim (Nolo).

Using Arrangements Without Getting Sued

Here are two things you can do that will most likely prevent a music publisher from complaining about your use of their arrangements:

- **Don't use new elements.** Don't use those elements of the music that the publisher has added or changed. For example if you want to use a work for which the publisher has added dynamic markings or guitar chord diagrams, leave out the elements the publisher has added or changed.

- **Create your own public domain version of the work.** If you don't have access to the original public domain version of the work, but you can find a number of different arrangements, you may be able to create your own public domain version of the work using the arrangements. You do this by carefully examining the arrangements and looking for the elements common to them all. These elements must have been taken from the original public domain version of the work. By copying just these elements, you can create your own public domain version of the work.

Is the Music a Collective Work?

Sheet music for public domain works is often published in collections containing many individual works. For example, the collection *Easy Classics to Moderns,* published in 1956 by Consolidated Music Publishers, contains the sheet music for 142 individual works by more than two dozen classical composers, almost all of which are in the public domain. Such a collection is called a collective work for copyright purposes.

When a music publisher collects and publishes together the sheet music for a number of public domain works, it may be entitled to claim copyright protection for the collective work it creates. But the publisher is entitled to only a very limited form of copyright protection. All that is protected is the *selection and grouping* of the preexisting public domain material, not the preexisting material itself. This is often called a "thin" copyright. The copyright status of the preexisting material used to create a collective work is unaffected by the collective work's existence. Thus, if the preexisting material was in the public domain, it remains in the public domain.

EXAMPLE: In 1987, Dover Publications published a collective work of music entitled *Alexander's Ragtime Band and Other Favorite Song Hits, 1901-1911*. The work consisted of exact copies of the original sheet music for 49 songs published between 1901-1911, all of which are in the public domain. Dover was entitled to claim a copyright for its selection of the music to include in the collection and include a copyright notice for the collective work, which it did. However, this collective work copyright only protects the collection as a whole. None of the individual pieces is protected. Their inclusion in the new collective work does not revive their expired copyrights.

CAUTION

Beware new arrangements. Sometimes, the material included in music collections consists of new arrangements of public domain songs. In this event, the individual pieces may be copyrighted if the changes in the new arrangements are substantial enough to merit copyright protection. In these cases the publisher is entitled both to a collective work copyright in the collection as a whole and copyright in the new arrangement of the public domain works.

However, not all collective works are entitled to even thin copyright protection. A collective work cannot obtain copyright protection at all if not even minimal creativity was required to compile it or if it doesn't contain sufficient material.

Minimal Creativity Required

A collective work is entitled to the limited copyright protection it receives only because the author/compiler had to use creativity and judgment to create it. For example, Dover Publications in the example above used creativity and judgment in selecting which of the thousands of songs published between 1901 and 1911 should be included in its collection of just 49 songs from that decade.

However, if a collective work was created without using even minimal creativity and judgment, it will not be entitled to any copyright protection at all—that is, it will be in the public domain.

How can you tell if a collective work contains sufficient creativity to be entitled to thin copyright protection? A collective work is copyrightable if either the selection or grouping of the material is minimally creative. In some collections, both the selection and grouping are minimally creative. In others, only one is.

A selection is minimally creative if it is based on the compiler's opinion about something subjective—for example, the compiler's selection of the "best" Bach fugues or the *100 Greatest Romantic Songs Ever Written*. Here, the compiler must use selectivity and judgment to decide which fugues are "best" and which of the thousands of romantic songs ever written are the "greatest."

But a selection is not minimally creative if it does not require individual judgment. For example, no judgment is needed to compile a collection consisting of *every* Bach fugue.

Similarly, the way the individual pieces in a collection are ordered or placed is entitled to copyright protection only if done in a way that requires the exercise of the compiler's subjective judgment. An ordering or placement is not entitled to copyright protection if done in a mechanical way. An alphabetical or chronological grouping is purely mechanical and not entitled to copyright protection. Thus, for example, a collection of Stephen Foster's songs placed in alphabetical order by title would not be entitled to copyright protection. But a grouping on some other basis could be—for example, from worst to best in the compiler's opinion.

Small Collections Not Protected

In addition to the minimal creativity requirement, a collective work must consist of more than a few elements to have copyright protection. The Copyright Office has stated that a collective work of fewer than four items does not meet this threshold. For example, a collection of three Beethoven sonatas could not hold a copyright as a collective work. It's very likely that courts would follow this rule, and you can too.

How Much of a Collective Work Can You Copy?

The thin copyright of a collected work protects only the selection and/or grouping of the material. None of the individual pieces in the collection are protected. This means you may copy any individual piece included in the collection, so long as it does not have a valid copyright as a new arrangement.

But you are not limited to copying just individual pieces. You may copy any amount of a collection as long as you don't copy the publisher's copyrighted selection and/or arrangement. Let's take as an example Dover Publication's collection *Alexander's Ragtime Band and Other Favorite Song Hits, 1901–1911,* mentioned above. The selection of 49 songs included in this collection is copyrighted, but the grouping is not because it is in alphabetical order. You may copy all 49 songs and sell them individually. This would not infringe on Dover's selection—that is, its decision as to which songs to include in a collection of 49 favorite songs originally published during 1901–1911. But you could not sell all 49 together, since this would be copying Dover's selection. You could, however, copy all 49 songs, add another 51 songs, and publish a collection of the *100 best songs 1901–1911.* Again, this would not be copying Dover's selection of 49 favorite songs, 1901–1911.

Let's consider an example where only the grouping is copyrighted. If a publisher published a collection of all of Stephen Foster's songs and grouped them by theme, it would have a copyright in the grouping, but not in the selection, because every Foster song has been included. No creativity was required to make such a selection. You could copy every song in the collection and group them in some other way without violating the publisher's copyright in its selection—for example, you could group them alphabetically or chronologically. But you could not claim copyright protection for your grouping, since chronological and alphabetical groupings are not protected by copyright law.

Again, however, what you may not do is copy the publisher's selection or grouping. This could get you sued. This is exactly what happened with regard to the collection *Easy Classics to Moderns* published by Consolidated Music Publishers, mentioned at the beginning of this section. Consolidated's collection included a selection of six piano pieces by Bela Bartok published under the title *Six Miniatures*. This was the first time these six pieces had ever been published together. One of Consolidated's competitors later published a collection of its own entitled *World's Favorite Classic to Contemporary Piano Music*. This collection included the same six Bartok pieces in the same order Consolidated had published

them. Consolidated sued the publisher for copyright infringement and won. The court held that the selection and grouping of the six Bartok pieces was original and that Consolidated's copyright was violated when all six were copied in the subsequent collection. *Consolidated Music Publishers, Inc. v. Ashley Publications, Inc.*, 197 F.Supp. 17 (S.D.N.Y. 1961).

Does the Music Have Public Domain Elements?

If you determine that the copyright in a piece of music has not expired and that it did not enter the public domain because of a faulty copyright notice, the work as a whole is not in the public domain. However, it may still contain elements that are in the public domain. These may be freely copied or otherwise used although the entire work may not.

Music Copied From Public Domain Sources

Composers have been borrowing from each other for hundreds of years. Here is a list of just a few well-known popular songs based on previously existing works, all of which are now in the public domain:

- "Goin' Home" (1922), based on the Largo from Dvorak's symphony *From the New World* (1893)

- "Hello Mudduh, Hello Faddah" (1963), based on Ponchielli's "Dance of the Hours," from the opera *La Gioconda* (1876)
- "Love Me Tender" (1956), based on "Aura Lee," by George Poulton (1861)
- "Marine's Hymn" (1919), based on a theme from the opera *Genevieve de Brabant,* by Offenbach (1868), and
- "Night on Disco Mountain" (1977), based on "Night on Bald Mountain," by Mussorgsky (1887).

Any portion of a song or other musical composition copied from a public domain source is itself in the public domain. Incorporating it into a new song does not revive its copyright status. Only the new material, if any, added by the composer of the new song is copyrightable. For example, the lyric written by Alan Sherman for the comic song "Hello Mudduh, Hello Faddah" is copyrighted, while the melody (based on a public domain opera) is not. Anyone can write a song based on this public domain melody, but they cannot use Sherman's lyric without permission.

Ideas

Ideas are not protected by copyright, only the particular way a creative person expresses his or her ideas is protected. For example, the idea to write a song about young love is not copyrightable. Only the

particular way a composer expresses this idea is protected.

Simple Melodies

Extremely short simple melodies are generally not copyrightable. For example:

- A three-note phrase consisting of C, D flat, C, sung over a background C note played on the flute. Finding that the phrase lacked sufficient originality to merit copyright protection, the court quoted the musical expert in the case, who described it as a "common building block tool" that was "used over and over again by major composers in the 20th century, particularly the 1960s and 1970s." The six-second phrase was "sampled" by the hip-hop group Beastie Boys on one of its albums. *Newton v. Diamond*, 388 F.3d 1189 (9th Cir. 2004).
- A four-note musical phrase consisting of the notes A, G, F, and C. Noting that this identical phrase appeared in many other songs, the court concluded that to grant a copyright in such a "musical commonplace" would improperly curb musical composition generally. *Granite Music Corp. v. United Artists Corp.*, 532 F.2d 718 (9th Cir. 1976).
- An advertising jingle for a brand of beer consisting of the words "Tic Toc," juxtaposed by "Time for

Muehlebach" scored to the notes C and G to produce the sound and tempo of a clock ticking. *Smith v. Muehlebach Brewing Co.*, 140 F.Supp. 729 (W.D. Mo. 1956).

- The melody for the song "Johnny One-Note" (excluding the break). *Compendium of Copyright Office Practices*, Section 403.

In addition, melodies copied from other previously existing musical works are not copyrightable. Obviously, such melodies are not original.

Song Titles

Song titles ordinarily are not copyrightable. For this reason, many songs have the same or similar titles (see Chapter 13 for detailed discussion of titles).

Musical Forms

Musical forms and structures are all in the public domain. For example, the traditional AABA 32-bar structure for popular songs is in the public domain. Anyone can write a song in this format.

Information That Is Common Property

Certain types of musical information are called common property, which means they are available to everyone and are always in the public domain. This includes diatonic and chromatic scales and standard chords.

Chord charts consisting of standard chords may be copyrightable as compilations, even though the individual chords are in the public domain. That is, the selection and arrangement of the chord chart as a whole may be copyrighted. Method books consisting of public domain chords, scales, exercises, and public domain music likewise may be copyrightable as compilations.

Sources of Public Domain Sheet Music

There are dozens of websites that contain downloadable public domain sheet music. These include:

- Historic American Sheet Music (https://library.duke.edu/digital collections/hasm)
- The Choral Public Domain Library (www.cpdl.org/wiki)
- The Lester S. Levy Sheet Music Collection (http://levysheetmusic. mse.jhu.edu)
- Library of Congress Music for the Nation—American Sheet Music, 1870–1885 (www.loc.gov/collections/ american-sheet-music-1870-to-1885/ about-this-collection)
- Musopen (https://musopen.org)
- Mutopia Project (www.mutopiaproject.org)
- Petrucci Music Library (https://imslp.org)

- Public Domain Info
  (www.pdinfo.com)
- Sheet Music Fox
  (www.sheetmusicfox.com)
- Sheet Music Online
  (www.sheetmusic1.com), and
- University of California at Berkeley
  California Sheet Music Project
  (http://people.ischool.berkeley.
  edu/~mkduggan/neh.html).

The following U.S. music libraries are
good sources for public domain music:

- Berklee College of Music
  (https://library.berklee.edu)
- Columbia University Gabe M.
  Wiener Music & Arts Library
  (https://library.columbia.edu/
  libraries/music.html)
- Eastman School of Music of
  the University of Rochester
  (www.esm.rochester.edu/sibley)
- Free Library of Philadelphia
  (www.freelibrary.org)
- Harvard University (https://library.
  harvard.edu/libraries/loeb-music)
- Indiana University William and
  Gayle Cook Music Library (https://
  libraries.indiana.edu/music-library)
- Johns Hopkins University Arthur
  Friedheim Music Library (http://
  musiclibrary.peabody.jhu.edu/home)
- Library of Congress Music Division
  (www.loc.gov/rr/perform/guide)

- New York Public Library for the
  Performing Arts (www.nypl.org/
  locations/lpa)
- University of California, Berkeley,
  Jean Gray Hargrove Music Library
  (www.lib.berkeley.edu/libraries/
  music-library)
- University of California, Los Angeles,
  Music Library (www.library.ucla.edu/
  location/music-library)
- University of Chicago Music
  Collection (www.uchicago.edu)
- University of Michigan Music Library
  (www.lib.umich.edu/music-library)
- University of Washington Music
  Library (www.lib.washington.edu/
  music), and
- Yale University Irving S. Gilmore
  Music Library (https://web.library.
  yale.edu/music).

Sound Recordings

In the early part of the 20th century,
composers and music publishers made
most of their money from the sale of
sheet music. Of course, this is no longer
true. Today, most of the money in music
is made from the sale of recordings of
musical performances.

Legal protection for a recording of
a musical composition is completely

separate and distinct from protection for the composition itself. Legally speaking, the recording is a separate work in its own right, consisting of the performance of the composition and the work of the record producer in fixing the performance in a recording.

Sound Recordings Made Before Feb. 15, 1972

For the most of the 20th century, sound recordings received no protection under the federal copyright law. It was not until February 15, 1972 that they became protectable under the Copyright Act of 1909. However, this change in the law did not apply to recordings fixed before that date.

Before February 15, 1972, sound recordings were protected under state law. These state laws consisted of a hodgepodge of state anti-piracy statutes and uncodified common law copyright and unfair competition laws. The scope of this state law protection varied from state to state, and even within states, leading to great uncertainty. For example, it was unclear whether state law provided an exclusive right to publicly perform pre-1972 recordings. Moreover, such state law protection was scheduled to continue through 2067.

The lack of federal copyright protection for pre-1972 recordings ended on October 11, 2018 when the Classics Protection and Access Act ("CPA Act"; 17 U.S.C. § 1401) was signed into law. The CPA Act establishes a unique regime of copyright protection for pre-1972 sound recordings, including a *sui generis* digital performance right and a provision allowing for permission-free noncommercial uses of orphan recordings. Moreover, as a result of the CPA Act, all pre-1923 sound recordings will enter the public domain fairly soon: January 1, 2022.

Term of Protection

Prior to the CPA Act, state law protected all pre-1972 sound recordings, wherever created, and this protection was scheduled to end no later than February 15, 2067. The CPA Act provides pre-1972 sound recordings with a basic federal copyright term of 95 years from the year of publication, plus a "transition period" of three to 15 years. The transition period is three years for sound recordings first published before 1923, five years for sound recordings first published 1923–1946, and 15 years for sound recordings published between 1947 and 1956. Protection for all other pre-1972 sound recordings, including those previously unpublished, expires on February 15, 2067.

Thus, all sound recordings first published before 1923 will enter the public domain on January 1, 2022. This will be a banner day for the public domain. Sound recordings first published between 1923 and 1946 enjoy 100 years of federal copyright protection. Sound recordings first published between 1947 and 1956 obtain 110 years of protection. Sound recordings first published between 1957 and February 15, 1972 are protected until February 15, 2067. Sound recordings never published before February 15, 1972 enter the public domain on February 15, 2067; this is so even if they are published before that date.

Publication History of Work	Copyright Term
First Published Before 1923	Enters public domain Jan. 1, 2022
First Published 1923–1946	100 years after publication
First Published 1947–1956	110 years after publication
First Published 1957–Feb. 15, 1972	Enters public domain Feb. 15, 2067
Unpublished before Feb. 15, 1972	Enters public domain Feb. 15, 2067

Noncommercial Use of Orphan Recordings

One big problem with using older works that are still under copyright is that it can be difficult or impossible to track down the copyright owner to obtain permission. Such works are often called "orphan works" because no one knows who owns them.

The CPA Act contains a new mechanism allowing the public to make noncommercial uses of pre-1972 sound recordings without obtaining permission from the copyright owner if three conditions are satisfied:

1. the person "makes a good faith, reasonable search for, but does not find, the sound recording" either in the records of the U.S. Copyright Office, or "on services offering a comprehensive set of sound recordings for sale or streaming";

2. the person files a notice identifying the sound recordings and the nature of the use in the Copyright Office; and

3. within 90 days after the notice "is indexed into the public records of the Copyright Office," the rights owner does not file a notice opting out of the noncommercial use (the opt-out notice must be filed within 90 days after a notice of noncommercial use is listed in Copyright Office records).

The CPA Act does not define "noncommercial use," but it does provide that, "merely recovering costs of production and distribution of a sound recording resulting from a use otherwise permitted under this subsection does not itself necessarily constitute a commercial use of the sound recording." Moreover, "the fact that a person engaging in the use of a sound recording also engages in commercial activities does not itself necessarily render the use commercial." 17 U.S.C. Section 1401(c).

For more information, visit the U.S. Copyright Office website at www. copyright.gov/music-modernization/ pre1972-soundrecordings.

Sound Recordings Made or Published After Feb. 15, 1972

All sound recordings published—that is, distributed to the public—on or after February 15, 1972 and before 1978 are protected by copyright for 95 years from the publication date. Unpublished recordings made during this time period continue to be protected by state law.

A new federal copyright law took effect on Jan. 1, 1978 that gave protection to both published and unpublished sound recordings created anytime during or after that date. The copyright for such works lasts for 95 years from the publication date or for 70 years after the composer dies. As a practical matter it makes little difference which term applies right now since the earliest such recordings will enter the

public domain is the year 2049 (for works created by composers who died in 1978; see Chapter 18 for a detailed discussion of copyright terms).

However, there is one small group of recordings made after 1972 that is in the public domain: those published between January 1, 1978 and March 1, 1989 that contained no valid copyright notice on the recording or album cover. The copyright notice for a sound recording consists of a capital "P" surrounded by a circle, the year of publication, and the name of the copyright owner. After March 1, 1989 copyright notices were made optional.

Recordings published during this ten-year period without a valid notice may have entered the public domain. However, not all have done so, and it can be very difficult to determine which ones have. (See Chapter 19 for a detailed discussion.)

Term of Copyright Protection for Post-1972 Sound Recordings in the U.S.	
Year Work Published	Length of U.S. Copyright Term
1972–1977	95 years from publication
1978 and later	Life of the author plus 70 years; 95 years from publication for works made for hire, anonymous, and pseudonymous works

Sound Recordings on the Internet

Millions of sound recordings have been converted into digital form and placed on the Internet. A digital copy of a sound recording is a derivative work. Making the copy and making it publicly available over the Internet without the copyright owner's permission constitutes copyright infringement unless both the sound recording and the underlying composition are in the public domain. Claims that the wholesale copying of sound recordings on the Internet is a fair use have been rejected by the courts; most notably in a case involving Napster, a website that provided music file-sharing software to Internet users and facilitated unauthorized downloading of sound recordings. The Napster website was shut down as a result. *A&M Records, Inc. v. Napster, Inc.*, 239 F.3d 1004 (9th Cir. 2001).

Of course, people continue to upload and download music files without permission, committing copyright infringement. Recording industry groups have filed lawsuits against individuals who do this.

U.S. Government Sound Recordings

One substantial body of sound recordings that are in the public domain are those made by U.S. government employees as part of their jobs or by nonemployees working for the government. (See Chapter 3 for a detailed discussion.)

The U.S. National Archives, located in and around Washington, DC, has more than 90,000 sound recordings; the bulk of these are spoken-word recordings, not musical recordings. These recordings are primarily from U.S. government agencies, but there are also some from private, commercial, and foreign sources.

The National Archives has an extensive website (www.archives.gov) that contains detailed information about its audiovisual holdings.

CAUTION

Even if a sound recording of a person's voice is in the public domain, using the speaker's voice for advertising purposes —for example, in a radio commercial— could violate his or her right of publicity. See Chapter 20 for a detailed discussion.

Sound Recordings Dedicated to the Public Domain

Some sound recordings have been dedicated to the public domain by their creators. This is often done by the use of Creative Commons licenses (see Chapter 17 for a detailed discussion of such licenses). For example, professional musician Kimiko Ishizaka created studio-quality recordings of Bach's Goldberg Variations, dedicated them to the public domain by using the Creative Commons CC0 license, and made them available for free download at www.opengoldbergvariations. org. You can search for such material using the Creative Commons search engine at https://search.creativecommons.org.

Links to other music recording dedicated to the public domain can be found at:

- Internet Archive Audio Collection (https://archive.org/details/audio)
- Mutopia Project (www.mutopiaproject.org)
- Project Gutenberg Recorded Music (www.gutenberg.org/browse/ categories/3), and
- Wikipedia (https://en.wikipedia.org/wiki/ Wikipedia:Sound/list).

Art

Part I: Original Works of Art 121

What Good Is Public Domain Art? 121

Using Public Domain Art 121

The Problem of Access 123

Deciding If Original Art Is in the Public Domain 124

Has the Art Been Published? 125

When Art Becomes Published 125

Limited Publications 127

Finding the Date and Country of Publication 127

Has the Copyright in the Art Expired? 129

Is the Art in the Public Domain Due to Lack of a Copyright Notice? 129

Is the Artwork Eligible for Copyright Protection? 130

Art Lacking Minimal Creativity 130

Artistic Ideas, Styles, and Techniques 131

Works Lacking Human Authorship 132

Useful Articles 132

Jewelry and Other Applied Art 133

Fabric Designs and Clothing 134

Typeface Designs 135

Art Created by U.S. Government Employees 136

Art Dedicated to the Public Domain 138

Do You Intend to Use the Art in Advertising or on Merchandise? 138

Is the Art Protected by a Design Patent? 139

Sources of Original Art 140

Part II: Art Reproductions 140

Is the Original Work of Art in the Public Domain? 141

Has the Reproduction Been Published? 141

Has the Copyright in the Reproduction Expired? 142

**Is the Reproduction in the Public Domain Due to Lack
of a Copyright Notice?** 142

Does the Reproduction Lack Originality? 142

    Reproductions Other Than Photographs 143

    Photographs of Public Domain Artwork 144

    Digital Reproductions 146

Is the Reproduction Dedicated to the Public Domain? 147

Will You Use the Reproduction in Advertising or on Merchandise? 147

Are Elements of the Reproduction in the Public Domain? 148

Sources of Art Reproductions 148

This chapter will help you determine if a work of art is in the public domain. It is divided into two parts:

- Part I covers original works of art, and
- Part II covers reproductions of artworks, such as photographs of original works of art.

Original art and art reproductions require different steps to decide if they are in the public domain. This is because both original works of art and reproductions are considered by the copyright law to be works of authorship entitled to their own separate copyright protection, if they satisfy the legal requirements discussed below. A reproduction can even maintain copyright protection after the original enters the public domain.

> ⃝! CAUTION
> **Many works that are in the public domain in the United States are still protected by copyright outside the country, and vice versa.** This chapter covers only the public domain in the United States. For a detailed discussion of the public domain abroad, see Chapter 16.

Part I: Original Works of Art

This portion of the chapter covers original works of art, which include:

- original paintings, drawings, and sculpture

- the ornamental or artistic features of useful articles, such as furniture and other items that we use in daily life, and
- works of artistic craftsmanship—also called applied art—such as ceramics, glassware, and toys and fabric and clothing designs.

What Good Is Public Domain Art?

The works of Michelangelo and Rembrandt are yours to use for free because they are in the public domain, as is a vast amount of other art created through the ages.

Using Public Domain Art

The fact that a work of art is in the public domain can make your life easier in a variety of ways. To illustrate, let's compare two well-known paintings, one that is in the public domain and one that is not: the *Mona Lisa* by Leonardo Da Vinci and *American Gothic* by Grant Wood. The *Mona Lisa* is of course in the public domain because it was completed in 1506 and was published before the first copyright law came into existence, in 1790. Copyright is still claimed in the famous Grant Wood painting of a farm couple, created in 1930. This copyright claim will last until 2026. (See Chapter 18 for more on how long copyright protection lasts.)

The *Mona Lisa* is owned by the French government and hangs in the Louvre Museum in Paris. Unlike many museums, the Louvre permits the public to take photographs of its public domain paintings without advance permission. However, such a photo would probably not be of professional quality because you are not allowed to use a flash and the *Mona Lisa* is kept inside a large glass case. In any event, traveling to Paris for this purpose might be too expensive or inconvenient.

Photo by the author, October 2013

Fortunately, because the *Mona Lisa* is in the public domain, you can copy, distribute, or display an existing professional-quality photograph of the *Mona Lisa* without obtaining permission from the Louvre Museum or the French government. You may, however, have to obtain permission from the photographer who took the picture.

In contrast, because copyright is still claimed in Grant Wood's *American Gothic* (though disputed by some academics), you cannot reproduce a photo of the painting without obtaining permission from Wood's heirs. When a painting or other artwork is under copyright, the copyright owner has the exclusive right to create copies of it, including photos.

In addition, because the *Mona Lisa* is in the public domain, you may create your own copy of it—for example, draw or paint it from memory or from a photograph. You can publish or otherwise distribute your copy without seeking permission from anyone—for example, place it on T-shirts. This is not the case with *American Gothic*.

Grant Wood, American 1891–1942, *American Gothic*, oil on beaverboard, 1930, 74.3 x 62.4 cm, Friends of American Art Collection, All rights reserved by The Art Institute of Chicago and VAGA, New York, NY, 1930. Photograph ©2000. The Art Institute of Chicago. All Rights Reserved.

Moreover, because the *Mona Lisa* is in the public domain, you may create a new derivative work from it without obtaining permission. A "derivative" work is a work based on or adapted from a preexisting work. For example, you could create a *Mona Lisa* sculpture, animated cartoon character or computer icon, or even paint a copy of the *Mona Lisa* with a beard (Marcel Duchamp did this in a painting called *L.H.O.O.Q.*). The only limit on how you may use the *Mona Lisa* is your own imagination. Tens of thousands of derivative works have been created from the *Mona Lisa*. Someone in Japan even created a copy of the *Mona Lisa* made out of toast. See the Wikipedia article "*Mona Lisa replicas and reinterpretations*" for many examples of ways people have used the *Mona Lisa* image (https://wikivisually.com/wiki/Mona_Lisa_replicas_and_reinterpretations).

None of these things may be done with *American Gothic* without first obtaining permission. (The only possible exception might be creating a parody version of the painting, which could constitute a fair use not requiring permission; however, this is far from clear, and you could get sued for doing it; see Chapter 22.)

The Problem of Access

Theoretically, once a work of art enters the public domain it can be copied freely by anyone for any use. However, to make a copy you must first have access to the original. And here lies the problem: Owners of works of art in the public domain are under no obligation to give anyone access to copy the work. Even when a work of art is in the public domain, the canvas, marble, clay, or other physical substance in which it is embodied is still owned by somebody—whether a museum, gallery, or private collector. Since a work of art is a piece of personal property as well as a work of authorship, the owner enjoys

Collage artist Claudine Hellmuth created this collage using various public domain materials, including old postage stamps (purchased on eBay), an old railroad schedule, the title from a 1911 sheet music (found in a secondhand bookshop), and a drawing of a woman (copied from a Dover book of public domain drawings). Hellmuth's book *Collage Discovery Workshop* (North Light Books) describes how to create collage art from public domain materials. Other examples of her work can be viewed at her website (www.collageartist.com).

all the rights of any personal property owner. Copyright protection may expire or never exist in the first place, but personal property rights attach to all works of art and last forever.

Private owners of public domain works of art are under no obligation to allow anyone into their home to make copies of the art or even to view it. And most major museums in the United States restrict the public from taking photographs of their collections. Some museums forbid photography entirely or permit only amateur photographs that are of low quality and therefore not publishable. Other museums instruct visitors that they may take photos for personal use only. Still others require visitors to sign camera permits in which they agree not to reproduce any photos they shoot in the museum.

If you want a high-quality publishable photograph or other copy of a painting or other artwork, you must ask the museum to provide you with one. You will be charged a fee for this and usually required to sign a license agreement restricting how you may use the photograph or other copy (see Chapter 2). Such licensing fees are a major source of income for many art museums. Moreover, many museums will not agree to license their works for products that might compete with their own products, such as calendars and note cards.

Deciding If Original Art Is in the Public Domain

RESOURCE

What if the work is not in the public domain? If you find that the work you want to use is not in the public domain, you may be able to use it anyway under a legal exception called "fair use" (see Chapter 22). If you do not qualify for this exception, you will need to obtain permission to use the work. For a detailed discussion of how to obtain copyright permissions refer to *Getting Permission: Using & Licensing Copyright-Protected Materials Online & Off*, by Richard Stim (Nolo).

CAUTION

Despite the legal rules discussed below, be aware that it is common practice for the estates of well-known artists to claim that the late artist's works were never published, no matter what the actual facts are. This will usually provide a longer term of copyright than if such works were published—the life of the artist plus 70 years. Moreover, the art could not have fallen into the public domain due to lack of a copyright notice. It may be difficult and costly to refute such claims.

Has the Art Been Published?

The first question you must answer is whether the artwork was published and, if so, when. This will govern when the work enters the public domain.

Art is published for copyright purposes when the copyright owner, or someone acting on his or her behalf, makes it available to the *general* public. In other words, any interested member of the public may obtain a copy; or, in the case of one-of-a-kind artworks, at least has an opportunity to obtain the work. *Burke v. National Broadcasting Co.*, 598 F.2d 688 (1st Cir. 1979).

When Art Becomes Published

One of the following actions must be taken for artwork to be considered published for copyright purposes.

General Distribution of Copies of the Work

Art is published for copyright purposes whenever copies are made available to the general public. Such copies may consist of photographs, postcards, prints, lithographs, castings from a statue, and other reproductions.

> EXAMPLE: A Picasso sculpture commissioned by the City of Chicago was deemed published for copyright purposes when pictures of a large model of the sculpture were published in Chicago newspapers and national and international magazines, and postcards of the model were sold to the public. *Letter Edged in Black Press, Inc. v. Public Building Commission of Chicago*, 320 F.Supp. 1303 (N.D. Ill. 1970).

Most of the world's most famous artworks have been photographed and the photos published in books, museum catalogs, postcards, and other ways. All such artwork has been published for copyright purposes. But a work need not be famous to be published this way. Any work of art that has been photographed and distributed in this way has been published for copyright purposes.

Offering the Work for Sale to the General Public

A work of art is also published when it is offered for sale to the general public—for example, by the artist, through an art dealer, a gallery, or in a public auction. It does not matter whether a transaction is actually completed. The simple act of offering the artwork for sale qualifies as publication for copyright purposes. The date the article is offered for sale becomes its date of publication. *Roy Export Co. Establishment v. CBS, Inc.*, 672 F.2d 1095 (2d Cir. 1982). The only qualification is that the offering must be to the general public. Sales or offerings to a restricted group of potential buyers do not result in publication.

EXAMPLE: Grandma Moses created a painting entitled *Over the River to Grandma's House* and exhibited it to the public in her studio. An unidentified buyer came by and purchased it that same day. A court held that this constituted publication of the work. *Grandma Moses Properties, Inc. v. This Week Magazine,* 117 F.Supp. 348 (S.D.N.Y. 1953).

Disseminations With No Restrictions

Artwork is also published when it is sold, lent, gifted, or otherwise distributed to a select group of people, or even one person, provided that the artist has placed no restrictions on reproducing, distributing, or selling the work, or copies of it, to the general public. The reason for this rule is that such a work may ultimately become available to the general public. That is, the person or group that receives the work may eventually make it available to the public.

EXAMPLE: Assume that Grandma Moses was commissioned by a wealthy art collector to create a painting. Upon completion, the painting was delivered to the collector and Grandma was paid. Grandma placed no restrictions on what the collector could do with the painting—for example, he could offer it for sale to the public or sell photographs of it. This transaction published the painting for copyright purposes.

Allowing a Work to Be Copied by the Public (Before 1978)

Simply putting a work on display and allowing the public to copy it is not enough to make the work published for copyright purposes, as long as the work was created after 1977. Before then, a work of art was considered published if it was displayed to the public and the public was allowed to copy it freely. This would have been the case where a piece of art was displayed in a public park, art gallery, or museum and there was no effort to stop people from making replicas, drawings, photos, or other artworks based on the original work.

An artwork was not considered published if the general public was allowed to view the piece, but was prevented from making copies or replicas of it, by, for example, placing guards near the object to prevent copying of the work.

EXAMPLE: English painter W. Dendy Sadler created a picture called *Chorus,* and later exhibited it to the public at the Royal Academy in London for three months. The U.S. Supreme Court held that the exhibition of the work did not result in its publication for copyright purposes because the Royal Academy's bylaws barred the public from copying works on exhibition and there were officers present in the gallery to enforce the rule. *American Tobacco Co. v. Werckmeister,* 207 U.S. 284 (1907).

As a practical matter, it will be difficult for you to determine whether a work of art displayed in public prior to 1978 has been published. It would be necessary to review the copying policies of every museum or gallery where it was shown to determine if copying was allowed in any of them. So, unless you're prepared to do some extensive research, you should assume that pre-1978 paintings, drawings, and similar works have not been published solely because they were publicly displayed.

On the other hand, sculptures, frescoes, friezes, and other artworks permanently displayed in public places such as parks and plazas and exteriors of public buildings before 1978 likely would be considered published, since the public is ordinarily allowed to freely copy such works.

Beginning in 1978, the law changed. Any display of a work after 1977—even if copying was allowed—will never result in publication of the work for copyright purposes.

Limited Publications

Publication occurs for copyright purposes only when any interested member of the public can obtain a copy of the work—for example, can purchase a photo or bid on the work at a public auction or sale. In contrast, publication does not occur where a work is only made available to a definitely selected group of people for a limited purpose and without the right of further diffusion, reproduction, distribution, or sale. This type of limited distribution is called "limited publication" and is not considered publication for copyright purposes. *White v. Kimmel*, 193 F.2d 744 (9th Cir. 1952).

Examples of limited publications include where:

- an artist distributes prints or copies of his or her work to colleagues for comment with the understanding that the copies are not to be sold or further reproduced or distributed, or
- copies of an artist's work are distributed to newspapers or magazines for review or criticism (however, if the work was printed in a newspaper or magazine it would be published).

Finding the Date and Country of Publication

If you determine that a work of art has been published, you must also determine when and where it was published before you decide when its copyright protection ends. Many artworks contain dates, but these are usually the date the work was created, which may not be the same year it was published.

As a practical matter, it may be difficult to determine the exact date a painting, sculpture, or other work of art was first published—that is, was first offered for sale or first copied. This is particularly true for works of art that are centuries old. Such works may be offered for sale and copied over and over again through the years. However, it is not necessary to determine the exact date when a work was first published. It is sufficient if you can determine that it was published in the United States over 95 years ago, or published outside the United States any time before 1909. If it was, the work is in the public domain. Works published for the first time in the United States less than 95 years ago but before 1964 are also in the public domain if their copyright was not renewed. (See Chapter 18 for a detailed discussion.)

> **TIP**
>
> **Art published after 1963 cannot be in the public domain due to copyright expiration.** But it could be public domain for other reasons, such as failure to use a copyright notice or because it's ineligible for copyright in the first place.

Probably the easiest way to determine if a work of art was published during the dates mentioned above is to search for a published photographic reproduction. If you can find a photo of the work in an artbook, art catalog, postcard, or newspaper it must have been published at least as of the date of the photo. The country the photo was published in will be the country of publication of the original artwork as well.

Art reference works may also be helpful. For example, they may tell you when and in what country a work was offered for sale to the public (another way art is published for copyright purposes). Other useful resources to finding both the date and country of publication of a work of art include:

The Library of Congress Card Catalog. If the artwork has been reproduced in a book, magazine, or other work, it may be listed in the Library of Congress card catalog. The catalog entry will usually show both the country and date of publication. You can check the catalog in person at the Library in Washington, DC, or online through the Library's website (https://catalog.loc.gov).

The Internet. There are thousands of websites devoted to art. There may be a website that provides a detailed publication history of the work you're interested in. Do a search using the artist's name and the name of the work of art. A list of useful art websites is contained at the end of Part I.

Copyright Office Records. If either the original artwork or a reproduction was registered with the U.S. Copyright Office, checking Copyright Office registration records will reveal when and where it was published. These records can be researched online (see Chapter 21). However, many published artworks are not registered with the Copyright Office, so there may be no record for them.

Art Museums. An art museum that collects the artist's works may be helpful.

You can find art gallery/museum links at: www.easysurf.cc/museum.htm. *The Official Museum Directory,* by the American Association of Museums, lists more than 15,000 museums in the United States and is revised annually. See www.officialmuseumdirectory.com/OMD.home.

If you are unable to determine the date and country of publication of the artwork, you will not be able to determine if its copyright has expired or if it is in the public domain due to lack of a valid copyright notice. However, you don't need the date and country of publication to determine whether it is in the public domain because it is ineligible for copyright protection. So skip to the section on copyright notice, below, and see if it is in the public domain on this basis. If not, you should assume the work is not in the public domain.

Has the Copyright in the Art Expired?

Copyright protection does not last forever. When it ends, the work enters the public domain. Some art published as recently as 1963 could be in the public domain. But some art created over 100 years ago or more could still be protected by copyright.

The greatest single body of public domain art comes from works for which the U.S. copyright term has expired. But determining whether a copyright has expired can be complex. You'll need to determine which of several possible copyright terms apply to the work in question.

Copyright terms are the same for all copyrighted material, including art, music, and writings, so they are discussed in detail in Chapter 18.

Is the Art in the Public Domain Due to Lack of a Copyright Notice?

SKIP AHEAD
Before reading this section, you must determine whether the artwork has been published for copyright purposes. If the art was never published it doesn't need a copyright notice. You don't need to read any more of this section.

If the artwork was published before 1989, it could be in the public domain if it lacks a copyright notice. Examine the work carefully to determine if it has a notice—the familiar © symbol or the word "Copyright" or abbreviation "Copr."—and the name of the copyright owner—for example: © Ralph Raphael. If the artwork was published before 1978, the notice didn't have to contain a publication date.

If it was published between Jan. 1, 1978 and March 1, 1989 a publication date was required, except for jewelry, toys, and other useful articles containing pictorial or graphic works.

The notice can be hand drawn or painted anywhere on the front or back of a canvas or piece of drawing paper or anywhere on a sculpture or piece of applied art such as jewelry or toys.

If the work has no notice, it could be in the public domain. Since many artists failed to place copyright notices on their works, many artworks published before 1989 have entered the public domain for this reason. Read Chapter 19 for detailed guidance on how to determine whether a published work is in the public domain because it lacks a valid copyright notice.

Is the Artwork Eligible for Copyright Protection?

Even if you determine that the artwork has a proper copyright notice and its copyright protection has not expired, it could still be in the public domain. Some types of artwork can never be protected by copyright; they will be in the public domain unless other laws protect them like, for example, trademark law.

Art Lacking Minimal Creativity

Art must be minimally creative to be protected by copyright (see Chapter 2 for a detailed discussion of creativity and copyright). However, the amount of creativity required is very slight. Almost any work satisfies the creativity test. It can have substantial or little artistic merit or aesthetic value. Copyright protects everything from the most accomplished painting or sculpture by a professional artist to a child's finger painting.

However, according to the U.S. Copyright Office, there are some types of artwork that completely lack creativity and are, therefore, ineligible for copyright protection. These include:

- common representational symbols, such as a spade, club, heart, diamond, star, yin yang, fleur-de-lys, or the like
- two- or three-dimensional geometric figures or shapes such as a hexagon, ellipse, cone, cube, or sphere
- simple coloration—for example, a textile design consisting simply of the colors green and blue
- arrows and other directional or navigational symbols
- common patterns, such as standard chevron, polka dot, checkerboard, or houndstooth designs

- well-known and commonly used symbols such as the peace symbol, gender symbols (♀♂), simple emoticons such as the typical smiley face (☺) or the like; and
- standard industry designs, such as the caduceus, the barber pole, food labeling symbols, or hazard warning symbols. *Compendium of U.S. Copyright Office Practices*, Section 313.4(J) (3d ed. 2014).

Copyright Office views are not binding on the courts, but it makes good sense to follow its views. They are given some deference by the courts and if you are sued for using a particular artwork, it will help you defend yourself if you followed a Copyright Office guideline.

Although these types of artistic creations are not individually protected by copyright, they may obtain copyright protection if they are combined in a new, creative way. For example, a mobile or collage consisting of a number of geometrically shaped pieces such as spheres and cones may obtain copyright protection as a whole even though the individual pieces would, under Copyright Office definitions, be in the public domain. In addition, all of these works could be protected by state and federal trademark laws if they are used as part of the packaging design used to sell a product or service.

Artistic Ideas, Styles, and Techniques

Copyright law protects only the particular way an artist expresses his or her ideas, not the ideas themselves. For example, the idea of painting a bowl of fruit is not protected by copyright. Anyone can paint a bowl of fruit, but you cannot copy the exact way another artist paints a bowl of fruit unless the work is in the public domain. For example, Cezanne's famous paintings of bowls of fruit are almost all in the public domain and can be copied freely. Likewise, the idea of creating a doll whose face has an upturned nose, bow lips, and evenly spaced eyes is in the public domain. However, the particular way this idea has been expressed in the Barbie doll is protected by copyright. *Mattel, Inc. v. Goldberger Doll Manufacturing Co.*, 365 F.3d 133 (2d Cir. 2004).

Similarly, artistic styles are always in the public domain. For example, anyone can create a painting in the cubist or impressionist style. Copyright only protects the exact way an artist expresses an artistic style. For example, cubism is in the public domain, but a particular painting by cubist painter Georges Braque is not.

Artistic techniques are also not protected by copyright. This includes, for example, two-point perspective or the drawing techniques an artist uses to create the illusion of a sphere on a two-dimensional surface such as a piece of paper. Anyone is free to use these techniques, which have been around for centuries.

Works Lacking Human Authorship

Copyright protects only works created by human beings. Thus, for example, the U.S. Copyright Office says that a mural painted by an elephant would not be copyrightable. Works produced by mechanical processes or random selection, without any contribution by a human author, are also not protected by copyright. For example, a floor covering featuring a multicolored pebble design that was produced by a mechanical process in unrepeatable, random patterns is not protected by copyright. Similarly, a work owing its form to the forces of nature is not protected by copyright—for example, a piece of driftwood is not protected by copyright even if it has been polished and mounted; neither is the appearance of actual animal skin, or cut marks, defects, and other qualities found in natural stone. A living garden of wildflowers was also not protectable because it lacked a human author.

However, the presence of human "choices" would make a work of art created by a machine protected by copyright. For example, spin art is protectable because the person using the spin art machine decides what colors to use and when to drop the paint onto the spinning platter.

Useful Articles

"Useful articles" are items whose intrinsic function is utilitarian—for example, automobiles, boats, household appliances, furniture, work tools, and clothing. The utilitarian or mechanical aspects of useful articles are not protected by copyright—for example, the serrated edge of a knife is not protected by copyright.

Two-Dimensional Representations of Useful Articles Protected by Copyright

A two-dimensional representation of a useful article—for example, a drawing, painting, or photograph of a chair—is protected by copyright even though the useful article is not. But copyright only extends to the drawing, painting, or photograph, not to the useful article itself. That is, you can't copy a copyrighted painting of a chair, but you may build the chair itself. Thus, for example, an inventor's copyright in drawings for a new type of pistonless engine only protected the drawings themselves, not the inventor's idea depicted in the drawings of how to create such an engine. *Rozenblat v. Sandia Corp.*, 79 Fed. App'x. 904 (7th Cir. 2003).

However, the design of a useful article or work of applied art is subject to copyright protection if:

- it contains pictorial, graphic, or sculptural features, and
- such features can be identified as existing independently of the utilitarian object in which they are embodied.

Copyright protects such design features if they are physically or conceptually separable from the useful article.

According to the U.S. Copyright Office, examples of two- and three-dimensional features that typically satisfy the test include:

- a painting on a dinner plate
- a portrait painted on a cigar box
- an artistic print on wrapping paper or a paper bag
- an artistic pattern woven into a rug
- a carving on the back of a chair
- a decorative hood ornament on an automobile, and
- an artistic scroll work framed as a fireplace screen.

SEE AN EXPERT

Because it can be very difficult to determine whether the artistic features of a utilitarian object are protected by copyright, it's advisable to seek legal advice before copying such an object for commercial purposes.

Patent and Trademark Protection for Useful Articles

In some cases, the purely decorative or ornamental aspects of a useful article may qualify for protection as a trademark or be protected by a design patent.

Trademark protection would be available where the decorative aspects of an article are used to advertise or sell a product—a good example is the distinctive shape of a Coke bottle. Patent protection is available where a useful article contains novel and unobvious ornamental features.

Jewelry and Other Applied Art

"Applied art" refers to works of artistic craftsmanship such as jewelry, toys, and wall plaques. Unlike useful articles, their intrinsic purpose is artistic or decorative, rather than utilitarian.

Copyright protects the artistic aspects of a work of applied art as long as they are minimally creative and original. The protected aspects of such a work may be either sculptural or pictorial in nature— for example, carving, cutting, molding, casting, shaping the work, arranging the elements into an original combination, or decorating the work with pictorial matter such as drawings or paintings.

However, works of applied art that are not minimally creative are not protected by copyright. For example, a jeweled pin consisting of three parallel rows of stones is not protected by copyright, while a pin consisting of a sculpted bee is. Reason: Placing three stones one over the other is not even minimally creative, while sculpting a bee most definitely is. But most jewelry designs are minimally creative and protected by copyright.

Even if the individual design elements used to create a piece of jewelry are in the public domain, the jewelry may still be protected by copyright if a minimal amount of creativity was required to select and combine those elements. For example, a court held that a gold and silver ring with a bridge-like motif was copyrightable even though the elements—a channel of princess-cut diamonds on the shank of the ring, the suspending of a marquis-shaped diamond above the shank to create the "bridge" effect, and use of flared gold supports to hold the marquis diamond in a tension setting—were all familiar designs in the public domain. The court stated that these elements were combined so as to create a more stylistic and flowing look than any prior bridge ring. *Weindling International Corp. v. Kobi Katz Inc.*, No. 00CIV2022(JSR) (S.D.N.Y. 2000).

The utilitarian or mechanical aspects of a work of applied art are not protected by copyright. For example, the purely functional clasp on a jeweled pin is not protected by copyright, while the design of the pin itself may be.

Fabric Designs and Clothing

Fabric designs are protected by copyright, but only if they are original and minimally creative. Copyright protection has been extended to a plaid design consisting of intersecting diamonds and to pansy and rose designs. However, standard designs that have been around for years are in the public domain—for example, polka dots or traditional plaids.

Clothing and dress designs ordinarily are not protected by copyright. In the words of one court, "it is accepted copyright law that a garden variety article of wearing apparel is intrinsically utilitarian and therefore a nonprotected by copyright useful article. Equally non-protected by copyright are the elaborate designs of the high fashion industry, no matter how admired or aesthetically pleasing they may be." *Whimsicality Inc. v. Rubie's Costumes Co.*, 721 F.Supp. 1566 (E.D.N.Y. 1989).

However, it is possible for specific ornamental or design elements contained in clothing to be protected by copyright, even though the piece of clothing as a whole is not—for example, a detailed embroidery, or a two-dimensional drawing or graphic work affixed to a portion of a garment might be protected by copyright. For example, the U.S. Supreme Court has held that surface decorations on cheerleading uniforms consisting of arrangements of colors, shapes, stripes, and chevrons were eligible for copyright protection if they were sufficiently original. *Star Athletica, LLC v. Varsity Brands, Inc.*, 137 S.Ct. 1002 (2017).

As a general rule, clothing designs can't be protected under the state and federal trademark laws. This is because trademark law doesn't protect functional objects such as clothing. However, clothing designers can rely on trademark laws to protect their brand names and logos—for example the company name "Levi's."

All of this means that clothing designers have little legal protection against "style piracy." The fashion industry has been asking for a special form of legal protection for clothing designs for years, but Congress has yet to act.

Typeface Designs

A "typeface" is the design or style of the letterforms used for printing type. A "font" is a typeface of a particular style and size. Typefaces were originally carved from wood and then cast in metal. Today, of course, typefaces are created on computers and added to word processors and other programs used to create and print documents.

Many typefaces have been around for hundreds of years, but there are many others that have been designed quite recently. Regardless of when they were created, typefaces or fonts are not protected by copyright in the United States. This is so whether they are generated by a computer program or represented in drawings, hard metal type, or any other form. In other words, they are in the public domain. One very significant result of this rule is that a public domain work does not receive a new copyright when it is reprinted in a new typeface. Both the words and the typeface are in the public domain. Thus, for example, you are free to copy a public domain writing you find on the Internet even if the person who posted it on the Web changed the font from the original.

Font Software Is Protected by Copyright

Font software (computer programs used to generate typefaces) can be protected by copyright. But this protection is limited to the computer code. It does not extend to the output these programs create: the typefaces themselves. Moreover, some font software programs have been dedicated to the public domain. (See Chapter 8 for a detailed discussion of public domain software.) Theoretically, this means that even though font software may be protected, you should still be able to copy the font itself—for example, by drawing or photographing it or creating your own program to generate a similar font. Unfortunately, things are not so simple—typefaces may be protected by licenses or laws other than copyright.

Other Protections for Typefaces

The large companies that sell font software don't want people copying their fonts, even though they aren't protected by copyright. For this reason, they usually include licensing agreements along with their programs. Among other things, these licenses typically bar users from making any unauthorized copies of the fonts generated by the program. The enforceability of such provisions is questionable. (See Chapter 2 for a detailed discussion of this issue.)

In addition, a few font software companies have obtained design patents for some of their fonts. For example, Adobe obtained design patents for its Garamond, Minion, and Utopia typeface families. You can usually tell if a font program has been patented: Ordinarily, the word Patent or the abbreviation Pat. and the patent number will appear on the packaging or in the program itself.

It's likely, however, that few typefaces qualify for design patent protection. This is because a typeface must be both novel and nonobvious to qualify for a patent. Few typefaces are either—most consist of reworkings of preexisting designs.

Finally, you should be aware that state and federal trademark laws protect some of the names given to fonts. For example, the name Helvetica is a protected trademark. This means that although the font itself may not be protected, the name could be. So, although the Helvetica typeface may be freely copied, the name may not be used to advertise the typeface to the public. (See Chapter 20 for a detailed discussion of trademarks.)

Art Created by U.S. Government Employees

Works of authorship created by U.S. government employees as part of their job are ordinarily in the public domain. This includes works of art and art reproductions. However, there are some exceptions. For example:

- The U.S. Postal Service has been legally entitled to claim copyright in postage stamp designs at least since 1970, when the former Post Office was remade into an independent corporation. However, the Service did not begin to claim copyright in its stamp designs until 1978. You'll find copyright notices on sheets of stamps published during or after 1978. However, if you reproduce pre-1978 public domain postage stamps in color, the reproduction must be at least 50% larger or 25% smaller than the original stamp. Black and white reproductions can be any size. Copyrighted postage stamps may be used in editorial matter in newspapers, magazines, journals, books, stamp catalogs, and stamp albums without obtaining permission from the U.S. Postal Service. If an uncanceled postage stamp is depicted in color, it must be less than 75% or more than 150% of life size.

Graf Zeppelin 1933 air mail stamp.

- Federal government agency seals, logos, emblems, and insignias may not be reproduced on articles—for example, on T-shirts—without government permission. This includes, for example, the NASA insignia logo (the blue "meatball" insignia) and the Presidential Seal. In addition, such items may not be used in advertisements, posters, books, stationery, plays, motion pictures, telecasts, or on any building in a manner that conveys a false impression of sponsorship or approval by the U.S. government or any department or agency. This prohibition is intended to help prevent fraud.

- U.S. currency may be reproduced in black and white or in color, but only if the reproduction is one-sided, less than 75% or more than 150% the size of actual currency, and if all the negatives, plates, digitized storage medium, and everything else used in the creation of the image are destroyed after final use. On the other hand, U.S. coins may be reproduced in photographs, illustrations, movies, and slides in any size.

- Special federal laws protect the characters of the Woodsy Owl used by the Department of Agriculture, the Crash Test Dummies used by the Department of Transportation, and Smokey Bear used by the U.S. Forest Service. These may not be reproduced without permission.

Moreover, certain organizations that you might think are part of the U.S. government are not considered to be so. This includes the Smithsonian Institution and all of its branches and the National Gallery of Art in Washington, DC. Both are independent quasi-governmental entities that are entitled to claim copyright in the works their employees create, and in fact do so.

Information concerning art owned by the U.S. government can be accessed from the General Services Administration website, at www.gsa.gov.

Art Dedicated to the Public Domain

Artists need not enjoy copyright protection if they don't want it. Instead, they may dedicate their work to the public domain. This means they give up all their rights in the work forever and anyone may use the work without asking their permission.

There is no prescribed formula for dedicating a work to the public domain. The artist or other copyright owner simply has to make clear his or her intentions. For example, stating "This work is dedicated to the public domain" on the work would be sufficient. It's not even necessary to make the dedication in writing. It could be done orally, but it's always best to write something down to avoid possible misunderstandings.

However, it is not at all common for artists to dedicate their work to the public domain; so it's not likely you'll encounter any.

Do You Intend to Use the Art in Advertising or on Merchandise?

Even if a work is in the public domain—that is, not protected by copyright—it may receive some legal protection under state and federal trademark laws. These laws can prevent someone from using a work of art in advertising, product packaging, or on merchandise such as T-shirts, mugs, and plates.

A trademark is any word, symbol, device, logo, or symbol that identifies and distinguishes one product from another. A service mark is the same as a trademark, except it is used to identify a service rather than a product. Trade dress means the total image and overall appearance of a product or service—for example, the shape, size, color or color combinations, texture, or graphics.

Any work of art can function as a trademark, service mark, or aspect of trade dress. This includes, for example:

- a statue used to identify a restaurant
- the image of a dog listening to a gramophone used to identify RCA recordings, and
- the unique star shape used to identify Mercedes cars.

Even art that doesn't qualify for copyright protection may be trademarked. For example, copyright does not protect simple ornamentation such as chevron stripes. However, such stripes could be protected by the trademark laws if they are used as a product logo or part of a product's packaging, as in the chevron logo used by the Chevron Corporation for its gas stations.

Trademark laws may also protect the nonfunctional aspects of product shapes and containers. For example, trademark protection has been extended to the shape of a Coke bottle and the front grill on a Rolls-Royce.

For artwork to receive trademark protection, it must be used to identify or distinguish a product or service that is currently being sold to the public. Typically, the owner of a trademark will help the public identify it by using a trademark notice on or near the trademark. A trademark notice may consist of the symbols ®, TM, SM, or the words "Registered in U.S. Patent and Trademark Office" or "Reg.U.S. Pat & Tm. Off." If you see such a notice anywhere on or near any work you want to use, be sure to check to see if it is a protected trademark.

But keep in mind that trademark protection does not confer an absolute monopoly on the use of the mark. Even if a work of art or design is trademarked, you may still use it without permission for purposes other than advertising or product packaging or on merchandise. Indeed, you may still, in many situations, be able to use it for some advertising or merchandise purposes. (See Chapter 20 for a detailed discussion of trademarks.)

Is the Art Protected by a Design Patent?

Federal patent law protects inventions—everything from new types of mousetraps to satellites. This book does not cover inventions. You may be surprised to learn, however, that patent law can also protect the ornamental design of a useful article such as a clock or cement mixer. This is where design patents come in.

A design patent may be used to protect a new, original ornamental design embodied in a manufactured object. The design can be a surface ornament such as a pattern on a beer mug or may consist of the shape of the article itself such as the shape of a Rolls-Royce automobile or silverware set.

Unlike copyright protection, patent protection is not automatic: one must apply for a patent from the U.S. Patent and Trademark Office in Washington, DC, a process that can take years. Three basic requirements must be met to obtain a design patent:

1. The design must be novel—that is, the exact same design must not have been used before.
2. The design must be nonobvious—that is, the design may not be one that a designer of ordinary capability who designs articles of the type involved could be expected to devise.

3. The design must be ornamental—it must create a pleasing appearance and not be dictated by purely functional considerations.

Most designs don't qualify for design patent protection because they are not novel or nonobvious. But, if the government issues a design patent, it lasts for 14 years from the filing date if the application was filed before May 13, 2015; design patents resulting from applications filed after May 13, 2015 last for 15 years.

In the past, design patents haven't been very popular. They were expensive and difficult to get and many of them were invalidated by the courts because they failed to satisfy the novelty or non-obviousness requirements. However, courts have been taking a more liberal view toward design patents in recent years and their popularity is increasing.

How can you tell whether a useful object is protected by a design patent? One way is to look for a patent notice. Although not mandatory, patent owners typically place patent notices on their works: the word "Patent" or "Pat." followed by the patent number. However, patent notices are not always used, so the absence of a notice does not conclusively mean the object is not patented.

Another easy way to determine if a design patent protects a manufactured object is to ask the manufacturer. A more difficult way is to conduct a patent search—a search of the U.S. Patent and Trademark Office's records. Such searches can be conducted online or at special patent and trademark depository libraries.

Finally, since pre-2015 design patents only last for 14 years, you can safely assume any object that has been sold to the public for more than 14 years is not protected by a design patent. You can usually determine how long an item has been sold by contacting the manufacturer. Another way to determine the age of a design patent is to conduct a patent search.

Sources of Original Art

You can find museum listings at Art Cyclopedia (www.artcyclopedia.com/museums.html). Other helpful art websites include Art History Resources on the Web (http://arthistoryresources.net/ARTHLinks.html), and Art and Art History (https://libguides.colostate.edu/art).

Part II: Art Reproductions

Because of the difficulty of obtaining access to original works of art, most people have to rely on reproductions. These include (but are not limited to) photographs, prints, lithographs, photo-engravings, collotypes, silk-screen prints, mezzotints, and three-dimensional reproductions of sculpture.

When such reproductions are in the public domain, you may freely copy and reproduce them and create new works based upon them *provided that the original artwork is also in the public domain*. For example, a public domain photo of an artwork that is also in the public domain can be freely used on a website. Using computer software such as *Photoshop*, you may also freely alter the image and copy and reproduce it.

RELATED TOPIC

What if the work is not in the public domain? If you find that the work you want to use is not in the public domain, you may be able to use it anyway under a legal doctrine called "fair use." If your intended use doesn't qualify as a fair use, you will need to obtain permission to use the work. See Chapter 22 for a detailed discussion of your options where you determine a work is not in the public domain.

Is the Original Work of Art in the Public Domain?

As explained below, some art reproductions are copyrighted and some are not. But, one rule applies to all reproductions: If the original artwork is not in the public domain, the reproduction is not either. You must always determine the copyright status of the original before deciding whether the reproduction is copyrighted. (For a detailed discussion of copyright protection for original artworks, see Part I, above.)

It is possible for a reproduction to be in the public domain while the original artwork is still protected by copyright. For example if a photograph of a famous copyrighted artwork lacks originality, it will be in the public domain. However, if the original artwork is still protected by copyright, the reproduction cannot be used without permission from the copyright holder of the original. But there will be no need to obtain a separate permission from the creator of the reproduction.

Has the Reproduction Been Published?

The answer to this question determines how long the copyright lasts and whether it has to contain a copyright notice. As with any work, an art reproduction is published when it is made available to the general public on an unrestricted basis. For example, a photo of a public domain painting is published when it is offered for sale to the general public in an art book, postcard, poster, or slide. The same rules apply to art reproductions and photographs. Read Chapter 6 for a detailed analysis of publication.

Has the Copyright in the Reproduction Expired?

The copyright in an art reproduction published as recently as 1963 could be in the public domain. The copyright in many unpublished reproductions expired in 2003. The rules for how long copyright lasts are the same for all types of work. Read Chapter 18 for a detailed discussion of copyright duration to see if the work you are interested in using has entered the public domain because its copyright expired.

Is the Reproduction in the Public Domain Due to Lack of a Copyright Notice?

If the copyright in a reproduction has not expired, it could still be in the public domain if it fails to comply with copyright notice rules. You should carefully examine the reproduction to see if it contains a copyright notice—a © symbol or the word "copyright" or the abbreviation "Copr." and the copyright owner's name. Copyright notices for photographs published before 1978 don't need to have a publication date. Art reproductions published from Jan. 1, 1978 through March 3, 1989 do need a publication year date, except for postcards, greeting cards, stationery, jewelry, toys, dolls, and useful articles.

If the work lacks a notice and you know it was published before 1989, it may have entered the public domain. Unfortunately, it is not always easy (or even possible) to determine if such works are in the public domain. (See Chapter 19 for a detailed discussion.)

SKIP AHEAD

If the reproduction was never published, or published after March 1, 1989, it doesn't need a copyright notice and you can skip Chapter 19.

Does the Reproduction Lack Originality?

If copyright protection for an art reproduction has not expired and it has a proper copyright notice, it may still be in the public domain for another reason: lack of originality. A reproduction of a public domain work of art is entitled to copyright protection only if it is original. It cannot be simply an exact copy of the original artwork. Reproductions that lack originality are in the public domain. There are undoubtedly a vast number of art reproductions that are not protected by copyright on this basis—these may include reproductions created as recently as last week. If the original artwork is also in the public domain, these reproductions may be freely used.

TIP

Here we examine the originality requirement for works other than photographs and digital copies. We deal with these categories separately below because photographs present special problems that have yet to be resolved by the courts.

GRAY AREA

Determining whether an art reproduction contains sufficient originality to be protected by copyright is a judgment call and reasonable minds can differ. If you're not sure whether a reproduction merits copyright protection, refer to Chapter 1 for detailed guidance on how to deal with foggy areas in the law of the public domain.

Reproductions Other Than Photographs

Reproductions other than photographs include lithographs, photoengravings, and three-dimensional reproductions of sculpture. The amount of originality required for such works to receive copyright protection is fairly small. All that is required is that the creator of a reproduction contribute something more than what the courts have called "a merely trivial variation" on the original public domain work. The contribution must be a substantial variation, "something recognizably his [the creator's] own." *Alfred Bell & Co. v. Catalda Fine Arts*, 191 F.2d 99 (2d Cir. 1951).

For example, mezzotint engravings of public domain old master paintings were found protected by copyright because the engraver had to use skill and judgment to create the engravings—that is, the engraver had to decide how to portray the paintings through the use of different lines and dots on a metal plate producing varying degrees of light and shade. Such engraving was a very different operation than creating the original public domain paintings with a brush and paints. Thus, the engravings were not mere "slavish" copies. They required an independent act of creation by the engraver. *Alfred Bell & Co. v. Catalda Fine Arts,* above.

On the other hand, purely trivial or minuscule variations are not enough to make a reproduction protected by copyright, even if they require great technical skill and effort. For example, one court ruled that a plastic version of a public domain cast iron mechanical coin bank was not protected by copyright because the plastic bank was substantially the same as the public domain cast iron version, except that it was made from plastic and was slightly smaller. *L. Batlin and Son, Inc. v. Snyder*, 536 F.2d 486 (2d Cir. 1976).

Similarly, art reproductions made by purely mechanical or photomechanical processes are not protected by copyright. This includes photocopying—for example, a photocopy of a public domain pen-and-ink drawing is not protected by copyright as an art reproduction. Both the original drawing and the photocopy are in the public domain. On the other hand, a photocopy of a montage made of several public domain drawings would be protected by copyright.

Likewise, the act of transferring a work of art from one medium to another is not by itself sufficient to give copyright protection to the copy. Rather, a copy in a new medium is protected by copyright only where the copier makes some identifiable original contribution. For example, transferring a painting on canvas to a coffee mug or plate does not by itself result in a copyrighted reproduction.

> EXAMPLE: In the late 1960s, John McConnell created the first "Earth Flag" by copying a photograph of the Earth taken by Apollo astronauts onto a piece of blue fabric. The flag became a well-known symbol of the environmental movement. Some 30 years later, the Alamo Flag Company created and sold an almost identical flag. The company that McConnell licensed his flag design to sued Alamo for copyright infringement and lost. The court held that the original Earth Flag was in the public domain because it was not a copyrightable work of authorship. The photo of the earth McConnell used was taken by government employees and no creativity was required to reproduce it on a flag-size piece of cloth. The flag was nothing more than a public domain photo transferred from paper to fabric. As such, it was itself in the public domain and could be freely copied. McConnell did not have a copyright over the idea of creating a flag with a photo of the earth—like all artistic ideas, this was in the public domain. *Earth Flag Ltd. v. Alamo Flag Co.*, 153 F.Supp.2d 349 (S.D.N.Y. 2001).

Photographs of Public Domain Artwork

Photographs of public domain artwork deserve special treatment. Except for those relatively rare occasions where we go to museums or art galleries, most of us rely on photographs to view public domain artworks. These may be published in websites, art books, art slides, art exhibition catalogs, postcards, or posters. Legal protection for photographs in general is discussed in Chapter 6. This section focuses solely on the question of whether photographs of public domain art works are protected by copyright as art reproductions.

The most significant court decision on this question held that photographs of public domain paintings lack originality and are therefore in the public domain. The case involved the Bridgeman Art Library Ltd., a company that has obtained the exclusive rights to license photographs of hundreds of public domain art masterpieces from various museums. Corel Corp. allegedly obtained more than 150 images from the Bridgeman collection and published them without obtaining Bridgeman's permission. The images were included on clip-art CD-ROMs and placed on the Corel website where they could be downloaded for a few dollars each.

Bridgeman sued Corel claiming that the unauthorized duplication of the photos was copyright infringement. The court held that no infringement was involved because the photos were in the public domain. The court found that the photos lacked originality and therefore could not be copyrighted as art reproductions. As noted above, a reproduction of a public domain work of art is protected by copyright only if there is some nontrivial variation on the original public domain work. The court noted that the whole purpose of taking the photos was to make "slavish copies" of the public domain originals—that is, to reproduce the underlying public domain works with absolute fidelity. While this took both effort and skill, it did not require originality. The photos stood "in the same relation to the original works of art as a photocopy stands to a page of typescript, a doodle, or a Michelangelo drawing." *Bridgeman Art Library Ltd. v. Corel Corp.*, 25 F.Supp.2d 421 (S.D.N.Y. 1999).

Relying on *Bridgeman*, the U.S. Copyright Office refuses to register "a photograph that is merely a 'slavish copy' of a painting, drawing, or other . . . work." For example, the Copyright Office will not register a high resolution photo of the *Mona Lisa* that is virtually identical to the painting.

The *Bridgeman* case attracted much attention in the art world at the time. Today, it seems to be largely ignored by museums, art book publishers, photo archives and other owners of photographs of public domain art. These parties routinely include copyright notices on photographs of public domain artworks. However, since the Copyright Office will not register these photos, such copyright claims are unenforceable in court. These notices are used to discourage the public from freely using photos of public domain art.

In reaction to the *Bridgeman* decision, companies, museums, and other organizations that publish art photos are relying on license agreements more than ever—that is, they require people who purchase or obtain permission to use their photos to agree to a license (a type of contract) limiting how they may use the photos. In this way, they can sue for breach of the license agreement if someone violates the terms of the license. However, there are limits on the effectiveness of licenses. For example, in the *Bridgeman* case, Corel was able to obtain the photos from a third party without signing a license.

The *Bridgeman* case only dealt with photos of two-dimensional artworks —paintings, frescoes, and drawings. Photos of three-dimensional works such as sculpture may be protectable as art reproductions because there are many ways to photograph a three-dimensional object, particularly a large one—choices as to lighting, angle, and so forth that may add originality to the reproduction.

Moreover, the *Bridgeman* case has no application at all to cases where a photographer makes something other than a "slavish copy" of a public domain work—that is, a reproduction as faithful to the original as photographic technology allows. For example, a photo of the *Mona Lisa* would be protected by copyright if the photographer lit it in such a way that only *Mona Lisa*'s face was visible, not the background.

Digital Reproductions

The most common way of creating a digital reproduction is to use a computer scanner to create a digital copy of a photograph of the artwork. In some cases, the original work is scanned rather than a photograph—for example, an original drawing could be scanned. It is also possible to create exact reproductions of three-dimensional works of art such as sculpture using computer scanners and 3D printing technology.

As mentioned above, art reproductions made by purely mechanical means such as photocopying cannot obtain copyright protection. It follows logically, then, that a photograph of an original work of art intended to be an exact copy of the original should not have copyright protection. For this reason, the U.S. Copyright Office has refused to register many scanned images of public domain artworks. However, some companies that own digital copies of public domain artworks continue to claim copyright in them. Such claims are probably spurious, but you might still be threatened with a lawsuit if you treat such companies' digital copies as public domain. (See Chapter 1 for detailed guidance on how to deal with such public domain problem areas.)

Moreover, if a scanned image of a public domain artwork is altered in some way, it may acquire copyright protection. For example, a person who scans a photo of a landscape painting by John Constable could change the color of the sky, move the location of a brook, or even remove a human figure. This sort of thing is easily done with computer technology. Such changes represent new authorship that is protected by copyright.

Is the Reproduction Dedicated to the Public Domain?

People who create protected-by-copyright art reproductions need not enjoy copyright protection if they don't want it. Instead, they may dedicate the reproduction to the public domain. This means they give up all their rights in the work forever and anyone may use the work without asking their permission.

There is no prescribed formula for dedicating a work to the public domain. The creator or other copyright owner simply has to make clear his or her intentions. For example, stating, "This work is dedicated to the public domain" on an art photo would be sufficient. It's not even necessary to make the dedication in writing. It could be done orally, but it's always best to write something down to avoid possible misunderstandings.

Be careful, however, where a creator sends mixed messages. For example, if a photographer states that his art photos are in the public domain, but then attempts to restrict how the public may use them—for example, by saying "This work is public domain but may not be posted on the World Wide Web without my permission." When a work is dedicated to the public domain, the author may not restrict how it is used. A statement like this leaves it

unclear whether the author really intended to dedicate the work to the public domain. It's wise to seek clarification from the creator or ask permission for the restricted use.

Similarly the use of the phrase "copyright free" by the author need not mean the work is dedicated to the public domain. The words "copyright free" are often used to describe photos and clip-art that are under copyright but are sold to the public for a set fee rather than under a royalty arrangement.

⃝! CAUTION
Dedicating an art reproduction to the public domain does not mean that the original work of art enters the public domain as well. You must be sure the original artwork is in the public domain before deciding to use a reproduction that has been dedicated to the public domain. (See Part I, above.)

Will You Use the Reproduction in Advertising or on Merchandise?

An art reproduction in the public domain may receive some legal protection under the state and federal trademark laws if someone is using it in advertising, product packaging, or on merchandise such as

T-shirts, mugs, plates, etc. If this is the case, you may be prevented from using the reproduction for similar purposes. Read Chapter 20 for a detailed discussion of the trademark laws.

Are Elements of the Reproduction in the Public Domain?

Art reproductions receive limited copyright protection. Even if an art reproduction as a whole is not in the public domain, it will likely contain individual elements that are in the public domain. These may be copied freely even if the work as a whole may not be.

All that is protected in an art reproduction is the new authorship added to the original public domain work. For example, a fabric designer reproduced public domain designs on a fabric in such a manner that by arranging varying colors the flat surface looked like three-dimensional embroidery. Copyright only protected the three-dimensional effect, not the elements of the design directly copied from the public domain designs. *Millworth Converting Corp. v. Slifka*, 276 F.2d 443 (2d Cir. 1960).

You are always free to copy the original public domain work. But you don't have to go back to the original. You can copy the copy so long as you don't copy the original elements that make the copy different than the original. For example, you can use a mezzotint engraving of the *Mona Lisa* to paint your own version of the *Mona Lisa*. But you can't make an exact copy of the engraving—that is, copy each line and dot made by the engraver.

Sources of Art Reproductions

Some websites that will assist in locating public domain art reproductions include:

- Art History Resources on the Web (http://arthistoryresources.net)
- Dover Publications (http://store.doverpublications.com)
- The Famous Artists (www.thefamousartists.com)
- Art Images for College Teaching (https://quod.lib.umich.edu/a/aict)
- The Chicago Art Institute (www.artic.edu/image-licensing)
- J. Paul Getty Museum (www.getty.edu/art/collection), and
- Metropolitan Museum of Art (www.metmuseum.org/art/collection).

Photography

What Good Are Public Domain Photographs? 150

Deciding Whether Photographs Are in the Public Domain 150

Has the Photograph Been Published? 151

Finding the Date and Country of Publication 152

Has the Copyright in the Photograph Expired? 154

Is the Photograph in the Public Domain Due to Lack of a Copyright
Notice? 154

Is the Photograph Eligible for Copyright? 155

Has the Photograph Been Dedicated to the Public Domain? 157

Does the Photograph Contain Copyrighted Materials? 158

Will You Use a Photograph for Commercial Purposes? 160

Sources of Public Domain Photographs 161

Photographs include any product of the photographic process, such as prints, negatives, slides, and filmstrips. Since the invention of photography in 1839, billions of photographs have been taken, many millions of which are in the public domain.

> ⚠ **CAUTION**
>
> **Many works that are in the public domain in the United States are still protected by copyright outside the United States, and vice versa.** This chapter covers only the public domain in the United States. For a detailed discussion of the public domain abroad, see Chapter 16.

What Good Are Public Domain Photographs?

Everyone likes to look at photographs. They are constantly being used in websites, books, magazines, newspapers, posters, postcards, and even in documentary films. Nobody knows how many photos have been posted on the Internet, but the number must be well into the billions.

Ordinarily, you need to obtain permission to use someone else's copyrighted photograph. This permission usually isn't free. For example, high-end stock photo agencies—companies that specialize in licensing photos to the public—usually charge at least $150 per photo, often much more. Famous photos may cost thousands of dollars to use. If you want to use a photo more than once, additional fees may have to be paid.

When a photo is in the public domain, you are free to copy, reproduce, display, or alter it without obtaining permission from anyone. For example, you can use it in a book or article or post it on your website. However, there are some exceptions to this rule: Permission may be needed if the photo contains people or trademarks and you intend to use it for advertising or on merchandise.

Public domain photos are not always free, because you may have to pay a fee to obtain actual or digital copies of them, but they are usually much cheaper than copyrighted photos. Moreover, there are thousands and thousands of public domain photos that can be obtained for free online and from books, newspapers, and magazines sitting on library or archive shelves.

Deciding Whether Photographs Are in the Public Domain

The first step in determining the public domain status of a photograph is to decide if it has been published.

Free Pictures: Worth a Thousand Words

Emmy Werner, a developmental psychologist at the University of California at Davis, wanted to write a book about the experiences of children during World War II. She realized that including pictures taken of children during the war would greatly enhance the book. So she traveled to the National Archives in College Park, Md., where she was given access to hundreds of photos of children taken during World War II by the U.S. Army Signal Corps. All these photos were in the public domain because they were taken by U.S. government employees—soldiers whose job was to document the war. She chose about 40 photos to include in her book. She had a private company duplicate the photos at a cost of from $5 to $10 each. This was the only expense involved. Because the photos were in the public domain, she did not have to obtain permission to use them or pay any permission or license fees. Werner's book, *Through the Eyes of Innocents: Children Witness World War II*, was published in early 2000. The moving photo below of two children is from the frontispiece of the book.

Has the Photograph Been Published?

To determine how long a particular photograph retains copyright protection, you must determine whether it was published properly under the rules of copyright law and, if so, when. The answer to these questions will determine how long the copyright in the photo lasts.

Like any work of authorship, a photograph is published for copyright purposes when the copyright owner, or someone acting on his or her behalf, makes the photo available to the *general* public. In other words, any interested member of the public may obtain a copy. *Burke v. National Broadcasting Co.*, 598 F.2d 688 (1st Cir. 1979).

For example, photographs are published when they are reproduced in newspapers, magazines, books, postcards, sets of slides, greeting cards, posters, T-shirts, mugs, or any other item that is sold or otherwise made available to the general public.

Of course, many photographs have never been made available to the general public, including many that are quite old. For example, your own family snapshots collected in a family photo album likely have never been published. Moreover, photos are not deemed published when they are displayed to the public in an art gallery or museum.

Finding the Date and Country of Publication

If you determine that the photograph you're interested in has been published, you should also determine the year of publication and the country where it was first published. Both these factors will affect how long the United States copyright in the photo lasts (see Chapter 18).

Date of Publication

You just need to know the year, not the exact date, the photo was first published. You can usually determine the publication date from the work itself. First, look for a publication date in the copyright notice. Photos published before 1978 didn't have to include a publication date in their

copyright notices, but they often had them anyway—for example, © 1986 by Kim Kodak. Photos published 1978–1989 did need a publication date in the notice. (See Chapter 19 for a detailed discussion of copyright notices.)

Photos are sometimes published alone, as in a postcard. In this event, they will often contain their own individual copyright notices. However, photos are also often published as part of a larger work—for example, books, magazines, and newspapers. Photos published in this way will sometime have their own notice, but often they won't. In this event, the copyright notice for the larger work will provide you with the publication date for the photo (books, magazines, and newspapers have always needed a publication date in their copyright notices). However, be sure to check any photo credit or acknowledgment section in the work to make sure the photo wasn't previously published before it was included in the work you have.

If the photo lacks a copyright notice with a date, you'll have to look elsewhere for clues about the publication date. Try the following:

Examine the Work for a Date. Examine the work in which the photo was published —for example, a newspaper—for a publication date. Most published works contain some indication of when they were published. Look on the title page, the masthead, the page after the title page, and anywhere else that seems logical.

Check the Library of Congress Card Catalog. Check the Library of Congress card catalog to see if it has as a record for the larger work in which the photo was published or for the individual photo itself. You can do this in person at the Library in Washington, DC, or online through the Library's website (https://catalog.loc .gov). The Library's catalog contains the publication dates for millions of works in the Library's collection.

Check Copyright Office Records. If either the individual photo or the larger work in which it was published (if any) was registered with the U.S. Copyright Office, checking Copyright Office registration records will reveal the publication date. These records can be researched online (see Chapter 21). However, not all published works are registered with the Copyright Office, so there may be no record for it.

Check Reference Works. There are hundreds of reference works that may be able to tell you when a work was published. Go to a public or university library with a good reference section and ask the reference librarian for assistance.

Research the Photographer. Researching the photographer or the author of the larger work in which the photograph was published may reveal the publication date. If the photographer or author is well known, a biography or critical study may have a detailed publication history for his or her works.

Use the Internet. Search the Internet using the name of the photographer, the name of any larger work in which the photograph was published, and the name of the author and publisher of that work. There may be a website devoted to the photographer, author, or even to the particular work, or some online reference with detailed information about the work.

Contact the Publisher. If the photo was published in a larger work such as a book or newspaper, contact the work's publisher and ask them to tell you when the work was first published.

Country of Publication

Unfortunately, a work's country of publication is not listed in the copyright notice. However, most published works typically say where they were published or printed. You can often find this information on the same page as the copyright notice. If you can't find the country of publication from the work itself, try using the resources listed above—they will ordinarily provide the country of publication as well as the publication date.

Has the Copyright in the Photograph Expired?

Once you determine if a photo has been published, you can figure out whether its copyright has expired. When copyright expires in a work, it enters the public domain. The greatest single body of public domain photos available for use in the United States is works for which the U.S. copyright term has expired.

Unfortunately, determining whether a copyright has expired can be somewhat complex. You'll need to determine which of several possible copyright terms apply to the work in question. Photos published as recently as 1963 could be in the public domain. On the other hand, photos created more than 100 years ago (and more) could still be protected by copyright.

The length of a copyright is the same no matter what type of work is involved (photos, art, writings, music, etc.), so they are discussed in detail in Chapter 18. Turn to that chapter now to determine whether the copyright in a photo you're interested in has expired.

SKIP AHEAD

If the photograph you're interested in was published after 1963, its copyright protection has not expired. If you wish, you may skip to Chapter 18, however, and read that chapter if you want to know exactly when the photo's copyright will eventually expire.

Is the Photograph in the Public Domain Due to Lack of a Copyright Notice?

SKIP AHEAD

Before reading this section, you must determine whether the photograph you want to use has been published for copyright purposes. If the photo was never published, it doesn't need a copyright notice and you don't need to read any more of this section.

If a photo was published before 1989, it could be in the public domain if it lacks a copyright notice. A copyright notice for a photograph must contain three elements—the familiar © symbol, the word "Copyright" or the abbreviation "Copr.," the publication date, and the name of copyright owner—for example:

© 1965 by Amos Adams

Examine the photo carefully to determine if it has a notice. It can be anywhere on the front or back of the photo. Photos are very often published as part of larger works—for example, in books, magazines, and newspapers. It's sufficient that the larger work has a copyright notice—the individual photos included within it need not have their own notices (though they often do). For example, a notice in the name of a magazine will cover all the photos in the magazine. However, there is one exception to this rule: Photos contained in advertisements published in magazines, newspapers, and similar works must contain their own copyright notices.

You can usually find the notice for a book on the page immediately following the title page or on the title page itself. Copyright notices for magazines, newspapers, journals, and other periodicals are usually found on the title page, the first page of text, or under the title heading. The notice may also appear in a magazine's masthead.

Read Chapter 19 for detailed guidance on how to determine whether a published work is in the public domain because it lacks a valid copyright notice.

Is the Photograph Eligible for Copyright?

Certain types of photographs are ineligible for copyright protection. These may be copied or otherwise freely used unless your use violates publicity rights, trademark rights, or if the subject of the photograph is copyrighted.

Photographs Lacking Originality

Only photographs that are original can have copyright protection. There are three ways a photograph is deemed to be original:

- There may be originality in the way the photograph is made—for example, such elements as choice of time and light exposure, camera angle or perspective, deployment of light and shadow from natural or artificial light sources, and effects achieved by use of filters and developing techniques.
- There may be originality in the arrangement of the people, scenery, or other subjects depicted in the photograph.
- A copyright may be created because the photograph records a scene unlikely to recur—for example, a battle between an elephant and a tiger. *Bridgeman Art Library Ltd. v. Corel Corp.*, 25 F.Supp.2d 421 (S.D.N.Y. 1999).

The vast majority of photographs qualify as sufficiently original under one or more of these criteria. This includes, for example, a photo of the New York Public Library, which a court ruled qualified for copyright protection under the first criterion listed above. Photographs made from photo footage of the John F. Kennedy assassination taken by an amateur cameraman named Abraham Zapruder were also considered protected, under the third criterion listed above.

However, there are some types of photographs that lack originality:

- prints from a photographic negative
- a photograph of a photograph that is an exact copy of the original, and
- a photograph that is an exact copy of a page of text or other printed matter.

Photographs that lack originality are not protected by copyright. However, this does not necessarily mean that they may be freely used. A print, negative, or photograph of a preexisting photograph can only be freely copied or otherwise used if the original negative or photograph is in the public domain. If not, permission is needed from the copyright owner of the original photograph. Similarly, a photograph of a page in a book may not be freely used unless the book is in the public domain.

Mechanical Copies of Public Domain Photographs

A public domain photograph can be copied by mechanical means using a photocopy machine or a computer scanner, which makes a digital copy that can be stored on a computer and printed out.

A photocopy of a public domain photo is also in the public domain, because a photocopier applies no originality to the public domain work. The only exception is where the copier alters the settings on the photocopy machine to create something other than an exact copy of the original photo.

A computer scan of a public domain photograph that is an exact copy of the original is also likely in the public domain. Such a digital copy is fundamentally no different from making a photocopy of a photograph with the photocopy machine. Again, the only exception would be where

the person making the scan changes or alters the original public domain photograph—for example, changes a black and white photo into color. Such alterations are easy to do with computer technology and can obtain copyright protection for the altered copy. But only the changes can be copyrighted, not the original photo.

GRAY AREA

People who create digital copies of public domain photographs by computer scanning often claim copyright in the copies. These claims are probably spurious where the digital copy is an exact or "slavish" copy of the original photo. Nevertheless, you could get sued for copyright infringement if you copy such digital copies. See Chapter 1 for detailed guidance on how to deal with such public domain gray areas.

Photographs by U.S. Government Employees

Works of authorship created by U.S. government employees as part of their job are ordinarily in the public domain, including photographs. For example, the photos taken by astronauts while on the moon are in the public domain—as are all other NASA photos—as well as tens of thousands of photos taken during World War II by the U.S. Army Signal Corps.

However, photographs of federal government agency seals, logos, emblems, and insignias may not be reproduced on articles —for example, on T-shirts—without government permission. This includes, for example, the NASA insignia logo and the Presidential Seal. In addition, such photographs may not be used in advertisements, posters, books, or stationery in a manner that conveys a false impression of sponsorship or approval by the U.S. government or any government department or agency.

Moreover, certain organizations that you might think are part of the U.S. government are not considered to be so. These include the Smithsonian Institution and all of its branches and the National Gallery of Art in Washington, DC. Both are independent quasi-governmental entities that are entitled to, and do, claim copyright in works created by their employees. (See Chapter 3 for a more detailed discussion.)

Photos Lacking Human Authorship

Only works of authorship created by, or under the direction of, human beings are protectable. This means that only photos taken by human beings are copyrightable. Thus, for example, a court held that a "selfie" taken by a monkey was not protectable. (*Naruto v. Slater*, 888 F.3d 418 (9th Cir. 2018).)

You can find the photo here: https://en.wikipedia.org/wiki/Monkey_selfie_copyright_dispute.

Has the Photograph Been Dedicated to the Public Domain?

Hundreds of thousands of photos have been dedicated to the public domain by their creators. This is often done through the use of Creative Commons licenses (see Chapter 17 for a detailed discussion of such licenses). One well-known source for such photos is Flickr: The Commons (www.flickr.com/commons). Any member of the public may upload a photo to The Commons and dedicate it to the public with a Creative Commons CC0 license. Other websites that contains hundreds of thousands of photos dedicated to the public domain through CC0 Licenses include:

- Pixabay.com (www.pixabay.com)
- Unsplash (https://unsplash.com), and
- Wikimedia Commons (https://commons.wikimedia.org/wiki/Main_Page).

You can search for such material using the Creative Commons search engine at https://search.creativecommons.org.

Some well-known professional photographers have also dedicated their work to the public domain. For example, Carol Highsmith, a decorated photographer whose work was featured on United States Postal Service stamps, donated 19,000 photos she took of landmarks across the country to the Library of Congress. The Library makes them available to anyone with no restrictions on their use.

There is no prescribed formula for dedicating a work to the public domain. It is not necessary to use the Creative Commons CC0 license. The creator or other copyright owner simply has to make clear their intentions. For example, stating, "This work is dedicated to the public domain" on a photo would be sufficient. It's not even necessary to make the dedication in writing. It could be done orally, but it's always best to write something down to avoid possible misunderstandings.

Be careful, however, where a creator sends mixed messages. For example, if a photographer states that their photos are in the public domain, but then attempts to restrict how the public may use them—for example, by saying "this work is public domain but may not be posted on the World Wide Web without my permission." When a work is dedicated to the public domain, the author may not restrict how it is used. A statement like this leaves it unclear whether the author really intended to dedicate the work to the public domain. It's wise to seek clarification from the creator or ask permission for the restricted use.

Similarly the use of the phrases "copyright free" or "royalty free" by the photographer need not mean the work is dedicated to the public domain. These words are often used to describe photos that are under copyright, but are sold to the public for a set fee rather than under a royalty arrangement.

Does the Photograph Contain Copyrighted Materials?

Even if a photograph is in the public domain, you may not be able to use it if the subject matter in the photo is protected under copyright law.

Nature Is Public Domain

Nobody "owns" the natural world around us. For example, anyone can photograph Yosemite National Park, a human face, or a natural object such as a vodka bottle. However, a photo of a natural object is entitled to copyright protection if it contains sufficient detail to make it minimally creative. In that case, you don't have the right to copy such a photo. *Ets-Hopkin v. Skyy Spirits, Inc.*, 323 F.3d 763 (9th Cir. 2003).

For example, anybody can create a photograph of a peach. Although peaches are in the public domain, a photo of a peach that makes creative use of lighting or perspective cannot be copied without permission. You could also infringe on a prior peach photo if you took your photo yourself, but copied the way the prior photo looked. *Yankee Candle Co. v. The Bridgewater Candle Company*, 259 F.3d 25 (1st Cir. 2001).

Photos of Copyrighted Works

Photographs are often made of copyrighted works of authorship such as paintings, drawings, and sculptures. Less frequently, photographs may also be taken of other types of works of authorship such as the pages in a copyrighted book. Such photographs are derivative works— new works created by transforming a preexisting work. The owner of the preexisting work has the exclusive right to create such derivative works for as long as his or her work is protected by copyright.

It is possible for a photograph of a work of art such as a painting to be in the public domain while the art itself is still protected by copyright. In this event, you would need to obtain permission from the copyright owner of the work of art to reproduce or otherwise use the photograph (but no permission would be needed from the owner of the photograph).

EXAMPLE: Sam finds a photograph of Grant Wood's painting *American Gothic* that was published as a postcard in 1960. The copyright in the postcard was not renewed on time, so it entered the public domain on January 1, 1979 (see Chapter 18 for detailed explanation of copyright renewal requirements). However, the original Grant Wood painting is not in the public domain. This means that permission to reproduce the postcard would have to be obtained from Grant Wood's estate, but not from the photographer.

Architectural Photographs

Although buildings can be protected by copyright (see Chapter 9), they may always be photographed without permission if they can be viewed from a public place— for example, a public street. When an architectural photograph enters the public domain it may ordinarily be used freely without permission from the owner of the copyright in the building itself. But there is one possible exception: If the building serves as a trademark—that is, it helps identify a product or service sold to the public—a photograph of it may violate the trademark laws if the photograph is also used as a trademark. For example, the distinctive pyramid-shaped Transamerica building in San Francisco serves as a trademark for the Transamerica Corporation. Using a photo of the building to advertise or promote a product or service could violate Transamerica's trademark rights. This could be so even if the photo was not protected by copyright.

You don't have to worry about permissions if the subject of the photograph and the photograph itself are in the public domain—for example, a public domain photograph of the *Mona Lisa*. The *Mona*

Lisa has always been in the public domain, so a public domain photo of it may be used freely.

Will You Use a Photograph for Commercial Purposes?

There are some special legal concerns where a photograph contains people or trademarks. A trademark usually consists of a word, phrase, logo, or other graphic symbol used to identify a product or symbol. Trademarks include product logos, brand names, company names, product packaging, or the distinctive shape of a product such as a Coke bottle. If you see the ® or TM symbols in a photograph you know it contains a trademark.

If you intend to use a photograph containing people or trademarks for advertising or other commercial purposes—for example, on merchandise such as T-shirts, coffee mugs, dishes, and ashtrays—you need to make sure that your use does not violate state right of publicity laws or state and federal trademark laws. Such violations could occur even though the photograph is in the public domain, meaning not protected by copyright.

For example, there are likely hundreds of photographs of Elvis Presley that are in the public domain (all those published before 1964 that never had their copyright renewed). Even so, you can't use such a photo in an advertisement for a product or service without consent from the Presley estate. Doing so will likely get you sued for violating Presley's right of publicity.

Similarly, there are many photographs containing the Coca-Cola name and logo that are in the public domain. Even so, you may not use such a photo for any advertising or commercial purpose without violating the Coca-Cola company's trademark rights.

In contrast, right of publicity and trademark laws are not violated when you use a photograph containing people or trademarks for noncommercial purposes—that is, editorial or informational uses, such as using a photo in a news story, nonfiction book, or documentary photo or video.

RELATED TOPIC

Right of publicity and trademark laws are discussed in detail in Chapter 20.

Sources of Public Domain Photographs

Links to dozens of sources of public domain photographs can be found at the Wikimedia website at https://meta.wikimedia.org/wiki/Help:Public_domain_image_resources. Some particularly useful resources for public domain photos include:

- Library of Congress Prints and Photographs Online Catalog (www.loc.gov/pictures)
- The George Eastman Museum of Photography and Film (www.eastman.org)
- Flickr Commons (www.flickr.com/commons)
- New York Public Library Digital Collections (https://digitalcollections.nypl.org)
- National Archives and Records Administration Archive Research Catalog (www.archives.gov/research/search)
- Pixabay.com (https://pixabay.com), and
- Wikimedia Commons (https://commons.wikimedia.org/wiki/Main_Page).

Movies and Television

Part I: Films 165

What Good Are Public Domain Films? 165

Has the Film Been Published? 166

    Film Distribution Methods 166

    Determining Publication Date and Country 167

Has the Copyright Expired? 168

    Films Published in the United States Over 95 Years Ago 168

    Films First Published in the United States Before 1964
        and Not Renewed 169

Is the Film in the Public Domain Due to Lack of a Copyright Notice? 176

Is the Film Protected by Copyright? 176

    U.S. Government Films 176

    Copies of Public Domain Films 177

Does the Film Contain Copyrighted Visual Art? 178

**Do You Plan to Use the Film for Advertising or Other Commercial
Purposes?** 179

Part II: Television Programs 179

Has the Television Program's Copyright Expired? 180

    What Is Publication? 180

    Were Television Programs Published When Syndicated? 180

    What Should You Do? 181

**Is the Television Program in the Public Domain Due to Lack
of a Copyright Notice?** 182

Is It a U.S. Government TV Program? 182

Video Dedicated to the Public Domain 182

Does the Program Contain Copyrighted Visual Art? 183

Will You Be Using Public Domain TV Programs for Advertising
   or Other Commercial Purposes? 183

Sources of Public Domain Films and TV Programs 184

If a picture is worth a thousand words, a moving picture must be worth at least ten thousand. But the cost of purchasing or licensing moving images for your own projects is also much higher. One can easily spend thousands of dollars for a few short clips of archival material. But there are many ways to save money on archival clips by using the public domain. Public domain movies are discussed in Part I and television programs are discussed in Part II.

> **CAUTION**
>
> **Many works that are in the public domain in the United States are still protected by copyright outside the United States, and vice versa.** This chapter only covers the public domain in the United States. For a detailed discussion of the public domain outside the United States, see Chapter 16.

Part I: Films

What Good Are Public Domain Films?

Unless you're a silent film fan, it's not likely that your favorite movie is in the public domain. Few sound films made by the major Hollywood studios are in the public domain. Most public domain films consist of silent films, obscure or low-budget sound

films made before 1964, nontheatrical films such as educational films and industrial films made before 1964, and films made by the U.S. government. However, this amounts to a huge treasure trove of public domain film footage that may have a variety of uses and save you substantial money.

When a film enters the public domain, you are free to use it in any way you wish without obtaining permission from the former copyright owner. For example you may:

- show the film to the public (there is one movie theater in Los Angeles that shows only silent films, many of which are in the public domain)
- make copies of the film and sell them to the public
- remake the film (for example, the 1937 public domain film *A Star Is Born* has been remade three times), and
- copy portions of the film and use the clips in new films videos, websites, video games, apps, or any other way you can think of.

> **RESOURCE**
>
> **What if the work is not in the public domain?** If you find that the film you want to use is not in the public domain, you may be able to use it (or at least part of it) anyway under a legal exception called "fair use" (see Chapter 22). If you do not qualify for this exception, you will need to obtain permission

to use the work. For a detailed discussion of how to obtain copyright permissions refer to *Getting Permission: Using & Licensing Copyright-Protected Materials Online & Off,* by Richard Stim (Nolo).

Has the Film Been Published?

Copyright protection begins when a film or other work is officially published and ends when it enters the public domain. The first step in determining whether a particular film is in the public domain is to determine its publication date.

Like any work of authorship, a film is published for copyright purposes when the copyright owner or someone acting on his or her behalf makes copies available to the *general* public. In other words, any interested member of the public may obtain a copy. *Burke v. National Broadcasting Co.,* 598 F.2d 688 (1st Cir. 1979).

Publication occurs only when copies of a film are made available to the public for purchase, rental, or loan. Showing a film to the public in theaters or on television does not constitute publication for copyright purposes. This is true even if thousands or millions of people have seen the film.

Film Distribution Methods

Before the invention of the VCR, copies of theatrical films were almost never sold to the public. Instead, they were leased or rented to film distributors and theater owners. The process worked like this: Once the film was produced, prints of the film were transferred to an independent film distributor that made several hundred copies and sent them to its branch offices (also called "exchanges") around the world. The exchanges entered into film rental agreements with exhibitors who then showed the films to the public. Before 1949, several major studios owned their own distribution companies and theaters.

Because films were rarely made available for public sale, determining an official publication date has been difficult for these older films. However, a consensus has developed among copyright experts, the film industry, and the courts that films were published for copyright purposes when copies were placed in exchanges for distribution to theater operators. *American Vitagraph, Inc. v. Levy,* 659 F.2d 1023 (9th Cir. 1981). It is safe, then, to assume that any film that has been distributed and shown to the general public in movie theaters has been published for copyright purposes.

For films that were sold to the public, like educational films sold to schools, publication began at the time they were first offered for sale or rental to the public.

Films are also published when DVD copies are sold or rented to the public. However, the consumer DVD player is such a relatively recent technology that this form of publication is largely useless for our purposes. (The same holds true for films made available for rental or purchase online or via cable television subscription services.) In other words, a film must have been published long before the VCR or DVD became commonplace for it to be in the public domain. The only exceptions are those films published on videotape during the 1970s and 1980s without a copyright notice—but there are probably very few films in this category. Films that are released directly to video, bypassing a release in theaters, are published for copyright purposes when they are first offered for sale to the general public.

Determining Publication Date and Country

If you have a copy of the film, take a look at the copyright notice—the symbol © or word copyright followed by a year date and name of the copyright owner—for example: © Copyright 1935 Paramount Pictures, Inc. The date in the notice is the date the copyright owner states the film was first published. You can ordinarily find the copyright notice for a film either at the beginning or end of the film as part of the title or credits. If you have a videotape or DVD of a film, a copyright notice may be printed on the packaging. However, this may not always be the date the film was first published.

If you don't have a copy of the film, the easiest way to determine whether or when a film was published is to use the Internet Movie Database website at www.imdb.com. This will give you the year the film was "released," which would ordinarily have been the year it was placed in exchanges for distribution. The Internet Movie Database contains detailed historical information on more than 200,000 films and videos. If you check the "release information" link you can often find the exact date the film was released, which is more information than you really need, because knowing the year is sufficient.

If the film you are searching for is not on the database, there are a number of printed film guides that may help. Perhaps the best one-volume film guide is *Halliwell's Film Guide 2008* (HarperCollins UK). If you can't find a reference to a film in *Halliwell's* or a similar one-volume guide, try consulting the multivolume *AFI Catalog of Feature Films*, published by the American Film Institute. The most comprehensive national filmography, it consists of a series of volumes providing documentation on all films produced in the United States from 1893 to 2011. A library with an outstanding film collection or film archive may have a copy.

If none of these methods result in finding a publication date, you will be able to determine the publication date for a film by examining copyright registration records—provided that the film was registered with the U.S. Copyright Office (not all films were; see Chapter 21). However, this is usually not necessary, since the history of motion pictures has been so well documented in books and on the Internet.

In addition to the publication date, you need to know the country in which the film was first published. Check the Internet Movie Database (www.imdb.com). It will ordinarily indicate a film's country of origin and may also show the film's release dates in various countries. The various film reference works discussed above may also prove helpful. Checking the Copyright Office registration records for the films will also reveal the country of origin, copyright owner, and publication dates for a film. (See Chapter 21 for a detailed discussion.)

You may have problems checking the status of British films, because they were often released with different titles in the United States and Great Britain. The Internet Movie Database will usually show these alternate titles. Also, a book called *The British Film Catalogue 1895–1994,* by Denis Gifford, lists more than 15,000 British films, often including their U.S. titles. This book is out of print, but you may be able to find it in a good collection of film materials or purchase it from used booksellers.

Has the Copyright Expired?

Once you have determined the official publication date of a film, you can determine whether its copyright protection has expired. Remember, once copyright has expired, the work of art has entered the public domain and may be used for any purpose without paying a fee to the creator or former owner of the product (with a few possible restrictions detailed later in this chapter).

The largest single group of public domain films are those whose copyright has expired. Generally, these are older films, but some films published as recently as the early 1960s are in the public domain. Copyright duration in general is discussed in detail in Chapter 18. Read that chapter now to get a general background. Then read the rest of this section, which applies these general rules specifically to films.

Films Published in the United States Over 95 Years Ago

All films published in the United States more than 95 years ago are in the public domain. Since sound films did not become popular until the 1927 release of *The Jazz Singer,* all these public domain films are silent films. However, there are many works of interest in this group, including famous films by Charles Chaplin, Buster Keaton, and Harold Lloyd. Even those silent movies that aren't artistically exciting may contain interesting historical footage.

RESOURCE

For an excellent introduction to the glories of the silent film era, see *The Parade's Gone By*, by Kevin Brownlow (University of California Press).

All newsreels published over 95 years ago (of which there were many) are also in the public domain. These were collections of filmed news events, much like today's television news, and are the only film record we have of the early years of the 20th century. They are a treasure trove of public domain film footage on thousands of subjects, from early attempts at flight to the rural electrification of the country and the creation of the automobile. Be aware, however, that many early newsreels contain phony recreations of historic events rather than authentic on-the-scene footage, and their creative lineage is difficult to trace.

Unfortunately, film preservation experts estimate that 85% of all silent films have been lost. Many were simply thrown away, while many others were allowed to deteriorate until their chemically unstable nitrate film stock turned to dust. For a detailed study of the sad history of film preservation, see *Nitrate Won't Wait*, by Anthony Slide (McFarland & Company).

RELATED TOPIC

See below for more reference materials on how to locate public domain silent films.

Films First Published in the United States Before 1964 and Not Renewed

Under the copyright law in effect at the time, all films published over 95 years ago, but before 1964, received an initial copyright term of 28 years. They were also eligible to receive a second term of 67 years if the copyright owners (or someone acting on their behalf) filed a renewal application with the Copyright Office during the 28th year after publication. If the copyright owner failed to do this, the film entered the public domain on January 1 of the 29th year after the year it was published.

EXAMPLE: The original (nonmusical) version of the movie *A Star is Born* was published in 1937 but not renewed during 1965. As a result, it entered the public domain on Jan. 1, 1966. Had it been renewed, it would have been protected by copyright for 95 years, or until the end of 2032.

The compilers of the *Film Superlist* (see below) estimate that about 20,000 theatrical films are in the public domain because they were never renewed. One third of all films published between 1912 and 1939 were not renewed. Of course, most of these were silent films that were not renewed because their owners viewed them as having no value after the introduction of films with sound. Nevertheless, there are a number of well-known films made during the late 1920s, 1930s, 1940s, and 1950s that are in the public domain because they were not renewed. These include:

- *A Star Is Born* (1937), directed by William Wellman and starring Janet Gaynor and Fredric March
- *The General* (1927), directed by and starring Buster Keaton
- *The Gold Rush* (1925), directed by and starring Charlie Chaplin
- *McLintock!* (1963), starring John Wayne
- *Of Human Bondage* (1934), starring Bette Davis, and
- *Nothing Sacred* (1937), starring Carole Lombard.

The major Hollywood film studios—Metro-Goldwyn-Mayer, Paramount, Warner Brothers, Universal, Columbia, RKO, and Twentieth Century Fox—generally took care to renew their films, although even they sometimes made mistakes. For example, MGM missed renewing some films released in 1950

and Universal did not renew 11 features copyrighted during the summer of 1938.

More commonly, however, it was small studios and independent producers who neglected to renew their films. This was particularly likely where they were no longer in business by the time renewal was required (28 years after the film was first released). Some studios that are notorious for failing to renew their films are Hal Roach Studios, Chesterfield, Invincible Pictures, and KBS Films.

Particularly likely not to be renewed were "B" pictures (low-budget films), such as low-budget Westerns, horror films, exploitation films, and serials. These include many early John Wayne Westerns, B-movies such as *Teenagers From Outer Space* (1959), and Francis Ford Coppola's first directorial effort—a "nudie cutie" film called *Tonight for Sure* (1961).

Even more likely not to have been renewed are nontheatrical films—that is, films never meant to be shown in movie theaters, such as industrial films, training films, and educational films. (Make sure, however, that such films were sold or leased to the public—if not, they were not published for copyright purposes and, therefore, they didn't have to be renewed. The copyright for such unpublished films will not expire for many years.)

To determine whether a film has been renewed, you ordinarily must search U.S. Copyright Office records. You can do this yourself or hire the Copyright Office or a private search firm to do it for you. (See Chapter 21 for a detailed discussion of copyright renewal searches.) However, there are special problems posed by films that were not renewed. These problems exist in part because film is a collaborative medium combining many different works of authorship.

The Film Superlist

You can avoid going to the trouble of checking U.S. Copyright Office renewal records yourself or hiring someone to do it for you if you can find a copy of a multivolume publication called *The Film Superlist: Motion Pictures in the U.S. Public Domain*, created by Walter E. Hurst; updated edition by D. Richard Baer, Hollywood, Calif.: Hollywood Film Archive, 1991. The Copyright Office published three special cumulative volumes showing all the registrations (more than 100,000 titles) made for motion pictures for the years 1894–1939, 1940–49, and 1950–59. The compilers of the *Superlist* have taken these volumes, researched the renewal records, and listed in them which films were renewed. Each *Superlist* book has an appendix with search reports conducted by the Library of Congress verifying nonrenewal of some of the most significant films. Unfortunately, the *Superlist* is out of print. Copies can be obtained from used booksellers and found in some research libraries.

Even if the film was not renewed, there are several problems you must resolve before you can finally decide whether the film is in the public domain.

Problem 1: Was the Film First Published Outside the United States?

Before 1996, thousands of foreign films published during 1923–1963 entered the public domain in the United States because they were never renewed. These included such classics as *Grand Illusion* (France, 1937), *Breathless* (France, 1959), *The Bicycle Thief* (Italy, 1949), *The Blue Angel* (Germany, 1931), *The Third Man* (United Kingdom, 1949), and *Yojimbo* (Japan, 1962).

However, a law took effect on January 1, 1996 that automatically restored copyright protection for most foreign works—including films—that fell into the public domain because they were not renewed on time. The full term of copyright protection was restored to all these films. Ordinarily, they are protected for 95 years from the date of publication. (See Chapter 18 for a detailed discussion of copyright terms.) This law greatly decreased the number of films in the public domain in the United States.

Copyright restoration applied to any film first published outside the United States during 1923–1963 if:

- at the time of publication the film had at least one author that was a citizen or resident of a country other than the United States (the author of a film is usually a film studio or production company—for example, Germany's famed UFA Studios)

- the film was first published outside the United States and not published in the United States until 30 days after the initial foreign publication, and
- the copyright term for the film had not expired under the copyright laws of the country in which it was first published.

The great bulk of foreign films published during 1923–1963 that were never renewed satisfy these requirements and are no longer in the public domain. In fact, it is usually a waste of time to determine whether such films were renewed or not. You should simply consider that any film in this category has a valid copyright for 95 years from the date of publication. However, see "No Copyright Restoration for Some Foreign Films," below, for some films that have not had their copyrights restored.

If the country of origin for a film is somewhere in Western Europe, you can safely assume that the copyright is intact in the United States. If the film originated outside of Western Europe, it may not have qualified for copyright restoration because it was in the public domain in its home country. But to determine this, you'll have to research the copyright law of this country. (See Chapter 16 for a discussion of copyright terms in many foreign countries.)

No Copyright Restoration for Some Foreign Films

There is one group of foreign films that were not renewed on time that still do not qualify for copyright restoration: Those that had entered the public domain in their home countries as of Jan. 1, 1996. Copyright terms for films in most Western European countries last at least 70 years (usually much longer), so virtually no films from these countries fall into this group. But, many non-European countries—for example, Japan—protect films for as few as 50 years. Some films from these countries may have entered the public domain in their home countries as of January 1, 1996 and therefore not been eligible for restoration of their U.S. copyrights. As a result, they remain in the public domain in the United States. (See Chapter 15 for a detailed discussion.)

In addition, some foreign films entered the public domain in their home countries due to a failure to comply with legal requirements. For example, seven films released in Mexico in the late 1940s were in the public domain in that country because they were never registered with the Mexican government (a formality that is no longer required). The films entered the U.S. public domain because they were never renewed, and their copyrights could not be restored because they were public domain in Mexico. *Alameda Films v. Authors Rights Restoration Corporation, Inc.*, 331 F.3d 472 (5th Cir. 2003).

Problem 2: Is the Film Based on a Preexisting Work?

Many films are based on preexisting works, particularly novels, plays, and short stories. For example, the 1940 Cary Grant film, *His Girl Friday,* is based on the famous 1928 play *The Front Page*.

It is possible for a film to enter the public domain because it was not renewed on time, but for the work it was based on to still be protected because it was renewed on time. When this happens, the preexisting work remains protected by copyright, as do those portions of the film based on the copyright-protected previous work. As a practical matter, this means you cannot use the film without obtaining permission from the copyright owner of the preexisting work.

For example, the film *His Girl Friday* was not renewed and therefore entered the public domain in 1969. However, the play *The Front Page* was renewed and will be protected by copyright until the year 2024. This means that the film *His Girl Friday* is basically unusable unless you obtain permission from the copyright owners of *The Front Page*. But you don't need to obtain permission from the producers of *His Girl Friday.*

The upshot of all this is that whenever you determine that a film has not been renewed on time, you must also check to see if it was based upon a preexisting work.

Screenplays Become Public Domain When Films Do

Does a screenplay upon which a film is based enter the public domain when the film does? This is not an idle question. If the screenplay does not enter the public domain when the film does, you would need permission from the owner of the screenplay to use the public domain film. Several screenplay owners argued that their screenplays did not enter the public domain because the screenplays were not published when the films were made and distributed. As unpublished works, the screenplays didn't have to be renewed and still had copyright protection even though the films made from them were in the public domain because they were not renewed on time.

Federal appellate courts in both New York and California have rejected this argument. In cases involving the films *McLintock!* and *The Little Shop of Horrors,* the courts held that the publication of a film publishes as much of the screenplay as is used in the film. This means that you can safely assume that the portion of the screenplay used in the film enters the public domain when the film does. *Shoptalk, Ltd. v. Concorde-New Horizons, Corp.,* 168 F.3d 586 (2d Cir. 1999); *Batjac Productions, Inc. v. Goodtimes Home Video Corp.,* 160 F.3d 1223 (9th Cir. 1998).

The Saga of *It's a Wonderful Life*

Undoubtedly the most famous film that ran afoul of the preexisting works rule discussed above is the Christmas classic *It's a Wonderful Life*, starring James Stewart and directed by Frank Capra. This 1947 film was never renewed and was thought to have entered the public domain for this reason in 1976. Spelling Entertainment, the owner of the studio that made the film, apparently believed that it was in the public domain and initially made no effort to enforce its copyright. Because the movie was thought to be in the public domain, television stations all around the country began playing it repeatedly during the Christmas season and ironically, this is why the film, not a hit when it was first released, became so popular.

However, in 1996 Spelling Entertainment had a change of heart and decided that *It's a Wonderful Life* was not in the public domain. Spelling asserted this because it was based on a short story that was still protected by copyright. Whether this claim is legally valid is not clear. The movie contains so few elements from the short story that it's quite possible that a court would rule that it's not really based on it at all. Nevertheless, Spelling sent warning letters to television stations not to air *It's a Wonderful Life* without permission. Fearing a lawsuit, the stations complied.

In summary, we really don't know whether *It's a Wonderful Life* is in the public domain or not. But we do know that if you use it without permission you'll risk getting sued by Spelling.

If it was, you must determine if that work is also in the public domain. You can freely use the film only if the preexisting work is also in the public domain.

To do this, you must determine if and when the preexisting work was published. Read Chapter 3 for detailed guidance on how to determine whether novels, plays, short stories, and other written works are in the public domain. If the preexisting work was published less than 95 years ago but before 1964, you'll have to check Copyright Office records to see if it was renewed. You can do this yourself (many of the records can be searched on the Internet) or hire someone to do it for you. (See Chapter 21 for a detailed discussion of copyright renewal searches.) If the preexisting work was not renewed, it is in the public domain.

If the preexisting work is still under copyright, you'll have to wait until it expires before you can use the film based upon the prior work, or make an arrangement with the owner of the preexisting work to use it. Usually this means you have to pay a fee to obtain a license for use.

How can you tell if a film is based upon a preexisting work? If you have a copy, look at the credits. They will usually indicate whether the film was based on a prior work. Also, check the listing for the film on the Internet Movie Database (www.imdb.com)—the writer's credit area will usually show if the film was based on a prior work. You can also determine this by checking the American Film Institute catalogs mentioned above as well as many other film encyclopedias. Copyright Office registration records will also reveal this information (see Chapter 21 on how to obtain copies of such records). Another useful guide is the book *Filmed Books and Plays*, by A.G.S. Enser (Andre Deutsch Limited), which lists books and plays from which films have been adapted.

Problem 3: Is the Music in the Public Domain?

Most theatrical films contain music, including background music and songs. It may seem amazing, but no court has ever decided the question of whether the music included in a film that was not renewed is also in the public domain.

Film music presents a hornet's nest of unresolved copyright problems—for example, no one knows for sure if music

was published for copyright purposes when it was included in a film. Before 1978, music ordinarily was published only when copies of sheet music were distributed to the public. Recording or playing music in public didn't constitute publication. (See Chapter 4.) Because it's unclear if film music was published when the film was, no one knows for sure how long the copyright in such music lasts or if it had to be renewed.

The simplest way to avoid these problems is not to use music contained in films that lost their copyright protection because they were not timely renewed.

But if you want to use such music, you must first check Copyright Office renewal records to see if the music was separately renewed. In many cases songs (and even background music) written for films were separately copyrighted and registered with the Copyright Office. If renewed, this music would still be under copyright, even though the film it was first used in is not. Look in the Copyright Office records under the composer's name, the name of the movie, the name of the film studio, and the name of any songs. These renewal records can be searched online. (See Chapter 21 for a detailed discussion of how to do renewal search.) If there is no renewal record for the film music, you may elect to use it. It probably is in the public domain, but be aware that there is an element of risk involved.

GRAY AREA
See Chapter 1 for a detailed discussion of how to deal with public domain gray areas such as use of music in films that have not been renewed.

Is the Film in the Public Domain Due to Lack of a Copyright Notice?

Any film first published in the United States before March 1, 1989 had to have a copyright notice on it or it entered the public domain, unless the lack of notice was excused or cured. A copyright notice consists of the symbol ©, the word "Copyright" or the abbreviation "Copr." followed by the date the film was published and the name of the copyright owner—for example, Copyright 1940 RKO Pictures, Inc.

It's not likely you'll find many films published before 1989 without a copyright notice. Most films were so expensive to make that their owners took great care to ensure they contained copyright notices. Probably the most famous American film published without a copyright notice is the 1968 horror classic *Night of the Living Dead*. This film entered the public domain the moment it was published without a notice and can be used by anyone for any purpose except if one of the actors' right of publicity is involved.

Foreign filmmakers failed more often than Americans to place copyright notices on their films, since notices were not required in most foreign countries. There used to be many foreign films in the public domain in the United States because they lacked a copyright notice. However, the copyright in the great majority of these films was automatically restored on January 1, 1996 under the law discussed above.

If you do find a film first published in the United States without a notice, read Chapter 19 to determine if it is in the public domain.

Is the Film Protected by Copyright?

Certain categories of films are never protected by copyright and are in the public domain regardless of when they were published.

U.S. Government Films

You may be surprised to learn that Uncle Sam, not Sam Goldwyn, is the largest film producer in the United States. The various branches of the U.S. government have produced thousands of films—everything from World War II combat footage made by the U.S. Army Signal Corps to training films for expectant mothers.

All films created by U.S. government employees as part of their job automatically enter the public domain the moment they are created. Technically, even secret films created by the government are in the public domain, but they are protected by other laws from use by the public.

Films created for the government by nonemployees are also in the public domain unless the government allowed the nonemployee to claim copyright in the film. If the government film has a copyright notice, it is likely that the private vendor who created it holds the rights to the film.

Copies of Public Domain Films

An exact copy of a public domain film cannot hold a copyright. This is true even where a film is transferred from one format to another—for example, from 35-millimeter film to DVD.

Thus, a company that makes exact copies of public domain films and sells them to the public cannot hold a copyright in the material. Some companies specialize in making copies of public domain films and newsreels and reselling them. Of course, they can charge you for buying a copy of the material. Many of these companies will try to license the copies to you in an effort to restrict how you use it.

However, people and companies that make and sell copies of public domain films often make changes or add new elements to the films. For example, a new soundtrack may be added to a silent film in the public domain, a black and white film in the public domain may be colorized, or a public domain film may be dubbed from English into another language. Changes such as these are protected by copyright if they are minimally creative. (See Chapter 2 for a detailed discussion of creativity and copyright.)

Not only are new soundtracks and colorizations copyrightable, but courts have held that "panned and scanned" versions of wide-screen films are copyrightable as well. "Pan and scan" means creating a reduced-size version of a film so it will fit on a television screen. The process is copyrightable because minimally creative artistic decisions must be made about how much of each frame should be chopped off. Remixing or making a stereo version of a one-channel film soundtrack is also copyrightable since creativity must be employed to remix and balance the sounds. *Maljack Productions, Inc. v. UAV Corp.*, 964 F.Supp. 1416 (C.D. Cal. 1997).

However, copyright protection only extends to changes, not to the original public domain film. For example, if remixed soundtrack music is added to a public domain film, you can still use the original film; just don't use the copyrighted soundtrack without permission. However, it's hard to see how you could use a pan and scan version of a public domain film without violating the copyright in the panning and scanning.

People who make such changes to public domain films often register their new versions with the Copyright Office. For this reason, when you check Copyright Office registration and renewal records for a film, you'll often find original copyright records and renewal records for a new version of film that was itself never renewed. For example, the original version of Buster Keaton's 1927 silent classic *The General* was never renewed, and therefore entered the public domain in 1956. However, in 1953, Raymond Rohauer, a film collector and distributor, created a new version of the film that contained new editing, an introduction, and music. This version was registered with the Copyright Office in 1953 and renewed on time in 1981. The changes made in this new version of *The General* are still under copyright, but the original film remains in the public domain, as are those original elements included in Rohauer's version.

Does the Film Contain Copyrighted Visual Art?

Films sometimes include footage of copyrighted works of visual art—for example, paintings, sculptures, photographs, posters, and toys. It's possible for a film containing such footage to be in the public domain while the work of visual art is still protected by copyright. This could occur, for example, where the copyright in the film was not renewed while the copyright in the artwork was renewed, or the artwork was never published and therefore didn't have to be renewed, or where the film was made by a U.S. government agency.

If the artwork appears in the film for only a few seconds, or is unidentifiable because it is obscured or out of focus, you don't need to obtain permission to use it. These uses of art in a film constitute a fair use. (See Chapter 22 for a detailed discussion of fair use.) However, if the art is still under copyright, permission may be needed from the copyright owner.

In this event, it is prudent to check to see if the art really is still protected by copyright. (See Chapter 5 for a detailed discussion of copyright protection for art.) It may be difficult to identify the artist or copyright owner if the art is not identified in the film or is not well known. There is no need to include a copyright notice for any artwork that appears in a film. The studio that made the film may have a record of who created it, but it's unlikely you could obtain access to such records.

If you're unable to determine whether or not the art is in the public domain, the safe course is to remove the footage containing the art, or obscure it, or obtain permission to use it from the copyright owner (if you can find the owner).

Do You Plan to Use the Film for Advertising or Other Commercial Purposes?

There are some special legal concerns where a film contains people or trademarks. A trademark usually consists of a word, phrase, logo, or other graphic symbol used to identify a product or service. Trademarks include product logos, brand names, company names, product packaging, or the distinctive shape of a product such as a Coke bottle.

If you intend to use a film containing people or trademarks for advertising or other commercial purposes—for example, in a television commercial—you need to make sure that your use does not violate state right of publicity laws or state and federal trademark laws. Such violations could occur even though the film footage is in the public domain—that is, not protected by copyright.

For example, the footage of the actor Jack Nicholson in the film *Little Shop of Horrors* is in the public domain because the film was never renewed. Even so, you can't use such footage in a TV commercial for a product or service without consent from Nicholson. Doing so will likely get you sued for violating Nicholson's right of publicity.

Similarly, there are probably many public domain films containing the Coca-Cola name and logo. Even so, you may not use such footage for commercial purpose without violating the Coca-Cola company's trademark rights.

In contrast, right of publicity and trademark laws are not violated when you use public film footage containing people or trademarks for noncommercial purposes—that is, editorial or informational uses, such as using it in a documentary. (Publicity and trademark laws are discussed in detail in Chapter 20.)

Part II: Television Programs

Television programs were initially broadcast over the air and recorded on videotape or film (kinoscopes). Later, they were distributed on videocassettes and DVDs. Today, television programs and videos from all eras are streamed over the Internet and available for digital download. Television programs do not include movies that were transferred to videotape after they were first shown in theaters (such videos follow the rules outlined in Part I above).

The good news about television programs is that there are thousands of them made by the U.S. government that are in the public domain. The bad news is that it may be impossible to determine whether many commercially broadcast TV shows are in the public domain or not.

RESOURCE

What if the work is not in the public domain? If you find that the television program you want to use is not in the public domain, you may be able to use it (or at least part of it) anyway under a legal exception called "fair use" (see Chapter 22). If you do not qualify for this exception, you will need to obtain permission to use the work. For a detailed discussion of how to obtain copyright permissions refer to *Getting Permission: Using & Licensing Copyright-Protected Materials Online & Off*, by Richard Stim (Nolo).

Has the Television Program's Copyright Expired?

Television broadcasting began in earnest in the late 1940s. Any television programs, published in the United States from this time until the end of 1963 that were not renewed on time 28 years after their first publication are now in the public domain. Television programs published in 1964 or later didn't have to be renewed and ordinarily receive 95 years of copyright protection. They won't enter the public domain for many decades.

Copyright duration rules are discussed in detail in Chapter 18, and how to determine whether a copyright was renewed is covered in Chapter 21.

However, before you turn to those chapters, there is an unresolved threshold question that must be considered: Were any television programs published for copyright purposes before 1963? If not, they didn't have to be renewed and are not in the public domain. Unfortunately, there is no definitive answer to this question.

What Is Publication?

A television program is published for copyright purposes when the copyright owner, or someone acting on his or her behalf, makes it available to the *general* public. In other words, any interested member of the public may obtain a copy. *Burke v. National Broadcasting Co.*, 598 F.2d 688 (1st Cir. 1979).

Broadcasting a program on television does not constitute publication. Copies of the TV program must be distributed to the public. Of course, television programs are published when they are sold or leased to the public in videocassette tapes. But commercial sales of TV programs to the public didn't begin until long after 1963. Only TV programs published before 1964 can be in the public domain because they were not renewed on time.

Were Television Programs Published When Syndicated?

Given the nature of the broadcasting industry at the time, the only way television programs could conceivably have been published before 1964 is if they were taped or filmed and the tapes or films were syndicated. Syndication occurs when a television program is licensed to local television stations. After popular television programs were initially broadcast on the networks they were frequently syndicated, often years after the initial broadcast. A perfect example is the *I Love Lucy* television series, which was filmed before a live audience during the 1950s and has been in syndication ever since.

However, most programs such as talk shows, sporting events, news, and variety and game shows were only aired once and never syndicated. Programs such as these have never been published for copyright purposes.

Unfortunately, two federal trial courts have held that syndication did not amount to publication. This was because the syndication agreements prohibited the television stations from making copies of the TV programs or from licensing them to other stations. *Paramount Pictures Corp. v. Rubinowitz*, No. CV 81 0925 (E.D.N.Y. 1981); *NBC v. Sonneborn*, 630 F.Supp. 524 (D. Conn. 1985).

These decisions by federal trial courts are not binding on other courts, which might have a different view. Moreover, some leading copyright experts believe they were wrongly decided. However, they are not encouraging. The best that can be said is that as of now there is no clear answer as to whether syndication of a television program amounts to publication.

What Should You Do?

So, what should you do? The conservative course of action is to assume that programs syndicated before 1964 are not in the public domain, even if they were not timely renewed. This means that no television programs are in the public domain because their copyrights have expired.

The riskier course of action is to rely on the assumption that programs syndicated in 1964 and earlier have been published for copyright purposes. Therefore, if they were syndicated before 1964, they had to be renewed 28 years later or they entered the public domain. This means you must find out if the program was syndicated before 1964. You must then research the Copyright Office renewal records to find out if the program was renewed. This is easy to do because most of the records you need are available online at the Copyright Office website. (See Chapter 21 for a detailed discussion of researching copyright renewals.)

However, even if the program was not renewed, your problems are not over. The program may still not be in the public domain. This would be the case where the television program was initially published outside the United States before 1964 or the program was based on a preexisting work such as a novel or play that is still under copyright. In addition, it's unclear whether music used in television programs that were not renewed is in the public domain.

Is the Television Program in the Public Domain Due to Lack of a Copyright Notice?

Any television program first published in the United States before March 1, 1989 without a valid copyright notice may be in the public domain. A copyright notice consists of the symbol © or the word Copyright followed by the date the program was published and the name of the copyright owner—for example, Copyright 1980 CBS, Inc.

It's unclear whether television programs were published for copyright purposes when they were syndicated. But publication would have occurred where television programs were made available to the public for sale or rental on videocassettes. But note carefully that such sales or rentals must have occurred before March 1, 1989. After that date no notice is required on any published work.

There are probably not large numbers of television programs that were published before March 1, 1989 without a copyright notice. One notable exception is the television series *Star Trek*, which was broadcast its entire first year without a copyright notice. However, this did not result in those programs entering the public domain, because a court held that they had not been published for copyright purposes when initially broadcast or syndicated. *Paramount Pictures Corp. v. Rubinowitz*, No. CV 81 0925 (E.D.N.Y. 1981).

Even if the program was published without a notice, it may not be in the public domain. The lack of notice could have been excused. See Chapter 19 for a detailed discussion of copyright notice requirements.

Is It a U.S. Government TV Program?

Fortunately, there is one group of television programs that are definitely in the public domain: Those created by U.S. government employees as part of their jobs. U.S. government agencies have created tens of thousands of television programs on a wide variety of topics. These include works created by officers or employees of the Corporation for Public Broadcasting (CPB) and the Public Broadcasting Service (PBS). However, programs created by independent producers hired by PBS or CPB may be copyrighted.

Video Dedicated to the Public Domain

Copyright owners may relinquish their rights in a work by dedicating it to the public domain. Few theatrically released films or television programs have been dedicated to the public domain. But much other, less-valuable video and film footage has been dedicated to the public domain. This is often done through the use of Creative Commons licenses (see Chapter 17 for a detailed discussion of such licenses). Such video is available on websites such as YouTube (www.youtube.com) and Vimeo (www.vimeo.com).

You can search for such material using the Creative Commons search engine at https://search.creativecommons.org.

Does the Program Contain Copyrighted Visual Art?

Television programs sometimes include footage of copyrighted works of visual art—for example, paintings, sculptures, photographs, posters, and toys. It's possible for a film containing such footage to be in the public domain while the work of visual art is still protected by copyright. This could occur, for example, where the program was made by a U.S. government agency.

If the artwork appears in the program for only a few seconds, or is unidentifiable because it is obscured or out of focus, you don't need to obtain permission to use it. These uses of art in a television program constitute a fair use. (See Chapter 22 for a detailed discussion of fair use.)

However, if the art is still under copyright, permission may be needed from the copyright owner if it appears in its entirety or in a close-up shot for more than a few seconds. In this event, it is prudent to check to see if the art really is still protected by copyright. (See Chapter 5 for a detailed discussion of copyright protection for art.)

It may be difficult to identify the artist or copyright owner if the art is not identified in the film or is not well known. There is no need to include a copyright notice for any artwork that appears in a television program.

If you're unable to determine whether or not the art is in the public domain, the safe course is to remove the portion of the program containing the art, obscure it, or obtain permission to use it from the copyright owner (if you can find the owner).

Will You Be Using Public Domain TV Programs for Advertising or Other Commercial Purposes?

There are some special legal concerns where a television program contains people or trademarks. A trademark usually consists of a word, phrase, logo, or other graphic symbol used to identify a product or service. Trademarks include product logos, brand names, company names, product packaging, or the distinctive shape of a product such as a Coke bottle.

If you intend to use a television program containing people or trademarks for advertising or other commercial purposes—for example, in a television commercial—you need to make sure that your use does not violate state right of publicity laws or state and federal trademark laws. Such violations could occur even though the program is in the public domain—that is, not protected by copyright.

In contrast, right of publicity and trademark laws are not violated when you use public domain film or television programs containing people or trademarks for noncommercial purposes—that is, editorial or informational uses, such as use in a documentary. Publicity and trademark laws are discussed in detail in Chapter 20.

Sources of Public Domain Films and TV Programs

The following Internet resources can help you find public domain films and video:

- The National Archives and Records Administration (NARA) (www.archives.gov)
- NASA (www.nasa.gov)
- The George Eastman Museum of Photography and Film (www.eastman.org)
- Library of Congress Motion Picture, Broadcasting and Recorded Sound Division (http://lcweb.loc.gov/rr/mopic)

- Museum of Modern Art Department of Film and Video (www.moma.org)
- UCLA Film & Television Archive (www.cinema.ucla.edu)
- Silents Are Golden (www.silentsaregolden.com)
- Kino International Corp. (www.kinolorber.com)
- Movies Unlimited (www.moviesunlimited.com)
- Prelinger Archive (https://archive.org/details/prelinger), and
- The Film Detective (www.thefilmdetective.com).

Caution Using YouTube Videos

Digital copies of thousands of films and videos have been uploaded to YouTube. com and labeled as public domain. Some of these works are in the public domain for the reasons described above—copyright expiration, U.S. government works, or dedication to the public domain. However, many of these videos labeled public domain are simply pirated copies of works that are still under copyright. YouTube itself does no vetting to determine if any material uploaded to its website is public domain or not. You use such material at your own risk.

Computer Software

Is the Software Dedicated to the Public Domain? 186

How to Tell Whether Software Is Dedicated to the Public Domain 187

Software Not in the Public Domain 188

Potential Problems Using Public Domain Software 190

Was the Software Created by the U.S. Government? 190

Has the Copyright in the Software Expired? 191

When Is Software Published? 191

**Is the Software in the Public Domain Due to Lack of
a Copyright Notice?** 193

Sources of Public Domain Software 193

Although computers and the software they use are relatively new technologies, a surprisingly large amount of software is in the public domain. This is because many software creators have elected to dedicate their programs to the public domain.

Anyone is free to use public domain software any way they desire. You can freely copy it, modify or adapt it to create new software, give it away, or even sell it to the public. It can be placed on websites or the source code can be printed in computer programming textbooks. The only limit to what you can do with public domain software is your own creativity and imagination.

Public domain software falls into the following categories:

- software dedicated to the public domain
- software created by the U.S. government
- software whose copyright has expired, and
- software in the public domain because it was published before 1989 without a valid copyright.

Each category is discussed in turn below. Public domain elements contained in copyrighted software are discussed later in this chapter.

Is the Software Dedicated to the Public Domain?

Software dedicated to the public domain accounts for, by far, the largest amount of software available without copyright restrictions. Much of it can be found on the Internet or in computer programming texts, which often contain code dedicated to the public domain that programmers are encouraged to copy.

While copyright protection is automatically given to a new creative work, the author or owner of the work is free to reject that protection and dedicate a product to the public domain. By doing so, the author gives up all ownership rights in the work, which allows anyone to copy or use the work in any way they want to without obtaining permission.

Dedication of a work of authorship to the public domain is more common with computer software than for any other type of work. There is a long tradition in the software programming community of sharing work with others and not seeking to profit from the work. These programmers simply want to create good software and experience the satisfaction of having others use and appreciate it.

Of course, software giants like Microsoft don't dedicate their software to the public domain. Individual programmers working on their own—hobbyists, students, academics, and others with a strong libertarian streak—have created most software dedicated to the public domain. Public-domain-dedicated software is usually not a slick, commercial-looking product, but it may still get the job done. In fact, it may work better than a commercial product designed for the same purpose.

Authors who dedicate software to the public domain give up all their copyright rights. This means you can use their software any way you wish without restriction. You can revise it and incorporate it into other software, charge the public for copies of it, or do anything else you wish.

How to Tell Whether Software Is Dedicated to the Public Domain

There is widespread confusion in the software community about what the words "public domain" mean. Many people believe that public domain software is software that is given away for free. This is not the case. Both public domain software and software protected by copyright can

be given away for free—for example, on the Internet. Indeed, most of the software given away for free on the Internet is not in the public domain.

So long as it's free, why should you care whether software is in the public domain or not? Because only public domain software can be used by anyone for any purpose. Copyrighted software, even if you obtained it for free, is still controlled by the copyright owner. You could, for example, be prevented from reselling or altering the software without permission of the copyright owner.

There is no official form for dedicating a creative work to the public domain. The author must simply state clearly somewhere on the work that no copyright is claimed in the work—for example "This program is public domain" or other words to this effect.

If the software has been dedicated to the public domain, you will ordinarily find a statement like this on the software itself. It may be on one of the first screens you see as the software is loading into your computer, or in a file on the program known as a "README" file or in the Frequently Asked Questions (FAQ) file or a manual distributed with the program.

Some software creators employ a Creative Commons CC0 license to dedicate their works to the public domain. This dedicates a work to the public domain by waiving all the owner's right in a work, to the fullest extent permitted by law. If the waiver isn't effective for any reason, the CC0 acts as a license granting the public a nonexclusive, royalty-free license to use the work for any purpose. You can search for such material using the Creative Commons search engine at https://search.creative commons.org. See Chapter 17 for a detailed discussion of such licenses.

If the words "public domain" appear on software, you would have a very strong defense if the owner later claimed the software wasn't really in the public domain and attempted to sue you for copyright infringement. Indeed, you'd very likely win the lawsuit. But you still might have to go through the trauma and expense of a lawsuit. It's best to make sure in advance that the software is really in the public domain and avoid even the possibility of getting sued later on.

For this reason, examine all the documentation that comes with the program to make sure its creator really intended to dedicate it to the public domain. You should be tipped off that the creator either didn't really intend to dedicate the program to the public domain or may simply be confused about what the words "public domain" mean if:

- you are required to agree to a license restricting how you use the program
- you are asked to register the software
- any type of restrictions are imposed on your use of the software
- the software is described with any of the words listed in the following section, or
- the creator places a copyright notice on the software.

In this event, you should contact the creator and ask if the software has been dedicated to the public domain. Explain that this means not only is the software free, but that it is not protected by copyright and can be used by the public in any way, even sold. (Most software contains some kind of contact information for the creator, whether an email address, website, or postal address.)

Software Not in the Public Domain

Following is a list of terms commonly used to describe software that is distributed for free but is *not* in the public domain. The software is copyrighted and users are often required to agree to license agreements (whose terms are usually quite generous). If the software you're interested in is described with one of these terms, it isn't in the public domain.

There is nothing wrong with using such software, but you should be aware that it comes with legal restrictions on how it is used. Make sure you understand these restrictions. They will usually be spelled out in a README file, license agreement, manual, or other documentation included within the software or inside its packaging.

- **Free software.** Free software (also called freeware) is open source software that is licensed under the most commonly used open source license—the GPL (General Public License). Like all open source software, free software may be freely used, but is not necessarily available for free—that is, without financial cost.

- **Shareware.** Shareware refers to a method of marketing software by making trial copies available to users for free. If users wish to keep the software, they are supposed to pay the shareware owner a fee. Shareware is fully protected by copyright and may be used only in the manner and to the extent permitted by the owner.

- **Open source software.** Open source software is copyrighted and can either be sold or given away. However, it must be distributed under an open source license that guarantees users' rights to read, use, modify, and redistribute the software freely. The source code must be made available so users can improve or modify the program. Many parts of the UNIX operating system, (including the Linux program) were developed this way. For more information, see https://opensource.org.

- **Copyleft software.** This software contains a provision requiring users who publicly distribute modifications to license them as open source software.

- **Semifree software.** This is software that is not free but comes with permission for individuals to use, copy, distribute, and modify it so long as they do so solely for nonprofit purposes.

Profiting From Government Software

Because it's in the public domain, U.S. government software can be freely copied and distributed to the public (*unless the government places restrictions on its use for security or other reasons*). It can even be sold for a profit. That is what Ralph Carmichael, a retired NASA employee, has done. He obtained copies of 23 programs developed by NASA for use by aeronautical engineers, airplane designers, and aviation technicians. Some of these programs had been given by NASA to major airplane manufacturers, but few had been updated for the desktop computers that are in widespread use today. Many of the programs had never left NASA's labs. Carmichael updated the programs to run on desktop computers. He then copied the software onto a CD-ROM and is selling it through his own website for $99. This is perfectly legal because the software is in the public domain. You can find his website at www.pdas.com.

Potential Problems Using Public Domain Software

There is one potential problem when you use software that someone says has been dedicated to the public domain: It may actually be copyrighted. Anyone can place a copy of a program on the Internet and say that it has been dedicated to the public domain. This doesn't mean it really is. For this reason, it's wise to trace its history to make sure it really has been dedicated to the public domain. This is not something you need to worry much about if you just intend to use the program yourself. However, you should always do this before you publicly distribute the program or incorporate it into a program of your own you plan to publicly distribute. Most software lists the name of the person(s) who created it and provides contact information for them, whether an email address, website, or postal address. Contact the creators and verify that they really are the creators of the program, and they have dedicated it to the public domain. Make sure they understand what public domain means.

If you can't find any information about the creators of the program, ask the people in charge of the place where they got it from, who created it, and how they know it was dedicated to the public domain. For example, if you obtained the software from a website, contact the webmaster and ask for this information.

Was the Software Created by the U.S. Government?

Any work created by U.S. government employees as part of their job duties is in the public domain, including software. Creative works made for the U.S. government by outside contractors are also in the public domain unless the government allows the contractor to retain ownership in the product. (See Chapter 3 for a detailed discussion.)

Thousands of software programs have been created by U.S. government employees and contractors and are in the public domain. These include, for example, weather forecasting programs created by the National Weather Service, mapmaking programs created by the U.S. Geological Survey, and aeronautical programs created by NASA.

Although they are in the public domain, not all of these programs are publicly available. For example, the Department of Defense or the CIA probably have a good deal of top secret software that the public is not allowed to see. However, some government-created public domain software is available to the public. Some can even be downloaded from the Internet. For example, public domain software created by the U.S. Geological Survey that is used to view USGS geographic data can be downloaded from the USGS website at www.usgs.gov.

Has the Copyright in the Software Expired?

Copyright protection does not last forever. When it expires, the work enters the public domain. (See Chapter 18 for a detailed discussion of copyright expiration.)

The only software now in the public domain because of copyright expiration is software published before 1964 that was not renewed on time with the U.S. Copyright Office during the 28th year after publication. This software entered the public domain at the start of the 29th year after publication. For example, a program published in 1960 that was not renewed during 1988 entered the public domain on January 1, 1989. You must check U.S. Copyright Office renewal records to determine if a renewal registration was filed for a software program (see Chapter 21). Of course, not much software was published before 1964, and what was published probably has little or no value today. Moreover, note that this rule applies only to published software. Copyright protection for all unpublished software, whenever it is written, will last over 70 years, because unpublished works are protected for the life of the author plus 70 years.

When Is Software Published?

Software is published for copyright purposes when it is sold, licensed, rented, lent, given away, or otherwise distributed to the public. Selling copies to the public through the Internet, selling a program at a widely attended computer show, and selling or licensing it for use by educational institutions are all examples of publication.

Are Computer Languages Protected by Copyright?

Although no court has ruled on whether high-level computer languages like C++ can themselves be protected by copyright, they are almost certainly in the public domain. The Copyright Office is so sure of this that it refuses to register a work consisting solely of a computer language. No one has challenged this Copyright Office policy.

Therefore, anyone is free to write any program in any computer language. Although the language itself is not protected, a particular program written in that language is. Similarly, the English language is not copyrighted, but a poem written in English can be.

Protecting Software by Other Means

Copyright law is not the only legal means available to protect computer software. Because so many elements contained in most software programs can't be copyrighted, software developers usually supplement their copyright protection with other forms of protection. These include:

- patents—the federal law that protects inventions
- licenses—contracts restricting how you may use software, including when you can copy it
- trade secrets—state laws protecting valuable information that is not generally known, and
- trademarks—federal and state laws protecting product names, logos, and designs.

You ordinarily don't need to worry about any of these types of legal protections when software has been dedicated to the public domain, created by the U.S. government, or had its copyright expire because it was published before 1964 and not renewed. It's theoretically possible, but not likely, that software published before 1989 without a valid copyright notice could be protected by a license or trade secrecy.

However, you should worry about these types of protection if you're interested in copying elements of a software program that are not protectable by copyright, particularly if it is relatively new or popular software. The elements of the software that are not protected by copyright could still be protected by one or more of these other means. As a result, copying them could get you sued.

Understanding all these complex laws and how they apply to software is a difficult task. Explaining them in detail would take a book in itself. This is why it's important for you to consult a knowledgeable attorney before copying software not in the public domain as a whole.

However, publication occurs only when software is made available to the general public on an unrestricted basis. Distributing copies of software to a restricted group of users does not constitute publication. For example, sending copies to a few friends or beta testers would not constitute a publication. Similarly, a court found that software used by a company's salespeople solely for sales presentations for customers was not published. *Gates Rubber, Inc. v. Bando American*, 798 F.Supp. 1499 (D. Colo. 1992).

Is the Software in the Public Domain Due to Lack of a Copyright Notice?

Another relatively small group of public domain software is software published in the United States before March 1, 1989 without a valid copyright notice. Before March 1, 1989 all works initially published in the United States had to contain a copyright notice or they entered the public domain unless the lack of notice was excused for some reason.

A copyright notice consists of a "c" in a circle or the word "Copyright" or abbreviation "Copr.," the year of publication, and the copyright owner's name—for example: © 1985 by Phil Fates.

Copyright notices for software can be found in a variety of places, including:

- the package or box the software comes in
- the manual and other written documentation
- the computer disks or other media containing the software, and
- the computer screens.

If you don't find a copyright notice in any of these places on software published before March 1, 1989 the software could be in the public domain. Unfortunately, it can be difficult to know for sure, because there are a number of exceptions to the notice requirement. See Chapter 19 for a detailed discussion of copyright notices and the public domain.

Sources of Public Domain Software

Thousands of websites have public domain software. The following are some of the most popular:

- www.freewarefiles.com
- www.freewareweb.com
- https://sourceforge.net, and
- www.gnu.org.

Architecture

What Good Is Public Domain Architecture?... 196

Architectural Plans... 197

    Have the Plans Been Published?.. 197

    Has Copyright in the Plans Expired?.. 199

    Are the Plans in the Public Domain Due to Lack of a Copyright Notice?...... 199

    Were the Plans Created by U.S. Government Employees?................ 199

    Are the Plans Original?.. 200

    Is It Okay to Use Copyrighted Plans?... 200

    Sources of Architecture Plans.. 202

Constructed Buildings 202

    Was the Building Constructed Before December 1, 1990?............... 202

    Was the Building Constructed After December 1, 1990?................. 203

    Is the Building Protected by Trademark or Patent Laws?................ 205

You may be surprised to learn that copyright law not only protects words, pictures, and music, but also architecture, which includes:

- the plans, blueprints, renderings, drawings, or models for buildings and other structures (referred to here as "plans"), and
- actual constructed buildings themselves.

Luckily, however, most buildings and many plans are in the public domain. Copyright protection differs for plans and buildings, and the two are covered separately below.

CAUTION

Many works in the public domain in the United States are still protected by copyright abroad, and vice versa. This chapter covers only the public domain in the United States. For a detailed discussion of the public domain outside the United States, see Chapter 16.

What Good Is Public Domain Architecture?

Architects have been copying from each other for millennia. Take a look at the buildings around you and it's very likely you will see echoes of public domain architecture. Older public buildings such as courthouses, libraries, banks, post offices, and city halls—with their reliance on columns and arches—frequently copy ancient Greek and Roman architecture.

Visit any major university, and there's a good chance you'll see buildings modeled after medieval cathedrals, such as Salisbury or Westminster in England. Look at the skyline of any modern city and you'll see skyscrapers whose design is heavily influenced by the work of such 20th century architectural giants as Walter Gropius, Mies van der Rohe, and Philip Johnson.

Many of the most famous buildings in America are copied from, or heavily influenced by, prior works. For example, the design of the Lincoln Memorial is similar to the Parthenon in Athens, while Thomas Jefferson's design for his home, Monticello, was heavily influenced by the work of the 16th century Italian architect Andrea Palladio.

Perhaps the most extraordinary modern examples of copying of public domain buildings can be seen in Las Vegas, Nevada. Along the famed Las Vegas "Strip" one can see copies of Egyptian pyramids, the Casino at Monte Carlo, and the Paris Opera House. Most extraordinary of all is the New York, New York Casino and Hotel. It contains one-third scale replicas of many of the most famous buildings in the Manhattan skyline, including the Empire State Building and the Chrysler Building.

New York, New York, Hotel and Casino, Las Vegas, Nevada. © copyright 1999 by Joe Schwartz.

Architectural Plans

Once architectural plans enter the public domain, they may be freely copied and distributed and new buildings may be built from them. Copyrighted plans may not be copied, but in many cases buildings can be constructed based on the plans without obtaining permission from the copyright owner.

Have the Plans Been Published?

You must first determine whether the plans you're interested in have been published and, if so, when. This will determine how long their copyright protection lasts and what rights the copyright holder has to protect and determine how those plans are used.

Like any other work of authorship, architectural plans are published for copyright purposes when the copyright owner, or someone acting on his or her behalf, makes the plans available to the *general* public. In other words, any interested member of the public may obtain a copy. *Burke v. National Broadcasting Co.*, 598 F.2d 688 (1st Cir. 1979).

Publication occurs, for example, when plans are published in newspapers, magazines, books, advertising brochures, promotional flyers, or otherwise made available to the general public. However, the following activities do *not* result in publication of architectural plans:

All this copying is perfectly legal because all buildings constructed before 1990 are in the public domain. Millions of architectural plans for existing buildings and those yet to be built—along with other types of structures—are also in the public domain. Modern-day architects are free to draw upon this architectural heritage in any way they desire—from outright imitation like that seen in Las Vegas to far more sophisticated and subtle forms of borrowing.

Nonarchitects such as building contractors and ordinary people who just want to build a home or other structure can also benefit from the public domain. Millions of architectural plans and blueprints are in the public domain and may be freely copied and used to build new structures without someone having to go to the time and expense of hiring an architect.

- where a person engages an architect to create custom plans for a building and the plans are not made available to the general public
- where copies of plans are sent to potential contractors and subcontractors for bidding purposes or to actually construct a building
- where copies of plans are placed in public files, such as filed with a local zoning board or planning department, or
- where photographs of a building are published—for example, in a magazine, newspaper, or book.

Date of Publication

If you determine that the plans have been published, you should also find out the date of publication. The date in the copyright notice for the plans themselves or the work in which the plans were published—for example, an architecture book—is the date of publication. If there is no copyright notice, but you have nonetheless determined that the plans have been published, you'll have to look elsewhere for clues about the publication date. Try the following:

- **Examine the work for a date.** Examine the plans and the work in which the plans were published—for example, a brochure or book—for a publication date. Most published works contain some indication of when they were

published. Look on the title page, the page after the title page, and anywhere else that seems logical.
- **Check the Library of Congress.** Check the Library of Congress card catalog to see if it has as a record for the plans themselves or the work in which they were published. You can do this online through the Library's website (https://catalog.loc.gov). The Library's catalog contains the publication dates for millions of works in the Library's collection.
- **Check Copyright Office records.** If either the individual plans or any larger work in which they were published was registered with the U.S. Copyright Office, checking Copyright Office registration records will reveal the publication date. These records can be researched online. (See Chapter 21.) However, not all published works are registered with the Copyright Office, so there may be no record for it.
- **Check reference works.** There are hundreds of reference works that may be able to tell you when a work was published. Go to a public or university library with a good reference section and ask the reference librarian for assistance.
- **Contact the architect.** Contact the architect or the architectural firm that created the plans and ask when they were published.

- **Use the Internet.** Search the Internet using the name of the architect, the name of any larger work in which the plans were published, and the name of the author and publisher of that work. There may be a website devoted to the architect, or some online reference with detailed information about the plans.

Country of Publication

You also need to know the country in which the plans were published. If this isn't readily apparent by examining the plans themselves or any larger work in which they were published—for example, an architecture book—try using the resources listed above.

Has Copyright in the Plans Expired?

Copyright protection does not last forever. When it ends the work enters the public domain where it will forever remain. Plans published as recently as 1963 could be in the public domain. However, the copyright for plans published any time after 1963 will not expire for many decades.

If the plans were published before 1964, carefully review Chapter 18 for a detailed discussion of how to determine whether the copyright has expired. If the plans have never been published, they could have entered the public domain as early as Jan. 1, 2003. See Chapter 18 for a detailed discussion.

Are the Plans in the Public Domain Due to Lack of a Copyright Notice?

If the plans were published before 1989, they could be in the public domain if they lack a valid copyright notice—the familiar "c" in a circle ©, publication date, and name of copyright owner. In one case, for example, the plans for five different styles of tract homes entered the public domain when they were published without a copyright notice in advertising brochures, promotional flyers, and a newspaper advertising supplement. *Donald Frederick Evans & Assocs. v. Continental Homes*, 785 F.2d 897 (11th Cir. 1986).

Read Chapter 19 for detailed guidance on how to determine whether a published work is in the public domain because it lacks a valid copyright notice. If the plans have never been published, they do not need a notice and you need not read Chapter 19.

Were the Plans Created by U.S. Government Employees?

All works of authorship created by U.S. government employees as part of their jobs are in the public domain. This rule applies to architectural plans as well as to all types of writings (see Chapter 3). The National Archives houses the plans for 28,000 U.S. government buildings across the country, such as post offices, courthouses, and military installations. For information on these holdings visit www.archives.gov/publications/general-info-leaflets/26-cartographic.

The National Archives also has an extensive website at www.archives.gov.

Are the Plans Original?

Architectural plans are protected by copyright only if, and to the extent, they are original. Elements copied from other plans or constructed buildings that are themselves in the public domain are not protected. Thus, for example, standard design features that have been used over and over again for decades or centuries are not protected by copyright—for instance, the standard design for a Georgian window, with the window divided into several small panes, has been in use for centuries and is not protected.

Is It Okay to Use Copyrighted Plans?

If you've gotten to this point and determined that the plans are not in the public domain for any of the reasons described above, then they are protected by copyright. However, this doesn't necessarily mean you are barred from constructing a building based on the copyrighted plans. This depends on whether the plans are only copyrighted as a pictorial work or also receive copyright protection as an

"architectural work" under a special provision of the copyright law.

If the plans are only protected as a pictorial work, you can't photocopy or otherwise duplicate them without the copyright owner's permission. But you can construct a building based upon them. If the plans are protected as an architectural work, not only can't you photocopy them, but you can't construct a building based upon them either.

All Copyrighted Plans Are Protected From Copying

All copyrighted plans are protected as pictorial or graphic works—that is, they receive the same type of protection as a painting, photograph, or drawing. Any type of plan can be protected in this way, whether for a building or for any other structure such as a parking garage, bridge, dam, or walkway. Landscape architecture designs can also be protected.

This form of protection gives the copyright owner the exclusive right to copy, distribute, and create derivative works from the plans. For example, an architect who creates a building plan can sue for copyright infringement against anyone who copies the plans without permission.

However, there is a huge limitation on this form of copyright protection for plans: The copyright owner has no right to prevent others from constructing the work described in the plans. This is because the copyright owner of a drawing of a useful article (such as a building) can't prevent others from building the article. He or she can only prevent unauthorized copying of the drawing itself. *Demetriades v. Kaufmann*, 680 F.Supp. 658 (S.D.N.Y. 1988).

As a practical matter, however, it may be difficult (if not impossible) for you to construct a building or other structure based on preexisting plans without first making copies of those plans. The unauthorized making of the copies would constitute copyright infringement, even if the actual construction would not. In one case, for example, the defendant copied house plans on tracing paper and used the unauthorized copy to build the house. The copyright owner of the plans sued and the court held that the copying of the plans was copyright infringement, although the construction was not. The court issued an order impounding the unauthorized copies of the plans, which effectively shut down construction. *Demetriades v. Kaufmann*, 680 F.Supp. 658 (S.D.N.Y. 1988).

However, it might be possible for you to obtain multiple copies of the plans without making the copies yourself. For example, if the plans have been published in a book or magazine, you could obtain numerous copies of the book or magazine.

Some Plans Are Protected as Architectural Works

In addition to being protected as pictorial works, some architectural plans qualify for copyright protection as architectural works. In this event, the copyright owner of architectural plans has the exclusive right to construct a building based on the plans. A person who constructs a building based on such plans without authorization would be guilty of copyright infringement even if he or she didn't actually make copies of the plans.

This form of copyright protection for plans began on December 1, 1990 and applies only to buildings, which includes structures that are habitable by humans and intended to be both permanent and stationary, such as houses and office buildings. Also covered are other permanent and stationary structures designed for human occupancy such as churches, museums, gazebos, and garden pavilions. Structures not designed for human occupancy such as dams, chicken coops, or barns, are not covered; neither are elements of the transportation system such as highways, bridges, and walkways.

In addition, there are important limitations on the extent of this form of copyright protection for architectural plans:

- All plans created after December 1, 1990—whether or not they are published—are protected as architectural works.
- Unpublished plans created before December 1, 1990 are covered only if the building described in the plans was *not* actually built by December 1, 1990. If the building

described in the pre-1990 plan was still not built by Dec. 31, 2002 this form of copyright protection for the plans ended (but they would still be protected as pictorial works). If the building was constructed by that deadline, the full term of copyright applies—the plans would usually receive 95 years of copyright protection, but never less than 70. (See Chapter 18 for a detailed discussion of copyright terms.)

- Plans that were published before December 1, 1990 are not protected as architectural works.

Sources of Architecture Plans

The following resources may be helpful for locating public domain architectural plans:

- Columbia University Avery Architectural and Fine Arts Library (https://library.columbia.edu/ libraries/avery.html)
- Harvard University Graduate School of Design (www.gsd.harvard.edu)
- University of Florida, Architecture & Fine Arts Library (https://cms.uflib. ufl.edu/afa/Index.aspx)
- University of Nevada Las Vegas Architecture Studies Library (www.unlv.edu/units/architecture-library), and
- Dover Publications (https://store. doverpublications.com).

Constructed Buildings

Determining whether the design of a constructed building like the Empire State Building or White House is in the public domain is relatively easy. You just have to know whether the building was constructed before or after December 1, 1990.

Was the Building Constructed Before December 1, 1990?

Copyright does not protect any building constructed before December 1, 1990. This means that, unless the building is protected by trademark laws, anyone can photograph or draw such a building or other structure and construct a new building or structure based upon the picture or drawing they made. For example, this is what the creators of the New York, New York, Casino in Las Vegas did. The plans for such a building may also be used, but they may not be photocopied or otherwise duplicated unless they are also in the public domain.

However, structures other than buildings that were built before December 1, 1990 can be protected as works of sculpture if they serve no functional (that is, practical) purpose—for example, cemetery monuments are protected as artworks, as long as they are original.

Copyright protection is also available for separately identifiable sculptural or pictorial elements or ornamentation attached to a building—for example, statues, friezes, or frescoes. These kinds of structures or elements receive the same term of copyright protection as sculptures or other works of art. But only these artistic elements are protected, not the building itself. For example, if a building contains an ornamental frieze still under copyright, you couldn't copy the frieze, but you could copy the rest of the building. These types of structures or building elements built before December 1990 receive the same copyright protection as other works of art. (See Chapter 5 for a detailed discussion of when artworks enter the public domain.)

Was the Building Constructed After December 1, 1990?

Buildings constructed after December 1, 1990 are entitled to copyright protection as architectural works. This means they are protected against unauthorized reproduction. Only buildings receive such protection. "Buildings" means structures that are habitable by humans and intended to be both permanent and stationary, such as houses and office buildings. Also in-cluded are other permanent and stationary structures designed for human occupancy such as churches, museums, gazebos, and garden pavilions.

Structures not designed for human occupancy such as dams, dog houses, chicken coops, or barns are not covered;

neither are elements of the transportation system such as highways, bridges, and walkways.

Copyrighted Elements of Buildings

Copyright protection for buildings constructed after December 1, 1990 extends only to the "overall form as well as the arrangement and composition of spaces and elements of the design." This vague definition seems broad enough to cover just about any original design element in a building whose purpose is not purely functional (see below).

Copyright does not extend to any of the following:

- "Individual standard features." 17 U.S.C. Section 101. Such standard features include, for example, windows, doors, and other standard building components. However, windows, doors, and other features that are not "standard" presumably would be protected—for example, highly stylized or unusual windows, doors, or other components.
- Design elements that are functionally required. In other words, no copyright protection is available for those elements of a building whose purpose is to keep the rain and wind out or prevent the building from falling down. Only design elements whose purpose is aesthetic or decorative may be protected.

- Features that are essential or common to the architectural style involved.
- Elements dictated by building codes, topography, or engineering necessity.
- Standard configuration of spaces.

A two-step analysis is required to determine which elements of a building are protectable. First, the work should be examined to determine whether there are original design elements present, including overall shape and interior architecture. If such elements are present, go on to step two and examine whether the design elements are functionally required. If the design elements are not functionally required, the work is protected.

An outstanding example of a building whose overall shape and interior architecture are clearly original and nonfunctional is the Guggenheim Museum of Modern Art in Bilbao, Spain. The highly imaginative form of this building, designed by Frank Gehry, obviously serves an aesthetic, rather than functional, purpose.

In addition, as with all works of authorship, buildings are protected by copyright only to the extent they are original. Design elements copied from other buildings or standard in the field of architectural design cannot hold a valid copyright. Examples include common architecture moldings or the volute used to decorate the capitals of Ionic or Corinthian columns.

Guggenheim Museum of Modern Art, Bilbao, Spain. © copyright Rosmi Duaso/Time Pix.

Photographing Permissible

There is one important limitation on copyright protection for a building constructed after December 1, 1990. If a building is located in or visible from a public place (for example, the sidewalk), the owner may not prevent others from making, distributing, or displaying photographs, movies, paintings, drawings, or other pictorial representations of the building. You can use such architectural photographs, drawings, or other copies in almost any way you desire. For example, you could use them in books, magazines, posters, or postcards. There is one exception: If a building qualifies as a trademark, you can't use a picture, drawing, or other representation of it as a trademark—that is, to identify goods or services in advertising, product packaging, on merchandise, etc.

> **EXAMPLE:** Part of the movie *Batman Forever* was filmed at a building in downtown Los Angeles that contained sculptural elements such as a vampire figure on a series of towers. The designer of the towers sued the movie's producers for copyright infringement, claiming that the sculptural elements he designed were copyrighted and could not be used in the film without his permission. He lost. The court held that the towers were part of the building; since they were part of an architectural work, the public was entitled to photograph them without permission. The right to photograph publicly accessible buildings includes not just the building itself, but sculptural elements the building contains. *Leicester v. Warner Brothers, Inc.*, 232 F.3d 1212 (9th Cir. 2000).

If a building is not located in or visible from a public place, you need permission to photograph or otherwise copy it. Photographing such a building without permission constitutes copyright infringement. Moreover, entering private property without permission to photograph a building may cause you to be charged with trespassing. To avoid such claims, photographers, publishers, and filmmakers have the property owner sign a property release (also known as a location release) in which the owner agrees to permit the photographing or other copying.

RESOURCE

For a sample property release form, refer to *Getting Permission: Using & Licensing Copyright-Protected Materials Online & Off*, by Richard Stim (Nolo).

Is the Building Protected by Trademark or Patent Laws?

Some buildings are entitled to legal protection under the state and federal trademark laws. A few buildings have actually been patented. Such protection is available for buildings constructed before or after December 1, 1990 and—unlike copyright protection—is not limited to structures habitable by humans.

Trademark Protection for Buildings

The design or appearance of a building can be protected by state and federal trademark laws if it is used to identify and distinguish goods or services that are sold to the public. For example, trademark protection was extended to the distinctive design of White Castle hamburger stands, consisting of a white structure designed like a miniature castle. White Castle was able to prevent a competitor from using a similar design for a competing hamburger stand. *White Tower System v. White Castle System*, 90 F.2d 67 (6th Cir. 1937).

More than 50 years later, a court held that the design of the façade of the New York Stock Exchange building was an inherently distinctive trademark that could have been infringed upon by a replica at the New York, New York casino in Las Vegas. *New York Stock Exchange, Inc. v. New York, New York Hotel*, 293 F.3d 550 (2d Cir. 2002).

Distinctive decorative portions of buildings can also be trademarked, such as the golden arches that used to appear on all McDonald's hamburger stands.

However, most buildings don't qualify for trademark protection. The building must become associated in the public's mind with a particular product or service. One way for this to occur is for the building design to be used to market a product or service—for example, by using it on menus, letterheads, in newspaper and magazine advertising, and so forth. The distinctive design of the Transamerica Pyramid building in San Francisco is a good example of a building design that is used to market a service—in this case, Transamerica Corporation's financial and insurance services. The design has been registered as a trademark.

Distinctive interior design can also qualify for trademark protection. For example, the interior design of the decor used by the restaurant chain Taco Cabana was protected. *Two Pesos, Inc. v. Taco Cabana*, 505 U.S. 763 (1992).

Of course, most building designs are not used to identify a product or service and are not protected as trademarks. Also, keep in mind that trademark protection does not confer an absolute monopoly on the use of the mark. Even if a building design is trademarked, it still may be copied without permission in many situations without violating the trademark laws. Moreover, trademarks cannot protect the purely functional aspects of building design. (See Chapter 20 for a detailed discussion of trademarks.)

Design Patent Protection

Architectural designs and structures can also be protected by design patents. To qualify, the design or structure must be ornamental, nonfunctional, and not obvious—for example, a design patent was obtained for a spaceship-shaped restaurant building. However, this form of protection is not often used. (See Chapter 5 for a detailed discussion of design patents.)

Courtesy of White Castle System, Inc.

Maps

Has Copyright in the Map Expired? 208

Is the Map in the Public Domain Due to Lack of a Copyright Notice? 208

Was the Map Created by the U.S. Government? 209

Is the Map Eligible for Copyright Protection? 210

Are Elements of the Map in the Public Domain? 210

    Elements Copied From Other Maps 210

    Place Names 211

    Signs, Symbols, and Colors 212

    Geographic Features 212

Sources of Public Domain Maps 212

When we talk about maps we mean flat maps, atlases, globes, marine charts, celestial maps, and three-dimensional relief maps. Maps generally receive less copyright protection than most other graphic or pictorial works because they are used to describe as accurately as possible the physical world, a world that is itself never copyrightable.

Many maps are in the public domain, including hundreds of thousands of maps made by the U.S. government. These public domain maps may be freely copied, republished, used to create new maps, or for any other purpose.

RESOURCE

What if the work is not in the public domain? If you find that the map you want to use is not in the public domain, there may be parts of the material you can use, even if the entire work is not in the public domain. It may also be possible to use the entire work under a legal exception called "fair use" (see Chapter 22). If you do not qualify for this exception, you will need to obtain permission to use the work. For a detailed discussion of how to obtain copyright permissions refer to *Getting Permission: Using & Licensing Copyright-Protected Materials Online & Off*, by Richard Stim (Nolo).

Has Copyright in the Map Expired?

The copyright for all maps published in the United States before 1923 has expired. You may use these maps for whatever purpose you desire. They are in the public domain. The copyright for many other maps published less than 95 years ago but before 1964 has expired as well. In addition, many unpublished maps entered the public domain on January 1, 2003. (See Chapter 18 for a detailed discussion of copyright duration.)

You cannot know whether the copyright in a map has expired unless you know whether or not it has been published and the date and country of publication. The rules for publication of maps are the same as for written works—publication occurs when the work is made available to the general public. (See Chapter 3 for a detailed discussion.)

Is the Map in the Public Domain Due to Lack of a Copyright Notice?

A map published before 1989 could be in the public domain if it lacks a copyright notice. Examine the map carefully to determine if it has a notice. A copyright notice on a map must contain at least two elements—the familiar © symbol, the word "Copyright" or abbreviation "Copr.," and name of copyright owner—for example: © Mel Mercator. Maps published after 1977 must also include the publication year date in the notice. Maps published before 1978 did not need a date.

If the map has been published as part of a larger work—for example, in an atlas containing many maps or in a book, encyclopedia, magazine, newspaper, or other work—it is sufficient that the larger work has a proper notice. For example, a notice in the name of an atlas publisher will cover all the maps in the atlas.

SKIP AHEAD

If the work has a notice in the format described above, you can forget about it being in the public domain for lack of a notice. There is no need to read Chapter 19, which explains copyright notice requirements in detail.

However, if the work has no notice or if the notice lacks one of the elements described above, it could be in the public domain. Read Chapter 19 for detailed guidance on how to determine whether a published map is in the public domain because it lacks a valid copyright notice.

Unpublished maps have never required a copyright notice. So if the map you're interested in has never been published, you need not read Chapter 19.

Was the Map Created by the U.S. Government?

All maps created by U.S. government employees as part of their jobs are in the public domain. This includes all the maps created by the U.S. Geological Survey (USGS), the U.S. Forest Service, and the Bureau of Land Management. However, maps created by state and local government employees may be protected by copyright—for example, a map created by a state highway or forestry department, or a county tax map. *County of Suffolk v. First American Real Estate Solutions*, 261 F.3d 179 (2d Cir. 2001).

The USGS alone has nearly 90,000 maps available for sale. These include topographic maps, thematic maps, and even maps of the moon. Many more USGS maps are out of print and are available from the National Archives, libraries, or from map dealers. Since all these maps are in the public domain, it would be possible for a person or company to sell them to the public without having to pay the government any fees at all.

For information on how to order maps from the USGS, visit its website at www.usgs.gov/core-science-systems/usgs-library.

Map of California as an island, 1650, Library of Congress, Geography and Map Division.

Is the Map Eligible for Copyright Protection?

To be protected by copyright, a mapmaker's selection and arrangement of the elements that make up the map must be original and minimally creative. If the components selected to create the map are entirely obvious, the map will not be copyrightable. For example, an outline map of the United States showing the state boundaries is not copyrightable.

And a survey map of a building site that used standard cartographic conventions was not copyrightable since there was no originality used to show boundaries, zoning districts, plot lines, streets, elevations, and buildings. *Sparaco v. Lawler, Matusky & Skelly Engrs.*, 303 F.3d 460 (2d Cir. 2003).

GRAY AREA

It's far from clear what types of maps, other than simple outline maps, are so obvious as not to be protected by copyright. What may seem obvious to you may not seem so obvious to a mapmaker or publisher. See Chapter 1 for detailed guidance on how to deal with such public domain gray areas.

Are Elements of the Map in the Public Domain?

Even if a map as a whole is not in the public domain, it will ordinarily contain many individual elements that are in the public domain and may be freely copied. These public domain elements include the following:

Elements Copied From Other Maps

To create a new map, a cartographer will typically use preexisting maps as a starting point. Often, U.S. Geological Survey maps or other maps that are in the public domain are used. The cartographer selects and rearranges the information on these maps and adds new information to create a "new" map. For example, one mapmaker created real estate ownership maps by drawing the location of real estate tracts onto topographical maps obtained from the USGS. *Mason v. Montgomery Data, Inc.*, 967 F.2d 135 (5th Cir. 1992).

Fictional and Humorous Maps

Are maps of fictional places in the public domain? Can anyone use the famous map drawn by author William Faulkner of Yoknapatawpha County, the fictional area of Mississippi where most of his stories and novels took place? And what about the humorous maps of the late *New Yorker* Magazine cartoonist Saul Steinberg? His most famous joke map depicts the world from a New Yorker's point of view—the map presents a bird's eye view across a portion of the western edge of Manhattan (which dominates the map) and a telescoped version of the rest of the United States and the Pacific Ocean, to a red strip of horizon, beneath which are three flat land masses labeled China, Japan, and Russia.

Fictional or humorous maps receive far more copyright protection than ordinary maps that describe the real geographical world. They are more like works of art than maps. Unless they are in the public domain due to copyright expiration or lack of notice, copying such maps is not advisable. You could get sued and easily lose. This is what happened when Columbia Pictures copied many of the elements of Steinberg's New York map in a poster for the movie *Moscow on the Hudson*. Steinberg sued the movie studio for copyright infringement and won. *Steinberg v. Columbia Pictures Industries*, 663 F.Supp. 706 (S.D.N.Y. 1987).

A mapmaker's copyright extends only to the new authorship added to the preexisting materials, not material that is borrowed or copied from previous maps. Typically, this consists of the selection, arrangement, and presentation of the component parts of the map. The preexisting materials remain in the public domain and may be freely copied.

> **EXAMPLE:** A mapmaker created a map of an Idaho county by starting with a map prepared by the Idaho Highway Department that was in the public domain and adding to it the location and names of rifle ranges, landing strips, motorcycle and jeep trails, landmarks, and subdivisions, all obtained from other sources. The resulting map was a copyrightable "synthesis," but the elements copied from the Highway Department map remained in the public domain. *United States v. Hamilton*, 583 F.2d 448 (9th Cir. 1978).

Place Names

The names shown on maps for cities, streets, mountains, rivers, and other geographic features are always in the public domain. This is so even if a cartographer creates a place name. For example, a court ruled that the names a cartographer devised for over 200 lakes, streams, creeks, and tourist camps in the Sierra Nevada mountains of California were in the public domain. *Hayden v. Chalfant Press, Inc.*, 281 F.2d 543 (9th Cir. 1960).

Signs, Symbols, and Colors

Signs, symbols, and keys used on maps cannot obtain copyright protection, even if they are original. This includes, for example, the use of particular symbols to indicate the comparative populations of cities. *Andrews v. Guenther*, 60 F.2d 555 (S.D.N.Y. 1932).

Similarly, the use of particular colors to identify topographic features is not protected by copyright. For example, one can't copyright the use of the color green to delineate a forest, blue the sea, or brown a desert.

Geographic Features

Geographic or topographic features are facts or discoveries that are in the public domain. Thus, no one can hold a copyright on topographic features such as the shape of the state of Florida or on the location of boundaries, cities, or roads. This applies even to geographic features newly discovered by a cartographer. For example, if a cartographer discovers a river, island, or even a new shopping mall and depicts it on a map, the name and location would not be protected by copyright.

Sources of Public Domain Maps

These Internet resources may help you find public domain map information:

- Michigan State University links to major online mapping resources (http://libguides.lib.msu.edu/maplinks)
- University of Texas maps on other websites (https://legacy.lib.utexas.edu/maps/map_sites/map_sites.html), and
- Geography and Map Division of the Library of Congress (www.loc.gov/rr/geogmap).

Choreography

Deciding If Choreography Is in the Public Domain.. 214

Has the Choreography Been Fixed?... 214

Has the Choreography Been Published?.. 215

Has the Copyright in the Choreography Expired?... 216

Is the Choreography in the Public Domain Due to Lack
of a Copyright Notice?.. 216

Is the Choreography Eligible for Copyright Protection? 217

Sources of Public Domain Choreography 217

This chapter covers all forms of choreography, including ballet and modern dance. The owner of the copyright in a work of choreography has the exclusive right to perform it in public or grant licenses permitting others to do so. Such licenses usually cost money. But once a ballet or dance enters the public domain, anyone can perform it without obtaining permission from the former copyright owner. Public domain choreography can also be freely adapted and revised to form new dance works.

CAUTION

Many works that are in the public domain in the United States are still protected by copyright outside the United States, and vice versa. This chapter only covers the public domain in the United States. For a detailed discussion of the public domain outside the United States, see Chapter 16.

Deciding If Choreography Is in the Public Domain

RESOURCE

What if the work is not in the public domain? If you find that the work you want to use is not in the public domain, you may be able to use it anyway under a legal exception called "fair use" (see Chapter 22). If you do not qualify for this exception, you will need to obtain permission to use the work. For a detailed discussion of how to obtain copyright permissions refer to *Getting Permission: Using & Licensing Copyright-Protected Materials Online & Off*, by Richard Stim (Nolo).

Has the Choreography Been Fixed?

The first question you need to answer to determine whether choreography is in the public domain is whether or not it has been fixed in a tangible medium of expression. Only choreography that has been recorded in some concrete way can be in the public domain.

There are a variety of ways choreography can be fixed, including:

- on film or video
- written down using dance notation (the most popular forms of dance notation are Labanotation and Benesch; for a good introduction to such notation see www.dance notation.org)
- by writing down or recording a detailed verbal description
- by creating pictorial or graphic diagrams
- by using computer dance notation software programs, or
- by a combination of any of the above.

A good deal of choreography has been fixed using one of these methods. However, most choreography has never been fixed. Instead, it exists in the memories of dancers and choreographers and is passed down orally and by repetition from generation to generation.

Federal copyright law does not protect choreography that has never been filmed, written down, or otherwise fixed in a tangible medium of expression. But this does not mean that such unfixed works are in the public domain. To the extent a work is original, state copyright law—also known as common law copyright—protects unfixed choreography. Such state law protection lasts as long as the work remains unfixed; in other words, it could last forever. As a practical matter, though, it can be difficult to enforce legal rights in an unfixed work. Without a concrete record of the work (such as a film or dance notation) it can be difficult to prove the exact contents of the work. Nevertheless, such unfixed works are *not in the public domain* and using them without permission invites legal trouble.

SEE AN EXPERT

Seek legal advice from a copyright attorney before using an unfixed choreographic work without permission.

The remainder of this chapter covers federal copyright protection for choreography that has been fixed.

Has the Choreography Been Published?

If the choreography has been fixed in a tangible medium of expression, you must then determine whether it has been published. This will determine how long the copyright in the work lasts and whether it needed a copyright notice.

A choreographic work is published for copyright purposes when the copyright owner, or someone acting on the owner's behalf, makes the work available to the *general* public. In other words, any interested member of the public may obtain a copy. *Burke v. National Broadcasting Co.*, 598 F.2d 688 (1st Cir. 1979).

For example, a choreographic work is published if it is filmed and copies of the film are offered for sale or rent to the public. Likewise, a dance that is written down in Labanotation is published if copies of the writing are made part of a dance book that is offered for sale to the public. Distributions of copies of choreographic works to limited or restricted audiences do not count as publication. For example, providing copies of dance notation to the cast of a dance group is not a publication.

Has the Copyright in the Choreography Expired?

Copyright protection does not last forever. When it ends the work enters the public domain where it will forever remain. The copyright in a choreographic work expires when the copyright in the work in which it is fixed expires.

> **EXAMPLE:** If a dance has been filmed, the copyright in the dance expires when the film enters the public domain. This means, for example, that when the 1935 musical *Top Hat* enters the public domain in 2031, the famous dances it contains will also enter the public domain. Similarly, if a choreographic work has been fixed in a book of photographs, the work will enter the public domain when the book does.

Unfortunately, determining whether a copyright has expired can be somewhat complex. You need to determine which of several possible copyright terms apply to the work in question. Choreography published as recently as 1963 could be in the public domain. On the other hand, choreography created more than 100 years ago (and more) could still be protected by copyright.

The copyright terms are the same no matter what type of work is involved (writings, music, art, etc.). They are discussed in detail in Chapter 18. Turn to that chapter to determine whether the copyright in a work you're interested in has expired.

CAUTION

Beware the right of publicity.
If a film or photograph of a dance enters the public domain, you may copy the dance steps, but this doesn't mean you may freely copy a film or picture of the dancers. Doing so may violate their right of publicity if the photo or film is used for advertising or other commercial purposes. For example, you can't use a photo of Fred Astaire to advertise a product even if the photograph is in the public domain (see Chapter 20).

Is the Choreography in the Public Domain Due to Lack of a Copyright Notice?

Copyright expiration is not the only way choreography may enter the public domain. Choreography published in the United States before 1989 had to contain a copyright notice—the familiar "c" in a circle © or the word "Copyright" or abbreviation "Copr.," publication date, and name of copyright owner. Choreography published without such a notice could be in the public domain.

Examine the work carefully—whether a book, article, movie, video, or work in which the choreography has been fixed. If the work lacks a copyright notice or if the notice lacks one of the three elements described above (copyright symbol or word, publication date, copyright owner's name) it could be in the public domain.

Read Chapter 19 for detailed guidance on how to determine whether a published work is in the public domain because it lacks a valid copyright notice.

If the choreography has never been published, it needs no notice and you need not read Chapter 19.

Is the Choreography Eligible for Copyright Protection?

Not all choreography is protected by copyright under either federal or state law. For example, choreography copied from previous public domain choreographic works is not protected.

> **EXAMPLE:** Serge, a modern dance choreographer, finds a little-known modern ballet described in Labanotation in a book published in 1928. The book and the ballet it describes are in the public domain because the copyright expired. Serge copies the ballet step-for-step and claims credit for the "new" ballet. The ballet is later published in a written collection of Serge's works. However, because Serge copied the ballet from a public domain work, the ballet cannot be protected by copyright. It is in the public domain.

In addition, social dance steps and simple routines do not have copyright protection. For example, the basic waltz step, the hustle step, basic classical ballet movements—such as the second position—cannot be protected by copyright. Social dance steps, folk-dance steps, and individual ballet steps may be utilized as the choreographer's basic material in much the same way that words are the writer's basic material. *Horgan v. MacMillan*, 789 F.2d 157 (2d Cir. 1986). Thus, for example, the U.S. Copyright Office refused to register the "Carlton dance," made famous in 1990s sitcom *The Fresh Prince of Bel Air*, because it was a simple routine.

RESOURCE

For a detailed discussion by a dance expert of what elements of choreography are copyrightable, refer to the book *Choreographing Copyright: Race, Gender, and Intellectual Property Rights in American Dance*, by Anthea Kraut (Oxford University Press).

Sources of Public Domain Choreography

The leading resource for choreography materials is the Jerome Robbins Dance Division of the New York Public Library for the Performing Arts (www.nypl.org/locations/divisions/jerome-robbins-dance-division).

Databases and Collections

Part I: Databases...221

Is the Work a Database?...222

    Limited Copyright Protection for Databases 223

    Raw Facts in Databases Not Protected by Copyright................223

Does the Database Lack Creativity?..225

    Is the Arrangement of the Data Creative? 226

    Is the Selection of the Data Creative?..................................226

    Examples of Databases That Lack Creativity.........................226

Was the Database Created by the U.S. Government? 228

    Copyrighted Materials in Government Databases....................228

    Copyright Claims Outside the United States 229

    Privacy and Security Limitations..229

    U.S. Department of Commerce Databases 229

    State and Local Databases...230

Has the Copyright in the Database Expired?.............................230

Is the Database in the Public Domain for Lack of a Copyright Notice?........231

Is the Database Protected by Means Other Than Copyright? 231

    Licenses 231

    Trade Secrets..233

    Encryption...234

Part II: Collections of Public Domain Works...........................235

Are the Collected Materials in the Public Domain?.....................235

    Copyright Protection for Public Domain Collections 237

    Copying Collections of Public Domain Works 237

Does the Collection Lack Minimal Creativity? 238

Is It a De Minimis Collection? 239

Is It a U.S. Government Collection? 239

Has the Collection's Copyright Expired? 239

Is the Collection in the Public Domain for Lack of a Copyright Notice? 240

Is the Collection Protected by Means Other Than Copyright? 240

This chapter is about a special type of work of authorship: what the copyright law refers to as a "compilation." This is a work that is created by collecting data or materials that already exist.

There are two types of compilations:

- Raw data or facts—for example, a list of names, addresses, and phone numbers in a phone book. These are called databases.
- A collection of works of authorship, such as a collection of short stories, drawings, or photographs. These are called collections.

As you can imagine, there are millions of databases and collections. As this chapter explains in detail, such works can receive limited copyright protection if a minimal amount of creativity was required to create them. But many databases and collections fail the creativity requirement and receive no copyright protection at all. However, those databases and collections that are not copyrighted are not always freely available, because the people who created them may attempt to use means other than copyright law to protect them, such as licenses, trade secrecy, or encryption.

Part I covers databases and Part II covers collections.

> **CAUTION**
>
> **It is possible for a database or collection to be in the public domain in the United States but protected by copyright in a foreign country, and vice versa.** This chapter covers only the public domain in the United States. If you want to know whether a work is in the public domain outside the United States, see Chapter 16.

Part I: Databases

When a database is in the public domain and not protected by the other legal restrictions discussed in this chapter, you can use the data it contains in any way you want without obtaining permission from the person or entity that originally created the database—permission that often must be paid for. You can use the data to create and publish your own database or use it in any other way you desire. For example, you can take U.S. State Department statistics about worldwide terrorism and write your own article, book, or report on terrorism and even sell it at a profit. You could even post these statistics on your website to warn overseas travelers about dangerous destinations. (Most U.S. government databases are in the public domain.)

Unfortunately, determining which databases are and are not protected can require that you navigate a complex legal maze. For a variety of reasons explained below, many databases are not protected by copyright at all; and, even where copyright protection is available, it is extremely limited. As a result, database creators and owners frequently resort to other means to protect their works, including using licenses. The extent to which these other means of protecting databases are legally effective is not always clear.

However, it is clear that database owners have become increasingly aggressive in asserting ownership claims in their data. For example, the *New York Times* sued the online bookseller Amazon.com when it began posting the *Times's* weekly list of best-selling books on its website. The case was settled when the *Times* agreed that Amazon could post the list in alphabetical order, rather than by sales volume.

As a result, you should exercise caution before you copy any database. If you're not sure it is in the public domain, seek legal advice.

RESOURCE

What if the work is not in the public domain? If you find that the database you want to use is not in the public domain, you may be able to use it (or at least part of it) anyway under a legal exception called "fair use" (see Chapter 22). If you do not qualify for this exception, you will need to obtain permission to use the work. For a detailed discussion of how to obtain copyright permissions refer to *Getting Permission: Using & Licensing Copyright-Protected Materials Online & Off*, by Richard Stim (Nolo).

Is the Work a Database?

A database (also known as a fact compilation) is a work created by selecting and arranging facts. "Data" is just a fancy word for facts. The facts in a database can take any form—for example, they can consist of numbers, names, dates, addresses, or just about anything else.

EXAMPLE: Cynthia Powell, a romance novel fan in Michigan, created a website called the Romance Novel Database. Here she listed 244 romance novels and rates them by quality—five hearts is best, one heart is worst. Cynthia's website is a database consisting of 244 facts—the names of 244 romance novels—unprotected by copyright.

EXAMPLE: Key Publications, a publisher of phone book yellow pages, compiles a yellow pages directory for New York City's Chinese American community. Key selects which businesses qualify for inclusion in its yellow pages and arranges the directory into categories such as Accountants, Shoe Stores, and Bean Curd & Bean Sprout

Shops. Key's yellow pages are a database consisting of hundreds of public domain facts—the names, addresses, and phone numbers of Chinese-owned businesses in New York City.

You probably create databases all the time. For example, your personal list of phone numbers you frequently call is a database. So is a shopping list, Christmas card list, daily "to do" list, list of appointments, or checking account register. Other types of databases include such works as bibliographies, directories, price lists, real estate and stock listings, listings of scientific data, and catalogs of all types.

Prior to the computer age, databases typically took the form of a list or a paper card system or file. With the advent of computer technology, traditional hard copy databases have been eclipsed in importance by electronic databases.

Limited Copyright Protection for Databases

Databases receive limited copyright protection. All that is protected is the *selection and arrangement* of the material making up the database, *not the preexisting material itself.* This is sometimes referred to as a thin copyright.

For example, the only protected elements of Cynthia's romance novel list mentioned in the example, above, are her selection and arrangement of the names of the novels in her catalog and her ratings of them. Cynthia had to employ creativity and judgment in deciding which of the thousands of romance novels in existence belonged on her list of 244 novels and in deciding what rating each novel should receive. The exercise of this creativity and judgment is the type of authorship that can obtain copyright protection.

When we speak of a database as being in the public domain, we mean that—for one reason or another—the particular selection and arrangement is not protected by copyright. As explained below, the raw facts contained in a database can never be copyrighted but might be protected by other means.

Raw Facts in Databases Not Protected by Copyright

Since the copyright in a database extends only to the selection and arrangement of the facts, the raw facts or data themselves are never protected by copyright. The U.S. Supreme Court has stated that the raw facts may be copied at will without violating the copyright law. This means that a database creator is free to use the facts contained in an existing database to prepare a competing database. *Feist Publications, Inc. v. Rural Telephone Service Co.*, 499 U.S. 340 (1991). But the competing work may not feature the same selection and arrangement as the earlier database and must be minimally creative.

EXAMPLE: A website called Who's Alive and Who's Dead (www.whosaliveand whosdead.com) contains the birth and —where applicable—death dates for thousands of celebrities, political figures, sports stars, and others. This information is organized in a variety of interesting ways. For example, you look up your favorite television show and see when the cast members were born and if any are dead. This website is a simple database. The creators of this database are entitled to copyright protection for the way they have selected and arranged the material on their website. However, they do not have a copyright in the individual facts in their database—meaning they don't own the birth and death dates of celebrities. These facts are not protectable by copyright. Anyone writing an article or book about a celebrity can look up his or her birth date in the database and use that date in the article or book without obtaining permission from the creators of the database. There is no need to go back to the original sources the database's creators used to compile their database, such as newspaper obituary records or government records of births and deaths.

It may seem unfair that the facts contained in a database gathered at great trouble and expense may be used by others without violating the copyright laws. However, the purpose of copyright is to advance the progress of knowledge, not to enrich authors. If the first person to compile a group of raw facts acquired a monopoly over them, progress would be greatly impeded. This might not seem so serious if we were only talking about birth and death dates of celebrities. But many databases contain far more vital information that no one should be allowed to monopolize.

Opinions Are Not Facts

Facts themselves cannot be protected by copyright. This is particularly true for numerical or statistical data. However, some things you might think are facts in the public domain really aren't. At least that's what two federal appellate courts have held. These cases involved copying of databases containing pricing data. In one case, someone copied the price quotations in coin dealer newsletters. In the other, the prices for used cars listed in a used car price guide called the *Red Book* were copied. In both cases, the courts held that the individual price quotations involved were copyrighted because they were entirely subjective—they were simply estimates devised by the publishers of the guides. They represented the publishers' *opinions* of what the coins and used cars were worth, not what someone actually paid for them. The courts held that sufficient creativity was required to devise these estimates for them to be protected by copyright. *CCC Info. Servs., Inc. v. Maclean Hunter Mkt. Reports*, 44 F.3d 61 (2d Cir. 1994); *CDN Inc. v. Kenneth A. Kapes*, 197 F.3d 1256 (9th Cir. 1999).

But don't get the idea that raw facts in databases may always be freely copied. Database owners often try to use laws other than copyright to prevent the public from doing just that.

Does the Database Lack Creativity?

A work of authorship must be the product of a minimal amount of creativity to be protected by copyright. This requirement applies to databases as well as all other work. The amount of creativity required for a work to be protected by copyright is very small. A work need not be novel, unique, ingenious, or even any good to be sufficiently creative for copyright purposes. It need only be the product of a very minimal creative spark.

Most types of works easily satisfy the creativity requirement. However, many databases don't make the grade. The data contained in a database need not be presented in an innovative or surprising way, but the selection or arrangement cannot be so mechanical or routine that it requires no creativity at all. If no creativity was employed in selecting or arranging the data, the database is not eligible for copyright protection—that is, the selection and arrangement of the data will be in the public domain as well as the data itself.

This selection and arrangement may be copied freely unless it's protected through a means other than copyright.

In a landmark decision on databases, the U.S. Supreme Court ruled that the selection and arrangement of white pages in a typical telephone directory fails to satisfy the creativity requirement and is therefore not protected by copyright. The selection wasn't creative because the compiler of the phone book included all the residents and businesses in the geographic area covered. No selectivity was needed to do this. The arrangement wasn't creative because the phone book was arranged alphabetically. Alphabetizing a list of names and phone numbers is a purely mechanical act—that is, you just follow the alphabet. *Feist Publications, Inc. v. Rural Telephone Service Co.*, 499 U.S. 340 (1991). There are doubtless many other types of databases that are in the public domain for the same reason.

To tell if a database is sufficiently creative to be protected by copyright, you need to answer two questions:

1. Is the *arrangement* of the data minimally creative?
2. Is the *selection* of the data minimally creative?

A database is eligible for copyright protection if either the selection or arrangement is minimally creative. Of course, many databases satisfy both criteria.

Is the Arrangement of the Data Creative?

Famed "information architect" Richard Saul Wurman, in his classic book *Information Architects*, points out that there are only six ways to arrange data. You may use:

- location
- alphabet
- time
- number
- category, or
- hierarchy.

Common sense tells us that of these six methods only location, category, and hierarchy can require minimal creativity and can be protected by copyright. No creativity is involved in arranging a database by alphabet, time, or number. These types of organization are purely mechanical—that is, they require no exercise in judgment. You just have to know the alphabet, how to tell time, or count to arrange a database by these methods.

Is the Selection of the Data Creative?

The selection of the data in a database satisfies the minimal creativity test only if the compiler has:

- chosen less than all of the data in a given body of relevant material, regardless of whether it is taken from one or more sources, and

- the selection is based on the compiler's opinion about something.

For example, no selectivity is required to compile a directory of *all* the restaurants in New York City. The compiler of such a directory need not employ any judgment in deciding which restaurants belong in the directory.

But a list of the 100 "best" restaurants in New York City is minimally creative and protected by copyright. Here, the compiler must use selectivity and judgment to decide which 100 of the thousands of restaurants in New York City are "best."

Examples of Databases That Lack Creativity

Representatives of the U.S. Copyright Office have indicated that, in their view, the following types of databases will usually fail to satisfy the minimal creativity requirement. The Copyright Office's views don't have the force of law, but the courts likely would follow them.

- **Street address directories, alumni directories, membership lists, mailing lists, and subscriber lists.** Works such as these often require no more creativity to compile than the white pages in a phone book. This would be the case where (1) the material is arranged in alphabetical or numerical order, and (2) no judgment was needed to decide which names and addresses should be included.

EXAMPLES: An alphabetical list of all Harvard alumni, all the members of the ACLU, or all the subscribers to *Time* magazine; a mailing list in numerical order according to zip code of all persons who have contributed more than $1,000 to the Republican Party.

- **Parts lists.** An alphabetical or numerical list of all the parts in a given inventory clearly fails the creativity test: If the list is exhaustive, no selectivity is required to compile it; if it is arranged in alphabetical or numerical order, no creativity is required to arrange it.
- **Genealogies.** A genealogy (that is, a table or diagram recording a person's or family's ancestry) consisting merely of transcriptions of public records, such as census or courthouse records, or transcriptions made from headstones in a few local cemeteries, are also deemed by the Copyright Office to lack minimal creativity. On the other hand, the creativity requirement may be satisfied where the creator of a genealogy compilation uses judgment in selecting material from a number of different sources.
- **De minimis compilations.** De minimis in Latin means trifling or insignificant. A de minimis compilation is one that contains only a few items. The Copyright Office considers a compilation of only three items to be clearly de minimis and not protected by copyright. Even if a de minimis

compilation meets the minimal creativity requirement, the Copyright Office will refuse to register it. This means the compiler can't file a copyright infringement suit if anyone else uses their list of three or fewer things.

CAUTION

Beware of databases containing protected authorship. A database author may add additional material to a database that is protected by copyright. If such material is included throughout a database, it will be much more difficult and risky to copy the entire work or large chunks of it. By doing so, you would be copying not only unprotectable facts but the protected expression in the database as well.

EXAMPLE: Robert compiles a bibliography containing the titles, authors, and publishers of every book published in the United States on the Civil War (about 50,000 in all). The bibliography is simply in alphabetical order and lists every work in its category, so it probably lacks sufficient creativity to be protected by copyright. However, Robert also includes an introduction and annotates some of the selections with explanatory notes. Both the introduction and notes constitute expression that can be protected by copyright. Thus, if someone copied the entire bibliography they would be copying protected authorship, and therefore committing copyright infringement. Of course, anyone could still copy the individual bibliographic entries so long as they left the protected authorship alone.

Was the Database Created by the U.S. Government?

Most U.S. government databases are in the public domain. U.S. government employees and contractors have compiled millions of databases on nearly every conceivable subject. Many of these databases can be accessed through the Internet. For example:

- All types of population data can be found at the U.S. Census Bureau website at www.census.gov.
- Statistics on all aspects of the U.S. education system can be found at the Department of Education website at www.ed.gov.
- Statistics on crime and the justice system can be found at a Department of Justice website at https://bjs.gov.

The U.S. government has created a Web portal (www.usa.gov) containing links to its many websites.

Most of these and other U.S. government databases are in the public domain—that is, not just the data itself, but the selection and arrangement of the database, is free for the taking.

For example, you can take Census Bureau statistics about population growth in the United States, selected and arranged by state, race, education, and many other ways, and write your own report on U.S. population growth and even sell it at a profit. If your selection and arrangement

are minimally creative, you may even claim a copyright in your database, even though all the data came from a public domain source. You cannot, however, prevent others from using the public domain data.

However, the material in U.S. government databases is not always freely available. Some of it may be copyrighted in the United States, it might be copyrighted outside the United States, or there may be other legal restrictions on its use. Government databases ordinarily contain warning statements or lists of terms and conditions of use describing any limitation on use of the database. You need to read these carefully.

Copyrighted Materials in Government Databases

Some material on U.S. government databases has been created by outside contractors and is copyrighted by them. For example, a database containing millions of citations to medical articles maintained by the U.S. National Library of Medicine (NLM) contains a warning that states:

> This site contains resources which incorporate material contributed or licensed by individuals, companies, or organizations that may be protected by U.S. and foreign copyright laws.... All persons reproducing, redistributing, or making commercial use of this information are expected to adhere to the terms and conditions asserted by the copyright holder. (www.ncbi.nlm.nih. gov/home/about/policies.)

Copyright Claims Outside the United States

While works created by U.S. government employees are always in the public domain in the United States, the U.S. government is legally entitled to claim copyright outside the United States if the foreign country involved allows government materials to be copyrighted under its own laws. For example, the U.S. government may claim copyright protection for its materials in Canada or Great Britain because their laws provide copyright protection for most government works. Ordinarily, the United States does not assert such claims.

However, if the U.S. government claims copyright protection for a database outside the United States, you will have to get government permission to use it in a foreign country. You could be sued if you do not obtain permission.

Privacy and Security Limitations

Many U.S. government databases contain sensitive information that is not made publicly available—for example, databases maintained by the Department of Defense or the Department of Health and Human Services. Privacy and national security laws and regulations may prevent the data in such databases from being disseminated.

U.S. Department of Commerce Databases

The U.S. Department of Commerce runs something called the Standard Reference Data Program. This program creates publications and databases of technical data regarding metals, chemicals, industrial fluids and materials, and similar items for solving technical problems, research, and development by scientists and engineers. The Commerce Department is allowed to claim a copyright in such standard reference data so it can sell it and help earn extra income to support its programs. 15 U.S.C. Section 290e.

Private Databases Containing U.S. Government Materials

Many private publishers and other companies maintain and sell to the public databases that contain U.S. government data. These private companies may claim copyright protection for their selection and arrangement of the data in their databases if it is minimally creative, as described above. However, they often also require users to agree to licenses restricting how they may use the data. By using these licenses, they attempt to obtain far more legal protection for their databases than can be obtained under the copyright law. Whether these licenses are legally enforceable is unclear.

State and Local Databases

In addition, databases created by state and local government agencies are entitled to copyright protection if a minimal amount of creativity is evident. Thus, for example, a list compiled by your state department of fish and game about the places to catch fish can be copyrighted if minimally creative.

Has the Copyright in the Database Expired?

Like any other work of authorship, a database enters the public domain when its copyright expires, at which time its selection and arrangement no longer receives copyright protection. Databases published as recently as 1963 could be in the public domain due to copyright expiration.

Copyright duration rules are discussed in detail in Chapter 18. But before you can know whether a database's copyright has expired, you must first determine whether it has been published. This is because published and unpublished works receive very different copyright terms.

A database is published for copyright purposes when the copyright owner—or someone acting on his or her behalf—makes one or more copies of the work available to the *general* public. In other words,

any interested member of the public may obtain a copy. *Burke v. National Broadcasting Co.*, 598 F.2d 688 (1st Cir. 1979).

The copies don't necessarily have to be sold for a publication to occur—they can also be leased or rented, loaned, or even given away. For example, a telephone directory is published when it is given away to customers. Nor is it necessary for large numbers of copies to be distributed. So long as the work has been made freely available to the general public, it makes no difference if just one copy has been sold or distributed. *Gottsberger v. Aldine Book Publishing Co.*, 33 F. 381 (C.C.D. Mass. 1887).

Obviously, a database has been published if copies were made and offered for sale to the general public in bookstores, through mail order, or by any other means of public distribution. In contrast, a publication does not occur where copies are limited to a definitely selected group of people for a limited purpose without the right of further reproduction, distribution, or sale. For example, a customer list distributed to the sales employees of a company for marketing purposes, but carefully kept secret from the general public, would not be considered published.

Once you have determined the publication date, you should refer to Chapter 18 to determine if and when the database has entered the public domain.

Is the Database in the Public Domain for Lack of a Copyright Notice?

SKIP AHEAD
If the database was never published, it doesn't need a copyright notice. You don't need to read any more of this section.

If a database was published before 1989, it could be in the public domain if it lacks a copyright notice. Examine the database carefully to determine if it has a notice.

A copyright notice on a database must contain three elements—the familiar © symbol or the word "Copyright" or abbreviation "Copr.," the publication date, and name of copyright owner—for example: © DataBest, Inc. 1975.

If the database has a notice in the format described above, you can forget about it being in the public domain for lack of a notice. There is no need to read Chapter 19, which explains copyright notice requirements in detail. Go on to the next section.

However, if the database has no notice or if the notice lacks one of the three elements described above (copyright symbol © or word "Copyright," publication date, copyright owner's name), it could be in the public domain. Read Chapter 19 for detailed guidance on how to determine whether a published work is in the public domain because it lacks a valid copyright notice.

Is the Database Protected by Means Other Than Copyright?

Given the limitations on copyright protection for databases and the fact that many databases don't qualify for any protection at all, the owners of valuable databases often try to use other ways to protect their creations. These means are used not only to protect the selection and arrangement of the data, but also the data itself.

Licenses

A database license is a contract restricting what a person can do with the data. These licenses are commonly used to protect databases that are not made freely available to the public. People who use the database must agree in advance to the terms of the license.

Database licenses take many forms. Some are form contracts, while others are negotiated agreements tailored to particular individuals or institutions. They may appear in traditional print form, on a computer screen as part of software, online, or in a combination of these formats.

The terms of database licenses also vary, but they generally restrict or limit how the database can be used. For example, an online license typically dictates when the database can be downloaded or disseminated to others. These restrictions put limits on a user's ability to use the contents of the database beyond what copyright law allows.

Licenses also usually establish enforcement procedures and remedies should the licensee violate the terms of the license. Such terms can include terminating a subscriber's access, suspending services, or suing the subscriber for damages.

Are Licenses Legally Enforceable?

Many database owners resort to licenses when their databases cannot be protected by copyright law because they do not meet the standards for copyright protection outlined earlier in this chapter. In other words, they are probably in the public domain. Most courts have held that such licenses are legally enforceable.

> **EXAMPLE:** Matthew Zeidenberg purchased from a company called ProCD a CD-ROM containing a database of 95 million business telephone listings. This database was not entitled to any copyright protection at all because there was nothing even minimally creative about the selection or arrangement of the listings. ProCD simply took the contents of 3,000 telephone alphabetical directories and placed them on a CD-ROM. However, when Zeidenberg loaded the CD-ROM onto his computer, he was required to agree to a "click-wrap" license agreement obliging users to agree to certain restrictions before they could access the data on the disk. For example, the license barred purchasers of the CD-ROM from copying, adapting, or modifying the listings. Zeidenberg agreed to the license terms, but then went ahead and violated them by copying the listings and placing them on his website, where they were sold to the public for far less than ProCD charged. ProCD sued Zeidenberg for violating the license agreement and won. The court held that the license restrictions were legally enforceable even though the listings were in the public domain. *ProCD v. Zeidenberg*, 86 F.3d 1447 (7th Cir. 1996).

See Chapter 2 for more on the legal enforceability of licenses.

The Privity Limitation

An important limitation of database licenses is the legal requirement of privity. A license (or any other contract) is enforceable only against a person who signs it or otherwise agrees to it. People who don't agree to it are not legally bound by it.

> **EXAMPLE:** Applied Technologies of Wisconsin created a computer program, Market Drive, to help Wisconsin county assessors' offices compile real estate data, such as property addresses and the names of the owners, in an electronic database. The counties used the data for tax assessment purposes. Applied required the counties to license Market Drive from it; the license forbade them from releasing the raw data in the database created with Market Drive to others, even though this raw data was in the public domain. A company called WIREdata

attempted to obtain the raw data from the counties to create its own database for use by real estate brokers. A court held that Applied could not sue WIREdata for violating the license because it had never signed it, only the Wisconsin counties had. Applied could only sue WIREdata for copyright infringement, but this suit failed because the raw data WIREdata wanted was public domain. *Applied Technologies of Wisconsin v. WIREdata, Inc.*, 350 F.3d 640 (7th Cir. 2003).

So, if you can obtain access to a database without signing a license, you can't be sued for violating the license. Unfortunately, this may be difficult or impossible to do in many cases.

Trade Secrets

We've seen above that databases get extremely limited copyright protection or, in many cases, none at all. For this reason, database owners often attempt to use state trade secrecy laws to protect their works. For example, computer databases that are maintained by companies on their internal—that is, nonpublic—computer networks are usually protected as trade secrets. This form of legal protection may be used to supplement copyright protection. If the database cannot be protected by copyright, it may be the owner's main line of defense against unauthorized use.

What Is a Trade Secret?

A trade secret is information that is not generally known in the business community and that provides its owner with a competitive advantage in the marketplace. This can, and often does, include information in databases such as customer lists, formulas, and technical data of all kinds.

If a trade secret owner takes reasonable steps to keep the confidential information secret, the courts will protect the owner from unauthorized disclosures of the secret to others by:

- the owner's employees
- other persons with a duty not to make such disclosures, such as non-employees who work for the company and people who sign nondisclosure agreements promising not to disclose the secret
- industrial spies, and
- competitors who wrongfully acquire the information by means such as theft or bribery.

This means that the trade secret owner may be able to sue the person who stole or disclosed the secret and obtain an injunction (a court order preventing someone from doing something, like stealing or disclosing trade secrets) and damages. However, the trade secret owner must truly take steps to preserve the trade secret; the more widely known a trade secret is, the less willing the courts are to protect it.

Databases That Are Trade Secrets

Not everything can be a trade secret. The database owner must take reasonable steps to keep the data in the database secret—for example, carefully restrict access by keeping it in a password-protected computer system. Databases that are published or otherwise made available to the public cannot be protected as trade secrets; nor can databases that contain information that is generally known in the industry involved. Data that everybody knows cannot provide anyone with a competitive advantage. However, the information in a database need not be novel or unique to qualify as a trade secret. All that is required is that the information not be generally known by people who could profit from its disclosure and use.

Do You Have a Duty of Confidentiality?

Generally, it is very easy for you to know whether you might run afoul of someone's trade secret rights if you copy or otherwise use a database. First, the company or person who developed it must keep the database secret. In addition, your use or disclosure of the data must constitute a breach of an obligation to keep the material confidential. Such a confidential obligation may arise because you work for the person or company that developed the database. Or you agreed not to disclose

it—for example by signing a nondisclosure agreement. Or you must have improperly learned or obtained the data from someone else who had a duty not to disclose it. For example, you obtained a company's idea for a new product by bribing an employee of the company or by theft.

Encryption

Another form of protection for electronic databases is encryption—that is, encoding the data in an unreadable form that can be "unlocked" and read only with the proper key. This is not a legal protection, but it makes it difficult or impossible to obtain access to a database, even if it is in the public domain. The government has been encrypting its sensitive data for years. Powerful encryption technologies that can prevent unauthorized access to and changes in databases are now commercially available. Moreover, it is generally illegal for anyone to obtain access to a database or other work by circumventing technological measures such as encryption.

The Digital Millennium Copyright Act (DMCA; 17 U.S.C. § 1201) was enacted in 1998 to prevent computer hackers and others from circumventing technological measures designed to protect digital works, such as the use of encryption and passwords. In theory, the DMCA does not apply to public domain materials. The reality, however, has turned out to be very different. For example, the DMCA bars the sale or manufacture of products or services designed to defeat encryption. Thus, it would be illegal to sell a product to disable encryption even if it is only used to obtain free access to a public domain work. The U.S. Copyright Office has established certain exceptions to the DMCA, but they do not include obtaining access to public domain works. (SeeCopyright Office, "Exemption to Prohibition on Circumvention of Copyright Protection Systems for Access Control Technologies," 37 C.F.R. Part 201, at www.copyright.gov/fedreg/2012/77fr65260.pdf.)

Thus, the use of encryption technologies may make it impossible for you to obtain access to many databases that are in the public domain. And there may be nothing you can do about it.

Part II: Collections of Public Domain Works

Publishers and others are constantly collecting and republishing public domain materials. This includes, for example, collections of public domain fiction and poetry, drawings and other artwork, photographs, and sheet music. Often, a public domain work is readily accessible only because it has been republished (or published for the first time) as part of such a collection. An excellent example

is the website Public Domain Review (https://publicdomainreview.org), which publishes collections of a wide variety of public domain materials, including art, photography, and written works.

Collections of preexisting works of authorship are called "collective works" by the copyright law. But for the sake of convenience, we'll refer to them simply as collections. Collections differ from databases because they are created from works of authorship, such as writings, while databases are created from facts or data.

Good examples of collections are newspapers, magazines, and other periodicals in which separate articles are combined into a collective whole. However, the preexisting material in a collection can consist of any work of authorship, including any type of writing, music, photographs, or drawings or other artwork.

Copyright notices are routinely included on such collections. However, it's important for you to understand that copyright protection for collections of public domain materials is extremely limited, if it is available at all.

Are the Collected Materials in the Public Domain?

The first question you must answer to determine whether a collection is in the public domain is whether the works of authorship gathered together to create the collection are themselves in the public domain. When public domain materials are used, the author of the collection does not need to obtain permission to use them and neither do you. Here are some real examples of collections consisting of public domain materials:

- Fourteen public domain short stories culled from the more than 60 the author Frank Norris published during his lifetime were published together by Ironweed Press under the title *The Best Short Stories of Frank Norris*. Each story is a separate and independent work. However, Ironweed has created a new copyrighted collection by selecting and arranging the stories into a collective whole—that is, a collection of the best short stories of Frank Norris.

- The original sheet music for dozens of public domain songs originally published during 1901–1911 was collected and published together under the title *Alexander's Ragtime Band and Other Favorite Song Hits, 1901–1911* by Dover Publications. Dover's collection is entitled to copyright protection because it has selected and arranged the materials to form a new work—a collection of songs from 1901–1911.

- More than a hundred public domain postcards were collected and reproduced in a book called *Delivering Views: Distant Cultures in Early Postcards*, published by the Smithsonian Institution Press. Each postcard is a separate work of authorship, but the collection is nonetheless entitled to its own copyright protection because it is a new collection.

On the other hand, a collection may contain materials that are still protected by copyright. In this event, you need permission to use the materials in the collection. A good example is both the current print and online edition of the *Encyclopaedia Britannica*. Each article in the encyclopedia is protected by copyright and you need permission to copy or republish any of them.

To determine whether the materials included in a collection are in the public domain, turn to the chapter covering the types of works involved. For example, if the collection consist of written works, go to Chapter 3, covering writings. If the collection contains sheet music, turn to Chapter 4, covering music.

If you determine that the materials in the collection are copyrighted, the collection isn't in the public domain and you need not read the rest of this chapter. If, on the other hand, the materials are in the public domain the entire collection may be in the public domain as well, or it may receive the extremely limited copyright protection described below.

Copyright Protection for Public Domain Collections

When an author creates a collection consisting of public domain materials it may be entitled to copyright protection, but such protection is very limited. All that can be protected is the *selection and/or arrangement* of the preexisting material, not the preexisting material itself. In some cases both the selection and arrangement are copyrighted. In others, only one or the other is. This limited form of copyright protection is sometimes called a thin copyright.

> EXAMPLE: The copyright in Ironweed Press's Frank Norris short story anthology extends only to its selection and arrange-ment, not to the stories themselves. This means that anyone could reprint any one of the stories contained in the collection without violating Ironweed's compilation copyright. But another publisher could not, without Ironweed's permission, publish a book of the best short stories of Frank Norris using the exact same stories in Ironweed's book, printed in the exact same order.

As the above example shows, the copyright status of the preexisting material used to create a collection is unaffected by the collection's existence. Thus, if the preexisting material was in the public domain, it remains in the public domain.

When we speak of a collection as being in the public domain below, we mean that —for the reasons stated—the selection and arrangement are not protected by copyright.

Copying Collections of Public Domain Works

Since a thin copyright protects only the selection and/or arrangement of the material in a collection, none of the individual public domain works in the collection are protected. This means you may copy any individual work included in the collection. However, you may not copy the copyrighted selection and/or arrangement. This would occur where you copy the *entire* collection (or a substantial portion of it) and leave it unchanged.

This is exactly what happened with a collection called *Easy Classic to Moderns* published by Consolidated Music Publishers. The collection contained the sheet music for 142 individual piano pieces by more than two dozen classical composers, almost all of which were in the public domain. Consolidated's collection included a selection of six piano pieces by Bela Bartok published under the title *Six Miniatures*. This was the first time these six pieces had ever been published together. One of Consolidated's competitors later published a collection of its own entitled *World's Favorite Classic to Contemporary Piano Music*. This collection included the same six Bartok pieces. Consolidated sued the publisher for copyright infringement and won. The court held that the selection and arrangement of the six Bartok pieces was original and that Consolidated's copyright was violated when all six were copied in the subsequent collection. *Consolidated Music Publishers, Inc. v. Ashley Publications, Inc.*, 197 F.Supp. 17 (S.D.N.Y. 1961).

However, you may copy any amount of a collection as long as you don't copy the publisher's copyrighted selection and/ or arrangement. Let's take as an example Dover Publications' collection *Alexander's Ragtime Band and Other Favorite Song Hits, 1901–1911,* mentioned above. The selection of 49 songs included in this collection is copyrighted, but the grouping is not because it is in alphabetical order. You may copy all 49 songs and sell them individually. This would not infringe on Dover's selection—that is, its decision as to which songs to include in a collection of 49 favorite songs originally published during 1901–1911. But you could not sell all 49 together, since this would be copying Dover's selection. You could, however, copy all 49 songs, add another 51 songs, and publish a collection called *100 Best Songs 1901–1911*. Again, this would not be copying Dover's selection of 49 favorite songs, 1901–1911.

Let's consider an example where only the arrangement is copyrighted. A collection of all of Edgar Allan Poe's short stories (which are all in the public domain because their copyrights have expired) arranged by theme would have a copyright in the arrangement, but not in the selection, since every Poe story is included. No creativity is required to make such a selection. You could copy every story in the collection and group them in some other way without violating the publisher's copyright in its selection—for example, you could group them alphabetically or chronologically.

Does the Collection Lack Minimal Creativity?

A collection is entitled to limited copyright protection because the author had to use creativity and judgment to create it. For example, a person who compiled an anthology of the 25 "best" short stories of the 19th century would have to use creativity and judgment in selecting which of the thousands of short stories published during the 19th century belonged in the anthology, and in deciding on the arrangement (that is, order) of the stories.

However, if a collection was created without using even minimal creativity and judgment, it would not be entitled to any copyright protection at all—that is, the selection and arrangement of the work would be in the public domain.

How can you tell if a collection contains sufficient creativity to be entitled to thin copyright protection? A collection is copyrightable if either the selection or arrangement of the material is minimally creative.

A selection is minimally creative if it is based on the author's opinion about something subjective—for example, the author's selection of the "best" short stories written by O. Henry or the "100 Greatest Romantic Poems Ever Written." But an anthology of every short story O. Henry ever wrote would not be an example of a minimally creative selection.

An arrangement is entitled to copyright protection only if it is created in some nonmechanical way. For example, an alphabetical, chronological, or numerical arrangement is purely mechanical and not entitled to copyright protection. An arrangement on some other basis such as category or hierarchy could be—for example, an arrangement of O. Henry's short stories from the worst to the best in the editor's opinion, or according to a theme, would be copyrightable. (See above for a more detailed discussion of the type of arrangements that are entitled to copyright protection.)

Thus, for example, an anthology consisting of all the unpublished poems written by Dorothy Parker was found to be unprotectable because compiling such an anthology required no selectivity or judgment. Anyone could publish an identical anthology. *Silverstein v. Penguin Putnam, Inc.*, 522 F.Supp.2d 579 (S.D.N.Y. 2007).

Is It a De Minimis Collection?

In addition to the minimal creativity requirement, a collection must consist of more than a small number of elements to be copyrightable. The Copyright Office has stated that a collection consisting only of three or fewer items does not meet this threshold. For example, a collection of three one-act plays is not protectable as a collection. If the plays are in the public domain, the collection as a whole will be too.

Is It a U.S. Government Collection?

Collections compiled by U.S. government employees as part of their jobs are also in the public domain. But this rule does not apply to collection by state or local employees. (See Chapter 3 for a detailed discussion.)

Has the Collection's Copyright Expired?

Like any other work, a collection enters the public domain when its copyright expires. The copyright term for a collection begins to run when the work is created or published, not when the works it contains were created or published. The rules for determining whether a collection has been published for copyright purposes are the same as the rules for databases. Copyright terms for published and unpublished collections differ greatly, so read this section carefully. Once you understand these rules you can determine how long a copyright will last in a particular work by reading Chapter 18.

Is the Collection in the Public Domain for Lack of a Copyright Notice?

A collection published before March 1, 1989 had to contain a valid copyright notice. A collection published without such a notice may have entered the public domain. See Chapter 19 for a detailed discussion.

Is the Collection Protected by Means Other Than Copyright?

Because copyright protection for collections is so limited, people who create them often attempt to use means other than copyright to protect them. For example, some collections may be protected as trade secrets.

Far more common, however, is the use of licenses to protect collections. For example, legal publishers who collect public domain court decisions and place them online or on physical media typically require purchasers to agree to licenses restricting how they may use the materials. Among other things, these licenses typically bar users from republishing the decisions. If you violate the terms of the license, the publisher might sue you for breach of contract. (The publisher couldn't sue for copyright infringement, because the decisions are in the public domain.)

This is what happened when a website called Jurisline placed online thousands of legal decisions it copied from 60 CD-ROMs purchased from the legal publisher Lexis. Lexis immediately filed suit, claiming that the copying violated the terms of a license that the person who bought the CD-ROMs had agreed to. Following a preliminary trial court ruling that the license was legally enforceable, Jurisline settled the case by agreeing to remove from its website all of the legal decisions it had copied from the CD-ROMs. (See Chapter 2 for a detailed discussion of licenses.)

Titles

Titles of Copyrighted Works 242

No Copyright Protection for Titles 242

Protection for Titles Under Trademark and Unfair Competition Laws 242

Titles of Public Domain Works 246

Republishing a Public Domain Work 247

Public Domain Titles on Derivative Works 247

Using Disclaimers to Avoid Public Confusion 248

Titles Used on Merchandise and Other Products 249

The First Amendment and Titles 249

Shakespeare may have asked, "What's in a name?" but in today's world, a title can be as valuable as a work itself. For this reason, it's important to understand when titles can be legally protected and when they are in the public domain.

This chapter covers titles of literary and artistic works, including titles of books, magazines, newspapers, periodicals, journals, plays, movies, television shows, songs and other musical compositions, and sound recordings. Titles of copyrighted works receive more legal protection than those for works in the public domain, so we'll cover them first.

Titles of Copyrighted Works

If a work of authorship is still under copyright—that is, its copyright has not expired or been lost—its title may receive some legal protection, but only if it is very well known.

No Copyright Protection for Titles

Copyright law does not protect titles, even if the work itself is protected by copyright. This is because titles are not considered to be works of authorship with their own copyright protection. Instead, they merely describe and identify a work of authorship.

Protection for Titles Under Trademark and Unfair Competition Laws

Although titles are never protected by copyright, state unfair competition laws and state and federal trademark laws may protect them. If a title is protected, you may be legally prevented from using it.

Unfair competition and trademark laws are designed to protect the public from deception and preserve the goodwill that a company builds when it sells a product or service to the public.

For a title to be protected under these laws, it must meet two requirements:

- the title must be strongly identified in the public's mind with the underlying work; and
- the owner or publisher must prove that:
  - the public will be confused if the title is used in another work, or
  - the unauthorized use of the title dilutes or tarnishes the title's value as a trademark.

Let's look at each requirement separately.

Identification

For a title to be protected, it must be associated in the public's mind with one work. In other words, when a member of the general public hears the title, he or she automatically thinks of a single work. For example, if you hear the title *Star Wars*, it's likely you immediately think of the famous series of movies known by that name. Lawyers call this "secondary meaning."

Other examples of titles that have secondary meaning include:

- *Gone With the Wind*
- *Conan the Barbarian*
- *Jaws*
- *Top Gun*
- *Twin Peaks,* and
- *The Sensuous Woman.*

However, most titles of individual literary works don't have secondary meaning and are therefore not protected by unfair competition or trademark laws.

Whether a title has acquired secondary meaning is a judgment call that depends on a variety of factors, including:

- how long it's been used
- the amount of advertising and other publicity the title has been given, and
- the number of people who bought or viewed the work—the better known a work, the more likely it has acquired secondary meaning.

Ordinarily, a literary work must be published and widely circulated before its title can acquire secondary meaning. However, it is possible for a title to acquire secondary meaning before it's published where the work has been given substantial prerelease publicity.

It's not necessary that the public know the name of the author or publisher of the work for the title to have secondary meaning. It's sufficient that it identifies the title with the work itself.

How can you tell whether a title makes the grade and has achieved secondary meaning? It can be impossible to come up with a conclusive answer. If you're dealing with a title for an extremely well-known work like those listed above, secondary meaning has very likely been achieved. On the other hand, if the title is for a work that is so obscure or sold so poorly that only a few people have ever heard of it, there is no secondary meaning. In between these two extremes there is a vast gray area.

One way to help determine if a title has secondary meaning is to have a title availability search done. A private search firm researches the complete history of a title, showing you how it's been used in the past—for example, whether it's been used for movies, books, articles, or other works. Companies that sell liability insurance to producers of television shows and movies may require that such a search be done.

The best known title availability search company is CompuMark, in Boston. For details, see https://clarivate. com/compumark/solutions/trademark-searching, or call 800-692-8833.

SEE AN EXPERT

If you're unsure whether a title has achieved secondary meaning, consult with an attorney before using it.

Confusion

In addition, to prevent others from using a title, an author or publisher must prove that the public would likely be confused as to the source of the work. Public confusion exists if the public is deceived into buying one work, believing it to be another. Confusion also is found where the public is deceived as to the sponsorship or approval of a work. For example, if a film is called *Rocky VII*, the public is likely to believe the creators of the original *Rocky* film produced it or at least approved it.

Factors considered by the courts if someone challenges your use of a title include:

- whether the title has artistic relevance to the underlying work—that is, does the title describe or conjure up the work
- the design of the works involved
- the similarity between the two titles
- the similarity in the contents of the works
- how the works are marketed
- the care likely to be exercised by purchasers
- whether the defendant intended to confuse the public, and
- the distinctiveness of the prior title.

EXAMPLE: *Playboy* magazine brought suit to stop a competitor from using the title *Playmen* magazine and won. The court held that a likelihood of confusion existed because some consumers would mistake *Playmen* for *Playboy*. Moreover, even those consumers who wouldn't confuse one magazine with the other might believe *Playboy* and *Playmen* were both published by Hugh Hefner. *Playboy Enterprises v. Chuckleberry Publishing*, 486 F.Supp. 414 (S.D.N.Y. 1980).

Trademark Dilution

Trademark dilution occurs when the integrity of a famous trademark is "muddied" by an offensive association, either by a vulgar or insulting affiliation (tarnishment) or by a connection with a lesser product (blurring).

- **Tarnishment.** The image of a famous trademark is used in such a way that it image may be tarnished in the public's mind—for example, using the title "Braveheart" for a sexually explicit website.
- **Blurring.** A use that blurs the identity of a famous trademark—for example, using "Game of Thrones" on toilet paper.

Dilution is a vague concept, often used by companies to justify going after an offensive use of a trademark. Critical book or movie reviews or other editorial uses of titles are not considered dilution.

News reporting and commentary and other noncommercial uses are also exempted from the federal dilution law. A use is noncommercial if it does more than propose a commercial transaction. For example, a court held that the song title "Barbie Girl" did not dilute Mattel's trademark in the Barbie doll. The song was noncommercial speech because it lampooned Barbie's image—thus, the title did more than "propose a commercial transaction"—that is, act just to get consumers to buy the song. *Mattel, Inc. v. MCA Records, Inc.*, 296 F.3d 894 (9th Cir. 2002).

Series Titles

Titles of a series of works receive much more legal protection than titles of single works. These include titles of newspapers, magazines, and other periodicals; titles for a series of books—for example, the popular *Dummies* series of reference books or the series of novels known as the *Hardy Boys Mysteries*; titles of television series or a series of movies; and encyclopedia and dictionary titles.

Unlike titles of individual works, series titles can be registered as trademarks with the U.S. Patent and Trademark Office (PTO). When such a series title is registered, it is presumed to have secondary meaning. This makes it much easier for the owners of such titles to win trademark infringement suits.

Because of this, you should not use such a series title—for example, you should not use the words *Dummies Guide to ...* in a title. Doing so will likely result in a lawsuit that you will probably lose. Indeed, you'll likely be threatened with litigation if your title is similar, though not identical to, a well-known series title. For example, the *Wall Street Journal* recently threatened a student publication called *The Small Street Journal* with a lawsuit if it didn't change its name.

An easy way to tell if a series title has been registered is to check if the ® symbol is used near it. If it is, the title has been registered. However, the ® symbol is not always used for registered trademarks, so its absence doesn't necessarily mean the title is not registered. You can determine for certain if a title is registered by conducting a trademark search—that is, a search of the PTO's trademark registration records. You can do this yourself online or hire someone to do it for you.

RESOURCE

For a detailed discussion of trademark searches, see *Trademark: Legal Care for Your Business & Product Name,* by Stephen Fishman (Nolo).

Registering Movie Titles

The major Hollywood film studios have established their own private system of movie title protection and registration. Through the auspices of the Motion Picture Association of America (MPAA; www.motionpictures.org), a film industry trade group, they have established a title registration bureau. MPAA members (which include all the major film studios) and independent producers who are members may apply to register a film title. If the title has not been used, registration is granted. But if a subscriber objects that the title is confusingly similar to one of its own titles, the dispute is referred to an MPAA arbitration panel, which holds a hearing and issues a decision resolving the dispute. The studios and producers who use the registration system have agreed by contract to be bound by the panel's decision. However, the panel's decisions are not binding on the public, only on those who have agreed to participate in the registration system.

Use in Other Media

If the title of a copyrighted work has secondary meaning as described above—whether it is a title of an individual work or a series title—courts are particularly likely to protect it against unauthorized exploitation in different media. For example, the magazine *National Lampoon* was able to prevent the use of the words "National Lampoon" or "lampoon" in the title for a television series. *National Lampoon, Inc. v. American Broadcasting Cos.*, 497 F.2d 1343 (2d Cir. 1974). This is because the reason such a title is being used is not to describe the work, but to make the public believe that the creator of the original work is in some way connected with the new work.

CAUTION

Avoiding title lawsuits. Unless you're prepared to get involved in litigation, you should avoid using extremely well-known titles of non-public-domain works. This is true even though you think your use will not lead to public confusion or dilution. The prior user of the title may disagree with you.

Titles of Public Domain Works

When a work enters the public domain, its title receives much less legal protection than titles of works still under copyright. Ordinarily, the unfair competition and trademark laws described earlier in this section cannot protect the title of a public domain work, but there can be exceptions.

Republishing a Public Domain Work

If you republish a public domain work, you are ordinarily free to use the title to identify it. However, there is one very limited exception: If the title has acquired such strong secondary meaning that the public identifies it with its original publisher or other distributor, the title cannot be used in a way that deceives the public as to the source of the work.

Very few public domain titles qualify for protection under this exception because they don't have strong enough secondary meaning. Remember, the public must not only identify the title with the public domain work, it must also identify it with the original publisher or other source. This is very difficult to show. Only rarely does the public identify a work's title with a particular publisher or other source. For example, do you know who first published *Alice in Wonderland* or the Irving Berlin song "Alexander's Ragtime Band"? You probably recognize the titles, but not the sources.

Even where a title of a public domain work has acquired such strong secondary meaning, it may still be used so long as the public isn't misled into believing the original publisher or other source is behind the new publication. Ordinarily, you don't have to use a disclaimer; it's enough that the name of the new publisher or other distributor is clearly identified on the work.

EXAMPLE: A John Wayne movie called *McLintock!* entered the public domain when it was not renewed with the U.S. Copyright Office in the 28th year after its publication. About 20 years later, a video distributor called Goodtimes Home Video began selling a videocassette of the movie. The cassette contained a label clearly identifying Goodtimes as producer of the video. A court held this was sufficient to prevent public confusion about the source of the video. *Maljack Productions v. Goodtimes Home Video Corp.,* 81 F.3d 881 (9th Cir. 1996).

However, if you really want to make sure there is not even a possibility of public confusion, you can use a disclaimer.

Public Domain Titles on Derivative Works

What if you want to create a derivative (new) work based on a public domain work and use the work's title to identify it—for example, create a movie based on Mark Twain's novel *Huckleberry Finn* and call it *Huckleberry Finn*? Ordinarily, this doesn't pose a problem.

However, if someone has already created a similar derivative work with the same title, there could be trouble. The creator of the prior work might be able to prevent your use of the title on the grounds of unfair competition. He would have to prove in court that the public identifies the title with his particular derivative work (whether or not it also identifies the title with the public domain work).

This is hard to establish, at least where the public domain work is well known. In one case, for example, Walt Disney studios created an animated cartoon based on the public domain novel *Alice in Wonderland* and brought suit against the producer of a movie based on the novel that used the same title. The suit was unsuccessful because Disney was unable to show that, as far as movies were concerned, the public identified the title *Alice in Wonderland* solely with the Disney movie, not a film based on the book *Alice in Wonderland*. *Walt Disney Prods. v. Souvaine Selective Pictures, Inc.*, 192 F.2d 856 (2d Cir. 1951).

If a title of a derivative work based on a public domain work has attained such secondary meaning, you may be able to avoid liability for unfair competition or trademark violations by using a disclaimer making clear to the public that your work is not connected with the prior work (see below).

Using Disclaimers to Avoid Public Confusion

A disclaimer is a statement that makes clear to the public that even though your work has a title that is the same as or similar to the title of a previous work, the creator or publisher of the previous work has not produced or approved it.

Courts have held that even if the title of a public domain work has attained secondary meaning, anyone may use it so long as the title is used in a way that does not deceive or confuse the public. A good way to help avoid such confusion is to use a disclaimer.

If you're using a title of a work that is not in the public domain, use of a disclaimer may limit or avoid liability for unfair competition or trademark violations. Courts sometimes require the use of disclaimers rather than prohibit use of a title, so if you already have a disclaimer you're way ahead of the game.

Using a disclaimer may not always avoid problems with unfair competition or trademark laws, but it can only help. Such a disclaimer should be clearly written, prominently displayed, and permanently affixed to your work.

Here is an example of a disclaimer you can use when you republish a public domain work. It makes clear to the public that the original publisher of the work is not involved with your republication of the work:

> This work is not published by the original publishers of [TITLE OF WORK] or by their successors.

Where a title of a new work is the same as or similar to that of a copyrighted work, the words "based on" or "derived from" are often used in a disclaimer to make clear that the work doesn't owe its origin to the prior work with the same title.

> **EXAMPLE:** The producers of the film *Elephant Man* used the following disclaimer to make clear to the public that their film was not connected with a previous Broadway play of the same title:
>
> Based upon the life of John Merrick, The Elephant Man, and not upon the Broadway play or any other fictional account.

Titles Used on Merchandise and Other Products

Some titles are used on merchandise, such as cups, toys, T-shirts, and other clothing. This is often the case with movie titles such *Star Wars* or *Godzilla*. Titles used in this way may be registered with the U.S. Patent and Trademark Office. Such uses receive strong trademark law protection. You ordinarily need permission to use a well-known title on merchandise. If you don't, you'll likely receive a call or letter from a lawyer.

Titles of public domain works can also be used to identify goods and services. For example, the words *Moby Dick* could be used to identify a chain of seafood restaurants or a company could come up with a line of *Scarlet Letter* chocolates. Titles used in this way may receive trademark protection, but only against uses that would confuse the public or dilute the value of the trademark. For example, even if there is a *Moby Dick* seafood restaurant chain, you may continue to use the title for purposes not related to selling seafood.

The First Amendment and Titles

Trademark and unfair competition laws apply only to commercial uses of titles—that is, using them to identify products or services. Informational or "editorial" uses of a trademark do not require permission. These are uses that inform, educate, or express opinions or ideas protected under the First Amendment of the U.S. Constitution (protecting freedom of speech and of the press). For example, permission is not required to use a book title in a book review, even if the review is very negative.

Public Domain Elements in Copyright Writings

Ideas..252

    State Contract Law...254

    Trade Secret Law...254

    Federal Patent Law...256

Facts...256

    Legal Protection for Fictional "Facts"...257

    Legal Protection for Hot News...258

    The Merger Doctrine—When Ideas, Facts, and Their Expression Merge.....258

Unprotected Elements in Works of Fiction..261

    Themes..261

    Factual Settings...261

    Plots..261

    Stock Characters..262

    Standard Situations (*Scènes à Faire*)..264

    Literary Devices...265

Unprotected Elements in Works of Fact...265

    Research...265

    Interpretations...266

    Quotations...266

    Fictional Elements...268

    Organization of Material...269

If you have concluded that a work you want to use is protected by copyright, all is not lost. You cannot use the whole work, or substantial portions of it, without first obtaining permission from the copyright owner, and possibly paying a fee for its use. However, almost all copyrighted works contain elements that are in the public domain. These elements consist of things other than the actual words or other creative building blocks the author uses to create the work. Such public domain elements include:

- ideas, facts, systems, and discoveries
- a fictional work's themes, settings, plots, stock characters, and standard scenes, and
- a nonfiction work's research, interpretations, quotations, fictional elements, and unoriginal organization.

This chapter focuses on public domain elements in written works—that is, works consisting of words—because these kinds of works contain more public domain elements than any other. However, the basic principles discussed here apply to all types of copyrighted works.

Ideas

Copyright only protects the particular way authors express their ideas, not the ideas themselves. Ideas, procedures, processes, systems, methods of operation, concepts, principles, and discoveries are all in the public domain, free for all to use. (See 17 U.S.C. Section 102(b) for the exact wording of this statute.) There is a good reason for this: If authors were allowed to obtain a monopoly over their ideas, the copyright laws would end up discouraging new authorship and the progress of knowledge, which are the two goals copyright is intended to foster.

Copyright does not protect three kinds of ideas:

- **The idea to create a work.** The idea to create a particular type of work is never protected by copyright. For example, the idea to convert Jane Austen's classic public domain novel *Pride and Prejudice* into a story about Zombies is not copyrighted. Anyone can write a novel based on this idea and incorporate as much of Austen's work in it as they wish. The fact that Seth Grahame-Smith wrote a bestselling novel based on this idea called *Pride and Prejudice and Zombies* in 2009 does not prevent anyone from using the same idea. However, the material Grahame-Smith added to Austen's *Pride and Prejudice* to create his own Zombie version cannot be copied.
- **Creative building blocks.** The building blocks of creative expression are also in the public domain. If these were protected by copyright, it would be virtually impossible for anyone to

fashion a new creative work. What these building blocks consist of depends on the nature of the work involved. In the realm of fiction, they include a work's theme, settings, plot, stock characters and situations, and literary devices. In the case of a nonfiction work, they include the facts contained in the work.

- **Methods, systems, and processes.** In addition, copyright protection does not extend to methods of operation, systems, or processes. Thus, for example, copyright did not protect a bookkeeping system described in a book. Copyright protected the words the author used to describe the system, but not the system itself. Anyone was entitled to use the system without the author's permission, or even write another book about it, but could not copy the author's description without permission. *Baker v. Selden*, 101 U.S. 99 (1879).

When Does Copying Become Plagiarism?

Ideas, facts, research, concepts, principles, and discoveries are ordinarily in the public domain. So are the words contained in books and other writings that are in the public domain. This means you can copy or otherwise use these things without obtaining permission. But this doesn't necessarily mean you shouldn't provide credit for the source of such words, ideas, facts, or research. Failure to do so may constitute plagiarism.

Plagiarists are people who pose as the originators of words they did not write, ideas they did not conceive, or facts they did not discover. "Plagiarism" is not a legal term; it's an ethical term. Plagiarists who only copy public domain materials can't be sued for copyright infringement. But there still could be severe consequences. College professors and journalists have been fired because of plagiarism.

To avoid charges of plagiarism, authors of scholarly works (histories, biographies, legal and scientific treatises, student papers, etc.) must always give proper credit to the sources of their ideas and facts, as well as to any words they borrow. Authors of less serious works— for example, how-to books, newspaper or magazine articles, or blog posts—should always attribute direct quotations but may not always need to give credit for ideas and facts they borrow. (Authors of such works should discuss this with their editors or publishers.)

It is neither customary nor necessary for authors of works of imagination, such as novels, screenplays, or stage plays, to credit the sources of their inspiration, whether other works of imagination, newspaper accounts, or histories. But they should, of course, give proper attribution for direct quotations from public domain materials.

While copyright law does not protect ideas, they can receive legal protection in other ways.

State Contract Law

As a general rule, ideas are as free as air. However, if you promise to pay someone for telling you an idea, your promise may constitute an enforceable contract. This means that if you fail to pay as promised, the person who disclosed the idea may be able to sue you in court and collect the promised payment. The suit would be for breach of your contract, not for copyright infringement, and would be brought under your state's contract law. In real life, however, such suits are rarely brought because it's very unusual for people to agree to pay for ideas before they know what the ideas are.

Usually there is no express (stated) promise to pay for an idea. Instead, person A tells person B an idea without an advance promise from B to pay for it. B later uses the idea and A claims he should therefore be paid for it. Courts will sometimes hold that an implied (unstated) contract was created under these circumstances and make B pay A. However, A must prove that B actually received the idea from A and actually used it. Moreover, A must show that B agreed to pay for the idea, but did not expressly say so. This might arise on the basis of prior dealings between A and B (for example, B paid A for previous

similar ideas), or the custom in the trade A and B are engaged in.

In addition, most courts require that the idea be both novel and concrete. An idea is novel when it is not commonly known. An idea is concrete when it is ready for immediate use without any additional embellishment.

You don't need to worry about contract law protection for ideas you obtain from a book or other written work you buy or obtain from a library. You must have personal contact with the idea creator for an express or implied contract to be formed. That is, the idea originator must have personally told you the idea (either orally or in a writing directed to you) and you must have acted in such a way as to create an express or implied contract.

Trade Secret Law

There is a very important exception to the general rule that ideas, procedures, processes, systems, methods of operation, concepts, principles, and discoveries are in the public domain. All of these things can be protected under state trade secret laws.

A trade secret is information or know-how that is not generally known in the business community and that provides its owner with a competitive advantage in the marketplace. The information can be an idea, written words (such as an instructional manual), formula, process or procedure, technical design, list, marketing plan, or any other secret that gives the owner an economic advantage.

If a trade secret owner takes reasonable steps to keep the confidential information or know-how secret, the courts will protect the owner from unauthorized disclosures of the secret to others by:

- the owner's employees
- other persons with a duty not to make such disclosures, such as nonemployees who work for the company and people who sign nondisclosure agreements promising not to disclose the secret
- industrial spies, and
- competitors who wrongfully acquire the information such as through theft or bribery.

This means that the trade secret owner may be able to sue the person who stole or disclosed the secret and obtain an injunction (a court order preventing someone from doing something, like stealing or disclosing trade secrets) and damages. However, the trade secret owner must truly take steps to preserve the trade secret; the more widely known a trade secret is, the less willing the courts are to protect it.

Not everything can be a trade secret. Ideas and information that are public knowledge or generally known in the industry involved cannot be trade secrets. This is because things that everybody knows cannot provide anyone with a competitive advantage. However, information constituting a trade secret need not be novel or unique. All that is required is that information not be generally known by people who could profit from its disclosure and use.

Generally, it is very easy for you to know whether you might run afoul of someone's trade secret rights. First of all, the company or person who developed it must keep the idea secret. Ideas you find in published books, articles, and other works distributed to the public cannot be trade secrets. On the other hand, if you discover an idea in a closely guarded internal company memo marked "Confidential," you may not have the legal right to use or disclose it to the public.

In addition, your use or disclosure of the idea must constitute a breach of an obligation to keep the idea confidential. Such a confidential obligation may arise because you work for the person or company that developed the idea or you agreed not to disclose it, for example by signing a nondisclosure agreement. Or you must have improperly obtained the idea from someone else who had a duty not to disclose it. For example, you obtained a company's idea for a new product by bribing an employee of the company or by theft.

As mentioned above, you don't have to worry about trade secrecy when you're dealing with published works. The issue arises only when you're dealing with unpublished documents that contain economically valuable ideas or information that a person or company has sought to keep secret from competitors and the general public.

Federal Patent Law

This book is about works of authorship such as writings, movies, music, and art. However, you should be aware that ideas, methods, and systems embodied in inventions can be protected under U.S. and foreign patent laws. Inventions are not works of authorship and generally cannot be protected by copyright. In the United States, patentable inventions include:

- a process or method of getting something useful done (such as a genetic engineering procedure, a manufacturing technique, or computer software)
- a machine (usually something with moving parts or circuitry, such as a cigarette lighter, laser, or photocopier)
- a manufactured article (such as a tire, transistor, or hand tool)
- a composition of matter (such as a chemical composition, drug, soap, or genetically altered life form)
- the unique, ornamental, or visible shape or design of an object (such as a unique ornamental design of a lamp or desk), or
- an asexually reproduced plant.

Patents can also be obtained for methods of doing business that are implemented in the real world through technology like computers—for example, Amazon's "1-Click shopping" system.

Filing for and obtaining a patent from the U.S. Patent and Trademark Office grants an inventor a monopoly on the use and commercial exploitation of an invention for up to 20 years. That is, the inventor has the legal right to prevent others from making, using, or selling the invention claimed in the patent.

For example, an inventor who obtains a patent on a new type of mousetrap can prevent others from copying and selling the trap to others. But such an inventor could not prevent anyone from writing a book or creating a film or video about how to catch mice, even if the book, film, or video described how to use the inventor's new mousetrap.

 RESOURCE
For a detailed discussion of patents, see *Patent It Yourself,* by David Pressman and David Blau (Nolo).

Facts

Copyright does not protect facts, whether scientific, historical, biographical, or news of the day. If the first person to write about a fact had a monopoly over it, the spread of knowledge would be greatly impeded. Another reason why copyright law does not protect facts is that authors do not independently create facts; at most, they may discover a previously unknown fact. For example, Nicolaus Copernicus did not create the fact that the earth revolves around the sun when he wrote his landmark book, *De Revolutionibus Orbium Caelestium,* in 1543. This fact existed in nature and Copernicus discovered it through close observation and the exercise of his genius. Copyright does not protect discoveries. 17 U.S.C. Section 102(b).

So, the facts contained in works such as news stories, histories, biographies, and scientific treatises are not protected by copyright. Subject to the important limitation of the merger doctrine (discussed below), all that is protected is the author's original expression of the facts contained in such works—that is, the words the author uses to describe the facts and possibly the way he or she organizes or shapes the material. Thus, for example, anyone who writes a novel, play, or other fictional work based on Marilyn Monroe's life is free to cull the historical facts about her from biographies and other sources and use them in the fictional work. The events of Marilyn Monroe's life—for example, her marriages to baseball great Joe DiMaggio and playwright Arthur Miller—are unprotectable facts. Moreover, incorporating these facts into a fictional work does not give the author a copyright over them. Only the way the author expresses such facts, to the extent original, is protectable. *Whitehead v. CBS/Viacom,* 315 F.Supp.2d 1 (D.D.C. 2004).

However, state trade secret laws may protect economically valuable facts not generally known to the public that have been kept secret.

Legal Protection for Fictional "Facts"

One reason facts are not protected by copyright is that authors do not create them. Facts exist in nature or history. Authors simply discover them and express them in words. It's the author's words that are copyrighted, not the facts themselves.

However, "fictional facts" contained in a television show, movie, play, or novel *are* created by the author, as are the words used to express them. Such "facts" are entitled to copyright protection. For this reason, a trivia quiz book that contained detailed information about the *Seinfeld* television show was found to have infringed upon the producers' copyright. The book didn't ask questions about who acted in the program, who directed each show, or how many seasons it ran. These are nonfiction facts that are not protected by copyright. Instead, the book posed questions about the fictional events depicted during the episodes. These events were created by the authors of the shows and were copyrighted. *Castle Rock Entertainment v. Carol Publishing Group*, 955 F.Supp. 260 (S.D. N.Y. 1997). A similar result was reached where the authors of a 400-page lexicon of the *Harry Potter* books copied or paraphrased thousands of fictional facts from the seven-book series. *Warner Bros. Entm't Inc. v. RDR Books*, 575 F.Supp.2d 513 (S.D.N.Y. 2008).

In contrast, the creators of the board game Trivial Pursuit did not commit copyright infringement when they used the facts contained in two trivia encyclopedias to write the questions for their game. The facts contained in these encyclopedias—*The Complete Unabridged Super Trivia Encyclopedia*, volumes 1 and 2—were in the public domain, free for all to use. These books contained facts about geography, art, literature, sports, and history, not fictional facts such as contained in the *Seinfeld* TV show. Unlike the case of the authors of the *Seinfeld* show, the author of the encyclopedias did not create the facts expressed in his works. *Worth v. Selchow and Righter Co.*, 827 F.2d 569 (9th Cir. 1987).

CAUTION

Check the facts. Copyright protection for "fictional" facts makes it important for anyone using a fact from a work of authorship to make sure that what they are using is actually a fact. Failure to check whether a fact is actually a fact could cause you to unintentionally violate someone's copyright in a "fictional" fact.

Legal Protection for Hot News

Although facts are not protected by copyright, unfair competition laws in the 50 states might protect them in certain narrowly defined situations. For example, a court has held that hot news is protected under such laws if:

- a person or company generates highly time-sensitive factual information at some cost or expense
- another person's or entity's use of the information constitutes free-riding on the fact gatherer's costly efforts to collect the information
- the use of the information is in direct competition with a product or service offered by the fact gatherer, and
- other people free-riding on the fact gatherer's efforts would threaten its ability to stay in business.

EXAMPLE: It would probably be unlawful for a newspaper to copy news stories contained in a competing newspaper and print them as its own. But a company that used pagers to transmit to subscribers real-time NBA game scores and other information tabulated from television and radio broadcasts of basketball games did not commit misappropriation because there was no free-riding involved. The company collected the scores itself; it didn't steal them from the NBA. See *National Basketball Assoc. v. Motorola, Inc.*, 105 F.3d 841 (2d Cir. 1996).

The Merger Doctrine— When Ideas, Facts, and Their Expression Merge

Sometimes there is just one way, or are only a few ways, to adequately express a particular idea or fact. If the first person to write about such an idea or fact could copyright his or her expression, that would effectively create a monopoly over that idea or fact itself—that is, no one else could write about it without the author's permission. The copyright law does not permit this, since it would discourage authorship of new works and thereby retard the progress of knowledge. In these cases, the idea or fact and its particular expression are deemed to merge, and the expression—the way the author placed the words—is either treated as if it were in the public domain or given very limited copyright protection.

The merger doctrine applies mainly to factual works such as histories, biographies, and scientific treatises, rather than to works of imagination such as novels, plays, and poems. This is because the ideas and facts in factual works can often be expressed only in one particular way or only in a few ways, while the ideas contained in novels and similar works can usually be expressed in a wide variety of ways.

For example, assume you wish to write an unadorned factual account of Paul Revere's famous midnight ride during the Revolutionary War. You research Revere's life and create a work containing, in part, the following sequence of words:

On April 18, 1775, the Boston minutemen learned that the British intended to march on Concord with a detachment of 700 men. Paul Revere arranged for a signal to be flashed from the steeple of the Old North Church in Boston. Two lanterns would mean that the British were coming by water, and one, by land.

The particular selection and arrangement of words in the above paragraph appears to satisfy the three requirements for copyright protection: fixation, originality, and minimal creativity. (See Chapter 2 for a detailed discussion of these requirements.) Does this mean that if anyone used these three sentences without your permission they would be liable for copyright infringement? Because of the merger doctrine, the answer is probably not. This is because if anyone else wrote a brief factual account of Paul Revere's ride, it would necessarily have to contain sentences looking very much like those in your paragraph. This would be so even though the author had never read your account, because there are just not many different ways to express the facts described in your paragraph. For example, how many different words can an author use to explain that one lantern meant that the British were coming by land and two meant by sea? The facts pretty much dictate the form of expression here.

As a result, if your paragraph were protected by copyright, nobody else could ever write a factual account of Paul Revere's ride without your permission. Copyright law does not permit this kind of control, since it would effectively give you a monopoly over the facts concerning

Paul Revere's ride. To prevent this, the facts of Paul Revere's ride and the words you used to express them would be deemed to merge. Many courts would hold that your paragraph was in the public domain, and could be copied verbatim (or used in any other way) without your permission. Other courts would not go quite this far; they would give your paragraph limited protection by holding that your paragraph was protected from unauthorized verbatim copying, but nothing else. See *Kregos v. Associated Press*, 937 F.2d 700 (2d Cir. 1991).

In contrast, the merger doctrine would not be applied to a work of imagination—for example, a poem—about Paul Revere's ride. Consider this:

> *Listen, my children, and you shall hear*
> *Of the midnight ride of Paul Revere,*
> *On the eighteenth of April, in Seventy-five.*
> *Hardly a man is now alive*
> *Who remembers that famous day and year.*
> *He said to his friend, If the British march*
> *By land or sea from the town tonight,*
> *Hold a lantern aloft in the belfry arch*
> *Of the North Church tower as a signal light,*
> *One, if by land, and two, if by sea.*

These stanzas were written by Henry Wadsworth Longfellow more than 100 years ago and are thus in the public domain because the copyright has expired. But let's pretend, for purposes of our example, they were written just the other day.

This verse conveys almost exactly the same factual information as your paragraph above, yet the facts and expression would not be deemed to merge. Why? Because the author's words are embellished and highly distinctive. The sequence of words has not been dictated solely by the facts. Indeed, it is the unique word sequence itself, not the facts, that is the work's main attraction. No one must copy this particular word sequence in order to convey the same facts or to write another work of imagination about Paul Revere's ride. A person who copied even the first two lines would probably be found to have infringed on the copyright in the poem.

A work need not be written in poetic meter to obtain copyright protection. But the more distinctive an author's words, the more protection his or her work will receive. An elegantly written biography of Paul Revere will receive more copyright protection than an unadorned factual account.

GRAY AREA

You may have trouble determining when a work receives little or no copyright because of the merger doctrine. This is an issue about which reasonable minds can easily differ. See Chapter 1 for detailed guidance on how to deal with such public domain gray areas.

Unprotected Elements in Works of Fiction

Works of fiction include novels, short stories, poems, and plays. There are elements in works of fiction that do not secure copyright protection and are, thus, in the public domain.

Themes

In fictional works, the theme is simply its underlying idea, which is never protected. Only the original way an author expresses his or her theme is protected. For example, anyone can write a work expressing the theme of human against nature, but this doesn't mean you can copy wholesale from Ernest Hemingway's famous novel *The Old Man and the Sea.*

Factual Settings

A fictional work's factual setting—that is, the factual time and place in which the story occurs—is likewise not protected by copyright. For example, anyone can write a story set on the RMS *Titanic* or in New York City. However, the particular words an author uses to describe a setting are protected. Fictional settings are another matter, however. Where a story takes place in an entirely imaginary world—such as the world created by J.R.R. Tolkien in his *Lord of the Rings* novels—the setting is probably protected by copyright. You shouldn't copy such an imaginary setting without permission.

Plots

The plot of a fictional work—the sequence of events by which the author expresses her theme or idea—is a selection and arrangement of ideas. While ideas themselves are not protected, an author's selection and arrangement of ideas are protected as long as they are original, that is, independently created. Thus, a plot constitutes protected expression only to the extent it was independently created by an author.

Because there are, in reality, few independently created plots, it is rare for a plot to have copyright protection. One literary critic has noted that "authors spin their plots from a relatively small number of 'basic situations,' changing characters, reversing roles, giving modern twists to classic themes." *The Thirty-Six Dramatic Situations*, by Polti (The Writer, Inc.). For example, authors have recycled the time-tested plot of boy meets girl, boy gets girl, boy loses girl, boy gets girl back over and over again, throughout the centuries. Naturally, these basic plots are all in the public domain; otherwise, it would be very difficult, if not impossible, for anyone to create a "new" work of fiction.

Independently created variations or twists on basic plots would constitute protected expression. But there aren't very many new plot twists either. For example, can you think of any variations on the boy-meets-girl scenario that haven't been done before?

Although a plot itself usually cannot be protected by copyright, the particular way an author expresses a plot ordinarily is—that is, the particular words an author uses to flesh out and advance a plot are protected. For example, if Shakespeare's play *Romeo and Juliet* was protected by copyright (it isn't, of course, because it was created so long ago; see Chapter 18), anyone could write a play about young lovers from feuding families who commit suicide, but no one could copy the words Shakespeare used in *Romeo and Juliet* to express this plot.

Stock Characters

There are many standard character types that have developed in fiction over time—for example, the eccentric little old lady; the wicked stepmother; the tall, silent, strong cowboy; the two-fisted, hard-drinking private detective; the street-wise, fast-talking urban hustler. Because they are not original creations, these character types are not protectable by copyright; they are part of the stock of ideas that all fiction writers may draw upon. Again, however, the particular way an author describes a stock character is protectable to the extent it's original.

However, once a written work of fiction enters the public domain, any element of the work can be used without permission, including the characters.

Photo by the author, October 2013.

Some well-known characters take on a life of their own and end up appearing over a number of years in a variety of works, often in different media—for example, both novels and movies or television. The literary character Sherlock Holmes is a good example. Arthur Conan Doyle first created Holmes in a series of short stories in the late 19th century. Since then he has been the subject of numerous plays, movies, television shows, and even a novel based on the idea that Sigmund Freud cured Holmes of a cocaine addiction (*The Seven-Per-Cent Solution*, by Nicholas Meyer). All of the Conan Doyle stories and novels about Holmes originally published more than 95 years ago are in the public domain because their copyrights have expired. All the storylines, dialog, and character traits contained in these publications may be freely used. However, ten stories first published less than 95 years ago through

Distinctive Characters Are Not in the Public Domain

In contrast to stock characters, distinctive characters are *not* in the public domain, unless the work they are based on has entered the public domain. This means that no one can copy the particular original combination and selection of qualities—such as personality traits, physical attributes, and mode of dress—that make the character distinctive. An author's selection and combination of such distinctive qualities (ideas) is deemed to be copyrighted.

Unfortunately, there are no uniform standards for judging when a character is, or is not, sufficiently distinctive to be protectable. Copyright protection has been extended to such disparate characters as Tarzan, Amos & Andy, Hopalong Cassidy, and E.T., and denied to Sam Spade and the Lone Ranger. Is Sam Spade any less distinctive than Hopalong Cassidy? The only general rule is that "the less developed the characters, the less they can be copyrighted." *Nichols v. Universal Pictures Corp.*, 45 F.2d 119 (2d Cir. 1930).

Because the legal standards in this area are far from clear, never use a well-known character from a copyrighted work—either by name or detailed description—without first consulting a copyright attorney or disguising the character to such an extent that it is not recognizable. Even if the character doesn't seem sufficiently distinctive to you to merit protection, its creator and publisher may feel quite differently and sue you for copyright infringement. In one case, for example, the son of the late novelist Vladimir Nabokov filed suit when an author wrote and attempted to publish a fictional diary by Lolita Haze, the main character of Nabokov's novel *Lolita*. (The suit was settled and the book subsequently published to mixed reviews.)

Be particularly careful about using cartoon characters. Cartoon characters have a much easier time obtaining copyright protection than literary characters. For example, copyright protection has been extended to Superman, Batman, the Pink Panther, the Simpsons, and the entire stable of well-known Disney characters, including Mickey Mouse and Donald Duck.

1930 are still under copyright in the United States. Copyrightable story and character elements first introduced in these stories are under copyright and may not be used without permission of the Conan Doyle estate (unless the use constitutes a fair use).

The courts have held that these include the fictional facts that Holmes retired from his detective agency in 1926, Dr. Watson's background as an athlete, and Watson's second wife. *Klinger v. Conan Doyle Estate, Ltd.*, 755 F.3d 496 (7th Cir. 2014).)

This leads to an important question: When the first work in which a character appears enters the public domain, is the character available for use in new stories and contexts despite the fact that other works containing the same character are still under copyright? In other words, can you use the Holmes character even though he is portrayed in many works that are still copyrighted?

The answer is yes. You can copy the character as it appeared in its original public domain source. But you cannot copy any new traits or other character changes that were added in the later copyrighted works. For example, you can copy Sherlock Holmes as he appeared in the original Conan Doyle stories. But you can't copy any new material later authors added to their own works about Holmes that are still under copyright.

A character's name is never copyrightable by itself. However, a character's name may be a protected trademark law if it is used to identify the source of goods or services other than the literary work itself. Examples include Harry Potter, Indiana Jones, and Mickey Mouse.

> ## CAUTION
>
> **Other laws besides copyright law have been used to legally protect characters, particularly visual characters such as cartoon characters.** These laws include state and federal trademark laws and state unfair use and misappropriation laws (see Chapter 20).

Standard Situations
(*Scènes à Faire*)

There are certain sequences of events, scenes, situations, or details that necessarily follow from a fictional work's given theme or setting. The French call these *scènes à faire* (that which must follow from a certain situation). *Scènes à faire* are indispensable, or at least standard, in the treatment of a given topic. They flow conventionally from the situation being portrayed and are therefore in the public domain. Examples of *scènes à faire* include the following:

- A scene in the reality game show *Survivor* in which the contestants on a hostile deserted island who were deprived of food ate worms. *CBS Broadcasting, Inc. v. ABC, Inc.,* No. 02-CV-08813-LAP (S.D.N.Y. 2003).

- Scenes involving attempted escapes, flights through the woods pursued by baying dogs, and the sorrowful or happy singing of slaves, in a novel about slavery. *Alexander v. Haley*, 460 F.Supp. 40 (S.D.N.Y. 1978).

- Scenes involving hard-drinking Irish cops, drunks, prostitutes, vermin, and derelict cars, in a story about police work in the South Bronx. *Walker v. Time-Life Films*, 784 F.2d 44 (2d Cir. 1986).

- Treasure maps, ghost pirates, the "undead," ships flying black sails, skeletons, privateers, naval attacks, dark fog, the "pirate code," ghosts, sea monsters, "pirates searching for treasure," "cockiness, bravery, and drunkenness" among pirates, pirates who wear dark clothing and have facial hair, 10-year curses, and settings such as ships, port towns, and the Caribbean generally in the *Pirates of the Caribbean* series of films. *Alfred v. The Walt Disney Co.*, 388 F.Supp.3d 1174 (C.D. Cal. 2019).

However, to the extent they are original, the particular words an author uses to describe or narrate a *scène à faire* are protected by copyright, even though the idea for the scene is not. Thus, although any author can write a police novel that includes a scene involving a high-speed chase, he could not copy the words another author used to describe a similar chase in a previously published police novel.

Literary Devices

Literary devices such as the story-within-a-story, flashbacks, the epistolary novel (novels consisting of fictional letters), stream of consciousness, prosodic forms and rhetorical devices such as alliteration are all unprotectable ideas. These and most other literary devices are all in the public domain. Only the particular way an author uses such a device is copyrighted, not the device itself.

Unprotected Elements in Works of Fact

Works of fact include histories, biographies, political science, philosophy, law, the social and hard sciences, reference works, and similar works. This includes not just books devoted to these subjects, but magazines, journals, and periodicals as well. There are elements contained in works of fact that are in the public domain.

Research

The facts that an author discovers in the course of research are in the public domain, free to all. This is so even if an author spends considerable effort conducting the research. Copyright does not protect the fruits of creative research, no matter how grueling or time-consuming the research may have been. Copyright protects only the way an author expresses the facts.

> **EXAMPLE:** Otto Eisenschiml, a renowned Civil War historian, wrote a book on Abraham Lincoln's assassination. The book contained much original research, including facts obtained from police records that had never before been analyzed. Subsequently, a freelance writer wrote a magazine article on Lincoln's assassination that used many of the new facts unearthed by Eisenschiml.

The freelancer could have examined the police records himself, but he didn't. He simply used in his own article the facts as represented by Eisenschiml. Eishenschiml sued the writer and magazine for copyright infringement and lost. The court held that the facts he had unearthed were in the public domain. *Eisenschiml v. Fawcett Publications*, 246 F.2d 598 (7th Cir. 1957).

Interpretations

An author's interpretation of facts is itself a fact (or a purported fact) that is deduced from other facts. Interpretations are therefore also in the public domain. This is so whether or not they are really true. For example, an author's theory that the *Hindenburg* dirigible crashed because of sabotage was held to be in the public domain. This meant that a screenwriter was free to write a screenplay based on the idea that the *Hindenburg* blew up due to sabotage. *Hoehling v. Universal City Studios*, 618 F.2d 972 (2d Cir. 1980).

Quotations

The author of a news story, biography, history, oral history, or similar work may not claim copyright ownership of statements made by others and quoted in the work. This is because a verbatim quotation of what someone else says is not original.

EXAMPLE: The author of a book about motion pictures conducted an interview with Michael Wayne, John Wayne's son, and included quotes from the interview in the book. Subsequently, *Newsweek* magazine published an obituary of Wayne that used some of these quotations. The author sued *Newsweek* for copyright infringement and lost. The court held that the author held no copyright in the quotations because they were not original—that is, the author didn't say them, Michael Wayne did. *Suid v. Newsweek Magazine*, 503 F.Supp. 146 (D.D.C. 1980).

However, this doesn't mean that quotations are always in the public domain. If the quote is written down or otherwise recorded with the speaker's authorization, federal copyright law protects it.

Typically, the person who writes down or records the speaker's words will have the speaker's permission to use the quotes. Such permission may be express or implied by the fact that the speaker consented to an interview. In some cases, the interview subject may transfer his or her copyright rights to the interviewer. A written transfer agreement must be signed to accomplish this.

EXAMPLE: In the case involving Michael Wayne mentioned above, the author had Wayne sign a release giving him the right to use Wayne's words in his book. Michael Wayne could have sued *Newsweek* for copying his words without permission. However, it's highly likely such a lawsuit would have been unsuccessful. News organizations have broad latitude under the fair use privilege to use quotations without permission.

In addition, a conversation reconstructed by an author from memory, rather than quoted verbatim from written notes or a recording, may be protectable by the author (not the person who made the original remarks) if some originality was involved in reconstructing the conversation. *Harris v. Miller*, 50 U.S.P.Q. 306 (S.D.N.Y. 1941).

> **EXAMPLE:** Imagine that a famous writer named Evelyn writes a memoir about her experiences over many decades. She discusses all the famous writers and other interesting people she has known. She also includes in her book many fascinating and witty conversations she has had with the great and near great. However, none of these conversations contain verbatim quotations. Rather, she has reconstructed them from memory. She has embellished or even made up the words in these reconstructed conversations. Evelyn is entitled to a copyright in these reconstructions.

If a person creates a book of quotations that are in the public domain because they are copied from public domain books, articles, and other sources, the book may be a copyrighted compilation, although the individual quotations are not protected. *Quinto v. Legal Times of Washington*, 506 F.Supp. 554 (D.D.C. 1981). One or more of the individual quotations in such a book could be copied without the compiler's permission, but verbatim copying of the entire book would infringe on the compiler's copyright.

There are many instances where quotations *are* in the public domain. For example:

- A quotation by a federal government employee spoken as part of his or her duties is in the public domain. (See Chapter 3.) This includes official speeches by the president and members of Congress.

- Quotations that are written down and published enter the public domain when the copyright in the published work expires (see Chapter 18) or, in some cases, if the work is published without a valid copyright notice (see Chapter 19).

- Quotations that are simply short phrases may also be in the public domain (see Chapter 3).

- Quotations from public domain sources—for example, from a book whose copyright has expired, such as the King James Version of the Bible—are in the public domain. Republishing them in a new work does not revive their copyright.

In addition, for a quotation to be copyrightable, it must be written down or recorded *with the speaker's authorization*. A quotation recorded without the speaker's authorization is not protected by copyright. Good examples are the many phone conversations Linda Tripp had with Monica Lewinsky that Tripp secretly recorded without Lewinsky's permission (as part of the 1998 Clinton-Lewinsky scandal). Lewinsky's portions of these conversations are not protected by copyright. Unless they can be protected under state law (see below), they are in the public domain.

The above discussion applies only to quotations that are written down or otherwise recorded. What about things people say that are not written down or recorded at the time or soon after? Are they entitled to any legal protection? The federal copyright laws do not protect a quotation that is spoken by someone but not recorded in any way, but it might be protected under state law. State copyright laws, also called common law copyright, can protect works of authorship that have never been written down or otherwise fixed in a tangible medium of expression (see Chapter 2).

However, the extent of such protection is far from clear. Several state courts have been reluctant to extend such protection very far. For example, a New York state court refused to give state law protection to a conversation the author Ernest Hemingway had with his biographer A.E. Hotchner, which Hotchner reproduced in the book *Papa Hemingway* many years after Hemingway's death. The court held that for an oral statement to be protected by state law, the speaker would have to "mark off the utterance in question from the ordinary stream of speech" and indicate that he or she wished to exercise control over its publication. *Estate of Hemingway v. Random House*, 244 N.E.2d 250 (N.Y. 1968). Of course, people rarely do this in ordinary conversation.

GRAY AREA

The extent of legal protection for quotations that have never been written down or recorded is a gray area of the law. See Chapter 1 for a detailed discussion about how to deal with such public domain gray areas.

Fictional Elements

Fictional elements in otherwise factual works are entitled to full copyright protection. For example, a biographer who finds his subject's actual life story boring and embellishes his biography with a fictional love affair is entitled to copyright protection for the fictional portions of the work. *DeAcosta v. Brown*, 146 F.2d 408 (2d Cir. 1944).

However, if an author represents his work to be completely factual, he or she may not bring a copyright infringement suit against someone who relied on that representation and copied a portion of it thinking it was unprotectable fact when it was really protectable fiction. In other words, an author cannot trick the public into thinking that a fictional element is really factual and then sue for copyright infringement. *Houts v. Universal City Studios*, 603 F.Supp. 26 (C.D. Cal. 1984).

If the work involved is a news story, there need be no express statement in the story that it is completely factual. News stories are presumed by the public to be factual. *Davies v. Bowes*, 209 53 (S.D. N.Y. 1913). But if the work is a history or biography, the author must expressly state that the work is completely factual. For example, the author of a biography of Wyatt Earp was not allowed to sue for copyright infringement when someone copied fictional elements contained in the biography because the book stated that it was "in no part a mythic tale." *Lake v. Columbia Broadcasting System, Inc.*, 140 F.Supp. 707 (S.D. Cal. 1956).

This means that if the author of a history, biography, or other nonfiction work does *not* expressly state that the work is completely factual, a person who copies fictional elements from such a work could be liable for copyright infringement. One way to avoid such liability, of course, is to double-check the author's work to make sure you are only using facts.

Organization of Material

To write a factual work, the author must select and arrange the factual material.

The facts themselves are in the public domain, but the author's selection and arrangement of them can be copyrightable if it's original.

However, where the range of choices available to an author as to how to arrange the work is severely limited, there will be little or no copyright protection for the arrangement. For example, an author of a work of history who selects and arranges the historical facts in chronological order cannot claim copyright in such arrangement. Obviously, any other historian who wishes to write about the same events in chronological order—the most common method of organizing historical material—must follow a similar or identical selection and arrangement. Moreover, an historical chronology is itself a fact that is not copyrightable. *Norman v. Columbia Broadcasting System, Inc.*, 333 F.Supp. 788 (S.D.N.Y. 1971).

However, a historian who writes about an event in an unconventional—that is, a nonchronological—way, could likely claim copyright protection for his or her selection and arrangement. For example, if an author writes a history of the kings and queens of England and organizes the material on the basis of the monarchs' astrological signs, this eccentric selection and arrangement would likely be copyrightable. If a second author copied this same selection and arrangement, that author would likely be guilty of copyright infringement.

Copyrights Restored From Public Domain

The GATT Agreement 272

What Works Were Restored? 273

    Three Requirements for Restoration 273

    How Many Works Have Been Restored? 275

What Works Were Not Restored? 276

    Works in the Public Domain in Their Home Countries 277

    Works Simultaneously Published in the United States and Abroad 277

    Works Published in Countries With No U.S. Copyright Relations 278

Who Owns Restored Works? 278

Copyright Infringement of Restored Works 278

    Liability for Continuing to Use Restored Works 278

On January 1, 1996 something unprecedented in the history of American copyright law occurred. Because of an international trade treaty called GATT, millions of foreign works in the U.S. public domain had their copyrights restored. In other words, many works first published outside the United States were withdrawn from the public domain.

Among the foreign works whose copyright protection was restored were many masterpieces of world cinema, including *Grand Illusion* (France, 1937), *Breathless* (France, 1959), *The Bicycle Thief* (Italy, 1949), *The Blue Angel* (Germany, 1931), and *The Third Man* (United Kingdom, 1949).

Untold thousands of foreign musical works that used to be in the public domain in the United States also had their protection restored. This includes virtually the complete works of the great Soviet composers Sergei Prokofiev, Aram Khachaturian, and Dimitri Shostakovich.

No one can even guess how many foreign written works have had their copyrights restored, but the number must be enormous.

You need to clearly understand which foreign works have had their copyrights restored before you can conclude that any work first published outside the United States is in the public domain in the United States.

 SKIP AHEAD

If the work you're interested in was first published in the United States, it doesn't qualify for copyright restoration and you don't have to read this chapter. Nor does copyright restoration apply to any unpublished work.

The GATT Agreement

The copyright restoration came about as a result of longtime efforts by the U.S. government to enter into comprehensive international trade agreements reducing or eliminating tariffs and otherwise freeing up world trade. In 1994, the United States signed the General Agreement on Tariffs and Trade (known as GATT), an extensive international treaty dealing with many aspects of international trade. The GATT agreement required that the United States restore copyright protection for foreign works that had entered the public domain because the foreign copyright owners failed to comply with certain copyright formalities or because the United States had no copyright relations with the foreign country where the work was published.

The U.S. copyright law has, in fact, been rewritten to implement this provision, and works meeting the GATT requirements had their copyrights automatically restored on January 1, 1996. The United States Supreme Court has ruled that this retroactive copyright extension for foreign works does not violate the U.S. Constitution. *Golan v. Holder*, 556 U.S. (2012).

What Works Were Restored?

Foreign works in the public domain as of January 1, 1996 qualified for copyright restoration if they were published:

- between January 1, 1923 and March 1, 1989 without a proper copyright notice (see Chapter 19), or
- during the years 1923-1963 but never had their copyrights renewed by filing an application with the U.S. Copyright Office during the 28th year after publication (see Chapter 21), or
- in countries with which the United States had no copyright relations.

Three Requirements for Restoration

Any foreign published work falling into any one of the three categories listed above had its U.S. copyright automatically restored on January 1, 1996 if it met all three of the following requirements:

- It had at least one author who was a citizen or resident of a country other than the United States that has copyright relations with the United States, which includes all the countries of the world except for Eritrea, Ethiopia, Iran, Iraq, and San Marino.

- It was *first* published in a country with which the United States has copyright relations, but not published in the United States within 30 days following the foreign publication.
- Its copyright protection had not expired under the copyright laws of the country of foreign publication as of January 1, 1996 (see below).

Works meeting these requirements receive the same term of copyright protection in the United States that they would have had if they had never entered the public domain.

EXAMPLE: Assume that in 1950, Thames Press, a British publisher, published in Great Britain a novel called *Sticky Wicket*, by the English writer John Jones, who died in 1970. Thames failed to file a renewal registration for the book in 1978, and as result it entered the public domain in the United States on January 1, 1979. However, the U.S. copyright in the book was automatically restored by the GATT agreement on January 1, 1996. This is because the work was written by a British subject, first published in a country with which the United States has copyright relations, and the British copyright on the book had not expired as of 1995, because British copyrights last for the life of the author plus 70 years.

The book receives the same term of copyright protection in the United States that it would have had if a renewal been filed on time—a term of 95 years from the date of publication. The novel will be protected by copyright in the United States until December 31, 2045.

Where a Work Was First Published

Copyright restoration applies only to works first published outside the United States. There is no single source for finding where a work was first published. You may have to look in a variety of places and do extensive research. There is no one best way to make this determination. How you go about your research depends on the type of work involved, how much time you have, and whether you have access to the Internet. Here are some useful resources and techniques you can use:

Examine the work. If possible, obtain a copy of the work and examine it carefully. Books, magazines, newspapers, sheet music, films, maps, and other published works often say where they were published or printed. But even if the work you obtain shows it was published in the United States, it may not have been originally published here. Many works initially published outside the United States are republished in the United States. Very often, the work will indicate where it was first published.

If the work is in a language other than English or was translated into English from a foreign language, it likely was first published outside the United States, but this isn't always the case.

Check library catalogs. You may be able to determine whether a work was published by checking the Library of Congress Online Catalog at https://catalog.loc.gov. The catalog contains over 12 million records for books, magazines, newspapers, and other serials, cartographic materials, music, and visual materials in the library's collection. The library's records typically give a work's country of publication.

Check Copyright Office records. If the work was registered with the U.S. Copyright Office, checking Copyright Office registration records will reveal in what country it was first published. These records can be researched online. (See Chapter 21.) However, not all published works are registered with the Copyright Office, so there may be no record for it.

Check reference works. There are hundreds of reference works that may be able to tell you where a work was published. For example, in the realm of literature these include such works as *Contemporary Authors*, *Contemporary Literary Criticism*, and the *Dictionary of Literary Biography*, all published by Gale Research. Go to a public or university library with a good reference section and ask the reference librarian for assistance.

Research the author. Researching the author of the work may reveal where the work was published. First, determine the author's home country. Works by authors who are not U.S. citizens or residents are typically

Where a Work Was First Published (continued)

first published outside the United States and vice versa. However, this isn't always the case. If the author is well known, a biography or critical study may have a detailed publication history for his or her works.

Use the Internet. Many helpful reference works and information about authors and their works are available on the Internet. Do a Web search using the author's name, the name of the work involved, and the publisher. There may be a website devoted to the author or even to the particular work, or some online reference with detailed information about the work. Other specialized websites may prove helpful. For example, the Internet Movie Database, at www.imdb.com, lists the country of origin for most theatrical films.

Contact the publisher. Contact the work's publisher and ask them to tell you if the work was first published in the United States or abroad.

TIP

A useful rule of thumb: It's *very* likely that any work first published within the last 50 years in any foreign country other than Eritrea, Ethiopia, Iran, Iraq, or San Marino qualifies for copyright restoration. You can assume that such works are not in the public domain. Or, if you wish, you can research the work's publishing history to make sure.

How Many Works Have Been Restored?

Nobody has any idea of the exact number of foreign works that had their U.S. copyrights restored, but the number is large. This is because substantial numbers of foreign copyright owners failed to comply with U.S. copyright formalities. Foreign authors and publishers often failed to place copyright notices on their published works, since notices have never been required in most foreign countries. Even more common, however, they failed to renew works published before 1964. Renewal was required even for works published outside the United States. The Copyright Office estimates that only about 15% of pre-1964 published works were ever renewed. The percentage may be even lower for foreign works. The result of this noncompliance with U.S. copyright formalities was that millions of foreign works entered the U.S. public domain even though they were still protected in their home countries and most other countries.

No Restoration for Works by Americans

The copyright restoration law applies only to works with at least one non-American author. Works authored solely by Americans don't qualify, even if they were first published outside the U.S. An American photographer named George Barris found this out the hard way. In 1962, he took a series of photographs of Marilyn Monroe which were published that year in the British newspaper *The Daily Mirror*. Two or three years later an American artist used the photos in a collage without Barris's permission. Unfortunately, Barris never timely renewed the photos. So, by the time he got around to suing the artist and others for copyright infringement in the late 1990s, his photos had entered the public domain in the United States. The restoration law didn't help Barris because he was an American. Had he been British (or any other non-American), the copyright in the photos would have been restored on Jan. 1, 1996 and he could have had a successful lawsuit. Who said life was fair? *Barris v. Hamilton*, No. 96 CIV. 9541 (DAB) (S.D.N.Y. 1999).

Moreover, a surprisingly large number of works were in the public domain in the United States because it had no copyright relations with the country of publication.

For example, until 1973 the United States had no copyright relations with the Soviet Union. All works published before 1973 in the Soviet Union were in the public domain in the United States. Most of these works have now had their copyrights restored.

You can visit the Copyright Office website, at www.copyright.gov, and view lists the Copyright Office has compiled of some of the works whose copyrights have been restored. These lists were compiled from legal notices that foreign copyright owners filed with the Copyright Office informing the Office and the world that they intended to enforce their newly restored copyrights. Most of the works on the lists are foreign films and musical works. However, these lists represent only a tiny fraction of all the foreign works whose copyrights have been restored.

What Works Were Not Restored?

Don't get the idea that *every* foreign work has had its U.S. copyright restored. Millions of foreign works are still in the public domain in the United States. These include works in the public domain in their home countries, works simultaneously published in the United States and abroad, and works published in countries with no U.S. copyright relations.

Works in the Public Domain in Their Home Countries

A significant group of foreign works that does not qualify for copyright restoration is works whose copyright expired in their home countries as of January 1, 1996, the date U.S. copyright restoration took effect.

To know if this exception applies, you need to know the copyright term of the foreign author's country. You also need to know when the author died. This is because, in most foreign countries, the copyright terms for most works last for a given number of years after the author dies.

Copyright terms differ from country to country; they also differ according to the type of work involved. However, copyrights last for at least 50 years in almost all foreign countries, so this exception could only apply to works published before 1946. In the case of most individually authored works such as books, music, and art, copyrights in most countries last for the life of the author plus 50 years, or the life of the author plus 70 years.

> EXAMPLE: Ken published a song with a copyright notice in Canada in 1940. The song was never renewed and so entered the public domain in the United States on January 1, 1969. Ken died in 1942, so the song entered the public domain in Canada on January 1, 1993 because copyrights last for the life of the author plus 50 years in Canada. The song was in the public domain in Canada on January 1, 1996, so it didn't qualify for U.S. copyright restoration. It remains in the public domain in the United States.

Unlike Canada, virtually all Western European countries extend copyright protection for 70 years after an author dies. So this exception would apply only to works published by most European authors who died before 1926.

See Chapter 16 for a detailed discussion of foreign copyright terms.

Works Simultaneously Published in the United States and Abroad

Before 1989, U.S. publishers could obtain copyright protection in many foreign countries only by publishing a work simultaneously at home and in a foreign country that had signed a major international copyright treaty called the Berne Convention. The work had to be published in both countries within 30 days. American publishers commonly had their works published simultaneously in the United States and Canada or Great Britain. This fact was usually indicated on the same page as the copyright notice. These works do not qualify for copyright restoration because they are really American works that were also published abroad.

Works Published in Countries With No U.S. Copyright Relations

Works published in almost all foreign countries are entitled to full U.S. copyright protection. However, there are a handful of countries with which the United States has no copyright relations: Eritrea, Ethiopia, Iran, Iraq, and San Marino.

A work first published in any of these countries by a citizen or resident of any of these countries is not entitled to U.S. copyright protection. Nor does it qualify for copyright restoration. In other words, it is in the public domain.

Who Owns Restored Works?

The author initially owns the U.S. copyright in a restored work. The laws of the country where the work was first published defined who the author is. If the author died before January 1, 1996, ownership is determined under the inheritance laws of the author's country. U.S. federal courts, applying the law of the country of origin, decide disputes concerning initial ownership of restored foreign copyrights.

If the author at any time assigned, licensed, or otherwise transferred all or part of his or her rights, the transfer is supposed to be given effect according to the terms of the agreement. Disputes concerning copyright transfers must be resolved in U.S. state courts applying U.S. copyright law.

Copyright Infringement of Restored Works

No one can use a restored work *for the first time* after January 1, 1996 without obtaining the copyright owner's permission. "Use" means exercising any of the copyright owner's exclusive rights to copy, distribute, create derivative works from, or publicly display or perform the work. The owner of a restored work can bring a copyright infringement action against anyone who unlawfully uses the work after January 1, 1996 just as for any other work still under copyright.

But what if you used a restored foreign work before January 1, 1996, when it was in the public domain? There's no need to worry about this. You aren't liable for any uses you made of the work before 1996.

Liability for Continuing to Use Restored Works

Things are more complicated, however, if businesses or people used a restored work without permission before January 1, 1996 and *continued to use the work in the same way* after that date. Such people are called "reliance parties." They can't be sued for copyright infringement unless:

- the owner of the restored copyright sends them directly a Notice of Intent to Enforce Copyright, or
- the owner filed such a notice with the Copyright Office between 1996 and 1997, when such notices were permitted to be filed there.

The filing of a Notice of Intent to Enforce a Copyright starts a 12-month clock running, during which time the copyright owner is not allowed to enforce the copyright against the reliance party. During this 12-month period, the reliance party may sell off previously manufactured stock, publicly perform or display the work, or authorize others to do so. A reliance party cannot make new copies of the restored work during this period or use it differently than it was used before January 1, 1996, unless permission is obtained from the work's copyright owner.

After the 12 months are up, the reliance party must stop using the restored work unless a licensing agreement is reached with the copyright owner for continued use of the work. If the copyright owner filed the Notice of Intent to Enforce Copyright with the Copyright Office between 1996 and 1997, the 12-month period is already up.

If a licensing agreement is not reached and the reliance party continues to use the restored work, the copyright owner can sue for copyright infringement for any unauthorized uses occurring after the 12-month period expires. But a copyright owner cannot sue a reliance party for any unauthorized uses that occurred before the 12-month notice period ended, provided the party used the work the same way before January 1, 1996.

However, the rules are different if the reliance party created a derivative work from the restored work while it was in the public domain. In this event, the reliance party may continue to exploit the derivative work—and may do so forever, even after being sent a Notice of Intent to Enforce Copyright. But the reliance party must pay the copyright owner of the restored work a reasonable license fee for using the work after its copyright was restored. This is a mandatory license—that is, the owner of the restored work must let the reliance party exploit the derivative work so long as it is compensated.

EXAMPLE: In the 1950s, a Danish woodcarver named Thomas Dam created a troll doll out of rubber for his daughter. The doll proved very popular with children, and Dam eventually opened his own factory to manufacture and sell it. He exported the doll into the United States in 1961. Unfortunately, proper copyright notice was not included on the dolls and as a result they entered the public domain in the United States under the law then in effect. A few years later, Russ Berrie began manufacturing and selling a very similar troll doll in the United States. The Danish company that manufactured the authorized Dam trolls could do nothing about it at the time because the Dam troll doll was public domain in the United States. On Jan. 1, 1996 the U.S. copyright in the Dam troll doll was automatically restored. On Feb. 13, 2001 Dam gave Berrie a Notice of Intent to Enforce Copyright in the doll, and litigation ensued. The trial court held that the copyright in the doll had been restored and therefore Berrie had to stop selling his troll doll after Feb. 13, 2002, one year after it received Dam's Notice. Berrie appealed, and the court agreed that Dam's U.S. copyright in the troll doll had been restored. However, the court threw a wrench in the works because it held that it was unclear whether Berrie's troll doll was a derivative work based upon Dam's original troll doll. If true, this meant Berrie could continue to sell his doll in the United States, but would have to pay Dam reasonable compensation for its mandatory license. The matter was sent back to a trial court for a determination as to whether Berrie's doll was a derivative work, and the parties eventually settled. *Dam Things from Denmark v. Russ Berrie & Co., Inc.*, 290 F.3d 548 (3d Cir. 2002).

What to Do If You're a Reliance Party

If you're a reliance party—here's what you should do:

First, check Copyright Office records to see if the owner of the work filed an NIE with the Copyright Office during 1996-1997. The Copyright Office has posted a list of all filed NIEs on its website, at www.copyright. gov. You can also search for them by using the Copyright Office's online database, which is accessed from the same website.

If an NIE has been filed, stop using the work. You'll be liable for any unauthorized uses of the work that occurred 12 months after the NIE was filed, even though you were not aware of the filing. You could seek out the copyright owners of the restored work and obtain their permission to use it again. Be aware, however, that this could bring your infringement to the owners' attention and open you up to a lawsuit if you can't reach an agreement on licensing the work.

If no NIE was filed with the Copyright Office or sent to you directly, you may decide to continue to use the restored work. But you must use it in the *exact* same way as you did before 1996. You won't be liable for that kind of use until one year after the copyright owner sends you an NIE, if they ever do. Alternatively, you may stop using the work or obtain permission from the copyright owner to continue using it.

Notice of Intent to Enforce a Copyright Restored
Under the Uruguay Round Agreements Act (URAA)

1. Title: _____Sticky Wicket_____

   (If this work does not have a title, state "No title.")

   OR

   Brief description of work (for untitled works only). _____

   _____

   _____

2. English translation of title (if applicable): _____

   _____

3. Alternative title(s) (if any): _____

   _____

4. Type of work (e.g., painting, sculpture, music, motion picture, sound recording, book): _____book_____

5. Name(s) of author(s) ____Eric Blair_____

   _____

6. Source country: _____United Kingdom_____

7. Approximate year of publication: _____1935_____

8. Additional identifying information (e.g., for movies: director, leading actors, screenwriter, animator; for photographs: subject matter; for books: editor, publisher, contributors, subject matter): _____

   ___Published by Thames Press_____

   ___Edited by John Malcolm_____

9. Name of copyright owner (statements may be filed in the name of the owner of the restored copyright or the owner of an exclusive right therein):

   ___Sally Blair_____

   _____

10. If you are not the owner of all rights, specify the rights you own (e.g., the right to reproduce/distribute/publicly display/publicly perform the work, or to prepare a derivative work based on the work). _____

_____

_____

_____

11. Address at which copyright owner may be contacted. (Give the complete address, including the country, and an "attention" line, or "in care of" name, if necessary.)

___Sally Blair_____

___123 Mayfield Road_____

___Walton-on-Thames, Surrey_____

___United Kingdom_____

12. Telephone number of owner: ____123-555-6789_____

13. Telefax number of owner: _____123-555-8900_____

14. Certification and signature

I hereby certify that, for each of the work(s) listed above, I am the copyright owner, or the owner of an exclusive right, or one's authorized agent, the agency relationship having been constituted in a writing signed by the owner before the filing of this notice, and that the information given herein is true and correct to the best of my knowledge.

Signature: ____Sally Blair_____

Name (printed or typed): __Sally Blair_____

As agent for (if applicable): _____

Date: ____2/1/xx_____

Note: Notices of Intent to Enforce must be in English, except for the original title, and either typed or printed by hand legibly in dark, preferably black, ink. They must be on 8½" × 11" white paper of good quality, with at least a one-inch (or three cm) margin.

The Public Domain Outside the United States

Introduction..284

    Different Copyright Terms 284

    Different Coverage of Copyright Laws..285

    Moral Rights..285

    If a Work Is in the Public Domain in the United States but Not Abroad.......286

Copyright Duration in Other Countries...287

    European Union 287

    Canada..290

    China 292

    Japan 292

    Russia...293

The Rule of the Shorter Term...294

    Impact of Rule on U.S. Works...294

    Countries That Do Not Follow the Rule 295

Researching Foreign Copyright Laws 297

    Books..297

    Websites 298

To explain the rules of copyright around the world would take a whole book. Here, we give you a general idea of how long copyright lasts in most major countries and explain why many works created in the United States are still under copyright here, but in the public domain outside the United States.

> **CAUTION**
>
> **If you want to know whether a work is in the public domain in a foreign country you must research that country's copyright laws.** You can do this yourself with the aid of the resources listed at the end of this chapter, or hire an experienced international copyright attorney to help you.

Introduction

There is no single international copyright law that applies in all the countries of the world. Instead, each country has its own copyright law that operates within its own borders. However, through a series of international treaties, almost every nation has agreed to give citizens of other nations the same protection they give their own citizens.

This means that you must look at the laws of the country where you want to use the work to determine whether it is in the public domain. For example, if you want know whether a book published in Germany in 1925 is in the public domain in the United States, you must rely on U.S. copyright law for the answer. If you want to know whether the book is in the public domain in Germany, you must look to German copyright law. If you want to know whether the book is in the public domain in Canada, you must look to Canadian copyright law.

Because the copyright laws of various countries often differ dramatically, a work in the public domain in the United States is not necessarily in the public domain outside the United States.

Different Copyright Terms

In 1998, the United States amended its copyright law, bringing the length of copyright terms more in line with Western Europe. However, for works published before 1978, the U.S. copyright terms are still very different than most foreign terms. As a result, millions of works that are in the public domain in the United States are still under copyright in many foreign countries. For example, all the songs of Irving Berlin published over 95 years ago are in the public domain in the United States because the copyright has expired. However, all of these songs are still under copyright in Canada because Canadian copyright lasts for the life of the author plus 50 years (Berlin died in 1989). This means if you want to use the songs in Canada, you must obtain permission from Berlin's heirs.

However, because of something called the rule of the shorter term, works that are in the public domain in the United States are automatically in the public domain in many foreign countries as well, including most of Western Europe. Countries that use the rule of the shorter term treat works in the public domain in the United States as in the public domain in their own countries as well. (This rule is discussed in more detail later in this chapter.)

There are also many works that are protected in the United States but are in the public domain in many foreign countries because their copyrights have expired in those countries.

Different Coverage of Copyright Laws

There are also major differences in the types of works that can have copyright protection in the United States and many foreign countries. Here are just a few examples:

- U.S. government publications are in the public domain under U.S. copyright law, while many foreign governments, including the United Kingdom and Canada, claim copyright in their publications under their own copyright laws.
- In most of Western Europe, commercial databases are given a unique form of copyright protection prohibiting

unauthorized extraction of the data for ten years. This is not the case under U.S. law.

- In several countries, including the United Kingdom and China, copyright protection is granted to typography. If a public domain work is republished with original typography, the work may not be photocopied or otherwise reproduced in a manner that reproduces the typography, although the words of the public domain work can be copied by hand or typed. U.S. copyright law does not protect typography.
- In many countries, including the United Kingdom and Italy, copyright protection is granted to new typefaces. If a public domain work is republished with a copyrighted typeface, the work may not be photocopied or otherwise reproduced in a manner that reproduces the typeface, although the words of the public domain work can be copied by hand or typed. U.S. copyright law does not protect typefaces (see Chapter 5).

Moral Rights

Another major difference between U.S. copyright law and the copyright laws of most foreign countries is what are called moral rights, which consist of:

- the right of integrity—the author's right to control alterations of his or her work and to prevent its destruction
- the right of paternity—the right to be recognized as author of a work, or, if the author so chooses, the right to disclaim authorship, and
- the right of disclosure (also called the right of dissemination), which is the author's right to decide when to release his or her work into the public arena.

Moral rights last at least as long as a work's copyright and in many countries they last longer. In several countries, the rights of integrity and paternity last forever.

For example, because of moral rights, it may be illegal in some countries to:

- colorize a black-and-white movie, even if its copyright has expired
- republish a public domain work without identifying the author, or
- destroy or deface a work of art in the public domain.

United States copyright law gives some limited moral rights—the rights of attribution and paternity—to visual artists, but the rights don't apply to any works that are in the public domain in the United States.

Ordinarily, you don't need to worry about moral rights if you plan to republish a work that has been published and is now in the public domain in the country where you want to use it and you are careful to give credit to the author. However, if you plan to alter the work in any way, you could end up violating the author's moral rights unless you get permission for the changes.

Moral rights laws differ from country to country. To know how they may affect your use of a work in a particular country, you must research that country's copyright laws (or hire an attorney to do so for you). A list of foreign copyright law resources is provided at the end of this chapter.

Among the countries that recognize one or more of the moral rights described above are:

Argentina	Hungary
Australia	India
Belgium	Israel
Brazil	Italy
Canada	Japan
China	Netherlands
Czech Republic	Poland
France	Spain
Germany	Sweden
Greece	Switzerland
Hong Kong	United Kingdom

If a Work Is in the Public Domain in the United States but Not Abroad

What should you do if a work is in the public domain in the United States, but not in the public domain in a foreign country such as Canada or the United Kingdom? If you want to use the material copyrighted in that country, you'll have to get permission.

EXAMPLE: Repulsive Pictures creates a movie based on a play that is in the public domain in the United States, but not in Canada. Repulsive needs permission from the copyright owner of the play to distribute the movie in Canada.

If you fail to get such permission, you could be sued for copyright infringement in the foreign country. It might even be possible for the copyright owner to sue you in the United States for violating his or her foreign copyright rights.

To avoid such potential legal liability, some companies won't sell copies of works in the public domain in the United States in foreign countries where they are still protected by copyright. For example, Dover Publications, Inc., a U.S. company that publishes many public domain works in the United States, won't ship such works to any country in which they still have copyright protection.

Copyright Duration in Other Countries

Almost all of the world's developed countries have signed an international copyright treaty called the Berne Convention, requiring them to grant copyright protection for 50 years after an author dies. However, this is a minimum requirement. Most countries grant authors much longer copyright terms.

A chart showing the basic copyright terms of all the countries of the world can be found at the Wikipedia website at https://en.wikipedia.org/wiki/List_of_countries%27_copyright_lengths.

SEE AN EXPERT

This section explains the copyright terms of many of the largest countries. If the country you are interested in is not discussed here, refer to the end of this chapter for resources you can use to learn about its copyright term, or consult with a copyright attorney.

European Union

The European Union (EU) is a unique supranational union made up of most of the nations of Europe including Austria, Belgium, Bulgaria, Croatia, Cyprus, the Czech Republic, Denmark, Estonia, Finland, France, Germany, Greece, Hungary, Ireland, Italy, Latvia, Lithuania, Luxembourg, Malta, the Netherlands, Poland, Portugal, Romania, Slovakia, Slovenia, Spain, and Sweden. The United Kingdom is leaving the EU in 2020—a process dubbed "Brexit").

Among the EU's many accomplishments is establishment of a frontier-free internal market allowing for free movement of people, goods, services, and capital; and adoption of a single currency, the euro.

The EU nations have also standardized many aspects of their legal systems, a process called harmonization. This includes European copyright laws. Every EU country has its own copyright law, but they have all adopted a single set of copyright duration rules.

The Basic Copyright Terms

The copyright terms discussed below apply throughout the EU to any work authored by an EU national. It makes no difference if the work was published in an EU country, or a country outside the EU such as the United States. Thus, for example, a work published in the United States by a French national receives the same copyright term in the EU as if it were published in France or another EU country (but its copyright term in the United States would be determined under American, not EU, copyright law).

Works by Americans are also given these copyright terms within the EU unless the rule of the shorter term requires that the U.S. copyright term be applied. Subject to some minor variations, the copyright terms in all the EU countries are as follows (all terms run to the end of the calendar year):

- The general copyright term is the life of the author plus 70 years—this applies to both published and unpublished works. If a work has more than one author, the copyright term lasts for 70 years after the death of the last living author. If a work is published anonymously or the author uses a pseudonym, the copyright lasts for 70 years from the date of publication. However, if the identity of the real author is not in doubt, the copyright protection lasts for 70 years after the author dies.

- The copyright in movies lasts for 70 years after the death of the last of the following people: the principal director, the author of the screenplay, the author of the dialog, and the composer of any music created for the movie.

- Collective works such as magazines, periodicals, and encyclopedias are protected for 70 years from the date of publication. However, if the individual authors who have contributed to such a work are identified by name, the copyright continues until 70 years after the author's death. But, if the individual author was anonymous or used a pseudonym, the copyright lasts for 70 years from the date of publication, instead of 70 years from the author's death.

- If the copyright in an unpublished work has expired—because the author died more than 70 years ago—the first person to publish the work is entitled to a copyright in the work that lasts for 25 years from the first publication.

- Effective 2013, the copyright in performances and sound recordings in the EU lasts for 70 years after the performance or recording is published. The copyright in musical compositions with more than one author expires 70 years after the death of the last surviving author, be it the author of the lyrics or the composer of the music. Prior to 2013, the copyright term for performances and sound recordings in the EU was 50 years. Performances and recordings that were in the EU public domain as of November 1, 2013 under the 50-year term remain in the public domain. Thus, all recordings first published before November 1, 1963 do not enjoy the extended 70-year term of protection in the EU.

Restoration of Public Domain Works

Before the members of the EU harmonized their copyright terms in the late 1990s, most of the EU countries had copyright protection during the life of the author and for 50 years after his or her death. For example, this was the basic copyright term in the United Kingdom before January 1, 1996.

However, Germany had a much longer copyright term: The basic copyright term under German law was the life of the author plus 70 years after the author died. Germany refused to reduce its copyright term to the life of the author plus 50 years. So, to achieve a single uniform copyright term within the EU, the other EU countries had to change their copyright laws to match Germany's copyright term.

To achieve this uniformity, EU law requires that any work still under copyright in Germany on July 1, 1995 must be given the full German term of protection in every EU country. This is required even if it means restoring the copyright in a work that had previously entered the public domain. This required most of the EU countries to extend their copyright protection by 20 years.

> **EXAMPLE:** All of the works of James Joyce entered the public domain in the United Kingdom and most of the rest of Europe on January 1, 1991 (Joyce died in 1941). However, Joyce's works were still under copyright in Germany on July 1, 1995 because Germany allowed copyright protection to extend for 70 years beyond the death of the author. Under EU law, this meant that Joyce's works were entitled to 70 years of copyright protection throughout the EU. As a result, the UK copyright in Joyce's works was restored on January 1, 1996 and lasted until December 31, 2011.

As a result of this change, millions of works that had been in the public domain in most EU countries have had their copyrights restored for an additional 20 years. To prevent this copyright restoration from causing economic hardship, the EU nations adopted special copyright provisions allowing the owners of copies of restored works to sell their stock and to continue to publish derivative works based on restored works. These provisions vary from country to country.

Canada

The basic copyright term in Canada ends 50 years after an author dies. If a work has more than one author, the copyright lasts for 50 years after the last author dies. All copyright terms last until the end of the year in which the author dies and then continue for an additional 50 calendar years. However, different terms apply to the works listed below.

Photographs

The term of protection for photographs depends upon the author. There are three possible terms of protection:

- First, where the author is a human being (as opposed to a business entity such as a corporation), the copyright lasts for 50 years after the author dies.
- If the author of a photograph is a corporation in which the majority of voting shares are owned by a human being who is the author of the photograph, the copyright lasts 50 years after the photographer dies.
- If the author of the photograph is a corporation in which the majority of voting shares are not owned by a human being who is the author of the photograph, the copyright lasts 50 years after the photo was taken or derived.

Movies

Canadian copyright differentiates between films (including videos) that have a dramatic quality and those that do not. Films with dramatic quality usually have actors and tell stories. Theatrical films and videos ordinarily have dramatic quality. Examples of works that don't have a dramatic quality are home movies.

Films and videos that do not have a dramatic quality are protected for 50 years from the date of their creation. However, if they are published within 50 years from creation, the copyright lasts for 50 years from the date of publication.

Films and videos that have a dramatic quality are protected for the life of the author plus 50 years. It's not entirely clear who the author of a film is under Canadian copyright law. It appears to be either the person who shoots the film or controls how it is shot. This could be the film director or producer. So if you are considering the use of a work that falls into this category, you should determine the years when all of these people died (if they have). Only if they have all been dead for over 50 years should you treat the film as in the Canadian public domain due to copyright expiration.

Sound Recordings

The copyright in a sound recording lasts for 50 years from the end of the year in which the original master or tape was created. But this does not mean that the composition played in the recording is in the public domain, since copyright protection for the sheet music lasts for the life of the author and for 50 years after his death. If you want to use a public domain recording, you may still need permission from the song's creator or owner.

Canadian Government Works

Works created by Canadian federal and provincial government employees are protected by Crown copyright. Copyright in these works lasts for 50 years from the year of publication. Copyright in unpublished Canadian government works is perpetual—that is, it lasts forever. However, anyone may, without charge or request for permission, reproduce laws enacted by the Government of Canada, decisions and reasons for decisions of Canadian federal courts and administrative tribunals. The copier must exercise "due diligence"—in other words, reasonable care—to ensure the accuracy of the materials reproduced and that the reproduction is not represented as an official version.

Unknown Authors

The copyright in a work written by an anonymous or pseudonymous author lasts for either 50 years after publication or 75 years after creation, whichever is shorter. However, if the author's identity becomes known, the copyright will last for 50 years after the author dies.

Posthumous Works

A posthumous work is a work that was under copyright when its author died, but had not been published before his or her death. The duration of the copyright in these works depends upon their date of creation. For such works created after July 25, 1997, the term of copyright protection is the normal life-of-the-author-plus-50-year term. However, any of three different terms may apply if the work was created before July 25, 1997:

- If the author died and the work was subsequently published, performed, or delivered before July 25, 1997, the copyright lasts for 50 years after such publication.
- If the author died during the period from 1927 through 1997—and the work was not published, performed, or delivered before July 25, 1997—the copyright lasts until January 1, 2048.
- If the author died before 1927—and the work was not published before July 25, 1997—the work is in the Canadian public domain.

China

The basic copyright term in China lasts for the life of the author plus 50 years. If a work has more than one author, the copyright lasts for 50 years after the last author dies. The copyright in an anonymous or pseudonymous work lasts for 50 years from publication.

In cases where a copyright is owned by a business entity such as a corporation, the copyright lasts for 50 years from publication. If the work is never published, the copyright lasts for 50 years after it was created. These terms apply to works created by employees for their employers and works commissioned by business entities.

The copyright in a movie, television broadcast, or photograph lasts for 50 years from publication. If the work is never published, the copyright lasts for 50 years after it was created.

Sound recordings are protected for 50 years after publication. If a sound recording is never published, its copyright lasts for 50 years after it was created.

Computer software owned by an individual is protected for life plus 50 years. Software initially owned by a business entity (such as a corporation) receives a 50-year term, counted from the year the software is first made public. However, this term lapses 50 years after the year of creation if such software is not made public in that period.

The typographic arrangement of a book or periodical is protectable under Chinese law for ten years after the first publication of the work using the typographic arrangement.

Japan

The basic copyright term in Japan is the life of the author plus 50 years. If a work has more than one author, the copyright lasts for 50 years after the last one dies.

The copyright in an anonymous or pseudonymous work lasts for 50 years from publication. But if the author's pseudonym is as well known as his real name, the normal term of 50 years after the author's death applies.

In cases where a copyright is owned by a business entity such as a corporation, the copyright lasts for 50 years from publication, or, if the work has not been published, 50 years from creation. This term applies to works created by employees for their employers and works commissioned by business entities.

The copyright in a movie lasts for 70 years after publication, or, if it's not published, 70 years from creation. However, for movies released before 1970, the copyright term lasts until 38 years after the death of the director.

Prior to March 25, 1997, a photograph was protected for 50 years from the year it was made public or 50 years from creation, whichever was shorter. Starting on March 25,

1997, photographs received the regular life-plus-50-year term. However, photographs that were in the Japanese public domain as of March 25, 1997 under the old rule did not have their copyrights extended.

Sound recordings and television broadcasts are protected for 50 years after publication.

Finally, Japanese copyright provides an extension of copyright terms for works created or owned by nationals of the Allied Powers—that is, the nations who fought Japan in World War II. This extension applies to all works copyrighted when the war started—Dec. 7, 1941—or created or acquired during the war, which officially ended in September 1945.

Works created by Americans have their copyright protection extended by 3,794 days—for example, if a book was published in the United States during WWII, 3,794 days have to be added to the normal life-plus-50 Japanese copyright term. This means that such works are protected in Japan for the life of the American author plus 60.3 years, instead of life plus 50 years.

Russia

Russia (formally known as the Russian Federation) adopted its first copyright law in 1993. It provided for a basic copyright term of life of the author plus 50 years. If there were two or more authors, the copyright lasted until 50 years after the death of the last survivor. The copyright

A *Beauty*, Kitagawa Utamaro (1753–1808), color woodblock.

for a work published anonymously or under a pseudonym lasted for 50 years after the date of its authorized publication. If the author's identity was revealed, copyright protection lasted for the life of the author plus 50 years. The copyright for a work published for the first time after the author's death lasted for 50 years after its publication.

In 2004, all of these copyright terms were extended by 20 years. However, this extension was not retroactive—that is, works already in the Russian public domain as of January 1, 1993 remained there. Moreover, for the first time, these copyright terms were made applicable to all foreign works.

There are some further wrinkles in Russian copyright law. Before 1992, copyrights belonging to legal entities were valid for an unlimited period of time. When these legal entities were broken up following the collapse of the Soviet Union, their copyrights were automatically transferred to the Russian government. The new law abolished ownership of copyrights by entities. Copyrights owned by entities in existence before 1993 were given a 50-year term from creation or publication.

There are also wartime and rehabilitation extensions. If an author worked during World War II (known as the Great Patriotic War in Russia) or participated in it directly, the copyright term was extended by four years. Russian copyright law also provides that if an author was repressed and rehabilitated posthumously, the applicable copyright period begins on January 1 of the year following the year of rehabilitation.

As a result of these enactments, January 1, 1954 is the key date for Russian copyright protection. Any work published before that date is in the Russian public domain if (1) the author died before that date, and (2) the author's identity was known while it was under copyright. However, if the author was entitled to a wartime extension of copyright, January 1, 1950 is the key date instead of January 1, 1954. Works belonging to the former Soviet government or other Soviet legal entities published before January 1, 1954 are also public domain in Russia.

The Rule of the Shorter Term

When it comes to calculating how long the copyright in a foreign work lasts, many countries use something called the "rule of the shorter term." This rule provides that copyright in a work created or published in a foreign country lasts the *shorter* of either:

- the term the work receives in its home country, or
- the term the work would receive under the laws of the foreign country involved.

Impact of Rule on U.S. Works

A work created or first published in the United States that is now in the public domain in the United States will also be in the public domain in all countries that follow the rule of the shorter term. This will be the case even though the work would not be in the public domain under the foreign country's own copyright law.

For example, all works first published in the United States over 95 years ago are in the public domain in the United States and are, therefore, in the public domain in all the countries that follow the rule of the shorter term. Without the rule, many of these works would not be in the public domain in these foreign countries, based on their own copyright laws.

> EXAMPLE: Irving wrote and published a song in the United States in 1920. He died in 1960. The song entered the public domain in the United States on Jan. 1, 1996 (75 years after publication). The work is in the public domain in the Netherlands as well because it follows the rule of the shorter term. The U.S. copyright term for the song is shorter than the Dutch term of life plus 70 years.

The rule of the shorter term is particularly important for works first published in the United States less than 95 years ago but before 1964 that were never renewed. These works entered the U.S. public domain on the 29th year after publication and will be in the public domain in countries that use the rule of the shorter term.

> EXAMPLE: Nathaniel published a novel in the United States in 1950 but did not renew it 28 years after publication. As a result, the work entered the U.S. public domain in 1969. The work is in the public domain in France as well, even though a novel published in France in 1950 would not be in the public domain, since it would retain copyright protection for 70 years after the author dies. Because the novel was not renewed, the U.S. copyright term is far shorter than the French term.

Countries That Do Not Follow the Rule

Not every country in the world follows the rule of the shorter term. Unfortunately, there is no definitive list of those countries that do and do not follow the rule. Indeed, the status of the rule is unclear for many countries. However, the copyright statutes of the following countries specifically provide that the rule of the shorter term is *not* applied, or applied with exceptions:

- Andorra (exception: rule of shorter term applies to works in public domain in their countries of origin on June 10, 1999)
- Armenia (exception: rule of shorter term applies to works in public domain in their home countries of origin on June 15, 2006)
- Australia (exception: rule of shorter term applies to "published editions")
- Brazil
- China
- Colombia
- Iceland
- Indonesia
- Ivory Coast
- Lebanon
- Mexico
- New Zealand (exception: rule of shorter term applies to works in the public domain in their countries of origin on Dec. 15, 1994)

- Nigeria
- Oman
- Paraguay
- Philippines
- Saint Vincent and the Grenadines
- Switzerland
- Turkey (exception: rule of shorter term applies to works in the public domain in their countries of origin on Dec. 6, 1995), and
- Venezuela.

The following additional countries likely do not follow the rule of the shorter term for works initially published in the United States, although their copyright laws do not specifically so provide:

- Austria
- Bahrain
- Belgium
- Brunei
- Chile
- Costa Rica
- Cuba
- Denmark
- El Salvador
- Greece
- Guatemala
- Haiti
- Honduras
- Hungary
- Indonesia
- Ireland
- Israel
- Italy
- Japan
- Jordan
- Korea
- Malaysia
- Morocco
- Netherlands
- Nicaragua
- Norway
- Peru
- Portugal
- Singapore
- South Africa
- Spain
- Sweden
- Thailand, and
- Vietnam.

Canada. Canada does not apply the rule of the shorter term to works whose country of origin is one of its fellow NAFTA (North American Free Trade Association) members —that is, the United States and Mexico. It does apply it to the rest of the world.

Germany. German copyright law in this area is particularly complex because of the way that Germany applies various copyright treaties it entered into with the United States in past years. The impact of these treaties on the copyright term in Germany for works created in the United States is shown in the following chart.

For example, if a book whose country of origin was the United States was published in 1928, it would receive an initial 28-year U.S. copyright term. If not renewed, it would then enter the U.S. public domain. However, the book would be entitled to the then life-plus-50-year German term because the rule of the shorter term did not apply (assume the author died in 1968). In 1989, the book would not receive the life-plus-70-year German term because it was in the public domain in the United States. Had the book been renewed in 1956, its U.S. copyright would have been extended to 2018 and therefore qualified for the life-plus-70-year German term in 1989.

Year in Which U.S. Work Was Created	Length of German Copyright Term
May 15, 1892–Sept. 15, 1955	Life plus 50 years; if work still under copyright in United States and Germany on March 1, 1989, term increased by 20 years (life plus 70 years)
Sept. 16, 1955–Feb. 28, 1989	Shorter of life plus 50 years or U. S. copyright term; if work still under copyright in United States and Germany on March 1, 1989, term increased by 20 years (life plus 70 years)
March 1, 1989 and later	Life plus 70 years

The United Kingdom. The United Kingdom has applied the rule of the shorter term since July 1, 1996. However, the UK does not follow the rule for works that were under copyright before then. The basic copyright term for such works is the life of the author plus 50 years. For example, if a work was originally published in the United States in 1950, and the author died in 1980, the work remains under copyright in the UK until 2021. This would be so even if the work was in the public domain in the United States as of 1979 due to nonrenewal.

Researching Foreign Copyright Laws

Following are some suggested resources you can use if you need to research the copyright law of a foreign country.

Books

The best book available in English on international copyright law is the two-volume treatise *International Copyright Law and Practice*, edited by Lionel Bently. It's published by Matthew Bender and can be found in many law libraries. This work contains in-depth discussions of the copyright laws of most large countries. See *Copyright Law: World Study*, by Sybil Foreman, for a one-volume summary of the copyright laws of many major countries. For a one-volume overview of the basic legal principles of international copyright law, see *International Copyright: Principles, Law, and Practice,* by Paul Goldstein and P. Bernt Hugenholtz (2012).

An excellent book on Canadian copyright is called *Canadian Copyright Law*, by Lesley Ellen Harris. It's published by Wiley.

The standard work on British copyright law is *Copinger and Skone James on Copyright*, by Nicholas Caddick, Gillian Davies, and Gwilym Harbottle. It is published by Sweet & Maxwell.

Websites

A number of websites contain information on foreign copyright laws.

You can access copies of the copyright laws of almost all the countries of the world at the website of the World Intellectual Property Organization (a United Nations agency). The URL is www.wipo.int/wipolex/en.

The following copyright countries have useful government-sponsored websites:

- Australia (www.copyright.org.au)
- Canada (www.cipo.ic.gc.ca), and
- United Kingdom (www.gov.uk/topic/intellectual-property/copyright).

The Internet and the Public Domain

Two Preliminary Rules...300

    Rule 1: Works on the Internet Are Not Automatically in
        the Public Domain 300

    Rule 2: The Presence or Lack of a Copyright Notice Is Meaningless..........300

Internet Content in the Public Domain 301

    Works Not Protected by Copyright 301

    Works in the Public Domain Before Being Placed on the Internet 303

    Works Dedicated to the Public Domain..303

Potential Problems Using Public Domain Materials on the Internet 307

    Copyright Claims in Digital Copies of Public Domain Works 308

    Websites as Collective Works 308

    Use of Licenses to Protect Internet Content.....................................310

Hyperlinks and the Public Domain 312

Copyright and the Internet's Global Dimension..313

    Check Foreign Copyright Terms...313

    Use a Disclaimer 313

Most of the material on the Internet is not in the public domain, but much is. Unfortunately, material on the Internet is not always clearly or correctly identified as being in the public domain or protected by copyright. There is widespread confusion, among both purveyors and users, of content on the Internet, about what can be used for free and what must be licensed.

Two Preliminary Rules

Before we discuss in detail what works on the Internet are in the public domain, here are two simple rules you should learn. Applying them will help you avoid stupid mistakes.

Rule 1: Works on the Internet Are Not Automatically in the Public Domain

There is a widespread belief among people using the Internet that simply placing a work on the Internet automatically places it in the public domain. Many people wrongly believe that if they find something on the Internet they are free to download, copy, retransmit, and use it in any other way they like. No—this is simply not true. A work does not lose copyright protection just because it's on the Internet.

Although many works on the Internet are in the public domain, this is not simply because they were published in this medium. Rather, they are in the public domain for some other reason—for example, because their copyright expired, they are U.S. government works, or the copyright owner dedicated them to the public domain.

Rule 2: The Presence or Lack of a Copyright Notice Is Meaningless

There is no requirement that a copyright notice accompany a protected work on the Internet, just like material in any other format—a novel, for example. Put another way, as long as material is protected by copyright, it makes no difference whether or not it has a notice claiming copyright ownership. Of course, many people place copyright notices on their websites and on individual items posted on the Internet, such as photographs. If a work contains a copyright notice, you know someone *claims* it is copyrighted. While that claim may be valid, it also may not be. It's not uncommon for people to place notices on public domain materials, either out of ignorance or because they want to deceive others into thinking they own the materials.

Moreover, many websites contain a mix of copyrighted and public domain materials. The owners of these sites are legally entitled to use copyright notices. Unfortunately, there is no requirement that they indicate in their notices (or anywhere else) which portions of their site are copyrighted and which are in the public domain. As a result, these copyright notices can mislead people into believing that public domain materials are protected by copyright.

On the other hand, the *absence* of a copyright notice means nothing. Remember: use of copyright notices on the Internet is purely optional. People who don't use them don't lose their copyright rights, if they have any, in the published work.

Internet Content in the Public Domain

Never assume that anything you find on the Internet is in the public domain. Public domain works on the Internet fall into one of three broad categories:

- works not protected by copyright
- works that were in the public domain before they were placed on the Internet, and
- works dedicated to the public domain.

Any work you find on the Internet that does not fall into one of these categories is not in the public domain.

Works Not Protected by Copyright

Probably the largest category of public domain works on the Internet are those that are not eligible for copyright protection.

U.S. Government Works

All works of authorship created by U.S. government employees as part of their jobs are in the public domain. Almost all federal agencies have websites, and most of the material on them is in the public domain and free for the taking. This includes, for example, the excellent IRS website (www. irs.gov) and the U.S. Copyright Office website (www.copyright.gov).

For more information on the types of U.S. government materials that are in the public domain and additional Web links, refer to the following chapters:

- writings (see Chapter 3)
- artwork (see Chapter 5)
- photography (see Chapter 6)
- film and video (see Chapter 7)
- software (see Chapter 8)
- maps (see Chapter 10), and
- databases (see Chapter 12).

However, state, local, and foreign governments can claim copyright owner- ship in materials created by their employ- ees. For example, materials on a website maintained by your state motor vehicle agency may be copyrighted.

Even highly sensitive documents by super-secret government agencies—like the Central Intelligence Agency—are in the public domain. They are protected from disclosure by other laws. But once they are declassified and released, they are in the public domain.

Laws and Court Decisions

All laws, whether federal, state, local, or even foreign, are in the public domain in the United States. Written legal decisions by all American courts (whether federal or state) are also in the public domain. Copies of these decisions are available on various websites. However, some of these websites charge users subscription fees and require them to agree to licenses restricting how they may use these public domain materials. (For a detailed discussion, see Chapter 3.)

Databases

Millions of databases are on the Internet. Many of these are in the public domain because their selection and arrangement are not sufficiently creative to be protected by copyright. However, licenses, encryption, and other means are frequently used to protect such databases. (For a detailed discussion, see Chapter 12.)

Blank Forms

Many websites contain blank forms that users fill out to register with the site or order goods or services. Blank forms used solely to record information are in the public domain. (For a detailed discussion, see Chapter 3.)

Information That Is Common Property

Information that is common property is in the public domain. Examples include standard calendars, height and weight charts, tape measures and rulers, schedules of sporting events, and lists or tables taken from public documents or other common sources. 37 C.F.R. Section 202.1(d). Any such information on a website is in the public domain.

However, new material added to such works is protectable. For example, although a standard calendar is not copyrightable, photos, illustrations, or quotations added to a calendar can be protected. But copyright protection extends only to this new material, not to the standard calendar itself.

Website Format and Layout

The format and layout of a website is not protectable because it is a template of expression. Thus, for example, there is no copyright protection for the format of a Frequently Asked Questions (FAQ) page on a website. *Mist-On Systems, Inc. v. Gilley's European Tan Spa*, 303 F.Supp.2d 974 (D. Wis. 2002).

HTML

HTML (Hypertext Markup Language) for a website is copyrightable only if it's created by a human being. HTML code automatically created by website design software is not protected by copyright. Also, style sheet languages, such as Cascading Style Sheets, are not protectable because they are merely methods of formatting and laying out the organization of documents written in a markup language, such as HTML.

Typefaces

Typefaces are in the public domain in the United States. However, computer software used to generate typefaces is protected by copyright. (For a detailed discussion, see Chapter 5.)

Food and Drink Recipes

Food and drink recipes are also in the public domain. (For a detailed discussion, see Chapter 3.)

Works in the Public Domain Before Being Placed on the Internet

The other large body of public domain material on the Internet consists of copies of materials that were in the public domain before being placed on the Internet.

Digital copies of such public domain works have been posted on many websites. The vast majority of these works are in the public domain because their copyrights expired before they were placed on the Internet. Thousands of copyright-expired books, magazines, and other written works, photographs, maps, and old films and television shows have been scanned and placed on the Internet where the public can view them and, if they wish, download them to their own computers.

To determine whether a particular work was public domain before it was placed on the Internet, turn to the chapter covering that type of work and read the detailed discussion there. Each of these chapters also contains a list of websites on which public domain materials can be found:

- writings (see Chapter 3)
- music (see Chapter 4)
- artwork (see Chapter 5)
- architectural plans (see Chapter 9)
- maps (see Chapter 10)
- photography (see Chapter 6)
- film and video (see Chapter 7), and
- computer software (see Chapter 8).

Works Dedicated to the Public Domain

A good deal of material on the Internet has been dedicated to the public domain—in other words, the copyright owner has elected to give up his or her copyright protection. The author of any work that can be protected by copyright is free to reject that protection and dedicate the work to the public domain. By doing this, the author gives up all ownership rights in the work, which permits anyone to copy or otherwise use the work without permission.

Much of this dedicated material consists of computer software. See Chapter 8 for a detailed discussion of how to determine whether software has been dedicated to the public domain. There are also graphics, writings, and even sound files that have been dedicated to the public domain.

There is no prescribed formula for dedicating a work to the public domain. The author or other copyright owner simply has to make his or her intention to do so clear. For example, stating "This work is dedicated to the public domain" on a webpage would be sufficient.

> EXAMPLE: A website containing a number of simple graphics for use by website designers has an excellent unequivocal public domain dedication: "Anywhere you see my cute face on these pages—the graphics were created by me and are 100% public domain. Modify any way you wish, use as you see fit, business or personal. No link back required, or credit given to me for them. No strings!"

> CAUTION
> **Double-check the status of a dedicated work.** Anyone can put a digital copy of any work on the Internet and say it has been dedicated to the public domain. This doesn't necessarily mean it's true. For this reason, you need to be careful. Before you distribute such materials to the public—for example, by placing them on your own website—double-check to make sure they really have been dedicated to the public domain. Send an email to the webmaster (person in charge) of the site where you got the materials. Ask if the webmaster

or someone else created the material. If it was created by someone else, find out who and send this person an email asking if the person dedicated it to the public domain. Explain that this means that, not only is the material free, but that it is not protected by copyright and can be used by the public in any way, even sold.

Watch for Mixed Messages

Be careful, however, where an author sends mixed messages. For example, an author may state that his or her work is in the public domain but then may attempt to restrict how the public may use it by stating something such as, "This work is public domain but may not be used for commercial purposes without my permission." When a work is dedicated to the public domain, the author may not restrict how it is used. A statement like this leaves it unclear whether the author really intended to dedicate the work to the public domain. It's wise to seek clarification from the author or ask permission for the restricted use.

Similarly, use of the phrase "copyright free" does not mean the work is dedicated to the public domain. The words "copyright free" are often used to describe works (particularly photos and clip-art) that are under copyright, copies of which are sold to the public for a set fee rather than under a royalty arrangement. "Copyright free" is also used where copyrighted materials are licensed to the public for free.

Dedicating Works to the Public Domain Through the Creative Commons

The Creative Commons (www.creative commons.org) is a nonprofit corporation whose goal is "to cultivate a commons in which people can feel free to reuse not only ideas, but also words, images, and music without asking permission—because permission has already been granted to everyone." Since its founding in 2001, hundreds of millions of pieces of content have been published under Creative Commons licenses, including websites, photographs, instructional materials, scholarly research, comic strips, maps, sound recordings, and motion pictures.

One of the initial goals of the Creative Commons project was to help copyright owners abandon their copyrights. Creative Commons enables copyright owners to dedicate their work to the public domain by adopting the Creative Commons CC0 license. This can be done online through the Creative Commons website. Hundreds of organizations and many individuals have made use of the CC0 license to dedicate all types of materials to the public domain.

As Creative Commons makes clear on its website (https://creativecommons.org/choose/zero), when you use the CC0 license you give up all your rights in the work forever throughout the world. These include not just your copyright rights, but any other ownership rights as well, including publicity, privacy, and moral rights. Since the work is in the public domain, anyone can use it in any way they want, without asking you for permission or paying you for the use. They don't even have to give you credit for the work. Only a small minority of copyright owners (about 3%–4%) use CC0 licenses. To put the CC0 license into effect, you complete the online form at https://creativecommons.org/choose/zero. The website requires the copyright owner to provide its name and the title of the work. The owner must then check a "confirm" button agreeing to the terms of the license. By agreeing to the license, the copyright owner waives all of his or her copyright and neighboring and related rights in a work, to the fullest extent permitted by law.

However, Creative Commons recognizes that in many countries dedicating a work to the public domain is difficult or even impossible, and that the abandonment and waiver of copyright may not be deemed legally effective. In this event, the CC0 acts as a license from the copyright owner granting the public an unconditional, irrevocable, nonexclusive, royalty-free license to use the work for any purpose. This broad license functionally dedicates the work to the public domain if copyright abandonment is not allowed. See the Creative Commons website at https://creativecommons.org/publicdomain.

You can perform Internet searches for Creative Commons licensed materials by using the Creative Commons' own search engine at https://search.creativecommons.org. Alternatively, the advanced search options in Google allow you to restrict your searches to CC licensed items—go to www.google.com/advanced_search.

Dedicating Works to the Public Domain Through the Creative Commons (continued)

However, most people who use Creative Commons licenses do not dedicate their works to the public domain. Instead, they use one of several open content licenses developed by the Creative Commons. These licenses were developed to "let authors, scientists, artists, and educators easily mark their creative work with the freedoms they want it to carry." (Creative Commons, "What We Do" https://creative commons.org/about.)

Copyright owners may choose among one of the following six types of licenses that allow varying degrees of permission-free use of the work involved:

Attribution (CC BY). "This license lets others distribute, remix, tweak, and build upon your work, even commercially, as long as they credit you for the original creation. This is the most accommodating of licenses offered. Recommended for maximum dissemination and use of licensed materials."

Attribution-NoDerivs (CC BY-ND). "This license allows for redistribution, commercial and non-commercial, as long as it is passed along unchanged and in whole, with credit to you."

Attribution-Noncommercial-Share Alike (CC BY-NC-SA). "This license lets others remix, tweak, and build upon your work non-commercially, as long as they credit you and license their new creations under the identical terms."

Attribution-Share Alike (CC BY-SA). "This license lets others remix, tweak, and build upon your work even for commercial purposes, as long as they credit you and license their new creations under the identical terms. This license is often compared to 'copy left' free and open source software licenses. All new works based on yours will carry the same license, so any derivatives will also allow commercial use. This is the license used by Wikipedia, and is recommended for materials that would benefit from incorporating content from Wikipedia and similarly licensed projects."

Attribution-Noncommercial (CC BY-NCP). "This license lets others remix, tweak, and build upon your work non-commercially, and although their new works must also acknowledge you and be non-commercial, they don't have to license their derivative works on the same terms."

Attribution-Noncommercial-NoDerivs24 (CC BY-NC-ND). "This license is the most restrictive of our six main licenses, only allowing others to download your works and share them with others as long as they credit you, but they can't change them in any way or use them commercially."

Creative Commons-licensed material placed on the Internet is supposed to contain a Creative Commons logo consisting of two "C"s within a circle. Clicking on the logo sends the user to a "Creative Commons deed"—an easy to read brief description of the license. For more information on Creative Commons licenses refer to https://creativecommons.org/licenses.

Nonexclusive Licenses Are Not Public Domain Dedications

People and companies that post material on the Internet frequently grant users permission to use the material in particular ways without obtaining specific permission. For example, you'll often see a statement somewhere on a website's home page or on a "Terms and Conditions" page that the material can be downloaded for personal use. Some website owners even grant users permission to email the content to anyone in the world, as long as they do not charge for it.

Statements like this are what the copyright law terms nonexclusive licenses, permitting free public use of the material. But the materials are still protected by copyright and there are restrictions on how they may be used. This type of license does not dedicate the material to the public domain. Typically, commercial uses are not permitted.

When Public Domain Doesn't Mean Dedicated to the Public

Many (perhaps most) of the people who use the Internet don't really understand what the phrase "public domain" means. You'll often see it used in conjunction with works that clearly haven't been dedicated to the public domain and aren't public domain for any other reason. For example, there are tens of thousands of websites that contain copies of photographs of actors, fashion models, and other celebrities. These photos have been copied from various sources and placed on the Internet, where they are often recopied thousands of times. Virtually none of these photos are in the public domain.

Often, these sites contain statements that the images are "presumed," "deemed," "believed," or "assumed" to be in the public domain. For example, one such website contains the following statement:

ALL IMAGES FOUND WITHIN THESE PAGES WERE OBTAINED FROM THE WEB AND WERE DEEMED IN THE PUBLIC DOMAIN.

The people who make statements like this apparently believe that anything they find on the Internet is in the public domain and can be freely copied unless someone tells them otherwise. Of course, this is not true. A statement like this should tip you off that the materials on the site are very likely not in the public domain, and it won't protect the people who include these statements on their websites from getting sued for copyright infringement, or protect you from a lawsuit if you copy the material for use on your website.

Potential Problems Using Public Domain Materials on the Internet

People who place digital copies of public domain works on the Internet often claim that they are protected by copyright or attempt to use licenses to restrict how the public may use them. You need to understand how to recognize and deal with such claims.

Copyright Claims in Digital Copies of Public Domain Works

Obviously, you can't place a public domain book or photograph on the Internet. The work has to be reduced to digital form. This is typically done using a digital scanner.

Sometimes the people who create digital copies of public domain writings or photographs claim that the copies are protected by copyright, even though the original works are not. This is particularly common for photographs. For example, www.getty images.com, one of the largest stock photo agencies in the world, has digitized tens of thousands of public domain photos and placed them on its website. Getty claims that these digital copies are copyrighted. Getty puts copyright notices on these copies and requires anyone who licenses the photos to include the notices as well.

Any claim that digitally scanning a book or other text document is copyrightable is almost certainly not legally enforceable. This is so even if the typeface is changed or the text rehyphenated, spellchecked, or reformatted. These types of changes are not copyrightable because they do not meet a legal standard of being a minimally creative change to the original public

domain work. (See Chapter 3 for a detailed discussion.)

A stronger argument might be made that a digitally scanned photograph should be copyrighted. This would be the case, for example, where the original photo is altered—for example, where a black and white photo is colorized. But, if the digital copy is an exact copy of the original photo, copyright claims are much more difficult to justify. (See Chapter 6 for a discussion of this question for photographs in general, and see Chapter 5 for a discussion of copyright claims in photos of public domain artworks such as paintings.)

Websites as Collective Works

A collective work is a work created by selecting and arranging more than one work of authorship into a single new work. Good examples of collective works are newspapers, magazines, and other periodicals in which separate articles are combined into a collective whole. However, the preexisting material can consist of any work of authorship, including any type of writing, music, photographs, or drawings or other artwork.

Most websites that have public domain materials qualify as collective works.

Fortunately, these collective work copyrights usually don't pose much of a problem. This is because copyright protection for a collective work is extremely limited. All that is protected is the selection and/or arrangement of the preexisting material, not the preexisting material itself.

How Much of a Collective Work Website Can You Copy?

Since the copyright on a collective work protects only the selection and/or arrangement of the material, none of the individual public domain works in the collection are protected. This means you may copy any individual public domain work included in the collection. However, you may not copy the copyrighted selection and/or arrangement. This would occur where you copy the entire collection (or a substantial portion of it).

If you want to use a particular work from a website you must still check to see if it is in the public domain. If it is not, you must obtain permission, and often pay a fee, for using the work.

You are not limited to copying individual items. You may copy any amount of a collection as long as you don't copy the website creator's copyrighted selection and/or arrangement.

> **EXAMPLE:** Let's assume that a website called The Presidents Speak contains digital copies of 50 presidential speeches arranged in order from the best to the worst, according to the website creator's opinion. This selection and arrangement is copyrighted, but the speeches aren't because there is no copyright protection for speeches of any president. You are free to copy them all, so long as you don't duplicate

the selection and arrangement. For example, you could use them all in a website containing copies of 500 important historic speeches arranged chronologically. This would duplicate neither the selection nor arrangement of The Presidents Speak site.

Minimal Creativity Required

Not all websites qualify for even the minimal copyright protection afforded to collective works. A website is protected as a collective work only if the author/compiler had to use creativity and judgment to create it. If not even minimal creativity was employed to select and/or arrange the materials on a website, it will not be protected as a collective work.

How can you tell if a website contains sufficient creativity to be entitled to copyright protection as a collective work? A website is copyrightable as a collective work if either the selection or arrangement of the material is minimally creative. In some websites, both the selection and arrangement are minimally creative. In others, only one or the other is.

Selection

A selection is minimally creative if:
- it consists of less than all of the data in a given body of relevant material, regardless of whether it is taken from one or more sources, or
- it is based on the compiler's opinion about something subjective.

For example, a website consisting of a collection of the 100 "greatest" speeches by U.S. presidents would be copyrightable. The compiler of such a website would have to use his or her individual judgment to determine which 100 of the thousands of speeches by presidents were the greatest.

But a selection is not minimally creative if it does not require individual judgment. For example, no judgment is needed to compile a website containing a copy of every speech by President Obama.

Arrangement

Similarly, the way the individual items on a website are ordered or placed is entitled to copyright protection only if done in a way that requires the exercise of the website creator's subjective judgment. An ordering or placement is not entitled to copyright protection if done in a mechanical way. An alphabetical or chronological arrangement is purely mechanical and not entitled to copyright protection. Thus, for example, a collection of the sheet music for Stephen Foster's songs placed in alphabetical order by title would not be entitled to copyright protection for the grouping. But an arrangement on some other basis could be—for example, according to theme or from worst to best in the opinion of the website creator.

Use of Licenses to Protect Internet Content

A license is a type of contract that gives someone permission to do something. People who own copyrights often license their works—for example, a photographer will grant a license allowing a magazine or website to copy and publish a photo.

Licenses are being increasingly used by website owners to restrict how the public may use the content on the Internet. These licenses usually take one of two forms. Websites that require users to pay for access to the site's content often display the license agreement in a window or webpage and require the user to agree to the license terms by clicking a "yes" or "I agree" box before he or she can access the site. For example, the online database LexisNexis requires subscribers to agree to such licenses. Licenses such as these are sometimes called "click-wrap" licenses.

However, most websites don't require users to click a "yes" box or otherwise indicate that they have read and agree to the terms of the license. Indeed, the user isn't even required to read the license before accessing the website's content. Instead, the license is more or less hidden in a "Terms and Conditions," "Terms of Service," or "Terms of Use" page on the website. Only users who click on the Terms and Conditions link at the bottom of the site's home page will even know the purported license exists. These Terms and

Conditions typically include a statement that by simply using the website the user agrees to the restrictions listed in the Terms and Conditions. Or it may say that use of the website is conditioned upon agreement to the Terms and Conditions.

License Restrictions

Whatever form a website license takes, it ordinarily imposes restrictions on how the public may use the material on the site. Typically, users are permitted only to use the material for their personal use.

"Personal use" means that you may download the material to your own computer and read and view it and make a copy for yourself. You can't make multiple copies or republish the material on your own website or in some other form—for example, in a book or magazine. You also can't adapt the material into a new work.

Unfortunately, many websites that contain public domain materials attempt to use restrictive licenses. A good example is the stock photo agency Getty Images. Its massive photography collection contains thousands of public domain images. However, anyone who wants to use them must pay a fee and enter into a license agreement with Getty that restricts how the images may be used—for example, unless additional fees are paid, Getty's photos may not be used for commercial purposes, may not be altered, or used in a standalone downloadable file.

Are Licenses Enforceable?

Clearly, these websites are attempting to use licenses to obtain and keep control over public domain materials that are supposed to be free to us all. Is this legal? Unfortunately, the answer appears to be yes. To date, almost all courts have enforced these licenses.

What to Do About Licenses

You should carefully read any license agreement or terms and conditions posted on any website. It's possible that your intended use of the public domain materials on the site won't be prohibited by the license or terms. But, if it is, you'll have to obey the license's terms or face a possible lawsuit (or at least the threat of a lawsuit).

Probably the best advice is to try to obtain the public domain materials from another source that doesn't require you to agree to a license or have restrictive terms and conditions. The exact same public domain materials could be available on another website that doesn't use licenses or they could be available at a library or some other site in the real world.

If the material is not readily available elsewhere, try asking for permission for your intended use. Sometimes, permission is available for free or may be very inexpensive.

Hyperlinks and the Public Domain

A "hyperlink" consists simply of the address of a particular website or other location on the Internet. An individual Web address is not protected by copyright or any other law. It's as much in the public domain as a street address. For example, the Internet address of Nolo's website home page is www.nolo.com. Its street address is 950 Parker St., Berkeley, CA. Both addresses are public domain.

Moreover, since no copying is involved, placing a hyperlink to another website on your own website does not constitute a copyright violation. In the words of one court, "This is analogous to using a library's card index to get reference to particular items, albeit faster and more efficiently." *Ticketmaster Corp. v. Tickets.com*, No. CV 99-7654 HLH(BQRX) (C.D. Cal. 2000).

However, a collection of Web hyperlinks is a type of database (also called a compilation). Although the individual hyperlinks in a hyperlink collection are public domain and may be freely copied and used, the collection as a whole may be copyrighted. Some website owners expressly claim protection for their hyperlink collections in copyright notices or terms and conditions statements.

However, it is not necessary to use such a notice or statement to have copyright protection for a hyperlink collection. If such a collection qualifies for copyright, U.S. copyright law will protect it automatically the moment it is created.

But, as with collective works, this form of copyright protection is extremely limited. All that is protected is the selection and/or arrangement of all the hyperlinks in the collection, not the individual hyperlinks themselves. Even this won't be protectable if the selection or arrangement is not at least minimally creative. For example, a collection of every hyperlink online concerning the writings of the Brontë sisters arranged in alphabetical order wouldn't be minimally creative.

CAUTION

Domain names are not free to use. An Internet domain name is the unique part of an Internet address (Universal Resource Locator or URL). The Nolo URL, for instance, is www.nolo.com. The last part—nolo.com—is the domain name. Domain names are not protected by copyright, but this does not mean they can be freely used. Trademark laws often protect domain names. They must also be registered for use on the Internet. You can't use a domain name somebody else has already registered.

Copyright and the Internet's Global Dimension

One unique feature of the Internet is that it can be accessed from almost anywhere in the world. For example, a website maintained by a person or company in the United States can easily be accessed by people in Canada, France, South Africa, Brazil, and Japan.

The Internet's global dimension leads to a unique copyright problem: Many works are in the public domain in the United States, but not in a number of other countries. There are several reasons for this. The most important is that copyright terms differ in the United States and in many foreign countries (see Chapter 16). Thus, for example, all of Irving Berlin's songs published over 95 years ago are in the public domain in the United States because their copyrights have expired (see Chapter 18). However, these songs are still under copyright in Canada, where copyrights last for the life of the author plus 50 years—Berlin died in 1989 (see Chapter 16).

If you're located in the United States and place such a work on your website, it is possible that you could be sued for copyright infringement in a foreign country where the work is still under copyright. If the suit is successful, the foreign copyright owner may then be able to enforce the foreign judgment in the United States against your assets located here. It might even be possible for you to be sued in the United States for violating the copyright laws of a foreign country.

If you live in the United States and want to post public domain materials on your website, there are a couple of things you can do to limit the possibility that someone will accusing you of violating a foreign copyright law.

Check Foreign Copyright Terms

Chapter 16 covers the public domain in foreign countries. Read it carefully, particularly the section on the copyright term in the European Union (EU), which consists of most of Western Europe. If a work's copyright term has expired in the EU, it's in the public domain in almost all of the rest of the world as well. Very few countries have longer copyright terms than the EU. Generally, for copyright protection to expire in the EU, the author must have died more than 70 years ago (see Chapter 16).

Use a Disclaimer

Another approach is to use a disclaimer. Place a notice in large type and bold letters on your home page stating that the website is intended only for U.S. residents, or residents of countries where the work is in the public domain. Also state that the material on your site may be downloaded only from within the United States or the other foreign countries on your list. Here's an example:

> THIS WEBSITE IS INTENDED ONLY FOR INTERNET USERS RESIDING IN THE UNITED STATES. THE MATERIAL ON THIS WEBSITE MAY ONLY BE DOWNLOADED WITHIN THE UNITED STATES. ALL OTHER USES ARE PROHIBITED.

Disclaimers are used all the time on websites. For example, many websites that contain medical information contain disclaimers that the site can't take the place of a doctor. Whether website disclaimers are actually effective in avoiding liability is far from clear. However, they cost nothing to use and can only help. At the very least it shows that you are aware of the problem and are trying to protect the copyright owner's foreign copyright rights. This can only make you look better in the eyes of a judge or jury if your use of some material is challenged.

Copyright Protection: How Long Does It Last?

Works First Published in the United States 316

    Works Published Over 95 Years Ago.. 318

    Works Initially Published in the U.S. Less than 95 Years Ago
        and Before 1964 That Were Not Timely Renewed 319

    Works Published Between 1964 and 1977.. 322

    Works Published After 1977... 322

Copyright Term for Unpublished Works.. 324

    Unpublished Works Created Before 1978 and Published Before 2003........ 324

    Authors Dead More Than 70 Years.. 324

    Unpublished Works for Hire More Than 120 Years Old.................................... 325

    Unpublished Works Registered With the Copyright Office Before 1978 326

Works First Published Outside the United States 327

    Works Published Before 1978 328

    Works Published With a Valid Copyright Notice.. 328

    Works Published Before 1978 Without a Copyright Notice 329

    The Rule in the Western United States 329

    The Rule in the Rest of the United States.. 330

    What You Should Do... 330

Sound Recordings 331

    Works Published After 1977... 332

opyright protection does not last forever. When a work's copyright expires, it enters the public domain. Works with expired copyright protection form the largest category of works in the public domain.

Unfortunately, the law describing how long copyright protection lasts is ridiculously complex. There is no single time limit for copyright protection. This is because copyright laws have been amended many times, and the old time limits were often left in place or only modified. So we are left with a hodgepodge of different time limits for copyright protection.

To know whether the copyright for a work has expired, you need to know which term applies. This chapter shows you how to do just that. The discussion of copyright terms is divided into three sections:

- The first section covers works first published in the United States.
- The second section covers all unpublished works.
- The third section covers works first published outside the United States.

Before you can know how long any work's copyright lasts you must first determine whether or not it has been published and, if so, when. This is because copyright terms often differ depending on whether or not a work is published. If you haven't done so already, turn to the chapter covering the particular type of work involved—for example, writings, music, art, or photography—and read the detailed discussion of when the work is considered published for copyright purposes.

You also need to know whether the work was published in the United States or in a foreign country. U.S. copyright terms may differ for some foreign works.

TIP
Copyright runs in a calendar year.
All copyright terms run until the end of the calendar year in which they expire—that, is until December 31. For example, the copyright in a work that was published in the United States in 1923 expired on December 31, 1995 2018 regardless of what month and day during 1923 it was published.

Works First Published in the United States

This section covers the copyright terms for works that were first published in the United States.

Cheat Sheet: What's in the Public Domain Right Now

It's not necessary that you memorize all the copyright terms explained below. If you just want to know what material is in the public domain right now because of copyright expiration, you only need to learn four rules. Only works falling within these rules have had their copyrights expire. Note, however, that on Jan. 1, 2003 the copyrights for many unpublished works expired.

Rule 1: Everything Published in the United States Over 95 Years Ago Is in the Public Domain

Copyright protection for every work of authorship published before 1923 lasted a maximum of 75 years. All such works entered the public domain in 1998. Copyright protection for works published from 1923 through 1977 lasts a maximum of 95 years. Thus, starting in 2019, works published over 95 years ago began to enter the public domain in the United States. You can safely assume any work published over 95 years ago is in the public domain. This is so whether the work was first published in the United States or was originally published outside the United States and republished here.

Rule 2: Works Initially Published Less than 95 Years Ago But Before 1964 in the United States and Not Renewed Are in the Public Domain

Any work initially published in the United States less than 95 years ago, but before 1964, has had its copyright expire if the copyright wasn't renewed 28 years after publication.

Rule 3: All Unpublished Works by Authors Dead More Than 70 Years Are in the Public Domain

All unpublished works created by authors who died 70 or more years ago are in the public domain in the United States. This is so whether the author was American or a non-American. Unpublished works made for hire created more than 120 years ago are also in the U.S. public domain.

Rule 4: Foreign Works Published Over 95 Years Ago With Copyright Notices Are in the Public Domain

Any work published outside the United States over 95 years ago had its U.S. copyright expire if it contained a copyright notice when it was published.

Works Published Over 95 Years Ago

The great cutoff term for the public domain is 95 years. The copyrights for any works published in the United States more than 95 years ago have expired, and such works are now in the public domain in the United States.

This category includes many of the most famous public domain works.

Year of Publication	Date Work Enters U.S. Public Domain
1922 and earlier	Jan. 1998 and earlier
1923	Jan. 1, 2019
1924	Jan. 1, 2020
1925	Jan. 1, 2021
1926	Jan. 1, 2022
1927	Jan. 1, 2023
1928	Jan. 1, 2024
1929	Jan. 1, 2025
1930	Jan. 1, 2026
1931	Jan. 1, 2027
1932	Jan. 1, 2028
1933	Jan. 1, 2029
1934	Jan. 1, 2030
1935	Jan. 1, 2031
1936	Jan. 1, 2032
1937	Jan. 1, 2033
1938	Jan. 1, 2034
1939	Jan. 1, 2035
1940	Jan. 1, 2036

Every January 1, a new body of works published 95 years in the past enters the public domain. For example, all works published during 1925 will enter the United States public domain on January 1, 2021. Works published during 1926 enter the public domain on January 1, 2022, and so on (see the chart above). Public domain proponents refer to January 1 as "public domain day."

Determining whether a work is in the public domain can sometimes be a complex process, but not for this category of works. If you know a work was first published in the United States over 95 years ago, it is almost certainly in the public domain.

The only possible exception would be where the work was published over 95 years ago without the copyright owner's permission. Such a publication does not start the copy right term clock ticking. However, it's highly unlikely you'll ever run into this problem. There is no reported case where a copyright owner (or his or her heirs) has ever claimed that a work was not in the public domain because it was published over 95 years ago without permission. If such a claim was made and turned out to be valid, the work would receive the term of protection provided for unpublished works (if it was never subsequently published with the owner's permission).

Public Domain was Frozen for 20 Years

Before 1998, copyright protection for works published in 1977 and earlier lasted 75 years from the date of publication. This meant that all works published in 1923 were due to enter the public domain in 1999; those published in 1924 would have become public domain in 2000; those published in 1925 would have become public domain in 2001; and so on every year until all works published before 1978 entered the public domain.

However, in 1998 this process was frozen for 20 years when Congress passed the Sonny Bono Copyright Term Extension Act. This law extended all copyright terms by 20 years.

Works published between 1923 and 1978 are protected for 95 years from the year of publication. This freeze finally ended on January 1, 2019, when all works published during 1923 entered the public domain. Notable 1923 works that entered the public domain included *The Prophet* by Kahlil Gibran and the classic Harold Lloyd silent film *Safety Last*. The website HathiTrust has made over 50,000 titles from 1923 available in its digital library (www.hathitrust.org/additional-resources-public-domain-day-2019).

More works published over 95 years ago continue to enter the public domain each year. For example, on January 1, 2020 all works published in the U.S. during 1924 entered the public domain, including Herman Melville's classic novella *Billy Budd*, *The Magic Mountain* by Thomas Mann, and *A Passage to India* by E.M. Forster. On January 1, 2021 all works published during 1925 enter the public domain including *The Great Gatsby* by F. Scott Fitzgerald, *The Trial* by Franz Kafka, and *Mein Kampf* by Adlolf Hitler.

Works Initially Published in the U.S. Less than 95 Years Ago and Before 1964 That Were Not Timely Renewed

Many works first published in the United States less than 95 years ago but before 1964 are also in the public domain because their copyrights have expired. However, you'll usually need to check records at the U.S. Copyright Office to determine the public domain status of such works.

Copyright Duration Chart for Works First Published in the United States

Date and Nature of Work	Copyright Term
Published over 95 years ago	The work is in the public domain
Published in the United States over 95 years ago, but before 1964, and never renewed	The work is in the public domain
Published over 95 years ago, but before 1964, and timely renewed	95 years from the date of first publication
Published between 1964–1977	95 years from the date of publication (renewal term automatic)
Created 1978 or later (whether or not published)	Single term of life plus 70 years (but if work made for hire or anonymous or pseudonymous, 95 years from the date of publication or 120 years from date of creation, whichever ends first)
Created, but not published or registered, before 1978	Single term of 120 years from creation for unpublished works made for hire, and unpublished anonymous or pseudonymous works (that is, unpublished works written under a pen name)
Created before 1978 and published 1978–2002	Copyright will expire Dec. 31, 2047

Using Public Domain Calculators

Public Domain Sherpa (www.public domainsherpa.com) is an online copyright duration calculator that can tell you whether a work's copyright has expired.

However, great care must be exercised when using this calculator. If the data input into a calculator is wrong, the answer will be wrong too. This requires a good understanding of basic copyright principles—for example, what constitutes publication, notice requirements, and protection for derivative works. Use of a calculator may give the illusion of a clear answer when in fact the copyright status of a work is unclear.

This is because works first published before 1978 were protected for 28 years from the date of publication. This protection could be extended for an additional 47 years (the "renewal term") by filing a renewal registration with the Copyright Office. The initial and renewal terms together added up to 75 years of copyright protection, the maximum term of protection that used to be available. In 1998, the renewal term was extended from 47 to 67 years, but the extension didn't apply to works already in the public domain in 1998.

Until 1992, the renewal term could only be obtained by filing a renewal registration with the Copyright Office during the 28th year after a work was first published.

(After 1992, however, the renewal term was made automatic and the copyright owner did not have to file a renewal.) As you might expect, many authors, publishers, and other copyright owners failed to file a renewal for their works on time. The Copyright Office estimates that only about 15% of all works published before 1964 were ever renewed.

This means that all works first published in the United States less than 95 years ago but before1964 for which no renewal was filed are in the public domain.

> **EXAMPLE:** The John Wayne movie *McLintock!* was published in 1963, but no renewal was filed by the movie's copyright owner during the 28th year after publication. This meant that the movie entered the public domain on Jan. 1, 1992. Had a renewal been filed, the movie would have received an additional 67 years of copyright protection and been protected until December 31, 2058.

CAUTION

Exception to the renewal requirement for foreign works. There is one very important exception to the rule that works published before 1964 had to be renewed after 28 years or the copyright expired. This rule does not apply to most works that were first published outside the United States and were never renewed. This is so whether such works were later republished in the United States or were never published in the United States.

Such works used to be in the public domain, but most of them had their copyrights restored on Jan. 1, 1996. See Chapter 15 for a detailed discussion of this issue.

"Out of Print" Does Not Mean Out of Copyright

Some people mistakenly believe that when a book or other written work is "out of print" the copyright expires and the work enters the public domain. Not so. A book is out of print when its publisher is out of stock and it can't be obtained from normal distribution channels. This has nothing to do with the work's copyright status and certainly doesn't mean that the copyright has expired. A book published as recently as one year ago could be out of print, but the copyright will not expire for at least 70 years. Similarly, books and other works published decades ago are often out of print but their copyright has yet to expire.

It is impossible to know how long the copyright will last in a work first published in the United States less than 95 years ago and before 1964 unless you know whether a renewal registration was filed on time. You'll usually need to research the Copyright Office's records to find out. Many of the renewal records can be searched online. (See Chapter 21 for a detailed discussion of how to research copyright renewals.)

Works Published Between 1964 and 1977

The renewal requirement for published works discussed above means that a vast body of work entered the public domain 28 years after publication due to failure to comply with a mere technical formality. This seemed unfair to many people, and as a result the law was changed in 1992. The new law made copyright renewals automatic—in other words, the renewal term was obtained whether or not a renewal registration was filed. Renewal registrations were made purely optional.

This means that works first published in the United States between January 1, 1964 and December 31, 1977 receive 95 years of copyright protection whether or not a renewal was (or is) filed on time. The earliest any such work will enter the public domain because of expiration of copyright is January 1, 2060 (for works published during 1964).

Note, however, this change in the law was not made retroactive. In other words, the copyright was not resurrected for works initially published in the United States that were already in the public domain before 1992 because no renewal application was filed. They remain in the public domain.

Works Published After 1977

Works published on January 1, 1978 or later receive a very different term of copyright protection than those published before that date. A work published after 1977 is protected by copyright as long as the author is alive and for 70 years from the date of his or her death. If there are multiple authors, the copyright lasts for 70 years after the last surviving author dies. This means that the earliest any work published after 1977 will enter the public domain because of copyright expiration is January 1, 2049 (if the work was created and the author died during 1978).

Works made for hire—that is, works created by employees as a part of their job or by independent contractors who have signed a work-for-hire agreement—are protected for 95 years from the date of first publication, or 120 years from the date of creation, whichever comes first. The earliest any such work will enter the public domain through copyright expiration is January 1, 2074.

Works for which the author employed a pseudonym (pen name) instead of his or her real name or which were written anonymously (for example, the novel *Primary Colors*, which was later revealed to have been written by former *Newsweek* journalist Joe

Klein) receive the same copyright term as works made for hire. If a pseudonymous or anonymous author's identity is subsequently revealed to the Copyright Office, the work automatically switches to the life-plus-70-year copyright term.

So, the upshot of all this is that you'll have to wait until the year 2049 for any works published after 1963 to enter the public domain due to copyright expiration.

Otherwise, you'll need to search U.S. Copyright Office renewal records to know whether or not the work has been renewed; if not, it is in the public domain (see Chapter 21).

If the year in the notice is 1964 or later, the work's copyright will not expire for many, many years.

However, not all published works contain copyright notices. And copyright notices for the following types of works published before 1978 did not have to contain a date of publication: maps, original works of art and art reproductions, technical and scientific drawings and models, photographs, labels used on products and merchandise, and prints and pictorial illustrations (see Chapter 19).

In this event, you'll have to look elsewhere for clues about when the work was published. It may contain a date of publication somewhere else—for example, on the title page of a written work or the back of a photo, or on a film can. You can also check Copyright Office registration records. If the work was registered, the record will show the date of publication (see Chapter 21). However, not all works are registered with the Copyright Office. Contacting the publisher may work; or the publication date may be listed in a reference work such as an encyclopedia or author's biography.

Determining a Work's Publication Date

It's easy to determine the year a work was published if it contains a copyright notice. You just have to look at the year date in the copyright notice. (See Chapter 19 for a detailed discussion of copyright notices.) If the year in the notice is over 95 years ago, the work is in the public domain.

Sample 1911 Copyright Notice:

Copyright 1911 Ted Synder Co. Inc. 112 W. 38th St. N.Y.

If the year is less than 95 years ago but before 1964, the work will also be in the public domain if it was initially published in the United States and not renewed on time. When a work is republished following renewal, the copyright notice will often state that the work has been renewed and give the year of renewal. In such cases, you know the work is not in the public domain.

Sample Renewal Copyright Notice:

Copyright © 1946. Copyright Renewed 1973. Fred Albert Music Corporation/EMI

Copyright Term for Unpublished Works

Unpublished works—for example, unpublished manuscripts, photographs, home movies, and computer software—retain copyright protection for 70 years after the author dies. This is true for unpublished works by both American and foreign authors regardless of the country in which the unpublished works were created. However, there are some special rules for unpublished works created before 1978.

An unpublished work that is a work made for hire or a pseudonymous or anonymous work is protected for 120 years from the date of creation. The reason works by pseudonymous or anonymous authors are protected for 120 years instead of the life of the author plus 70 years is that it can be very difficult to discover exactly when such an author died, since his or her real name may not be publicly known.

Unpublished Works Created Before 1978 and Published Before 2003

If an unpublished work was created before January 1, 1978 the copyright in the work will last until 70 years after the death of the author. However, there is one special twist: If the work was published between January 1, 1978 and December 31, 2003 the copyright will not expire before December 31, 2047, no matter when the author died.

> **EXAMPLE:** The famed novelist Ernest Hemingway died in 1961, leaving behind an unpublished novel called *True at First Light*, which was published in 1999. The novel would be copyrighted until December 31, 2031 (70 years after Hemingway's death) if the ordinary term of 70 years after death applied. Because of this special rule, the copyright will last until December 31, 2047.

Authors Dead More Than 70 Years

On January 1, 2003 all unpublished works by all authors who died in the year 1932 or earlier entered the public domain. This rule applies to all unpublished works by authors dead more than 70 years, whenever or wherever created. It also applies to unpublished materials yet to be discovered. Obviously, this was a prodigious body of work. On January 1 of every year after that date another year's worth of unpublished works also enter the public domain. For example, on January 1, 2008 unpublished works by authors who died during 1937 entered the public domain; on January 1, 2020 unpublished works by authors who died during 1949 became public domain, and so on.

Determining When Authors Died

Since all unpublished works by authors dead more than 70 years are now in the public domain, you need to know when an author died to determine whether his or her unpublished works are public domain.

If the author is well known, reference works such as encyclopedias will probably reveal when (or if) he or she died. The *Encyclopaedia Britannica* is an excellent reference source for this sort of information. It can be accessed for free on the Internet at www.britannica.com and is of course available in libraries. Other Internet resources include the website www.biography.com, which provides the birth and death dates for more than 25,000 people; the Biographical Dictionary website at www.s9.com, which contains 28,000 birth and death dates; and Wikipedia (www.wikipedia.org), which also has much biographical information.

There are also dozens of biographical dictionaries that provide death dates for well-known people. Some of these are general, such as *Merriam-Webster's Biographical Dictionary*. Many specialize in people in particular fields, such as *Baker's Biographical Dictionary of Musicians*, by Theodore Baker and Nicolas Slonimsky (GALE Group).

The following chart shows the dates unpublished works by individual authors entered or will enter the public domain over the next several years.

When Unpublished Works Enter Public Domain	
Year the Author Died	Date All of the Author's Unpublished Works Enter the Public Domain
1949 or earlier	January 1, 2020 or earlier
1950	January 1, 2021
1951	January 1, 2022
1952	January 1, 2023
1953	January 1, 2024
1954	January 1, 2025
1955	January 1, 2026

Unpublished Works for Hire More Than 120 Years Old

Unpublished works made for hire are protected by copyright for 120 years after the date of creation. All unpublished works for hire created before 1883 (1882 and earlier) entered the public domain on January 1, 2003. In addition, a new year's worth of works continue to enter the public domain every January 1. For example, all unpublished works for hire created in 1883 entered the public domain on January 1, 2004, those created in 1884 entered the public domain on Jan. 1, 2005, and so on. These works enter the public domain one at a time depending on the year they were created. This differs from works not made for hire—all such works by an author enter the public domain 70 years after he or she dies.

A work is made for hire if it was (1) created by an employee as part of his or her job, or (2) created by nonemployees where the work was created at the hiring party's "instance and expense"—that is, the hiring party induced creation of the work and had the right to direct and supervise how the work was carried out. No writing was required for a work to be considered a work made for hire before 1978.

Date Works for Hire, Pseudonymous, and Anonymous Work Enter Public Domain	
Year in Which Work Was Created	Date Work Enters Public Domain
1899 or earlier	January 1, 2020 or earlier
1900	January 1, 2021
1901	January 1, 2022
1902	January 1, 2023
1903	January 1, 2024

Thus, for example, if an unpublished drawing created by the great American artist Thomas Eakins in 1900 were discovered today, it would be in the public domain if it was not a work made for hire because Eakins died in 1916. However, if the drawing was a work made for hire, it would remain under copyright until January 1, 2021.

Unpublished Works Registered With the Copyright Office Before 1978

Before 1978, authors of some types of unpublished works had the option of registering them with the Copyright Office as unpublished. Such works receive the same copyright term as works published before 1978, with such protection beginning on the date a copy of the registered work was deposited with the Copyright Office.

Not all unpublished works could be registered. The procedure was only available for unpublished lectures and similar works, "dramatic compositions" (plays), musical compositions, "dramatico-musical compositions" (musicals), motion picture screenplays, motion pictures other than screenplays, photographs, works of art, "plastic works" (sculpture and similar works), and drawings. Such items as unpublished writings other than lectures could not be registered; nor could art reproductions or sound recordings. This procedure was not often used except for works that did not qualify as published for copyright purposes, even though they were performed in public or broadcast to the public—for example, plays, screenplays, radio scripts, and teleplays. Copyright

Office records must be searched to determine if such works were registered.

If such a registered unpublished work was later published, no new copyright was obtained in the material, and copyright term for such material was not extended.

Works First Published Outside the United States

This section covers the term of U.S. copyright protection for works that were first published outside the United States.

Until 1996, copyright experts generally believed that works first published outside the United States received the exact same copyright term as works first published in the United States. However, during that year a federal appellate court in California held that this was not always so. As explained below, according to this court ruling, many works first published outside the United States before 1978 receive a very different copyright term than those published in the United States at the same time. It all depends on whether the work was published with a proper copyright notice.

The Saga of Huckleberry Finn

In 1990 the long-missing original hand-written manuscript of Mark Twain's classic 1885 novel, *The Adventures of Huckleberry Finn*, was discovered in an old steamer trunk stored in the attic of a house in Los Angeles. To the surprise of many literary experts, the manuscript contained a good deal of material that had never found its way into the published version of Twain's novel. Some material was cut by Twain to keep the book from being too long. Other scenes were apparently omitted to keep the novel from being too dark and disturbing for 19th century readers. Following a lengthy legal battle, it was determined that the copyright in the manuscript belonged to The Mark Twain Foundation. Such a battle was worth fighting because the unpublished material was not in the public domain, even though the copyright in the published novel expired in 1942. Because of the copyright duration rules discussed in this section, the unpublished material was under copyright at least until Dec. 31, 2002. This was so even though Twain died in 1910. As explained above, the ordinary copyright term for unpublished works—the life of the author plus 70 years after the author dies—didn't apply because the unpublished material was created before 1978. A new "comprehensive edition" of *Huckleberry Finn* containing all of the previously unpublished material was published in 1996. Because this unpublished material was published before 2003, its copyright was extended to Dec. 31, 2047.

Works Published Before 1978

The copyright duration for works first published outside the United States before 1978 may depend on whether the work involved contained a copyright notice. Copyright notices have never been required for published works in most foreign countries, but they were often used anyway.

A copyright notice valid under U.S. law consists of the © symbol or the word "Copyright" or abbreviation "Copr.," followed by the publication date and copyright owner's name. However, the date could be left off maps, original works of art and art reproductions, technical and scientific drawings and models, photographs, labels used on products and merchandise, and prints and pictorial illustrations.

Works Published With a Valid Copyright Notice

Any work first published in a foreign country before January 1, 1978 with a copyright notice receives the same copyright term in the United States as works published in the United States during these years (with one big exception, noted below, for works whose copyright was never renewed). The term begins with the year of publication of the foreign work. The copyright terms for such works are as follows:

- **Works published before 1923:** All these works received a 75-year U.S. copyright term and, therefore, are all in the public domain in the United States.
- **Works published 1923–1963:** The vast majority of these works received a 95-year copyright term, dating from the year of publication with a copyright notice.

Note that many works published during 1923–1963 used to be in the public domain in the United States because their U.S. copyrights were not renewed with the U.S. Copyright Office during the 28th year after publication. However, most foreign works published during 1923–1963 that were never renewed had their U.S. copyright protection restored in 1996 and are protected for a full 95 years. But a few foreign works didn't qualify for copyright restoration and are still in the public domain in the United States. These are primarily works that were in the public domain in their home countries as of Jan. 1, 1996. Also, works by Americans first published outside the United States during 1923–1963 are not eligible for copyright restoration. Thus, for example, photographs of Marilyn Monroe by an American photographer that were initially published in a British newspaper in 1962 with a copyright notice and not timely renewed 28 years later were not eligible for restoration. As a result, the photos were in the U.S. public domain. *Barris v. Hamilton*, No. 96 CIV. 9541 (DAB) (S.D.N.Y. 1999). (See Chapter 15 for a detailed discussion of restoration of copyrights in foreign works.)

- **Works published 1964–1977:** Any work first published outside the United States during the years 1964 through 1977 with a copyright notice receives a 95-year copyright term, from the date of publication with notice. This means that the earliest any foreign work published between 1964 and 1978 will enter the public domain in the United States because of copyright expiration is January 1, 2060.

Works Published Before 1978 Without a Copyright Notice

Many works first published outside the United States did not contain copyright notices because they were not required in the country of publication. Should these works be treated any differently than works first published outside the United States with a notice? This is a crucial question whose answer is far from clear. As a result, it's possible for a work first published outside the United States before 1978 without a copyright notice to be in the public domain in some states and still under copyright in others!

The Rule in the Western United States

Federal courts in the Ninth Judicial Circuit—which covers the states of Alaska, Arizona, California, Hawaii, Idaho, Montana, Nevada, Oregon, and Washington—have determined that works first published outside the United States without valid copyright notices should not be considered as having been published under the U.S. copyright law in effect at the time. *Twin Books v. Walt Disney Co.*, 83 F.3d 1162 (9th Cir. 1996). Because these works are viewed as unpublished for American copyright purposes, they receive the same copyright term as unpublished works: They are protected for the life of the author and for 70 years after his or her death.

> **EXAMPLE:** The artists Pierre-Auguste Renoir and Richard Guino created a series of sculptures that were first published in France in 1917 without a copyright notice. In 2003, the owner of the sculptures filed a copyright infringement suit in Arizona against a company that was selling bronze copies of them without permission. Under the Ninth Circuit rule, which applied in Arizona, the sculptures did not acquire U.S. copyright protection when published outside the United States, and were also

not in the U.S. public domain. The court concluded that such works receive the copyright term applicable to unpublished works, which lasts for 70 years after the death of the last surviving author. Renoir died in 1919, but Guino lived until 1973. Thus, the court held that the copyright for the sculptures lasted until January 1, 2043. *Societe Civile Succession Richard Guino v. Renoir*, 549 F.3d 1182 (9th Cir. 2008).

However, there is an important exception to this rule. If the work was later republished before 1978 with a valid copyright notice, whether in the United States or abroad, it received the same term of U.S. copyright protection as if it were first published in the United States that year. These copyright terms are listed in the previous section.

> EXAMPLE: The children's book *Bambi: A Life in the Woods*, by Felix Salten, was originally published in Germany without a copyright notice in 1923. It was then republished in Germany with a copyright notice in 1926. The 1926 publication triggered the 95-year copyright term provided for U.S. works published at this time. This means *Bambi* won't be in the public domain in the United States until 2022. Had *Bambi* not been republished with a copyright notice, it would have been protected for 70 years after Salten died. *Twin Books v. Walt Disney Co.*, 83 F.3d 1162 (9th Cir. 1996).

The Rule in the Rest of the United States

Most copyright experts don't agree with the decision reached by the Court of Appeals in the *Twin Books* case. They believe there should be no difference in copyright terms for works published in the United States or abroad. Although the court's ruling is a binding legal precedent that all trial courts located in the Ninth Circuit must follow, courts in other parts of the country are not required to follow it, and it is likely they won't. Thus, for example, if the case involving the Renoir sculptures discussed in the above example had been filed in New York instead of Arizona, it is likely that the New York federal district court would have held that the sculptures were in the U.S. public domain because they were published before 1923. However, to date no court outside the Ninth Circuit has ruled on this issue, so no one can be absolutely certain what courts outside the Ninth Circuit will do.

What You Should Do

So what should you do? Unless you're certain that the work involved will not be used or made available in any of the states that make up the Ninth Circuit (which notably includes California), the only prudent course is to follow both the Ninth

Circuit's ruling and the rule that most experts believe should be used.

Under this approach, a work first published outside the United States without a copyright notice before 1978, and never republished before 1978 with valid notice, would be treated as in the public domain only if (1) the author has been dead more than 70 years (the same rule as for unpublished works); and (2) the work was first published before 1923 (the same rule as for works published outside the United States with a valid notice).

> **EXAMPLE:** Assume that Pierre-Auguste Renoir created a sculpture that was first published in France without notice in 1917 and never republished with notice. The work would be in the public domain under the Ninth Circuit's ruling because Renoir died in 1919—more than 70 years ago; also, since the work was first published more than 95 years ago, it would be in the public domain under the rule likely to be followed in the rest of the country. Thus the work is in the public domain in the entire United States.

Obviously, figuring all this out can be very complex, time consuming, and in many cases impossible. A cheap and simple alternative to conducting a copyright investigation is simply to select an arbitrary year to use as a cutoff publication date for the public domain. Such a year must be

before 1923 and more than 70 years after the author likely died.

There is no hard and fast rule as to what date to use. You want the date to be early enough so that the author almost certainly died more than 70 years ago. If you assume that the youngest an author is likely to be when a work is published is age 20, and such an author is likely to live no longer than age 80, then your cutoff year should be 130 years ago. For example, in 2020, the cutoff year would be 1889. Any work published before then would be assumed to be in the public domain because if a 20-year-old published a work in 1889, he or she would likely have died by 1949, and such work entered the public domain in 2020.

Of course, the problem with this method is that it eliminates many works that were published later than 1881 that are in the public domain.

Sound Recordings

Sound recordings created after February 15, 1972 receive the same copyright term as any other work of authorship. However, sound recordings created before February 15, 1972 were not protected by federal copyright law. Rather, they were protected under state law. Such protection was scheduled to end by December 31, 2067.

The lack of federal copyright protection for pre-1972 recordings ended on October 11, 2018 when the Classics Protection and Access Act ("CPA Act"; 17 U.S.C. § 1401) was signed into law. The CPA Act provides pre-1972 sound recordings with a basic federal copyright term of 95 years from the year of publication, plus a "transition period" of three to 15 years. The transition period is three years for sound recordings first published before 1923, five years for sound recordings first published between 1923 and 1946, and fifteen years for sound recordings published between 1946 and 1956. Protection for all other pre-1972 sound recordings, including those previously unpublished, expires on February 15, 2067.

Thus, all sound recordings first published before 1923 will enter the public domain on January 1, 2022. Sound recordings first published between 1923 and 1946 enjoy 100 years of federal copyright protection. Sound recordings first published between 1947 and 1956 obtain 110 years of protection. Sound recordings first published between 1957 and February 15, 1972 are protected until February 15, 2067. Sound recordings never published before February 15, 1972 enter the public domain on February 15, 2067; this is so even if they are published before that date.

Sound Recordings Created Before February 15, 1972	
Publication History of Work	**Copyright Term**
First Published Before 1923	Work enters public domain Jan. 1, 2022
First Published 1923–1946	100 years after publication
First Published 1947–1956	110 years after publication
First Published 1957–Feb. 15, 1972	Work enters public domain Feb. 15, 2067
Unpublished before Feb. 15, 1972	Work enters public domain Feb. 15, 2067

Works Published After 1977

Works published in almost all foreign countries after 1977 receive the same U.S. copyright term as works published in the United States. This is true whether or not they contain a copyright notice. None of these works will enter the public domain due to copyright expiration for many decades. However, some works published abroad without a copyright notice during 1978 through 1989 may have entered the U.S. public domain due to the lack of a copyright notice (but not due to copyright expiration); see Chapter 19. The only exception is for works from countries with which the United States has no copyright relations. (See below.)

Works Published in Countries With Which the U.S. Has No Copyright Relations

Today, works published in almost all foreign countries are entitled to U.S. copyright protection. However, there are a handful of countries with which the United States has no copyright relations. These are:

Eritrea   Iraq
Ethiopia   San Marino
Iran

Works published in these countries by citizens of these countries receive no protection at all under U.S. law.

Copyright Notice Requirements

Copyright Notices and the Public Domain..336

Does the Work Lack a Valid Notice?..338

    The Copyright Symbol...338

    Publication Year 339

    Owner's Name...340

    Wrong Placement...342

Is a Copyright Notice Required?..342

    Unpublished Works 343

    Works Published After March 1, 1989 343

    Works Published Outside the United States...345

    Sound Recordings..345

    Contributions to Collective Works...345

    Derivative Works 346

Is the Omission of a Valid Notice Excused?..347

    Works Published by Licensees..347

    Notice Removed Without Owner's Permission 350

    Notice Omitted by Accident or Mistake Before 1978 350

    Only Small Number of Unnoticed Copies Distributed 1978–1989 351

    Corrective Measures Taken to Cure Omission for Works Published
        1978–1989 352

What If You Make a Mistake?...352

If you find a work published before March 1, 1989 without a copyright notice—the © symbol followed by the copyright owner's name and publication date—it could be in the public domain. This chapter shows you how to determine whether a work lacking a proper copyright notice is in the public domain in the United States.

SKIP AHEAD

You may skip this chapter if the work you are researching was published after March 1, 1989 or was never published. These works do not need copyright notices.

Copyright Notices and the Public Domain

One unusual feature of U.S. copyright law is that before March 1, 1989 all published works had to contain a copyright notice —the familiar © symbol or the word "copyright" along with the publication date and the name of the copyright owner. The punishment for failure to comply with this rule was severe: A work published before January 1, 1978 without a copyright notice automatically entered the public domain at the moment of publication unless one of the many exceptions discussed below applied.

EXAMPLE: Sally self-published a book of her poetry in 1975. Since she wasn't familiar with copyright law, she failed to place a copyright notice on the book. As a result, the work automatically entered the public domain upon the date of publication.

Works published without valid notices beginning in 1978, and continuing through March 1, 1989, did not automatically enter the public domain upon the date of publication. Instead, owners of such works were given five years after the publication to cure the omission. They automatically entered the public domain after that time if the owner failed to add a proper notice.

It is impossible to know how many works published before 1989 lacked proper copyright notices. Most American publishers routinely included copyright notices on their products. As a result, there aren't many famous works that were published without copyright notices. Perhaps the most famous work that entered the public domain because it was published without a notice is the children's book *The Tale of Peter Rabbit*, by Beatrix Potter. More often, notices were left off works that were thought to have limited or only temporary value—for example, advertisements, postcards, or newspapers.

However, before you start trolling libraries, archives, flea markets, and other places for works published without a copyright notice, be aware that there are several exceptions to the notice requirement. Because of these exceptions, discussed below, it can be very difficult to know for sure if a work lacking a valid notice is in the public domain or not.

To determine if a work without a valid copyright notice is in the public domain, you must answer three questions:

- Does the work lack a notice or is the notice invalid?
- If the work lacks a valid notice, is it because a notice was not required?
- If notice was required, is the lack of a valid notice excused?

The work will be in the public domain only if it lacks a notice or has an invalid notice, if a notice was required, and if none of the excuses for failing to have a notice apply.

Before moving ahead to answer these difficult questions, first make sure the work is not in the public domain for some other reason. Turn to the chapter covering the type of work involved—for example, writings, music, art, photographs—to make sure you have considered these other ways the work might have entered the public domain. For example:

- Is the work eligible for copyright protection? Works created by the U.S. government and certain other types of works are not copyrightable and are always in the public domain.

- Has the copyright expired? Any work published in the United States before 1923 is in the public domain because its copyright has expired.
- If the work was first published in the United States less than 95 years ago but before 1964, was the copyright renewed? All works published during this time period had to be renewed 28 years after publication or they entered the public domain. It's likely that most works published without a valid copyright notice during these years were never renewed (indeed, it's estimated that 85% of all works published before 1964 are in the public domain because they were never renewed). It will usually be much easier to determine that a work is in the public domain because it was not renewed than for lack of a valid copyright notice (see Chapter 21). Now, let's examine each question in turn.

GRAY AREA

In many cases, it will be impossible for you to know for sure whether a work is in the public domain because it lacks a valid copyright notice, though it may seem likely that it is. In these cases, refer to Chapter 1 for detailed guidance on how to deal with such public domain gray areas.

Does the Work Lack a Valid Notice?

➡️ **SKIP AHEAD**
The first step you should take is to check the work carefully to see if it contains a valid copyright notice. If it has a valid notice, you don't need to read the rest of this chapter.

Some published works contain some, but not all, of the required elements for a valid notice. If the omissions or errors in the notice are serious enough, the notice will not be legally valid. A work with an invalid notice is treated just the same as if it has no notice at all.

A valid copyright notice ordinarily contains three elements:

1. the copyright symbol, "©," the word "Copyright," or abbreviation "Copr."
2. the publication date (however, the date is not required for some types of works), and
3. the copyright owner's name.

These elements don't have to appear in any particular order (although they are usually in the order listed here).

In the past, courts were very strict about enforcing complex rules concerning the format and placement of copyright notices. Today, however, they tend to be much more lenient. A notice must contain a truly serious error or omission for the copyright to be invalidated.

The following errors or omissions will render a notice invalid:

The Copyright Symbol

A copyright notice must contain either the copyright symbol "©," or the words "Copyright" or "Copr." The word "Copyrighted" is also acceptable. If one of these is not present on the work, the notice is invalid.

Sometimes the copyright symbol is not in the proper form—for example, where the letter "c" is not completely surrounded by a circle. A letter "c" surrounded by parentheses, hexagon, or some other geometric form has been found acceptable by several courts. *Videotronics, Inc. v. Bend Elecs.*, 586 F.Supp. 478 (D. Nev. 1984). But courts have held that use of the letter "c" alone renders the notice invalid. *Holland Fabrics, Inc. v. Delta Fabrics, Inc.*, No. 85 Civ. 2398 (WCC) (S.D.N.Y. 1987).

There is one exception to the rule that a copyright notice must contain the © symbol or words "Copyright" or "Copr." Copyright notices for sound recordings are supposed to contain a capital P in a circle (℗) instead of the © symbol or the words "Copyright" or "Copr." A sound recording notice without the ℗ is invalid. The P stands for phonogram. However, the word "phonogram" may not be used in place of the ℗. But note that notices are only required for sound recordings published from February 15, 1972 through March 1, 1989.

Publication Year

Subject to the important exceptions noted below, the notice must also contain the date the work was published. The date can be in either Arabic or Roman numerals. A notice without a date is invalid. In addition, a copyright notice with a publication date more than one year in the future— that is, more than one year after the actual date of publication—is treated as if it had no notice at all. This is so even if only a small number of copies were distributed with the defective notice.

> **EXAMPLE:** Isaac's book was first published in 1987, but the copyright notice lists 1989 as the publication date. The notice is invalid.

On the other hand, where the publication date is for any year *prior* to the actual publication date, the notice's validity is not affected. However, the year stated in the notice becomes the official legal publication date for copyright duration purposes.

> **EXAMPLE:** Abraham's book was first published in 1948, but the copyright notice lists 1946 as the publication date. The notice is valid, but 1946 is now considered the date of publication for purposes of computing the duration of Abraham's copyright.

However, not all works need to have a publication date in their notice. Whether a date was required depends on the type of work involved and the date of publication.

Works Published Before 1978

If a work was published before 1978, it needs to have a year in the copyright notice only if it is a printed literary, musical, or dramatic work. Such works include books, magazines, periodicals, newspapers, lectures, speeches, plays, sheet music and musical scores, screenplays, and movies. Also included are sound recordings published from Feb. 15, 1972 through Dec. 31, 1977. (Sound recordings published before 1972 didn't need copyright notices.)

The following types of works published before 1978 didn't have to have a year in the copyright notice:

- maps
- original works of art and art reproductions
- technical and scientific drawings and models
- photographs
- labels used on products and merchandise, and
- prints and pictorial illustrations.

Greeting Cards, Stationery, Jewelry, Toys, and Useful Articles Published After January 1, 1978

Starting on January 1, 1978, the copyright law was changed to require a year in copyright notices for all types of works except greeting cards, postcards, stationery, jewelry, toys, dolls, and useful articles when they contain pictorial or graphic works. For example, a Christmas card with a drawing or photo of Santa Claus need not contain a publication date in the copyright notice. Useful articles are utilitarian items such as furniture, clothing, pottery, dishes, glassware, silverware, and rugs.

Although dates are not required in the notices for such works, they are often included anyway, or a publication date may be placed elsewhere on the work. If not, you may need to do some research. See below for a discussion of ways to determine the date a work was published.

New Editions and Derivative Works

When a published written work is later revised and republished as a new edition, the notice need only include the publication date and copyright owner of the revised edition. The same rule holds true when an original work is later adapted into a new work—for example, a novel is transformed into a screenplay or stage play. Such a work is called a derivative work.

Owner's Name

The copyright owner's name must also be included in the notice. The word "by" need not be used before the name, though it often is. The name can appear in almost any form, including:

- the copyright owner's full legal name (if the owner is a corporation, the word "Inc." need not appear in the notice)

- the owner's surname (family name) alone or with the owner's first initial
- an abbreviation, trade name, nickname, or initials by which the copyright owner is generally known (for example, IBM), or
- the owner's initials on photos, sculpture, art, or graphics published before 1978, even if the owner isn't generally known by those initials, as long as the full name appears somewhere on or in the work.

Omission of the copyright owner's name from a notice makes the notice legally invalid and will place the work in the public domain unless one of the exceptions discussed below applies.

EXAMPLE: A Massachusetts manufacturer of sewing machine parts published an illustrated catalog containing drawings of its parts. However, the copyright notice included in the catalog said only "copyright-1933." The company's name—the copyright owner—was omitted. A court held that the catalog entered the public domain when it was published due to the failure to include the copyright owner's name in the notice. This meant that one of the company's competitors was free to copy the drawings in its own catalogs. *W.S. Bessett, Inc. v. Germain,* 18 F.Supp. 249 (D. Mass. 1937).

However, minor spelling or other minor errors in a name in a notice do not affect the copyright's validity. For example, misspelling John Smith's name as "John Smythe" in a copyright notice would not affect the copyright's validity.

But what if the wrong name is used in the notice—that is, the person or company named in the notice is not really the copyright owner? This is obviously a much more serious error than misspelling the name. Nevertheless, the copyright law provides that if the work was published during January 1, 1978 through March 1, 1989 it is not placed in the public domain if the name in the notice is not the actual copyright owner.

The rule as to works published before 1978 is not entirely clear. The law mentioned above does not apply to these works. Fifty or 60 years ago courts would usually hold that a work entered the public domain if the person or company named in the notice was not the true copyright owner. In more recent years, however, courts have tended to be much more lenient. For example, a court held that sound recordings published in 1973 with the wrong name in the copyright notice did not enter the public domain. The court reasoned that no one was harmed by the improper name because the company listed in the notice referred all inquiries regarding the recording to the true copyright

---

Very Old Copyright Notices

If you examine books or other written works published in the United States before 1909 you'll find that the copyright notice looks different than as described above. It was not until 1909 that Congress required that a copyright notice include the word "copyright" or the © symbol along with the date of publication and copyright owner's name.

Between 1874 and 1909 copyright owners had the option of using the word "Copyright" along with the date the work was entered (filed) with the Library of Congress and the name of the party who entered it. Or, they could use a notice like the following, which was used for a book published in New York City in 1847:

Entered according to Act of Congress, in the year 1847, by Wm. H. Onlerdonk, in the Clerk's Office of the District Court for the Southern District of New York.

Between 1802 and 1874, all copyright notices had to be like or similar to the example above.

Of course, the copyright in all such works has expired (see Chapter 18). Therefore, it makes no difference whether they contain a valid notice. But the date in the notice helps make it clear that the copyright has in fact expired.

owner. *Fantastic Fakes, Inc. v. Pickwick Int'l, Inc.*, 661 F.2d 479 (5th Cir. 1981). To be on the safe side, you should assume that such works do not enter the public domain—that is, it is sufficient that they have any name in the notice, even if it turns out not to be the true copyright owner.

Wrong Placement

Subject to the exceptions explained below, a copyright notice can be placed anywhere on a work so long as it gives the public "reasonable notice of the claim of copyright." 17 U.S.C. Section 401(c). In other words, it can be placed anywhere a person could be reasonably expected to find it.

However, there are three important exceptions to this general rule for works published *before 1978*. Notices for such works must be in the locations indicated below or the notice is invalid:

- **Books:** On the page immediately following the title page or on the title page itself.

Sample Pre-1978 Copyright Notice

- **Magazines, newspapers, journals, and other periodicals:** On the title page, the first page of text, or under the title heading. The notice may also appear in a magazine's masthead.

National Geographic Magazine
Copyright Notice

- **Musical works:** On the title page or first page of music.

Sample Copyright Notice for Sheet Music

Is a Copyright Notice Required?

Even if the work you're interested in has no notice or has an invalid notice, it may not be in the public domain. This is the case if a notice is not required for the type of work involved. Copyright notices are required only for works that were published for the first time in the United

States before March 1, 1989. Notices are not required for:

- unpublished works
- works published after March 1, 1989, or
- works first published outside the United States.

In addition, contributions to collective works such as magazines and newspapers don't need their own copyright notices.

If you determine that a notice is not required, you don't need to read the rest of this chapter. If a notice is required and the work lacks a valid notice, go on to the next section to determine if the lack of a valid notice is excused.

After March 1, 1989 the law was changed so that any published or unpublished work has copyright protection, even without a copyright notice. Any work created after that date automatically obtains copyright protection. (See Chapter 2 for a detailed discussion of copyright law.)

Unpublished Works

Although authors occasionally place copyright notices on their unpublished works, they have never been legally required. The lack of a valid copyright notice does not place a work in the public domain. Publication has a specific legal meaning for each kind of creative work. To learn the requirements for publication, read the chapter on the specific type of work you are considering—for example, if the work you want to use is a photograph, read Chapter 6 on photographs to learn the legal definition of publication.

Works Published After March 1, 1989

Copyright notices were made optional as of March 1, 1989, bringing U.S. law in line with the laws of most foreign countries. As a result, a copyright notice is not required on any copies of a work published on or after March 1, 1989. This is so regardless of whether other copies of the same work were previously published before that date—in other words, if a work is published both before and after March 1, 1989 the copies published after that date don't need notices.

> **EXAMPLE:** Bruno self-published a book of poetry in 1988. The work contained a valid copyright notice. By 1990, the work sold out and Bruno published a second edition. However, this time he forgot to include a copyright notice. Even so, the book did not enter the public domain. Because the second edition was published after March 1, 1989 no notice was required.

Even though copyright notices are not required for works published after March 1, 1989, they are usually included anyway. There are a number of reasons for this, including:

- force of habit
- because including copyright notices helps make it clear to the public that the work is copyrighted, and
- because including a notice provides certain limited advantages if the copyright owner ever files a copyright infringement lawsuit, because the alleged infringer can't claim he or she didn't know the work was copyrighted.

But inclusion or exclusion of the proper notice has no bearing on when a work published after March 1, 1989 enters the public domain.

How can you tell whether a work was published after March 1, 1989? Here are some ways:

- Most published works are dated in some way. Examine the work carefully to see if it contains a publication date or some other evidence of when it was published.
- Look at the condition of the work. If it looks old, it was probably published long before 1989, which, after all, isn't very long ago. For example, a book with yellowing pages and a crumbling leather binding was likely published long before 1989.
- Do an Internet search under the author's name and the name of the work. There may be an entire website devoted to the author that provides a publication date. Or there may be

an online encyclopedia (for example, britannica.com) or other reference work or database that provides this information.

- If the work was registered with the U.S. Copyright Office, checking Copyright Office records will also reveal when it was published (see Chapter 21). However, many works were never registered.
- If the publisher or printer's name is listed on the work, contact the company and ask them when the work was published.
- The work may be listed in library catalogs. Turn to the chapter covering the type of work involved —for example, writings or music— and you'll find a list of library resources for that type of work.
- Various printed reference works may also reveal when the work was published. For example, a music or art encyclopedia may reveal when a particular work was published. A biography about the author may also have this information. Turn to the chapter covering the type of work involved—for example, writings or music—and you'll find a list of reference resources for that type of work. You may find more resources by visiting or calling the reference department of a good library.

If you cannot determine the publication date after following the steps outlined above, the safest course of action is to assume that a work was published after March 1, 1989, and is, therefore, not in the public domain.

Works Published Outside the United States

If the work you're interested in was first published outside the United States and lacks a valid copyright notice, it is still not in the public domain. Works published outside the United States from January 1, 1978 through March 3, 1989 without a valid notice used to be in the public domain in the United States unless the omission was excused by one of the exceptions explained below. However, the U.S. copyrights in almost all these works was automatically restored on January 1, 1996. (See Chapter 15 for a detailed discussion of this issue.)

Sound Recordings

Until 2018, sound recordings were not protected by federal copyright law. For example, phonograph records were not protected. Phonograph records and other recordings were protected by state law instead. For this reason, such works did not have to contain copyright notices. Federal copyright protection replaced state law protection in 1972. So sound recordings published in the United States from February 15, 1972 through March 1, 1989 did have to contain a copyright notice. A recording published during this time without a notice is in the public domain unless the omission is excused as described below. But this does not mean that the words or music on the recording are in the public domain. The music and lyrics reproduced on a sound recording need not contain a copyright notice. A notice is only needed to protect the recording of the performance of the music and lyrics, not the music and lyrics themselves.

> **CAUTION**
> **You do not need permission to use a sound recording that fell into the public domain because it lacked a proper copyright.** That means you do not need to obtain permission from the former copyright owner, performers, or record company to use the recording of the performance. But you would need to obtain permission from the copyright owner of the music performed on the recording.

Contributions to Collective Works

A collective work is a work that is created by selecting and arranging preexisting materials that are separate and independent works entitled to copyright protection in their own right. Examples of collective works include anthologies; newspapers, magazines, and other periodicals in which separate articles (with copyright protection of their own) are combined into a collective whole; and encyclopedias consisting of articles on various topics. Individual articles or other contributions to a collective work need not contain their own copyright notices. The single notice for the work as a whole is sufficient.

> **EXAMPLE:** Steve wrote an article on filmmaking and sold the right to publish it the first time to *Film Weekly Magazine.* He retained all his other rights and was, therefore, the copyright owner of the article. When his article was published in *Film Weekly* in 1988, it did not contain its own copyright notice in his name. The only notice in the magazine was the notice that *Film Weekly* placed on its title page in its own name. However, this was sufficient to satisfy the notice requirement for Steve's article.

However, there is one exception to this rule. Advertisements published in magazines, newspapers, and other collective works must contain their own copyright notices.

Derivative Works

A derivative work is one that is based upon or adapted from a preexisting work. Good examples are movies based on novels or plays, and translations and new editions of existing works.

What if an original work published with a proper notice is later incorporated into a derivative work that is published before 1989 and the derivative work lacks a notice? Is the original work thrown into the public domain along with the derivative work? The courts disagree with each other on this question. Some have held it does place the original work into the public domain. Others have said it doesn't, as long as the copyright owner of the original work did not intend to abandon his or her copyright through the publication that occurred without the proper copyright notice. *L&L White Metal Casting Corp. v. Joseph*, 387 F.Supp. 1349 (E.D.N.Y. 1975); *Baldwin Cooke Co. v. Keith Clark, Inc.*, 383 F.Supp. 650 (N.D. Ill. 1974), *aff'd* 505 F.2d 1250 (7th Cir. 1974). Because of this split among the courts, the safest course is to assume that the original work is not injected into the public domain. However, the new material added to the original work will be in the public domain unless the lack of a notice is excused.

> **EXAMPLE:** Sam finds two editions of a book on forensic science called *Murder for Blockheads*. The first edition was published in 1980 with a proper copyright notice. The second edition—a major revision—was published in 1988 without a copyright notice. Sam should assume that the failure to place a notice on the second edition—a derivative work based on the first edition—does not place the first edition into the

public domain. But the new material added to the second edition will be in the public domain unless one of the excuses discussed below applies.

Is the Omission of a Valid Notice Excused?

Even if a work published in the United States before March 1, 1989 lacks a valid copyright notice, it still may have copyright protection. This is because the omission may be excused. Before you can conclude that any work is in the public domain because it lacks a copyright notice, you must first determine that none of these excuses apply.

Works Published by Licensees

Most courts do not like to see an author of a creative work lose copyright protection because of failure to comply with a technical formality. This seems particularly unfair where the noncompliance wasn't even the copyright owner's fault. For this reason, the courts created a very important excuse, saving from the public domain many works published without notices. This excuse applies when a copyright owner grants a license to a publisher or anyone else to publish his work and, unbeknownst to the owner, the person fails to include a valid notice on the work.

This excuse came into being because several courts held that an agreement between the author and the publisher includes the implication—whether in writing or not—that the publisher would take whatever steps necessary to preserve the author's copyright protection. This, of course, included placing a valid copyright notice on all published versions of the work so that it would not enter the public domain. If a licensee failed to live up to this implied promise, the courts held that the faulty publication was made without the copyright owner's authority and therefore did not inject the work into the public domain. *Fantastic Fakes v. Pickwick International*, 661 F.2d 479 (5th Cir. 1981).

Not all courts have applied this exception in every case in the past and it's possible some might refuse to do so today. However, given the trend in the courts to be lenient to copyright owners who have failed to have valid copyright notices placed on their works, it's likely that most courts would apply this exception to save a work from the public domain. It's prudent, therefore, for you to act as though this exception does apply and not treat works falling within this exception as being in the public domain for lack of a valid notice. You'll never get into legal trouble if you follow this approach.

EXAMPLE: Sean, a short story writer, orally agreed in 1975 that the science fiction fan magazine *SciFan* could publish one of his stories one time only (what's called a nonexclusive license). Sean retained all his other copyright rights in the story—for example, the right to republish the story in anthologies, to create a movie from it, or to translate it into other languages. *SciFan's* publisher failed to include a copyright notice in the issue containing Sean's story. Although Sean's story was published without a notice, it's likely that a court would hold it's not in the public domain. By publishing it without a notice, *SciFan* breached an implied (unspoken) promise to Sean that it wouldn't do anything to harm his copyright rights in the story. This in turn meant that for copyright purposes the story was published without Sean's permission.

Rule Changes for 1978 and Beyond

Starting in 1978, a new copyright law took effect that tightened up the rules for works published without copyright notices by licensees. A work published without a valid notice between Jan. 1, 1978 and March 1, 1989 is saved from the public domain only if there was a *written license agreement* that required the licensee to include a copyright notice on the work. Without such a requirement in writing, the work entered the public domain unless one of the other exceptions discussed below applies.

EXAMPLE: In 1987, Mavis signed a contract with Hackneyed Publications granting it a license to publish her book in North America. Mavis retained all her other copyright rights. The contract contained a clause requiring Hackneyed to include a proper copyright notice on the book when it was published. Somehow, the notice was left off all the copies Hackneyed published in 1988. Even so, the work is not in the public domain because the unnoticed publication violated a written license agreement.

Because of this rule, if a work without a copyright notice was licensed, you can generally forget about it being in the public domain if it was published before 1978. If the work was published after 1978, you must obtain and read a copy of the license agreement to know for sure whether it's in the public domain. As a practical matter, this will often be impossible. Some license agreements are recorded with the U.S. Copyright Office, so you may be able to get a copy there (see Chapter 21). However, most licenses have never been recorded. It's doubtful that either the licenser/copyright owner or licensee would agree to give you a copy or otherwise help you establish that the work is in the public domain. After all, why should they risk losing copyright in the work?

If the Author Knew the Work Was Published Without Notice

However, there is an exception to this excuse: If the copyright owner/licenser knew that the licensee was publishing the owner's work without a valid notice and did not object or otherwise attempt to stop the publication, the owner can't later claim the licensee breached a promise to include such a notice. In this event, the work *will* be deemed to have entered the public domain by the courts.

> **EXAMPLE:** Assume in the example above that Sean was sent an advance copy of the issue of *SciFan* containing his story. Sean saw that the issue lacked a copyright notice but did not object to the publisher or attempt to halt the unnoticed publication. Sean's story would be deemed to have entered the public domain because it was published without a notice with his knowledge.

Authors Who Don't License Their Work

In addition, the rules discussed here only apply to copyright owners who *license* their work to be published by others—that is, sell some, but not all, of their copyright rights. *House of Hatten, Inc. v. Baby Togs, Inc.*, 668 F.2d 251 (S.D.N.Y. 1987). It does not apply, for example, to the following:

- A person who publishes his or her own work.

  > **EXAMPLE:** Assume that Grandma Jacobs, a well-known primitive artist, completed a painting and offered it for sale to the public in her Arizona studio in 1960. She failed to place a copyright notice on the work. The painting is considered to be published (see Chapter 5), so the failure to include a notice on it injected it into the public domain.

- Works created by employees and published by their employers.

  > **EXAMPLE:** Assume that David, a newspaper reporter employed by the *New York Inquirer*, wrote a lengthy expose of the meat packing industry that was published in the paper in 1985. The newspaper did not contain a copyright notice. Since David was an *Inquirer* employee, the story was a work made for hire for which the newspaper owned all the rights and was considered the author for copyright purposes. Therefore, the unnoticed publication injected the story into the public domain.

- Works for which the author transfers all of his or her copyright rights to the person or entity who publishes it (such a transfer is termed an assignment, not a license).

> **EXAMPLE:** Assume that Suzy, a novelist, created a novel called *Golgotha* and sold all her copyright rights to Acme Press. Acme, not Suzy, then owned the copyright in the novel. Acme published the novel without a valid copyright notice in 1968. The unnoticed publication injected the novel into the public domain.

In some cases it will be fairly obvious that a work has not been licensed. For example, any work written by an employee and published by the employer is not licensed (see the example above). Another area where licensing is uncommon is fine art. Painters and sculptors ordinarily do not license their work for publication by other people. Instead, they publish their works themselves by offering them for sale to the general public, museums, or galleries (see Chapter 5). As a result, a great deal of fine art has entered the public domain because artists often did not include copyright notices on their works. But note carefully that this applies only to art published in the United States before March 1, 1989. After that date a notice on the work was not necessary.

In other cases, you may be familiar with the work's publishing history. However, in many cases it will be very difficult, if not impossible, for you to know whether a work was licensed. The first thing you need to do in these cases is check to see if the work has been registered with the U.S. Copyright Office and, if so, obtain a copy of the registration application (see Chapter 21). This will show you if the publisher of the work is the same person or entity as the copyright owner. If so, the work has not been licensed and an unnoticed publication will place it into the public domain unless one of the other exceptions discussed below applies.

If the work has not been registered, it will be much harder to determine if it has been licensed. You'll need to contact the publisher or copyright owner. It's probably wise not to mention that you're investigating to determine whether the work is in the public domain. Doing this kind of research can be time consuming; therefore, it's only worthwhile for a very valuable work.

Notice Removed Without Owner's Permission

A published work does not enter the public domain if it originally had a valid copyright notice and the notice is later removed, destroyed, or obliterated without the copyright owner's permission. For example, a book whose title page has been torn out is not in the public domain if the page had a valid notice.

Notice Omitted by Accident or Mistake Before 1978

There is another, much more limited exception to the rule that works published before 1978 without a valid copyright notice are in the public domain. This is where the copyright owner failed to provide notice on a *particular copy or copies* by accident or mistake. Accident or mistake meant that there was an accident in the printing process or similar mechanical error.

This exception has been successfully invoked only where a notice was omitted due to a printing or similar mechanical problem. For example, lack of notice was excused where the printing plate on which a copyright notice appeared was damaged. *Strauss v. Penn Printing & Publishing Co.*, 220 977 (E.D. Pa. 1915).

Moreover, the exception applies only if the notice was left off only a very few copies of the total number published. For example, the exception was applied where the copyright notice was accidentally obliterated on five jeweled pins out of hundreds that were manufactured when the words Tiffany & Co were stamped over the notice. *Herbert Rosenthal Jewelry Corp. v. Grossbardt*, 436 F.2d 315 (2d Cir. 1970). People who unwittingly use a work like this have some legal protection because the owner of the work would have to prove that the user actually knew the lack of a copyright notice was a mistake but used the work anyway.

Only Small Number of Unnoticed Copies Distributed 1978–1989

A much broader exception than the accident or mistake rule was created for works published between January 1, 1978 and March 1, 1989. Copyright protection was not lost for such works if the notice was omitted from no more than a "relatively small" number of copies distributed to the public. It doesn't matter if the omission was by accident or on purpose.

The "relatively small" criterion was deliberately left vague in the copyright law in order to give courts maximum flexibility to decide the question on a case-by-case basis. Courts have held that omission of a proper notice from 1% and 4% of the total copies published satisfied the criterion. Courts have also ruled that the criterion was not met when notice was omitted from 10%, 22%, and 39% of the total number of published copies. When applying this criterion, courts ask whether notice was left off so many copies that a diligent copyright owner should have been aware of the problem.

The problem is to discover how many copies of the work you want to use were published without a notice. If you find a single copy that lacks a notice, it could be the only one and fall into the "relatively small" category. Such a work would not be in the public domain. If you can find multiple copies lacking a notice, it's likely that a proper copyright notice was omitted from a substantial number of copies. However, even then you can't be absolutely sure how many copies were published without a notice. The publisher may not know and probably wouldn't tell you if it did. This is yet another reason why it can be very difficult to know for sure whether a work published without a notice is in the public domain or not.

Corrective Measures Taken to Cure Omission for Works Published 1978–1989

If the work was published between January 1, 1978 and February 28, 1989 there is one final exception to the rule that publication without notice injected the work into the public domain: The copyright owner could take certain corrective steps to cure the omission. If this was done, the work did not enter the public domain.

To cure the omission, the copyright owner was required to:

- register the work with the U.S. Copyright Office within five years after the unnoticed publication
- send certified letters to all distributors of the work instructing them to return their old copies for replacement, or

offering to supply them with labels containing the proper copyright notice to affix to the copies, and

- if economically feasible, attempt to notify every purchaser that could be located that the work was protected by copyright.

If you find a work published during 1978–1989 without a valid notice you'll need to check the Copyright Office records to see if the work was registered within the five-year time limit. If it was registered, it's likely the work is not in the public domain. (See Chapter 21 for how to search Copyright Office records.)

If the work was not registered, it could be in the public domain unless one of the other exceptions discussed previously applies.

What If You Make a Mistake?

As the above discussion demonstrates, it can be difficult—often, impossible—to know for sure whether a work published without a notice is in the public domain or not. What if you make a mistake and use a work that you wrongly thought was in the public domain? In this event, the copyright law gives you some important relief.

If, unbeknownst to you, the failure to include a valid notice on a published work is excused because of any of the last four exceptions discussed above (that is, removal of notice, accident or mistake, small number of copies, or corrective measures taken to cure the omission), you will not be liable for damages for copyright infringement if you prove the following two things:

1. You were misled by the lack of notice into thinking the work was in the public domain.

2. Your copying was completed before you learned that the work had been registered with the Copyright Office (if it was). 17 U.S.C. Section 405(b).

EXAMPLE: In 2020, Sally obtained several copies of a self-published book by Sam. All the copies lacked a copyright notice but stated that they were published in 1988. Sally checked the Copyright Office records and discovered that the work had never been registered. Sally therefore concluded that the work was in the public domain because it was published before 1989 without a valid notice and no steps had apparently been taken to cure the omission. Sally then copied most of the book onto her website. Sam later discovered Sally's copying and filed suit for copyright infringement. Sally will not be liable for damages if she convinces the court that she reasonably believed in good faith that Sam's book was in the public domain.

Note carefully, however, that this rule applies only to authorized publications by the copyright owner. It won't apply, for example, where the copy lacking a notice was itself a pirated version of the original work, and it may be impossible for you to tell if the work you have is a pirated version or not.

Nor will it usually apply where a licensee published the work before 1978. It also won't apply where the work was published between 1978 and March 1, 1989 by a licensee and a written license agreement required that a notice be included on the work. Such publications by licensees are not considered to be authorized by the copyright owner. The book in the example above was not published by a licensee, since the copyright owner published it himself.

To convince a judge or jury that you acted reasonably and in good faith, you should, at the very least, always check to see if a work published without a notice between 1978 and March 1, 1989 was subsequently registered with the Copyright Office. If the work was published between 1978 and March 1, 1989 it is also a good idea to try to find more than a single copy without a notice and document your efforts to do so.

Traps for the Unwary

Should You Worry About Trademark or Publicity Problems? 356

The Right of Publicity 357

    What Is the Right of Publicity? 357

    Limitations on the Right of Publicity 357

    Right of Publicity for Dead People 360

    No National Right of Publicity Law 361

    Obtaining Publicity Releases 361

Trademarks 362

    How Do You Know If Something Is a Trademark? 363

    Trademarks and Public Domain Materials 364

    Limits on Trademark Rights 366

    Using Trademark Symbols: ®, TM, and SM 369

I f you intend to use public domain works in commercial advertising or on merchandise, you may face special problems. In these circumstances, simply proving that a particular work is in the public domain—meaning it lacks copyright protection—is not sufficient. You must also be sure, in many cases, that you are not using protected trademarks or images of people, living or dead.

Should You Worry About Trademark or Publicity Problems?

You need to read this chapter if you want to use a public domain work—particularly photographs or film footage—for the following purposes:

- in advertising for a product or service
- as part of a product's identification or packaging, or
- on merchandise such as posters, buttons, patches (whether or not they advertise a product), bumper stickers, T-shirts, postcards, running shoes, dishes, cups, clocks, games, and calendars that contain advertisements for products or services.

If you plan to use a public domain work in any of these ways, your use may violate state right of publicity laws if the work contains a person's picture, name, signature, likeness, or voice. Your use could violate state and federal trademark laws if the work contains a trademark.

You don't need to worry about the restrictions covered in this chapter if you're using public domain materials for informational, editorial, or entertainment purposes. Uses such as these—which inform or educate the public or express opinions—are protected under the First Amendment of the U.S. Constitution, which protects freedom of speech and of the press. You will not have a problem if you are using a public domain work in:

- literary works such as books, stories, and articles, whether or not they are fiction or nonfiction
- theatrical works such as plays
- musical compositions
- film, radio, or television programs (with an exception for trademarks used in commercial films and television programs, discussed in the section on trademarks, below)
- any form of news reporting such as newspaper or magazine articles on the news of the day, television news programs, documentaries on political or other newsworthy issues, campaign posters, or
- original works of art.

It makes no difference whether your project is profit or nonprofit. Either way, the First Amendment applies to you and you don't have to worry about the publicity and trademark issues covered in this chapter.

The Right of Publicity

The laws in a majority of states give people something called the right of publicity. This is not the right to be famous. Rather, it is the legal right to control how a person's name, likeness, or other elements of personal identity are used for advertising and other commercial purposes. Because of the right of publicity, companies or individuals must get permission before they can use a person's photo or name in an advertisement or TV commercial, and must usually pay for such permission.

If a public domain work, such as a photo, film, or video footage, portrays a person, the right of publicity may make it illegal for you to use it for advertising purposes without first obtaining the person's permission.

RESOURCE

The definitive work on the right of publicity is *The Rights of Publicity and Privacy,* by J. Thomas McCarthy (Thomson Reuters).

What Is the Right of Publicity?

A majority of states give all living human beings (and many dead ones) a right of publicity, which protects a person's identity or "persona" from unauthorized commercial exploitation. The right of

publicity protects against unauthorized commercial use of a person's:

- name (including nicknames and professional, former, and group names)
- image (including photographs, film, and videos)
- likeness (including drawings and portraits)
- signature, and
- voice.

Celebrities usually claim the right of publicity, but it applies to noncelebrities as well. Even politicians are covered.

If you violate a person's right of publicity, he or she can sue you for damages, which can be substantial, particularly if a well-known celebrity is involved.

Limitations on the Right of Publicity

The right of publicity is far from absolute. There are significant limitations on when it applies. Indeed, it often does not apply in situations where public domain materials are used.

Only Protects Against Commercial Uses

The most important limitation on the right of publicity is that it only protects against the *commercial exploitation* of a person's identity—that is, when you use a person's name or identity solely to help sell a product or service. For example, an artist violated the Three Stooges' right of publicity when he created a drawing of their faces and reproduced it on T-shirts. The court held that the artist's use was purely commercial—that is, solely to sell the T-shirts. *Comedy III Productions, Inc. v. Gary Sadreup, Inc.*, 25 Cal.4th 387 (Cal. Sup. Ct. 2001).

Entertainment, informational, or "editorial" uses are not protected by the right of publicity. These uses include anything that informs, educates, or expresses opinions protected under the First Amendment of the U.S. Constitution, which protects the freedom of speech and of the press. For example, California's right of publicity law does not apply to "a play, book, magazine, newspaper, musical composition, audiovisual work, radio or television program, single and original work of art, work of political or newsworthy value, or an advertisement or commercial announcement for any of these works … if it is fictional or nonfictional entertainment, or a dramatic, literary, or musical work." Cal. Civil Code Section 3344.1.

Common examples of uses that don't violate the right of publicity are using a person's name or photograph in a newspaper or magazine article (in print or online), an educational program, film, or nonfiction book. However, informational uses are not limited to nonfiction works. The First Amendment also protects fictional stories such as novels, plays, and movies.

For example, there are probably hundreds of photographs of Babe Ruth that are in the public domain because the copyright has expired (all those published over 95 years ago and those published as recently as 1963 that never had their copyrights renewed). You may freely use such a photo without permission in a biography of Babe Ruth, a history of baseball, a newspaper or magazine article on baseball records, a TV documentary about the roaring 1920s, or a novel or movie based on Babe Ruth's life. These are all clearly informational uses, but even if it's in the public domain, you may not use a photo of Babe Ruth in an advertisement without permission from Ruth's estate.

At the same time, however, some courts have held that uses that combine the commercial with the editorial do not violate these laws.

> **EXAMPLE:** *Los Angeles Magazine* published an article in which digital technology was used to alter famous film stills to make it appear that the actors were wearing 1997 fashions. The magazine used a still of the actor Dustin Hoffman, from the film *Tootsie*. The photo was altered so that Hoffman's head was placed on an image of a male model wearing an evening dress. The text on the page read "Dustin Hoffman isn't a drag in a butter-colored silk gown by Richard Tyler and Ralph Lauren heels." Hoffman sued the magazine for violating

his right of publicity, since it never got his permission to use his face in the article. Hoffman ultimately lost the case. The court held that although one of the purposes of the article was to help sell new fashions, it also contained humor, and visual and verbal editorial comment on classic films and famous actors. Thus, the article was not a purely commercial use of Hoffman's image. *Hoffman v. Capital Cities/ABC, Inc.,* 255 F.3d 1180 (9th Cir. 2001).

Incidental Use Exception

When a work such as a book or musical composition is in the public domain, anyone may copy it and sell or rent the copies to the public. In this event, it is legally permissible to use the author's name, photo, or identity in advertisements for the work. For example, when musical arrangements created and published by big-band leader Artie Shaw fell into the public domain, others were free to rerecord them and state in magazine advertisements for the recordings that the arrangements had been created by Shaw. They could also use pictures of Shaw to advertise their product. This did not violate Shaw's right of publicity. *Shaw v. Time-Life Records,* 38 N.Y.2d 201 (N.Y. 1975).

In addition, a media company may reproduce news items containing a celebrity's name or identity in its own advertising. For example, a photo of football player Joe Namath was featured on the cover of *Sports Illustrated* and later used in advertisements to sell subscriptions to *Sports Illustrated*. No permission was required because the initial use of the photo was editorial and the subscription ads were "merely incidental," indicating the nature of the magazine contents. *Namath v. Sports Illustrated*, 371 N.Y.S.2d 10 (N.Y. App. Div. 1975).

Insignificant or Fleeting Use Exception

The right of publicity is also not violated when a person's name or image appears only briefly and insignificantly in an advertisement. For example, courts have ruled that there was no publicity violation where:

- a photo of a police officer on a *Rolling Stone* magazine cover was shown for four seconds in a 29-minute television "infomercial" for a rock music anthology (*Aligo v. Time-Life Books, Inc.*, No. C 94-20707 JW (N.D. Cal. 1994)), or

- a photo used in an advertising brochure that showed a man standing behind a stack of lumber and wearing a hat and was so small and fuzzy he was unrecognizable. (*Epic Metals Corp. v. Condec, Inc.*, 867 F.Supp. 1009 (M.D. Fla. 1994).)

Crowd Shots Are Covered

A photograph, film, or video of a group or crowd of people may violate the publicity rights of any members of the group or crowd who can be individually recognized from the photo if the photo, film, or video is used for commercial purposes. In one case, for example, a company reproduced a team photo of the 1969 New York Mets baseball team on baseball jerseys it sold commercially. The Mets players sued the company for violating their right of publicity and won. The court held that each member of the Mets team had his own individual right of publicity which was violated when the group photo was sold to the public on the jerseys without the players' permission. *Shamsky v. Garan, Inc.*, 632 N.Y.S.2d 930 (N.Y. Sup. Ct. 1995).

One way to avoid this problem is to crop or retouch the work so that no individual can be recognized. Of course, this is not a viable option where you want the public to recognize the members of the group or crowd. In these cases, permission must be obtained from the subjects in the photo, film, or video.

In these cases, there is no direct connection between the use of the person's identity and the commercial purpose of the advertisement. In other words, the use of the person's image or name is so insignificant that the company or person who created the advertisement could not possibly profit from it commercially.

Right of Publicity for Dead People

The right of publicity always lasts for as long as a person lives. Moreover, in several states the right of publicity survives death. How long the right lasts varies from state to state—from as few as ten years to as many as 100 years after death. The publicity statutes of some of these states reach back to cover people who died long before the publicity law was enacted. For example, California's publicity statute applies to anyone who died within 70 years before it was enacted in 1985—that is, to anyone who died in 1915 or later. On the other hand, some state right of publicity statutes, such as that of New York, provide for no right of publicity after death.

You don't need to research each state's publicity law to figure out how far back the right of publicity goes. You can safely assume that anyone who died more than 100 years ago is not covered by any right of publicity—no publicity law goes back farther than this. But anyone who died after that could be protected in one or more states. For example, you don't have to worry about publicity rights if you want to use a photo of Abraham Lincoln in an advertisement, since Lincoln died in 1865 (though the tastefulness of such

States With Postmortem Right of Publicity		
State	**Duration of Postmortem Right of Publicity**	**Statute**
Washington	10 years if identity has no "commercial value"; 75 years if it does	Wash. Stat. §§ 63.60.010–63.60.040
Virginia	20 years	Va. Code § 8.01-40
Pennsylvania	30 years	42 Pa. Consol. Stat. § 8316
Florida	40 years	Fla. Stat. § 540.08
Illinois, Kentucky, Nevada, Texas	50 years	765 Ill. Comp. Stat. § 1075/30; Ky. Rev. Stat. § 391.170; Nev. Rev. Stat. § 597.790; Tex. Prop. Code Ann. § 26.012
Ohio	60 years	Ohio Rev. Code Ann. § 2741.02
California, South Dakota	70 years	Cal. Civ. Code § 3344.1; 70 S.D. Codified Laws § 21-64-2
Indiana, Oklahoma	100 years	Ind. Code § 32-36-1-8; 12 Okla. Stat. § 1448
Tennessee	10 years; or indefinite as long as persona is continuously exploited after death; two years of nonuse results in waiver of right	Tenn. Code §§ 47-25-1102-110

an ad may be debatable). Note that one state, Tennessee, allows the right to last indefinitely, as long as it is being exploited.

No National Right of Publicity Law

There is no single federal right of publicity law that applies in every state. Instead, those states that recognize the right have their own publicity laws, which may be very different from other states.

Obtaining Publicity Releases

If you want to use a public domain photo, film clip, video, or other work of authorship to advertise a product or service, you must obtain a publicity release from the subject, or the subject's heirs, if the subject died less than 100 years ago. A publicity release is a legally binding promise not to sue for violating a right of publicity. A release can be oral, but it's always wise to get it in writing because it is almost impossible to prove that someone gave you verbal permission if they later challenge you in court.

Since the works we're dealing with in this book are in the public domain—that is, not protected by copyright—you do not need to obtain permission from whoever used to own the copyright. But you will need a release from the individual or the heirs of an individual whose likeness you wish to use.

For a detailed discussion of how to obtain a publicity release and sample forms, see *Getting Permission: Using & Licensing Copyright-Protected Materials Online & Off*, by Richard Stim (Nolo).

The Restatement (Third) of Unfair Competition

As mentioned above, there is no single national right of publicity law. Each state has its own publicity law. However, a model law called the Restatement (Third) of Unfair Competition, Sections 46–49, has been very influential on the development of the right of publicity. It was drafted in 1995 by nationally recognized legal experts. It can be found at www.rightofpublicity.com. Reading this short model law will give you a good overview of the right of publicity.

Trademarks

A trademark is any word, symbol, or device that identifies and distinguishes a product or service. It is a violation of a trademark owner's rights to use the trademark in a commercial context in a way that confuses consumers—that is, makes them think that the trademark owner is in some way associated with your (or somebody else's) product or service. A trademark owner can sue someone who violates his or her rights and obtain monetary damages and a court order preventing the trademark from being used.

> **EXAMPLE:** Copyright does not protect simple ornamentation such as chevron stripes (see Chapter 5). However, the chevron logo used by the Chevron Corporation to identify its gas stations and petroleum products is protected by the state and federal trademark laws. Anyone who used the same or similar chevron design for a gas station sign or advertisement, or in the packaging or advertising for any petroleum-related product, would almost certainly violate Chevron's trademark rights. Use of the logo for such similar products or services would likely lead the public to believe that Chevron Corporation sponsored or was in some way associated with the product.

There are many different types of trademarks, including the following:

- **Brand names.** The most common form of trademark is a brand name—for example, *Coca-Cola* or *Apple Computer*. Brand names are usually words, although they can be a combination of words, letters, and numbers such as *7-UP*.

- **Slogans.** A combination of words used as a slogan for a product or service qualifies as a trademark— for example, "A diamond is forever" for diamond jewelry.

- **Logos.** A graphic image or symbol may serve as a trademark—for example, the McDonald's golden arches.

- **Titles.** Titles of literary works, especially newspapers and magazines, can be trademarks (see Chapter 13).

- **Trade dress.** Any distinctive combination of elements used in a product may serve as a trademark—for example, the combination of the yellow border and distinctive lettering used in *National Geographic* Magazine, or a website's distinctive combination of colors, graphic borders, and buttons.

- **Product configurations.** Distinctive product packaging that is primarily nonfunctional is protected as a trademark—for example, the distinctive shape of the Coca-Cola bottle.

- **Fictional characters.** Trademark law protects fictional characters used to sell products or services.

Trademarks used to identify services are also known as service marks. For example, Twitter designates a company that provides online messaging service. Normally, a trademark for a product appears on the product or on packaging, while a service mark appears in advertising for the service. Service marks have the same legal rights and follow the same rules as trademarks.

How Do You Know If Something Is a Trademark?

Most trademarks—such as brand names, slogans, and logos—are easy to spot because the trademark owner displays them in a distinctive manner, often using stylized lettering—for example, capitals or italics. The symbols ®, TM, or SM are also frequently used to identify trademarks. However, many trademarks are more difficult to discern, particularly trade dress, product configurations, colors, and other nontraditional trademarks.

Another way to tell if something is a trademark is to conduct a trademark search. Trademarks can be registered by their owners with the U.S. Patent and Trademark Office in Washington, DC (PTO), and with the Secretary of State offices of the 50 states. Registration is not required to obtain trademark protection, but it gives trademark owners many legal benefits if they file trademark infringement suits. You can conduct online searches of these trademark registration records to see if someone claims that a particular word, slogan, or other item is being used as a trademark.

You can do your own search for free on the Internet by visiting the U.S. Patent and Trademark Office's website at www.uspto. gov, or with Trademarkia (www.trademarkia.com), which provides free access to records of federally registered marks or marks that are pending. But the most thorough trademark searches are accomplished by professional search firms such as CompuMark (www. compumark.com) or TradeMark Express (www.tmexpress.com).

However, trademark searches are not foolproof, because a business may be able to claim that something is a trademark even if it is not registered.

Trademarks and Public Domain Materials

The vast majority of the time users of public domain materials don't need to worry about trademarks. There are only three common situations where you might violate someone's trademark rights when you use public domain materials:

- if you use public domain photos or other materials containing trademarks in advertising or on merchandise
- if you copy all or part of an existing trademark in a product's name or packaging, or
- if you use a trademarked character in advertising or on merchandise.

Trademarks in Public Domain Photos and Other Materials

A public domain photo, film, magazine, or newspaper advertisement may contain a trademark such as a product name, logo, or slogan—for example, a public domain photograph may contain a Coca-Cola sign. Since the photo is in the public domain— that is, is not protected by copyright— anyone may copy it or republish it without violating the photographer's copyright rights.

However, if you use such a photo in a manner that is likely to confuse consumers into believing that there is some connection or sponsorship between the Coca-Cola Company and you or someone else, you may violate the Coca-Cola Company's trademark rights in its name and logo. This could occur, for example, if you used such a photo on a T-shirt, coffee mug, or other merchandise or in an advertisement for a product or service such as a newspaper advertisement for a soft drink vending machine company. You would need to obtain Coca-Cola's permission for these types of uses. But other uses that are purely informational in nature wouldn't involve Coca-Cola's trademark rights.

Creating Product Names or Packaging

Individual words, names, short phrases, slogans, colors, simple geometric designs, distinctive lettering, standard symbols such as an arrow or a five-pointed star, and standard ornamentation such as chevron stripes are not protected by copyright—they are all in the public domain. You can copy items such as these freely without violating anyone's copyright rights.

However, state and federal trademark laws can protect all of these things if they are used to identify a product or service. If they do, and you use them in a commercial context without permission from the trademark owner, you could find yourself on the receiving end of a trademark infringement lawsuit.

For example, the words "Apple Computer" are not protected by copyright. But they are a trademarked brand name. You may not use these words as the name for a computer product or any other related product without violating Apple Computer's trademark rights. Again, however, these words may be used for purely informational purposes—for example, in an article on the history of the computer industry, or in a novel or play.

RESOURCE

For a detailed discussion of trademark issues see *Trademark: Legal Care for Your Business & Product Name,* by Stephen Fishman (Nolo).

Using Characters

Trademark law protects characters that are used to sell products or services or used on merchandise. Trademark can protect such a character's name, appearance, and costume. Trademarked characters can be:

- graphic cartoon characters such as Mickey Mouse
- literary characters, such as Dracula or Tarzan of the Apes, or
- characters portrayed by human actors in movies, plays, and television shows, often based on literary characters such as Dracula or Tarzan.

Trademarked characters may be associated with a specific product or service—for example, back in the 1990s and early 2000s, Jeeves the butler from the P.G. Wodehouse novels became associated with an Internet search engine.

Or a character—Dracula, for example—may be used to sell a variety of merchandise. Trademark permission is not required to reproduce a graphic character such as Woody Woodpecker for informational purposes such as in a magazine article or TV documentary about the history of cartoons. Likewise, using a photograph of an actor portraying Tarzan for an informational use such as in a news story does not require trademark permission.

Permission is required for the commercial use of a trademarked character in an advertisement or on merchandise. So long as a character has continuously been used as a trademark, it remains protected even if its original literary source is in the public domain. This is the case, for example, with the Tarzan character. Many of the Tarzan novels are in the public domain, but the name and appearance of Tarzan have been registered as trademarks and are used to sell a variety of merchandise. Companies such as PepsiCo, Toyota, and KFC have used the Tarzan character to advertise their products. If you use Tarzan for a commercial purpose without permission, you can expect to hear from his lawyers.

Note that if you use a photo or other representation of an actor portraying a character in an advertisement or for other commercial purposes, you need to obtain permission from the actor or you'll violate his or her right of publicity.

 RESOURCE

For detailed information about licensing trademarked materials for use on merchandise and sample license agreements, see *Getting Permission: Using & Licensing Copyright-Protected Materials Online & Off,* by Richard Stim (Nolo).

Limits on Trademark Rights

There are significant limitations on trademark protection. Using trademarks for informational or editorial purposes is always permitted. Moreover, the rights of trademark owners to control the trademark usually don't last forever—they end when a trademark is abandoned. Finally, there are some words or symbols that can't be trademarks because they are considered to be generic.

No Attribution Required

In a case involving documentary film footage, the U.S. Supreme Court ruled that people who use public domain materials don't violate trademark laws by failing to provide credit to the creator of the materials.

In 1949, Twentieth Century Fox hired Time, Inc., to produce a 26-episode television documentary about General Dwight Eisenhower's role in World War II. However, Fox failed to file a copyright renewal for the series in 1977, so it entered the public domain. In 1995, Dastar, a company that manufactured and sold music CDs, decided to enter the home video market. It purchased eight copies of the original 1949 series and copied and edited them into a new series of its own. Dastar's documentary was half as long as Fox's and contained a new narration. Dastar sold the documentary as its "Campaigns" series. Neither the documentary itself, nor its packaging, made any mention of the original 1949 series or Twentieth Century Fox or Time, Inc.

Fox sued Dastar for violating the federal trademark laws. It claimed that Dastar's failure to provide attribution for the copied material in its documentary amounted to "reverse passing off"—that is, Dastar was posing as the originator of the material in the documentary, when it really wasn't. The U.S. Supreme Court held that this trademark law doctrine does not apply to works of authorship that have passed into the public domain. Once a work becomes public domain, anyone may copy it without providing credit to the original author. *Dastar Corp. v. Twentieth Century Fox Film Corp.*, 539 U.S. 23 (2003).

The *Dastar* decision is a major victory for proponents of the public domain. As the Court noted in its opinion, requiring people who use public domain materials to give credit to their originators would have caused enormous practical problems. In many cases, it would be difficult to figure out who should be credited as the originator of a public domain work. For example, Fox's original 1949 documentary was actually created by Time, Inc., and then sold to Fox; but much of the war footage in the series was taken by unknown military cameramen, not by Time or Fox. So would Dastar have to give credit to Fox, Time, and the military cameramen? Fortunately, this attribution mess was avoided by the Supreme Court's decision.

No Permission Required for Informational Uses

Trademark infringement can occur only when someone's trademark is used without permission *as a trademark* to help consumers identify the source of goods or services. This can occur only in a commercial context—that is, where a trademark is used in advertising or on a product or merchandise.

Informational or "editorial" uses of trademarks are always permitted—especially where they are the only way to refer to or discuss a particular product or service. Uses such as these inform, educate, or express opinions or ideas protected under the First Amendment of the U.S. Constitution, which protects freedom of speech and of the press. For example, permission is not required to use the Chevrolet logo in an article describing Chevrolet trucks, even if the article is critical of the company. Similarly, permission is not needed if a Coca-Cola sign appears in a news report or documentary film.

However, it's not clear whether the use of trademarks in commercial motion pictures is informational and, as a matter of course, film studios and attorneys recommend clearance of all trademarks that appear in commercial TV and film. This is especially true if the trademark figures into the plot or title.

Trademark Abandonment

The fact that a trademark has an ® or TM or SM symbol next to it doesn't always mean it's a valid trademark. Many trademarks are no longer legally enforceable because they have been abandoned.

Trademark rights are created *only* when the mark is used in commerce—that is, to sell a product or service. Unlike copyright protection, which expires after a specified number of years, trademark protection lasts for as long as a business continuously uses a trademark to help sell goods or services. Many trademarks have been protected for over a century—for example, the Coca-Cola name and logo. However, trademark protection is lost if a company stops using a mark to identify products or services sold to the public. Any trademark is presumed to be abandoned if it hasn't been used to sell a product or service for more than three years.

Many public domain photos probably contain images of abandoned trademarks. The older the work, the more likely it is that the product or service for which the trademark was used is no longer being sold to the public.

One way to tell if a trademark has been abandoned is to call or write the company and ask if it is still being used. Another way is to conduct a trademark search. (For information on conducting trademark searches, refer to *Trademark:* *Legal Care for Your Business & Product Name,* by Stephen Fishman (Nolo), available online at www.nolo.com.)

Generic Words and Symbols

On rare occasions, trademark rights end if the public believes that the trademark is a generic term. For example, aspirin and escalator were trademarks that lost protection once the public used the names for all versions of these products, not for just one manufacturer's version. Nowadays, companies such as Kimberly-Clarke (manufacturer of Kleenex) and Dow Chemical (manufacturer of Styrofoam) aggressively oppose this loss of trademark rights (known as "genericide") by educating the public. For example, a journalist who mistakenly writes "styrofoam cup" may receive a letter or email from Dow indicating that its trademarked Styrofoam product is not used in cups (it's used primarily in boat and house insulation).

Moreover, certain words and symbols are deemed to be inherently generic. These are words or symbols commonly used to describe an entire category or class of products or services, rather than to distinguish one product or service from another. For example, the words "bread" and "computer" are generic. Generic words are in the public domain and cannot be registered or enforced under the trademark laws.

Using Trademark Symbols: ®, TM, and SM

Typically, the symbols ®, TM, or SM are used along with trademarks—for example, GROK®. The symbol ® indicates that a trademark has been registered at the U.S. Patent and Trademark Office (PTO). The "TM" symbol is not an official designation—it means that the company believes it has trademark rights. The "SM" symbol is the same as the "TM" symbol except it is used for service marks. The TM and SM have no legal significance other than the fact that the owner is claiming trademark rights. There is no legal requirement that the ® be used, but the failure to use it may limit the amount of damages that the trademark owner can recover in an infringement lawsuit.

When using a trademark in a text format for informational purposes, it is not necessary to include the ®, TM, or SM symbols. However, it is good trademark etiquette to distinguish a trademark from other text—for example, "The house was constructed with *Styrofoam* insulation," or "He always bathed with *Ivory Soap.*"

Researching Copyright Office Records

**Researching Copyright Renewal Records for Works Published
    Before 1964**..372

    What Are Copyright Renewals?...372

    How to Determine If a Work Was Renewed..375

    Hiring Someone to Do a Search for You...376

    Researching Copyright Renewals Yourself..377

    Searches for Works Published 1950–1963..381

    Renewal Searches for Works Published through 1949...................................382

Researching Copyright Registration Records...387

    Online Registration Records..387

    CCE Registration Listings..388

    Obtaining a Copy of the Registration Certificate...388

Millions of works first published in the United States less than 95 years ago and before 1964 are in the public domain because their copyrights were never renewed in the 28th year after they were first published. But to determine that a particular work is in the public domain ordinarily requires a search of records in the U.S. Copyright Office. This chapter shows you how to do just that. We also show you how to research other Copyright Office records that often contain valuable information for the public domain researcher.

Researching Copyright Renewal Records for Works Published Before 1964

This section shows you how to determine if the copyright for a work initially published in the United States less than 95 years ago and before 1964 was renewed. If it wasn't, the work is now in the public domain in the United States and many foreign countries as well.

→ **SKIP AHEAD**

If the work you're interested in was never published or was not published less than 95 years ago and before 1964, it cannot be in the public domain for failure to renew its copyright, and there is no reason to read this section. Skip to the next section.

What Are Copyright Renewals?

The U.S. copyright law in effect from 1909 to 1978 had a unique feature: there were two copyright terms instead of one. Any work published in the United States with a valid copyright notice automatically received copyright protection for an initial period of 28 years. In the 28th year a renewal notice had to be filed with the Copyright Office for copyright protection to be extended for an additional 28 years, which was called the renewal term. If no renewal was filed, the work entered the public domain.

The renewal term was later extended from 28 to 47 years and then again to 67 years. Here we are only concerned with works that were never renewed and entered the public domain in the 29th year after publication.

> **EXAMPLE:** Richard published a song in the United States in 1960, but failed to file a renewal application with the Copyright Office in 1988. As a result, the work entered the public domain in 1989 and can be used freely by anyone. Had Richard or his heirs renewed the work, it would have been protected for a total of 95 years—the 28-year initial term plus the 67-year renewal term—or until the end of the year 2055.

Only Works Published Less than 95 Years Ago and Before 1964 Are Affected

You only need to be concerned with copyright renewals for works that were first published in the United States less than 95 years ago and before 1964. Works published over 95 years ago are in the public domain whether or not they were renewed.

There is also no need to research renewals for any works published in 1964 or later. A 1992 amendment to the copyright law made renewals automatic for all works published during 1964–1977. All these works receive a 95-year copyright term. Works published in 1978 and later never had to be renewed. The copyright in such works usually lasts for the life of the author plus 70 years after his death. (See Chapter 18 for a detailed discussion of copyright terms.)

How Many Works Published Before 1964 Were Not Renewed?

How many works published less than 95 years ago and before 1964 are in the public domain because they were not renewed on time? No one knows for sure, but the Copyright Office estimates that only about 15% of all such works were ever renewed. The renewal percentage varies for the type of work involved. Most movies and many musical works were renewed, but most books and other written works were not.

The following chart shows the results of a survey conducted by the Copyright Office in 1960 to see how many works originally published and registered with the Copyright Office in 1931–32 were renewed during 1958–59.

Copyright Renewal Rates (1958–59)	
Type of Work	**Renewal Percentage**
Books	7
Periodicals	11
Lectures, Speeches, Sermons, and Other Works for Oral Delivery	0.4
Drama	11
Music	35
Maps	48
Works of Art	4
Technical Drawings	0.4
Art Prints	4
Movies	74

With the exception of maps, music, and movies, the vast majority of works published during 1931–32 were never renewed and are in the public domain.

A survey of the renewal rates for books published during 1923–1963 conducted by the New York Public Library in 2019 found that about 642,000 books were registered for copyright during these years. Of these, only about 162,000, or 25%, had their copyrights renewed. (See www.nypl.org/blog/2019/05/31/us-copyright-history-1923-1964.)

Why were so few works renewed? Sometimes it was due to ignorance of the renewal requirement or by mistake. Very often a work was not renewed because it was viewed as having no economic value 28 years after it was first published. But the fact that a work may have been viewed as worthless 20, 30, or 40 years ago doesn't necessarily mean it's valueless today. There are doubtless thousands of hidden jewels among the huge number of works that were not renewed.

However, most well-known works published less than 95 years ago and before 1964 were renewed. This includes, for example, the novels of Hemingway and Fitzgerald, the music of Irving Berlin and George Gershwin, and most classic movies such as *Gone With the Wind* and *Citizen Kane*. But such famous works represent only a tiny fraction of all the works published during this time.

Most Foreign Works Published Before 1964 Don't Need to Be Renewed

Renewal rules for works first published outside the United States are different than for works first published in the United States. Before 1996, works published in foreign countries *with a copyright notice* had to be renewed just like works published in the United States. Many such works were in the public domain because they were not renewed. However, the law was changed so that on January 1, 1996 most foreign works that had not been renewed had their copyright protection restored.

Any work first published outside the United States less than 95 years ago and before 1964 with a copyright notice has 95 years of copyright from its publication date, even if it was not renewed, as long as:

- the work was still under copyright on Jan. 1, 1996 in the country where it was first published, and
- at least one author is a citizen or resident of a country with which the United States has copyright relations, which includes almost all countries in the world. For a list of countries not included, see Chapter 15.

EXAMPLE: Sammy, a citizen of Ireland, published a poem in Ireland with a copyright notice in 1960. The poem was never renewed and therefore entered the public domain in the United States on January 1, 1989. However, the U.S. copyright in the poem was automatically restored on Jan. 1, 1996 and will last until December 31, 2055 (1960 plus 95 years equals 2055).

However, there are some foreign works that don't qualify for copyright restoration. These are works that are no longer under copyright in their home countries because the copyright has expired. In almost all foreign countries, copyrights last for 50 or 70 years after an author dies (Western Europe uses the life-plus-70-year term). Thus, if the author of the foreign work died long ago, the work may not have qualified for copyright restoration in the United States.

> **EXAMPLE:** Ken published a song with a copyright notice in Canada in 1940. The song was never renewed and so entered the public domain on January 1, 1969. Ken died in 1942, so the song entered the public domain in Canada on January 1, 1993 (copyrights last for the life of the author plus 50 more years in Canada). Because the song was in the public domain in Canada on January 1, 1996 it didn't qualify for copyright restoration. It remains in the public domain in the United States.

You need to know the copyright term of the foreign author's country and when the author died to know if this exception applies. See Chapter 16 for a detailed discussion of foreign copyright laws.

Nonrenewed Works Are in the Public Domain in Many Foreign Countries

Works that are in the public domain in the United States because they were not renewed are also in the public domain in most foreign countries, including most of Western Europe and Australia (but not the United Kingdom or Canada). This is because these countries use something called the "rule of the shorter term" in calculating how long the copyright for a work first published in the United States lasts in their own countries. Applying this rule, if the work is in the public domain in the United States because it was not renewed, it will be in the public domain in the foreign country as well. (See Chapter 16 for a detailed discussion.)

How to Determine If a Work Was Renewed

Most of the time the Copyright Office's renewal records must be checked to determine whether or not a work was renewed. There are several ways you can do this:

- you can have the Copyright Office conduct a search for you
- you can hire a private search firm to do a search, or
- you can conduct the search yourself.

You'll save money if you do it yourself. It will require some time and effort, but it is not necessary to have special training to perform a renewal search, and all of the records can be searched online.

Preliminary Information for Search

Before you do a renewal search yourself or hire someone else to do one, you should obtain the following information about the work:

- the title
- the author
- the year the work was published, and
- the country in which the work was first published.

If the work was published as part of a magazine, newspaper, periodical, anthology, or collection, you will also need to know the name, volume or issue number, and any other available identifying information for the magazine or other publication in which the work appeared.

Avoiding Searches for Republished Works

If the work has been republished more than 28 years after its original publication (in other words, after it should have been renewed) you may be able to avoid having to do a renewal search. If you have access to a copy of the republished work, take a good look at the copyright notice. Usually, the copyright notice for a republished work will indicate that the work was renewed. For example, the copyright notice for a recent paperback edition of the 1952 novel, *Shiloh,* by Shelby Foote says:

Copyright © 1952 by Shelby Foote

Copyright renewed 1980 by Shelby Foote

This tells you that the work was originally published in 1952 and was renewed in 1980, 28 years after publication. This means there is no need to check the Copyright Office renewal records. The work is not in the public domain.

However, there is no legal requirement that a renewed work's copyright notice state that the work was renewed. For this reason, you can't rely on the fact that a republished work does not state it has been renewed.

Hiring Someone to Do a Search for You

You may wish to hire someone to do such searches for you if you just don't want to take the trouble to do it yourself.

Hiring the Copyright Office

You can have the Copyright Office search its records for you. They charge $200 an hour for this service, and the minimum charge is for two hours, meaning the minimum cost is $400. Upon request, the Copyright Office will estimate the total cost of a search—the fee for the estimate is $200, which is applied to the search fee. Unfortunately, it takes the Copyright Office six to 12 weeks to conduct a search and report back to you. You can obtain much faster service by using a private search firm, as described below.

The Copyright Office will conduct an expedited search that takes just five business days, but this costs a minimum of $1,000. Again, you can obtain faster service by using a private search firm.

There is no advantage to using the Copyright Office. But if you decide to use it, you may have the Copyright Office commence a search by completing and submitting the online Search Request Estimate form, available at www.copyright.gov/forms/search_estimate.html. Alternatively, you may call the Records Research and Certification Section at 202-707-6850, or send an email to copysearch@loc.gov with the following information:

- the title of the work
- the author's name
- the copyright owner's name (usually listed in the copyright notice)
- the year of publication
- the type of work involved—for example, a book, play, or photograph, and
- the name, volume or issue number, and other identifying information for the periodical, if the work was published as part of a periodical or collection.

For more information, correspondence, or payment, contact:

Copyright Office GC/I&R/RRC
Attn: RCC
P.O. Box 70400
Washington, DC 20024
phone: 202-707-6850
(M–F, 8:30–5:00 eastern time)
fax: 202-252-3485
email: copysearch@loc.gov.

Hiring a Private Search Firm

Private search firms usually charge less than the Copyright Office and work faster. For example, CompuMark, the best known of these firms, charges $160 for a renewal search and will report back in three business days. This is a much better deal than paying $400 to the Copyright Office and having to wait up to three months for the results. The Durationator Copyright System charges as little as $75 to search a single title.

Following is a list of copyright search firms. CompuMark is by far the largest, oldest, and best known of these firms, but we are not endorsing any particular firm. Contact several to see which offers the best deal and/or service.

Durationator Copyright System
www.durationator.com
info@durationator.com

Government Liaison Services, Inc.
www.trademarkinfo.com

CompuMark
www.compumark.com/solutions/
trademark-searching/title-copyright-
entertainment-searches

Researching Copyright Renewals Yourself

Paying to do a renewal search can really add up if you need to search several titles. You can avoid paying these fees by doing the search yourself.

Your goal in conducting a copyright renewal search is to determine if Copyright Office records show that a work published less than 95 years ago and before 1964 was renewed 28 years after publication. If you can't find any record of a renewal, you may usually assume that the work has not been renewed and is therefore in the public domain. There are no records made of works that were not renewed, only records of works that were renewed.

However, researching renewals can be tricky, and if you're not careful you may overlook a renewal record for a work. Here are some special problems to be aware of:

Works Created as Part of Larger Works

Many works were created and published as part of larger works—for example:

- articles or stories published in newspapers, magazines, and periodicals
- photographs or drawings published in books, newspapers, magazines, and other works, and
- musical compositions published as part of a Broadway show, opera, revue, or other larger work.

Generally, there are no separate copyright renewal records for such works. Instead, you must look to see if the larger work was renewed. For example, if you want to know if an article that appeared in the *New Yorker* magazine was renewed, you'd need to check if that issue of the magazine was renewed. You'd look under the name the *New Yorker* for the year and date involved. If it was renewed, you should assume that article was renewed as well.

On the other hand, if the larger work was not renewed, don't assume that the portion of it you're interested in is in the public domain. Instead, try to see if it was separately renewed. For example, if you're interested in a photograph contained in a book published in 1950 and find no renewal record for the book, check the Copyright Office records to see if the photo was separately renewed. Look under the name of the photographer, if you can find it. Examine the book and photo carefully. See if the photo has its own copyright notice in the photographer's or other copyright owner's name. Check to see if there is an "acknowledgment" section in the book giving copyright information for the photograph.

Articles and other contributions to magazines and other periodicals were especially likely to be separately renewed, particularly if they contained their own copyright notices. The Copyright Office *Catalog of Copyright Entries* has a separate section called "Contributions to Periodicals" that lists renewals for articles.

Only if you find no renewal information for both the larger work and the portion you want to use, may you conclude it is in the public domain.

Works Incorporating Other Works

What if you want to use an entire work that contains many separate works of authorship? For example, you may want to post a book on the Internet that contains photographs, drawings, or other separate works of authorship. In this event, you should check to see if each work of authorship has been renewed. Use the approach described in the preceding section.

If, for example, you discover no renewal record for the text of a book you want to use—but there is a renewal on file for photographs included in the book—you'll either have to get permission to use the photographs or simply not use them.

Derivative Works

Derivative works are works that are based upon or adapted from previously existing works. Examples of derivative works include:

- movies adapted from novels or plays
- new editions or versions, of previously published works
- translations from one language to another
- works adapted into a new medium —for example, a photograph of a painting, and
- new arrangements of musical compositions.

A derivative work is a separate work for copyright purposes, even though it is based on the original work. Each work must have been renewed separately. Renewing a derivative work did not automatically renew the original work and vice versa. In other words, when a derivative work was renewed, the renewal only covered the new material added to create the derivative work. When an original work was renewed, the renewal only covered the original version of the work, not any derivative works created from it.

EXAMPLE: Arthur writes a novel in 1940 that Eugene adapts into a Broadway play in 1950. The novel is timely renewed in 1968 and the play in 1978. This means that neither is in the public domain.

If the derivative work is not renewed but the original work is, you can't use those portions of the original work contained in the derivative work.

EXAMPLE: Assume that Arthur's novel is renewed, but Eugene's derivative play is not. All the material in the play copied from the novel is still under copyright. Only the new material Eugene added to adapt the novel into a play is in the public domain—for example, new dialog and the way he cut and restructured the novel to function as a three-act play.

If the derivative work is renewed, but the original work is not, you can't use any of the new material in the derivative work.

EXAMPLE: Assume that Arthur's novel was not renewed, but Eugene's play was. Both the original novel and all the elements copied by Eugene to create his derivative play are in the public domain. But the new material Eugene added to create the play is still under copyright.

If you're dealing with a derivative work initially published in the United States less than 95 years ago and before 1964 based on an original work initially published in the United States during this time period, you must determine if both the derivative work and the original work were renewed.

 RELATED TOPIC

Derivative works present a particular problem when you wish to determine the copyright status of many movies. See Chapter 7 for a detailed discussion of these and other special issues that arise when researching copyright renewals for movies.

Changing Titles

Some works were originally published under one title, and then renewed 28 years later under another title. This was particularly common for movie and television cartoons, whose names were often changed for marketing purposes.

The book *Of Mice and Magic, a History of American Animated Cartoons*, by Leonard Maltin, lists many alternative cartoon titles. Movies also sometimes had different titles. Alternate titles for most films can be found through a search of the Internet Movie Database (www.imdb.com). The book *The Film Buff's Bible of Motion Pictures*, by Richard Baer, has an index of alternative titles.

New Matter Added to Public Domain Works

Often when public domain works are republished, new material is added to them. For example, a new edition of Shakespeare's plays may contain new annotations, drawings, or photographs. Such new material is entitled to copyright protection, even though the public domain material is not. The author or publisher of the new material is entitled to renew the copyright in it, but this does not mean the original public domain material has been renewed. It remains in the public domain.

When you search the Copyright Office records (particularly the online records) you may find a record for a registration or renewal of such new matter added to a public domain work. This can confuse you into believing that the original work is under copyright, when in fact it is in the public domain. Normally, the online records contain a listing of what new material was added to a work in the public domain. The registration or renewal only covers this new matter.

Here's an example: Nathaniel Hawthorne's novel *The Scarlet Letter* was originally published in 1850 and is therefore in the public domain because the copyright expired in 1879. However, the Copyright Office online records contain the renewal record for *The Scarlet Letter* shown in Figure 1.

The "Basis of Claim" line makes clear that the renewal only applies to the foreword written by Leo Marx and added to an edition of the novel originally published by Penguin in 1959 and renewed in 1987. The text of the novel itself remains in the public domain.

Collections of Public Domain Material

Sometimes, a number of public domain works are republished together in a new collection. For example:

- Twelve well-known ghost stories originally published during the 19th century were collected and published by Oxford University Press under the title *12 Victorian Ghost Stories*.
- The original sheet music for dozens of public domain songs originally published during 1901–1911 was collected and published together under the title *Alexander's Ragtime Band* by Dover Publications.
- Fourteen public domain short stories were culled from more than 60 stories author Frank Norris published during his lifetime and published together by Ironweed Press under the title *The Best Short Stories of Frank Norris*.
- More than 100 public domain postcards were collected and reproduced in a book called *Delivering Views: Distant Cultures in Early Postcards*, published by the Smithsonian Institution Press.

When public domain works are republished in this way their copyright is not revived, but the compiler of the collection is entitled to a copyright in the selection and arrangement of the public domain works (see Chapter 12). Such a copyright in a collection published from 1923 through 1963 could be renewed. But such a renewal only extended to the selection and arrangement of the collection, not to the original works themselves, which remain in the public domain.

Searches for Works Published 1950–1963

Researching copyright renewals for works published during 1950–1963 is relatively easy. The Copyright Office has placed all its renewal records for these years online and they can be accessed from the Copyright Office website at www.copyright.gov. The records may be searched by title, name, keyword, and registration or document number. Moreover, through a command keyword search, elements of any or all fields can be combined to search the records. Users can also search by type of work, such as sound recordings, dramas, motion pictures, or visual materials. The Copyright Office website contains an online tutorial explaining how to use the system at www.copyright.gov/records/tutorial.html.

Labeled View

The Scarlet letter. By Nathaniel Hawthorne, foreword by Leo Marx.

Relevance: ■ ■ ■ ■ ■
Type of Work: Text
Registration Number / Date: RE0000346132 / 1987-08-10
Renewal registration for: A00000427734 / 1959-07-27
Title: The Scarlet letter. By Nathaniel Hawthorne, foreword by *Leo Marx.*
Copyright Claimant: N A L Penguin, Inc. (PWH)
Basis of Claim: New Matter: foreword.
Variant title: The Scarlet letter.
Names: Marx, *Leo*
Hawthorne, Nathaniel, 1804-1864
NAL Penguin, Inc.

Figure 1: Renewal Record for *The Scarlet Letter*

The detailed online renewal record for the 1954 motion picture *On the Waterfront* is reproduced in Figure 2. Here's how to decipher this entry:

This record informs the world that a motion picture named *On the Waterfront* was originally published on July 29, 1954 and the registration was renewed on January 25, 1982. Since the renewal took place during the 28th year after publication, the work has been timely renewed and is not in the public domain. Its U.S. copyright will last until January 1, 2050 (the copyright in any work published in the United States from 1923 through 1963 that was timely renewed lasts for 95 years after publication).

Renewal Searches for Works Published through 1949

Conducting a renewal search for a work published less than 95 years ago through 1949 is more difficult than for works published between 1950 and 1963, because you have to search the renewal records contained in a massive series of catalogs called the *Catalog of Copyright Entries* (CCE). The CCE contains the registration and renewal records for all works published during these years.

Online CCE Records

Until 1978, all copyright renewals were processed and recorded on paper. Lists of renewed works were published annually or semiannually in the CCE, a series of hardcover books.

As a result, in the past, it was always necessary to find a library that had a copy of the CCE and manually search it or go to the Copyright Office and manually search their records. However, this is no longer the case. All of the 660 CCE volumes have been digitized and made publicly available on the Internet Archive at https://archive.org/details/copyrightrecords. The Copyright Office has created a helpful video showing how to access and use these records, available at www.copyright.gov/tutorials/records/cce.mp4. These records include a limited search capability based on the results of optical character recognition (OCR) of the scanned text.

In addition, several private organizations have made many of the renewal records available online independently of the Copyright Office. For example, Google, Inc., has scanned all 91 volumes of the CCE containing renewal records for books, pamphlets, and contributions to periodicals published from 1923 to 1978 and made them searchable online through Google Books at: https://books.google.com/googlebooks/copyrightsearch.html. Also, the Stanford University Library has created a searchable online database of all the copyright renewals for books published during the period 1923 through 1963. The URL is: https://exhibits.stanford.edu/copyrightrenewals. These records may be searched by title, author, registration date, and renewal date.

In addition, the New York Public Library has converted all the registrations and renewals listed in the CCEs for 1923–1963 to XML format and a tab-delimited format. These files are downloadable at: https://github.com/NYPL/cce-renewals and https://github.com/NYPL/catalog_of_copyright_entries_project.

On the waterfront. By Columbia Pictures Corporation.

Type of Work:	Motion Picture
Registration Number / Date:	RE0000115860 / 1982-01-25
	Renewal registration for: LP0000003901 / 1954-07-29
Title:	On the waterfront. By Columbia Pictures Corporation.
Copyright Claimant:	Columbia Pictures Industries, Inc. (PWH)
Variant title:	On the waterfront.
Names:	Columbia Pictures Corporation.
	Columbia Pictures Industries, Inc.

Figure 2: Renewal Record for *On the Waterfront*

The Copyright Office Card Catalog

If you go to the Copyright Office to do a renewal search, instead of using the CCE, you may use a huge card catalog the Copyright Office has created listing all copyright renewals. The Copyright Office considers the card catalog superior to the CCE because it has been updated over time to reflect corrections, updates, and cancellations. These updates do not appear in the Catalogs of Copyright Entries except for some hand-written annotations made in the two sets of the CCE's maintained in the Copyright Office. Currently, the Copyright Office is in the process of scanning the 9 million catalog card records from registrations recorded from 1871 to 1977 to create a digitized card catalog available online. A beta version of this digitized card catalog is available at www.copyright.gov/vcc.

What Years to Search

CCE catalogs were issued each year. Normally, you'll have to search the CCEs for several years to make sure no renewal was filed. This is because works published through 1949 could be renewed any time during the 28th year after publication. This one-year period was measured from the actual date of publication. For example, a work published on June 1, 1930 could be renewed anytime during June 1, 1957 through June 1, 1958. The renewal record for such a work could be found in the CCE for 1957 or 1958. For this reason, it will always be necessary to search at least two years' worth of CCEs to make sure no renewal was filed—those covering the 27th and 28th years after publication. In addition, just to be on the safe side, it's advisable to search the 29th year after publication as well. This is because due to processing problems timely filed renewals may not have been entered in the CCE until after the 28th year. The chart below shows which years to search.

Conducting a Search

The CCE is available in printed form through 1979, after which it was issued in microfiche form until 1982. It was discontinued after 1982 because the renewal records were placed online. The CCE is divided into parts according to the type of work. Depending on the year you search, there may be separate volumes for books, periodicals, music, dramas, maps, prints and labels, art, and motion pictures.

Each volume of the CCE contains entries for registrations made during a particular year, with the entries for renewals in a separate section, usually in the back. For most years, renewal data was compiled twice a year, so there are two separate renewal listings: one for the first six months of the year and one for the last six months. You need to check both listings.

Guide to Renewal Searches for Works Published 1923–1949			
Year of Publication	27th Year After Publication	28th Year	29th Year
1923	1950	1951	1952
1924	1951	1952	1953
1925	1952	1953	1954
1926	1953	1954	1955
1927	1954	1955	1956
1928	1955	1956	1957
1929	1956	1957	1958
1930	1957	1958	1959
1931	1958	1959	1960
1932	1959	1960	1961
1933	1960	1961	1962
1934	1961	1962	1963
1935	1962	1963	1964
1936	1963	1964	1965
1937	1964	1965	1966
1938	1965	1966	1967
1939	1966	1967	1968
1940	1967	1968	1969
1941	1968	1969	1970
1942	1969	1970	1971
1943	1970	1971	1972
1944	1971	1972	1973
1945	1972	1973	1974
1946	1973	1974	1975
1947	1974	1975	1976
1948	1975	1976	1977
1949	1976	1977	1978

For most years, renewals are listed by the name of the author or copyright owner. If you don't know the name of the author or copyright owner, you can look in the title index for each CCE volume. If a title is followed by an (R) it means the work has been renewed.

But note carefully: If the work was originally published as part of a larger work—for example, an article published in a magazine—you need to look to see if the larger work was renewed. You also must check to see if the individual article was renewed. If either the larger work or individual contribution has been renewed, the work is not in the public domain. The CCE has a separate section called *Contributions to Periodicals* that lists renewals for individual articles.

In addition, be aware that there is no standardization of alphabetizing or name usage in the CCE. For example, names beginning with "Mc" and "Mac" are alphabetized in various ways. A name like "Tschaikowski" may be spelled "Chaikovskii." Non-English names such as "de Mille" and "von Franz" may appear under both the prefix and the surname. A corporate entity such as "Walt Disney Productions" may appear under that form or under "Disney (Walt) Productions."

Following is the renewal record for the 1925 novel *The Great Gatsby*, by F. Scott Fitzgerald. It was found in the renewal section of the *Books* volume of the 1953 CCE.

FITZGERALD, FRANCIS SCOTT
The Great Gatsby © 10Apr25, A855444.
R109367, 23Mar53, Frances Scott
Fitzgerald Lanahan (C)

Let's decipher this entry line by line:

- The first line lists the author of the work (the famed novelist F. Scott Fitzgerald).
- The second line shows the title of the work. The © symbol followed by the date 10Apr25 means *The Great Gatsby*, was first published on April 10, 1925. The entry A855444 is the original Copyright Office registration number for the work.
- The third line begins with the entry R109367, which is the renewal registration number for the novel. The date 23Mar53 means the work was renewed on March 23, 1953.
- The entry "Frances Scott Fitzgerald Lanahan" on the third and fourth lines is the name of the copyright owner of the novel following the renewal. The (C) following her name means that she is the child of the deceased author.

This entry tells you that *The Great Gatsby* was timely renewed during the 28th year after its initial publication and therefore receives a 95-year copyright term. Its copyright expires on January 1, 2021.

Abbreviations Used in the CCE

Following is a list of the main abbreviations used in the CCE:

(A) author

a.k.a. also known as

(C) child or children of the deceased

© copyright claimed by

© (followed by date) year of publication as stated in copyright notice

ca. circa

comp. compiler, compiled by

d.b.a. doing business as

(E) executor(s) of the author

ed. edited by, editor, edition

(NK) next of kin of the author who is not living, there being no will

p. page, pages

(P) proprietor of a commercial print or label

(PCB) proprietor of a work copyrighted by a corporate body otherwise than as assignee or licensee of the author

(PCW) proprietor of a composite work

(PPW) proprietor of a posthumous work

pseud. pseudonym

(PWH) proprietor of copyright in a work made for hire

rev. revised by, reviser, revision

t.a. trading as

tr. translator, translated by

v., vol. volume, volumes

(W) widow of the author

(Wr) widower of the author

Researching Copyright Registration Records

When a work is registered with the Copyright Office, the copyright claimant must file an application form that contains some basic information about the work, such as who wrote it, if it was published, when and where it was published, and the nature of the authorship involved. When the work is registered, the Copyright Office stamps a registration number and seal on the application, which serves as the work's certificate of registration. This certificate contains a good deal of information about the work that may be very useful to determining whether it's in the public domain, including:

- the title, and whether it had any previous titles
- in the case of writings, whether the work was published as a contribution to a magazine, newspaper, or other serial publication
- the name of the author(s)
- where and when the work was published (if it was)
- the author's nationality or residence
- the name of the copyright owner, and
- whether the work is a derivative work or compilation and, if so, what new material was added to create the derivative work or compilation (see Chapter 3 for a detailed discussion of derivative works and Chapter 12 for a discussion of compilations).

Online Registration Records

Since 1978, some, but not all, of the information contained in copyright certificates has been placed in an online Copyright Office database. This is the same database that contains the online renewal

---

Here lies : an autobiography / Eric Ambler.

Type of Work: Text
Registration Number / Date: TX0001595748 / 1985-06-20
Title: Here lies : an autobiography / Eric Ambler.
Imprint: London : Weidenfeld and Nicolson, 1985.
Description: 234 p.
Copyright Claimant: Eric Ambler
Date of Creation: 1985
Date of Publication: 1985-06-13
Variant title: Here lies : an autobiography
Names: Ambler, Eric

Figure 3: Registration Record for a Book by Eric Ambler

records discussed above and is accessed and searched in the exact same way.

Figure 3 shows an example of the online registration record for a book by the late English author Eric Ambler. Among other things, this record tells when and where the book was published—in London in 1985. Information such as this enables you to determine how long the copyright in a work lasts.

When a public domain work is republished with new material, the registration record will ordinarily contain a brief statement of what the new matter consists of. This statement may be helpful to determine which parts of the work are and are not copyrighted. However, it's often too general to be of much help. So, to really determine what new material is contained, you must actually examine a copy of the republished work.

CCE Registration Listings

There are no online registration records, other than renewals, for works published before 1978. There aren't even online renewal listings for works published before 1950. However, the *Catalog of Copyright Entries* (CCE) contains summaries of the registration records for works published before 1978. As with the online records, these may be helpful to determine when and where a work was published, who the owner is, and what new matter was added to a republished public domain work.

Obtaining a Copy of the Registration Certificate

If you want to see all the information on a work's registration certificate, you can request a copy from the U.S. Copyright Office by calling the Records Research and Certification Section at 202-707-6787, or emailing copycerts@loc.gov. You must provide information needed to identify the work, including the title of the work, the registration number, and the year of publication or registration.

There is a $55 fee for this service.

Finding the work's registration number may be a problem. If the work was published and registered after 1978, you can check the Copyright Office online records. If the work was published before 1978, you may have to check the *Catalog of Copyright Entries* (CCE). The procedure to check for a registration number is largely the same, except that you're looking for the work's original registration record, not a renewal.

If you can't find the registration number, you can request the Copyright Office to do a search, but this will cost a minimum of $400.

For more information on obtaining access to Copyright Office records, see the Copyright Office publication called Circular 6, *Obtaining Access to and Copies of Copyright Office Records and Deposits*. You can download a copy from the Copyright Office website (www.copyright.gov).

What If a Work Is Not in the Public Domain?

Find Another Public Domain Work 390

Obtain Permission to Use the Work 390

Use the Work Without Permission on the Grounds of Fair Use 393

    What Is the Fair Use Privilege? 393

    When Is a Use a Fair Use? 394

    Parody 401

f you determine that a particular work you want to copy, adapt, or otherwise use is not in the public domain, you have three alternatives:

- Find something else that is in the public domain.
- Obtain permission to use the work.
- Use the work without permission, relying on the fair use privilege, which allows copyrighted material to be used for free in limited situations.

We discuss each option below.

Find Another Public Domain Work

As this book makes clear, millions and millions of works are in the public domain. If you find that a particular work is not public domain, you can simply forget about using it and continue searching for a work that is in the public domain. The next public domain work you find may be just what you're looking for. The drawback to this approach, of course, is that it can be time consuming and there is no guarantee you'll ever find a public domain work that meets your needs.

Obtain Permission to Use the Work

If you are dead set on using a particular copyrighted work, you can go ahead and do so if you obtain permission from the copyright owner for the use. Unfortunately, obtaining permission to use a copyrighted work can be a difficult and time-consuming process and usage is usually not free.

RESOURCE
For a detailed explanation of how to go about getting permission and all the forms you may need, refer to *Getting Permission: Using & Licensing Copyright-Protected Materials Online & Off*, by Richard Stim (Nolo).

Expect permissions to take anywhere from one to three months to negotiate and obtain. The first step is to learn how much a particular work would cost to use. Depending on your budget for obtaining permissions, the cost might make your decision for you, if it is beyond your means. Often copyright owners have a sliding scale of fees for different uses. Commercial uses are usually more costly than nonprofit uses.

It is best to obtain written permission before you begin using the copyrighted work. But you should absolutely obtain it before your project is completed. It is sometimes more difficult and more expensive to obtain permission after a book, film, or recording is completed. If the copyright owner becomes aware that you have a vested interest in obtaining permission (for example, your book is already in production), the price may rise. In addition, if you can't obtain permission, you'll have to redo the work, which is expensive and time consuming. The best policy is to start seeking all required permissions as soon as possible.

Obtaining permission involves these steps:

Step 1: Find Out Who Owns the Work

The first step is to find out who owns the copyright in the work you want to use. Sometimes, this task is simple. Often, you may be able to locate the rights owner just by looking at the copyright notice on the work. For example, if the notice reads "Copyright 2020, Jones Publishing," you would start by finding the Jones Publishing company. Sometimes, more detailed research is required. Copyright ownership may have passed through several hands since your copy of the work was published.

In addition, some kinds of works, such as film and recorded music, can involve multiple owners or rights holders, each

---

Orphan Works

One problem that constantly bedevils people who want to obtain permission to use copyrighted works is that the copyright owner cannot be identified or located. This is particularly common for older works with little economic value. Such works are often called "orphan works." The Copyright Office completed two studies of the problem in 2006 and 2015 and issued two reports ("Report on Orphan Works" (2006), and "Orphan Works and Mass Digitization: A Report of the Register of Copyrights" (2015), available at www.copyright.gov).

The Copyright Office has recommended that legislation be enacted protecting users of orphan works from copyright infringement lawsuits. Under the proposal, a person who uses an orphan work without permission would have to pay no more than "reasonable compensation" if the work's owner later surfaces and complains, provided that such user (1) performed a good faith search to identify and locate the owner before the work was used, (2) filed a Notice of Use with the Copyright Office, (3) provided attribution to the copyright owner, if reasonable under the circumstances, and (4) included a (yet-to-be devised) orphan works symbol with any distribution, display, or performance of the work.

The proposed legislation has not been enacted by Congress.

An outstanding free guide on how to deal with orphan works has been created by the Society of American Archivists. It's called "Orphan Works: Statement of Best Practices," and may be obtained from the organization's website at www2.archivists.org/standards.

with separate rights to different parts of the work. For example, in order to use a music recording, you would have to obtain permission from the record company, from the music publisher (the owner of the song), and in some cases from the performers.

The method of identifying owners differs from industry to industry. For example, photographic reproduction rights are often owned by stock photo organizations, while collectives known as performing rights societies own music performance rights.

Step 2: Identify the Rights You Need

The next step in getting permission is to identify the rights you need. Each copyright owner controls a bundle of rights related to the work, including the right to reproduce, distribute, and modify the work. Because so many rights are associated with copyrighted works, you need to specify the rights you need. This can be as simple as stating your intended use—for example, you want to reproduce a photograph in your book.

Step 3: Negotiate Whether Payment Is Required

Next, you need to determine whether payment is required for the permission. In most cases there are no standard fees for using a work.

Sometimes, the owner of the work will not require payment if the amount of the work being used is quite small or the owner wishes to contribute to an educational or nonprofit effort.

However, some types of permission almost always require payment. For example, using a photo owned by a stock photo agency usually requires a payment of $100 or more. Using a song in a commercial usually requires a payment of several thousand dollars. As a general rule, expect to pay at least $50 or more for each copyright permission.

Generally, fees are linked to the popularity of your work. Commercial uses, such as advertisements, cost more than nonprofit or educational uses. The fees for website uses may depend upon on the number of visitors to the site.

If you can't afford the permission fee, you'll have to find another work to use unless you decide to use it without paying, on the grounds of fair use. This is why it's so important to find out what the fee will be as soon as possible.

Step 4: Get It in Writing

Finally, get your permission agreement in writing. Relying on an oral or implied agreement is almost always a mistake. You and the rights owner may have misunderstood each other or remembered the terms of your agreement differently. This can lead to disputes. If you have to go to court to enforce your unwritten agreement, you'll have difficulty proving exactly what the terms are.

Use the Work Without Permission on the Grounds of Fair Use

The final—and riskiest—option is to use the work without obtaining permission on the grounds of fair use. The law allows the use of copyrighted material for free in limited circumstances when the use is considered a fair use. However, determining when a use is a fair use requires a delicate balancing of several rather vaguely defined factors, discussed below.

This is the problem with the fair use privilege—it's an amorphous area of the law and it's hard to be sure whether a use is or is not a fair use. Moreover, always keep in mind that claiming fair use will not keep you from being sued. It is simply a defense you can raise if a copyright owner, claiming you infringed their ownership rights, sues you. You'll win such a suit if the judge or jury concludes that your use is a fair use, but the expense and trauma involved could be enormous.

GRAY AREA

For a detailed analysis of how to weigh the risks involved in using a work without permission, see Chapter 1.

CAUTION

No fair use outside the United States. This discussion only covers using copyrighted material within the United States. The fair use provisions contained in American copyright law are unique. No other country in the world gives the public such broad latitude to use copyrighted works without permission. Some countries do allow limited unauthorized copying, but only for the purposes of private study or research, not for publication. In the United Kingdom, Canada, Australia, and New Zealand this limited copying privilege is called "fair dealing"; no country other than the United States uses the term "fair use." If you want to use a work outside the United States without permission, you need to refer to the law of the country involved. (See Chapter 16 for a detailed discussion of foreign copyright laws.)

What Is the Fair Use Privilege?

The purpose of the copyright laws is to advance the progress of knowledge by giving authors an economic incentive to create new works. Authors and their heirs are automatically granted the exclusive right to reproduce, adapt, perform, and display their works for many years; they are in effect, granted a monopoly over the use of their work.

However, there are situations where strict enforcement of an author's monopoly would hinder, rather than promote, the growth of knowledge. An obvious example is that of a researcher or scholar whose own work depends on the ability to refer to and quote from prior works. No author could create a new work if he or she were first required to repeat the research of every author who had gone before.

Of course, scholars and researchers could be required to bargain with each copyright owner for permission to quote from or refer to prior works. But this would likely prove so onerous that many scholars would hunt for another line of work, and the progress of knowledge would be greatly impeded.

To avoid this result, the fair use privilege was created. Under the fair use rule, an author is permitted to make limited use of another author's work without asking permission. All authors and other copyright owners are deemed by U.S. law to give their automatic consent to the fair use of their work by others. The fair use privilege is the most significant limitation on a copyright owner's exclusive rights.

When Is a Use a Fair Use?

The following four factors must be considered to determine whether an intended use of a copyrighted work is a fair use:

- the purpose and character of the use
- the type of work involved
- the amount and importance of the material used, and
- the effect of the use upon the market for the copyrighted work.

These factors are intended to be a highly flexible set of general guidelines. The courts do not apply them in a mechanical or numerical way. For example, a use is not always fair if three of the four factors above are met. Moreover, not all factors are equally important in every case and it's up to the courts to decide what weight to give them. This makes determining whether a use is a fair use a highly subjective and unpredictable exercise.

Copyright Office Fair Use Index

In a laudable effort to help the public understand the fair use rules, the U.S. Copyright Office has compiled an online Fair Use Index. It contains detailed summaries of most notable court decisions involving fair use, going back to 1846. Reading these summaries, which are searchable by type of work involved, can help you understand how courts apply the complex fair use rules. The Fair Use Index is at www.copyright.gov/fair-use.

The Purpose and Character of the Use

First, the purpose and character of your intended use must be considered. The test here is to see whether your own work merely serves as a substitute for the original or "instead adds something new, with a further purpose or different character, altering the first with new expression, meaning, or message." The U.S. Supreme Court calls such a use "transformative." *Campbell v. Acuff-Rose Music, Inc.*, 510 U.S. 569 (1994).

This is a very significant factor. The more transformative a work is, the less important are the other fair use factors that may weigh against a finding of fair use. Why should this be? It is because the goal of copyright to promote human knowledge is furthered by the creation of transformative works. "Such works thus lie at the heart of the fair use doctrine's guarantee of a breathing space within the confines of copyright." *Campbell v. Acuff-Rose Music, Inc*, 510 U.S. 569 (1994).

Following are very typical examples of transformative uses where copyrighted material is used to help create new and different works. These types of uses are most likely to be fair uses:

- **Criticism and comment**—for example, quoting or excerpting a work in a review or criticism for purposes of illustration or comment.
- **News reporting**—for example, summarizing an address or article, with quotations, in a news report.
- **Research and scholarship**—for example, quoting a passage in a scholarly, scientific, or technical work for illustration or clarification of the author's observations.

Parodies are also transformative uses that often qualify as fair uses.

Can Fair Use Apply Where Permission Is Denied?

If you ask copyright owners for permission to use their work and they refuse, can you then use it without permission on the grounds of fair use? The U.S. Supreme Court has said yes: "If the use is otherwise fair, no permission need be sought or granted. Thus, being denied permission to use a work does not weigh against a finding of fair use." *Campbell v. Acuff-Rose Music, Inc.*, 510 U.S. 569 (1994).

This means that even though you're certain that your intended use is fair, you can go ahead and seek permission for the use from the copyright owner because you want to avoid the possibility of expensive litigation. If the copyright owner proves to be unreasonable and withholds permission, you can then go ahead and use the material on the basis of fair use. But, of course, the copyright owner could still sue you. If the use really is fair, you would win the suit even though you had unsuccessfully sought permission.

Although not really transformative, photocopying by teachers for classroom use may also be a fair use because teaching also furthers the knowledge-enriching goals of the copyright laws.

Note that the uses listed above, with the possible exception of news reporting, are primarily for nonprofit educational purposes. Although some money may be earned from writing a review or scholarly work, financial gain is not usually the primary motivation—disseminating information or otherwise advancing human knowledge is.

If permission were required for these socially helpful uses (presumably for a fee), it is likely that few reviews or scholarly works would be written; neither the authors nor publishers of works that earn such modest sums could afford to pay for the necessary permissions. (Newspapers and popular news websites probably could afford to pay for permissions, but requiring them to do so in all cases would inevitably impede the free flow of information, and might also violate the free press guarantees of the First Amendment of the U.S. Constitution.)

In contrast, an author and/or publisher of a work created primarily for commercial gain usually can afford to pay for permission to use other's protected expression. It also seems inherently fair to require this person to do so. In the words of one court (quoting from congressional hearings), fair use "distinguishes between 'a true scholar and a chiseler who infringes a work for personal profit.'" *Wainwright Securities, Inc. v. Wall Street Transcript Corp.*, 558 F.2d 91 (2d Cir. 1977).

For these reasons, a judge or jury in a copyright infringement case would be less likely to find a valid fair use claim for a work that was published primarily for private commercial gain than for a nonprofit or scholarly work. However, the fact that your primary motive is commercial does not always mean you can't exercise the fair use privilege. If the other fair use factors are in your favor, the use may be considered a fair use. This is particularly likely where the use benefits the public by furthering the fundamental purpose of the copyright laws—the advancement of human knowledge.

EXAMPLE: The authors of an unauthorized "popular" biography of Howard Hughes quoted from two *Look* Magazine articles about Hughes. All four fair use rules were satisfied. Only a small number of words were quoted and the authors had provided proper attribution for the quotes. In addition, the copyright owner of the articles (who turned out to be Hughes himself) had no intention of using the articles in a book, so the use was not a competitive use. A court held that the quotations qualified as a fair use. Although the biography had been published primarily to earn a profit, it also benefited the public. The court stated that "while the Hughes biography may not be a profound work, it may well provide a valuable source of material for future biographers (if any) of Hughes or for historians or social scientists." *Rosemont Enters. v. Random House, Inc.*, 366 F.2d 303 (2d Cir. 1966).

The Type of Work Involved

To preserve the free flow of information, less copyright protection is given to factual works (scholarly, technical, scientific works, etc.) than to works of imagination (novels, poems, plays, etc.). Thus, authors have more leeway in using material from factual works than from fanciful ones, especially where it's necessary to use extensive quotations to ensure the accuracy of the factual information conveyed.

In addition, you will have a stronger case of fair use if the material copied is from a published work than from an unpublished work. The scope of fair use is narrower for unpublished works because an author ordinarily has the right to control the first public appearance of his or her expression.

EXAMPLE: A well-known literary biographer named Ian Hamilton attempted to write an unauthorized biography of the notoriously reclusive novelist J.D. Salinger. During his research in universities libraries, he found 44 unpublished letters written by Salinger. When Salinger learned that Hamilton intended to include extensive quotations from these letters in his biography, he filed suit for copyright infringement and won. The court held that the quotations did not constitute a fair use, in large part because Salinger, not Hamilton, had the right to decide if and when to first publish his private letters. *Salinger v. Random House, Inc.*, 811 F.2d 90 (1987).

Attribution Does Not Make a Use Fair But Should Always Be Provided

Some people have the mistaken idea that they can use any amount of material so long as they give the author credit. This is simply not true. Providing credit for a quotation or other form of copying will not, in and of itself, make the use of the quote a fair use. For example, if you quote an entire chapter from another author's book without permission, your use wouldn't be considered fair even if you give that author credit.

Although the Copyright Act does not explicitly require authors to provide attribution for quoted or paraphrased material, it is a factor that courts consider. It is likely that a judge or jury would look with disfavor on an author who attempts to pass off the work of others as his or her own and then has the nerve to cry "Fair use!" if the author is sued for copyright infringement. They might be inclined not only to find that the use is not a fair use, but to impose particularly heavy damages in an infringement suit. If you copy someone else's work, always give that person credit. Copying with attribution is a very good hedge against getting sued, or losing big if you are sued.

The fact that a work is unpublished does not mean it can never be the subject of fair use. If all the other factors are in favor of fair use, they may outweigh this factor.

However, the drafters of the copyright law and the U.S. Supreme Court have suggested that a user may have more justification for reproducing a work without permission if it is out of print and unavailable for purchase through normal channels. *Harper & Row Publishers, Inc. v. Nation Enterprises*, 471 U.S. 539 (1985). Thus, most courts give users more leeway when they quote from or photocopy out-of-print works. But this does not mean that any amount of material from out-of-print works may be used without permission.

The Amount and Importance of the Material Used

The more material you take the more likely it is that your work will serve as a substitute for the original and adversely affect the value of the copyright owner's work, making it less likely that the use can be a fair use. However, contrary to what many people believe, there is no preestablished limit for fair use. For example, it is not always okay to take one paragraph or less than 200 words from a written work or less than two bars from a song.

Copying 12 words from a 14-word haiku poem wouldn't be fair use. Nor would copying 200 words from a work of 300 words likely qualify as a fair use. However,

copying 2,000 words from a work of 500,000 words might be fair. It all depends on the circumstances—for example, it may be permissible to quote extensively from one scientific work to ensure the accuracy of another scientific work.

The quality of the material you want to use must be considered as well as the quantity. The more important it is to the original work, the less likely is your use a fair use.

> **EXAMPLE:** The *Nation* magazine obtained a copy of Gerald Ford's memoirs prior to their publication. The magazine published an article about the memoirs in which only 300 words from Ford's 200,000-word manuscript were quoted verbatim. The U.S. Supreme Court held that this was not a fair use because the material quoted—dealing with the presidential pardon of former President Richard M. Nixon—was the "heart of the book" and (as an editor described it) "the most interesting and moving parts of the entire manuscript." *Harper & Row Publishers, Inc. v. Nation Enterprises*, 471 U.S. 539 (1985).

> **EXAMPLE:** In the late 1970s a television advertising campaign was conducted to promote New York City. A song called "I Love New York" accompanied the commercials. The song consisted in part of the phrase, "I Love New York" repeated again and again, accompanied by the four notes D, C, D, and E. The television show *Saturday Night Live* created and performed

a comic sketch in which it copied the four notes and changed the lyric to "I love Sodom." The court held that the use was not a fair use even though *SNL* only copied four notes and the words "I love" from a song that contained a 45-word lyric and 100 measures. The court reasoned that the copying was not a fair use because these four notes were "the heart of the composition." *Elsmere Music, Inc. v. NBC*, 482 F.Supp. 741 (1980).

The Effect of the Use on Potential Market

The fourth fair use factor is the effect of the use upon the potential market for, or value of, the copyrighted work. You must consider not only the harm caused by your act of copying, but whether similar copying by others would have a substantial adverse impact on the potential market for the original work.

For example, in the case involving J.D. Salinger's unpublished letters, mentioned above, Salinger's literary agent testified at trial that Salinger could earn as much as $500,000 if he published his letters. Thus, if biographers were permitted to publish portions of his most interesting letters first, it could have cost Salinger substantial royalties. The court ruled this was not a fair use.

Since fair use is simply a defense to a copyright infringement lawsuit, it is up to the defendant—the copier—in an infringement case to show there is no harm

to the potential market for the original work. This can be difficult. The more transformative the subsequent work—the more it differs from the original and is aimed at a different market—the less likely will it be deemed to adversely affect the potential market for the original.

But you'll have a very hard time proving that there is no harm to the potential market for the original work if your own work is similar to the original and aimed at the same market. This makes it much harder for a court to view your use as a fair use.

Doing Your Own Fair Use Analysis

To determine whether an intended use is a fair use, you need to pretend you're a judge and carefully weigh each of the four factors discussed above. List each factor in turn on a piece of paper or your computer and see whether it favors or disfavors a finding of fair use. To help you, here are two well-known examples of how judges conducted fair use analyses:

EXAMPLE 1: In 1980, a professional photographer named Art Rogers made a photograph of a man and his wife holding eight puppies. Rogers owned the copyright in the photo and exhibited and licensed it many times. Well-known artist and sculptor Jeff Koons obtained a copy of the photo and decided to recreate it as a sculpture. He gave the photo to artisans in his employ who proceeded to make four astonishingly faithful three-dimensional copies out of wood. Koons sold three of the sculptures for $367,000. Rogers filed suit claiming that Koons had infringed on his copyright in his photo by creating the sculptures without his permission. Koons claimed the sculptures were a fair use. The court disagreed, concluding that all four fair use factors discussed above went against a finding of fair use.

Purpose and character of the use: The court concluded that the main reason Koons had the sculptures created was to sell them and make a lot of money. This militated against a finding of fair use.

Type of work involved: The photo was a creative and imaginative work, not a factual work like a biography. This also weighed against fair use.

Amount and importance of material used: Koons copied virtually the entire photo. This also weighed against fair use.

The effect of the use on the market value of the original: Although Koons's sculpture was in a different medium than Rogers's photo, the court held that it did have a detrimental impact on the potential market for the photo. The court reasoned that the existence of Koons's sculpture made it less likely that any other artist would be willing to pay Rogers for permission to make another sculpture based on the photo. Moreover, Koons could take and sell photographs of the sculpture, which would reduce the market for Rogers's original photo. *Rogers v. Koons*, 960 F.2d 301 (2d Cir. 1992).

EXAMPLE 2: In 1988 Dr. Margaret Walker wrote a biography of the late author Richard Wright, best known for his novel *Native Son*. Walker included in the biography ten brief quotations and five short paraphrases from unpublished letters Wright had written to Walker, and 14 short passages from Wright's unpublished journal. Wright's widow sued Walker and her publisher for copyright infringement for using the material without permission. The court held the use was a fair use. Here's how the court analyzed the four fair use factors:

Purpose and character of the use: This factor clearly favored Walker because her work was a scholarly biography. Walker's use was transformative because her "biography furthers the goals of the copyright laws by adding value to prior intellectual labor."

Type of work involved: Since the material used by Walker was unpublished, this factor weighed against a finding of fair use.

Amount and importance of the material used: This factor favored a finding of fair use because Walker used no more than 1% of the letters or journal entries Wright had written. Moreover, although the material Walker used enhanced the biography, it was not of earthshaking importance and certainly did not form the heart of the biography. No one would buy the biography in order to read these passages.

Effect on the market: Finally, the court held that the biography did not pose a threat to the potential market for Wright's letters or journals. Since so little material was copied, the biography could in no way supplant the letters or journals. *Wright v. Warner Books, Inc.*, 953 F.2d 733 (2d Cir. 1991).

Parody

A parody is a work of imagination that ridicules another, usually well-known, work by imitating it in a comic way. Peruse the humor section of your local bookstore and you'll find many examples, such as parody versions of well-known magazines like *Cosmopolitan* (called *Catmopolitan*). Someone has even published a parody of the SAT exam called the "NSAT" (No-Sweat Aptitude Test) and a book of parody sequels to famous literary works, including titles such as *A Clockwork Tomato*, *2000: A Space Iliad*, and *Satanic Reverses*.

To parody a work, it is usually necessary to copy some of the work's material so that readers will be able to recognize what's being parodied. However, it is rarely possible to get permission to parody or satirize someone else's work. Thus, parodies can exist only because of the fair use privilege. Recognizing this, courts have historically held that parody and satire deserve substantial freedom, both as entertainment and a form of social and literary criticism.

The U.S. Supreme Court, in a case involving a parody of the song "Pretty Woman" by the rap group 2 Live Crew has provided specific guidance on how the fair use factors discussed above should be evaluated in a parody case. *Campbell v. Acuff-Rose Music, Inc.*, 510 U.S. 569 (1994).

Purpose and Character of the Use

In *Campbell*, the U.S. The Supreme Court stated that the heart of a claim of fair use for a parody is that an author's preexisting work needed to be copied in order to create a new work that, at least in part, comments on or criticizes the prior author's work. However, a self-proclaimed parodist who copies a prior work merely to get attention or to avoid the drudgery in working up something fresh has a weak claim to fair use.

Does it matter that a parody might be seen to be in bad taste? The Supreme Court said no. All that matters is that the work can reasonably be perceived to contain a parodic element—in other words, it comments on or criticizes the original work in some way. Whether a parody is in good or bad taste does not matter to fair use. However, as a practical matter, the copyright owner of a work being parodied is probably more likely to complain if the parody is in bad taste. The fact that a parody is commercially motivated weighs against a finding of fair use, but it is not a deciding factor in and of itself.

Type of Work Involved

As a general rule, a use is more likely to be considered a fair use when the work involved is a utilitarian factual work like a newspaper account or scientific work rather than a work of imagination like a novel or play. However, this isn't usually the case with parodies. People rarely bother to parody boring utilitarian factual works that no one has ever heard of. Instead, they parody highly creative well-known works. This is so whether they are nonfiction or fiction. For this reason, the *Campbell* court stated that the type-of-work factor is not helpful in determining whether a parody is a fair use.

The Amount and Importance of the Material Used

To be effective, a parody must take enough material from the prior work to be able to conjure it up in the reader's or hearer's mind. To make sure the intended audience will understand the parody, the parodist usually has to copy at least some of the most distinctive or memorable features of the original work. But a parody composed primarily of an original work with little new material added is not likely to be considered a fair use.

Effect of the Use on the Market for the Prior Work

A finding that a parody has a detrimental effect on the market for, or value of, the original work weighs against fair use. However, the Supreme Court stated that a parody generally does not affect the market for the original work because a parody and the original usually serve different market functions. A parody is particularly unlikely to affect the market for the original where the copying is slight in relation to the parody as a whole.

But what if a parody is so scathing or critical of the original work that it harms the market for it? Does this weigh against fair use? The Supreme Court answered this question with a resounding no. Biting criticism is not copyright infringement, even if it effectively destroys a work both artistically and commercially.

Applying the Fair Use Factors

Applying these fair use factors is a highly subjective exercise. One judge's fair use might be another's infringement. A parody will probably be deemed a fair use so long as:

- the parody has neither the intent nor the effect of fulfilling the demand for the original
- the parodist does not take more of the original work than is necessary to accomplish the parody's purpose (the more recognizable the original work, the less needs to be taken to parody it), and
- the original work is at least in part an object of the parody (otherwise there would be no need to use it).

EXAMPLE: Disc jockey Rick Dees created and recorded a parody version of the song "When Sunny Gets Blue." Dees's version was called "When Sonny Sniffs Glue" and copied the first six of the song's 38 bars. Dees changed the song's opening lyrics—"When Sunny gets blue, her eyes get gray and cloudy, then the rain begins to fall" to "When Sonny sniffs glue, her eyes get red and bulgy, then her hair begins to fall." The composers of "When Sunny Gets Blue" sued Dees for copyright infringement and lost because the court held that the parody was a fair use. Here's how the court analyzed the three fair use factors that the U.S. Supreme Court said are important in parody cases:

- **Purpose and character of use:** The court noted that Dees's song was intended to poke fun at "When Sunny Gets Blue," something a parody must do to be a fair use. While the parody was created as part of a recording sold for a profit, the court held it was "more in the nature of an editorial or social commentary than … an attempt to capitalize on the plaintiff's original work."

- **Effect of the use on the market for the prior work:** The court held that the parody would not have a substantial effect on the market for "When Sunny Gets Blue" because it could not fulfill the demand for it. The court noted that "When Sunny Gets Blue" was a romantic nostalgic ballad, while the parody was a song about a woman who sniffs glue. It was not likely that consumers who wanted to hear a romantic ballad would purchase the parody instead of the original song.

- **The amount and substantiality of the portion used:** Finally, the court held that the parody copied no more of the original song than was necessary to conjure it up in listeners' minds. The court noted that "a song is difficult to parody effectively without exact or near-exact copying." *Fisher v. Dees,* 794 F.2d 432 (9th Cir. 1986).

Index

A

Abridgments and condensations, 66
Adaptations, 4
    of sheet music, 85–86, 95–96, 100
    See also Derivative works; New works
Advertisements in collective works, 155, 346
Advertising or other commercial purposes
    actor portraying character in, 366
    art reproductions used in, 147–148
    art used in, 133, 138–139
    buildings used in, 205, 206
    crowd shots in, 360
    fair use and, 396
    film or photograph of dance and, 216
    films used in, 179
    photographs used in, 150, 155, 160
    public domain materials containing
        trademarks in, 364
    sheet music copyright and, 84–85
    titles used in, 249
    TV programs and, 183–184
    voice used in, 116
    See also Commercials; Right of publicity;
        Trademarks
Agricultural fairs, copyrighted music at, 83
Annotations, 66
Anonymous or pseudonymous work
    Canadian copyright, 291
    Chinese copyright, 292
    Japanese copyright, 292
    Russian copyright, 293
    U.S. copyright, 322–323, 324

Anthologies, 73, 74
    copyright notices and, 346, 348
    renewal searches and, 376
    thin copyright and, 237, 238–239
    See also Collections (collective works)
Anticounterfeiting rules, federal, 49–50
Applied art, 121, 130, 133–134
Architectural photographs, 159, 204–205
Architectural plans, 196–202
    copyrighted as architectural works, 200,
        201–202
    copyrighted as pictorial works, 200–201
    derivative works created from, 200
    expiration of copyright in, 199
    lack of copyright notice and, 199
    originality required for copyright of, 200
    publication for copyright purposes, 197–199
    sources of, 202
    types of graphics or models included under,
        196
    types of structures included under, 200, 201
    by U.S. government employees, 199–200
    uses of public domain in, 196–197
Arrangement. *See* Selection and arrangement
Arrangements of music
    in collective works, 100, 107
    copyright claims made for, 95–96
    as derivative works, 379
    determining whether copyrightable, 98–105
    expert advice on whether copyrightable, 103
    fees for your own arrangements, 105
    strategies to avoid getting sued, 106
    types of copyrightable changes in, 100–105

using arrangements with expired copyrights, 97

using if copyright is claimed, 97–100

using original public domain version, 96–97

Art, original works

  access to public domain works, 123–124

  in advertising or on merchandise, 133, 138–139

  applied, 121, 130, 133–134

  claims of artists' estates, 124

  dedicated to public domain, 138

  as elements of buildings, 202–203

  eligibility for copyright protection, 130–138

  fabric designs and clothing, 134–135

  in films, 178

  ideas underlying, 131, 144

  lacking human authorship, 132

  lacking minimal creativity, 130–131

  lack of copyright notice and, 129–130

  with limited publication, 127

  photos of copyrighted works, 159

  publication for copyright purposes, 125–129

  sources of, 140

  structures protected as sculptures, 202

  techniques in, 131–132

  as trademarks, 133, 138–139

  in TV programs, 183

  typeface designs, 135–136, 285

  types of, 121

  by U.S. government employees, 136–137

  useful articles and, 132–133

  uses of public domain works, 121–123

  See also Design patents

Art museums, 12, 123–124, 129, 140, 145

Art reproductions, 121, 140–148

  copyright status of original work and, 125, 141

  dedicated to public domain, 147

  digital, 146

  expiration of copyright in, 142

  lack of copyright notice and, 142

  originality required for copyright, 142–146

  photographs of public domain artwork, 144–146

  publication for copyright purposes, 141

  with public domain elements, 148

  sources of, 148

  types of, 140

  by U.S. government employees, 136

  used in advertising or on merchandise, 147–148

ASCAP

  fees for music performances and, 82

  fees for your own arrangements and, 105

  website list of restored copyrights, 92

Assignment of copyright

  by independent contractor to U.S. government, 46

  lack of copyright notice and, 349–350

Attribution

  by authors of scholarly works, 253

  Creative Commons licenses requiring, 306

  fair use and, 397

  of ideas and facts, 253

  moral right of, 286

  orphan works and, 391

  public domain material and, 366–367

  of public domain writing, 36

  of quoted material, 253, 397

Audiovisual works

  right of publicity and, 358

  sheet music copyright and, 84–85

  See also Commercials; Films; Television programs; Videos

Author's date of death

  determining, 325

  See also Copyright terms

B

Berne Convention, 277, 287
Blank forms
    copyright and, 55–57
    filled out for using websites, 302
BMI
    fees for music performances and, 82
    fees for your own arrangements and, 105
Book digitization projects, 75–77
Books. *See* Written works
Brand names, 363, 365
    of clothing designs, 135
Bridgeman Art Library Ltd. v. Corel Corp.,
    144–146
Buildings. *See* Architectural photographs;
    Architectural plans; Constructed buildings

C

California Digital Library, 76
Canada
    copyright terms in, 290–291, 296, 297, 298
    counterpart to fair use in, 393
Cartoon characters, 263
CC0 license of Creative Commons, 5, 59, 117,
    157, 158, 305
CCE (*Catalog of Copyright Entries*), 382–386
    abbreviations used in, 386
    contributions to periodicals in, 378, 385
    Internet resources for searching of, 383
    works published before 1978 and, 388
"Cease and desist" letter, 15
Characters, fictional, 253, 262–264
    as trademarks, 363, 365–366
Charitable uses, of copyrighted music, 83
China, copyright terms in, 292
Chord charts, 111

Choreography
    determining whether in public domain, 214–217
    source of public domain materials, 217
City governments. *See* Local governments
Classics Protection and Access Act (CPA Act),
    113–115, 332
Click-wrap licenses, 28, 30, 232, 310
Clothing designs, 134–135
Collections (collective works), 73–74, 235–240
    advertisements in, 155, 346
    arrangements of music in, 100, 107
    chord charts and method books, 111
    compiled by government employees, 239
    copying individual public domain works in,
        237–238
    of copyrighted materials, 236
    copyright notice for, 346
    European Union copyright term for, 288
    expiration of copyright, 239
    lack of copyright notice and, 240
    minimal creativity and, 238–239
    protected by licenses, 240
    of public domain materials, 235–236
    of recipes, 58
    renewal of copyright, 381
    of sheet music, 95–96, 100, 106–109
    thin copyright of, 106, 107, 108, 237, 238–239
    as trade secrets, 240
    websites as, 308–310
Commercials
    music used in, 9, 84–85
    See also Advertising or other commercial
        purposes
Common law copyright. *See* State copyright law
Common property, information that is, 57
    musical, 111
    on a website, 302

Commons, intellectual, 7–9. *See also* Creative Commons

Competing with someone's business, 13. *See also* Unfair competition laws

Compilations, 73–74
  de minimis, 227, 239
  See also Collections (collective works); Databases

Complaint by someone claiming copyright, 15–17

Computer games, and sheet music copyright, 85

Computer languages, 191

Computer scanner. *See* Scanned images

Computer software, 186–193
  checking whether really in public domain, 190
  Chinese copyright terms for, 292
  confusion about "public domain," 187–188
  created by U.S. government contractors, 190
  created by U.S. government employees, 189, 190
  dedicated to public domain, 135, 186–188, 190
  expiration of copyright, 191–192
  free but not in public domain, 188–189
  to generate typefaces, 135–136, 303
  lack of copyright notice and, 193
  protected by means other than copyright, 192
  publication for copyright purposes, 191–192
  sources of public domain software, 193

Condensations, 66

Constructed buildings, 202–206
  artistic elements protected by copyright, 202–203
  constructed after December 1, 1990, 203–206
  constructed before December 1, 1990, 202–203, 205–206
  copyrighted elements of, 203–204
  design patent protection for, 206
  originality required for copyright, 204

  photographing or other copying of, 159, 204–205
  trademark protection for, 159, 204–206
  types of structures included under, 203

Contracts to restrict public domain, 28–31. *See also* Licenses

Cookbooks, 57–58

Copies
  exclusive right to make, 4
  See also Digital copies; Fair use; Photocopies

Copyleft software, 189, 306

Copyright
  creation of, 24–25
  definition of, 22
  exclusive rights given with, 4, 22, 394
  limitations on protection under, 25–26
  requirements for protection by, 22–24
  thin, 106, 107, 108, 223, 237, 238–239
  as type of property, 4
  works protected by, 22

Copyright claims, spurious, 26–27
  for digital copies of public domain photos, 156
  for digital reproductions of public domain artworks, 146
  for digital versions of public domain texts, 70
  handling, 15–17
  by state governments about laws, 28

"Copyright free," 59, 147, 158, 304

Copyright infringement
  of restored works, 278–282
  by uploading and downloading music files, 116
  See also Lawsuit for copyright infringement

Copyright law
  before and after 1978, 20, 24–25
  exclusive rights under, 4, 22, 394
  goal of, 6, 395, 396
  history of, 20–21, 22
  See also State copyright law

Copyright notice, 25
 before 1909, 341
 absence not informative, 10
 for advertisements in collective works, 155,
  346
 categories of works not requiring, 342–347
 on collective works, 346
 date of publication in, 61, 323, 338, 339–340
 derivative works and, 340, 346–347
 excused omission of valid notice, 347–353
 on films, 167
 on Internet, 300–301
 misuse of, 10, 25, 26–27, 74, 77–78
 misuse on photos of public domain art, 145
 name of copyright owner on, 340–342
 not conclusive even if registered, 101
 omitted for works published 1978–1989, 336,
  352
 omitted on small number of copies, 350–352
 optional since March 1, 1989, 25, 63, 115,
  343–345, 350
 on photographs, 154–155
 public domain and, 336–337
 removed without owner's permission, 350
 renewal of copyright stated on, 376
 on republished work, 376
 required elements in, 338–342
 required placement of, 342
 restoration of foreign works and, 345
 on sheet music, 88, 89–90, 93–94
 on sound recordings, 115, 338, 339, 345
 on state or local documents, 47
 unpublished works and, 343
 on useful articles, 339–340
 on work funded by government contract, 46–47
 works first published outside U.S. and,
  327–331, 345
 on written works, 63

Copyright notice, works in public domain due to
 lack of
 architectural plans, 199
 art reproductions, 142
 artworks, 129–130
 choreography, 216–217
 collections, 240
 computer software, 193
 databases, 231
 films, 176
 maps, 208–209
 photographs, 154–155
 sheet music, 93
 television programs, 182
 written works, 63
Copyright Office, 20–21
 card catalog of, 384
 Fair Use Index of, 394
 hired to research renewal records, 376–377
 obtaining access to records of, 388
 See also CCE (Catalog of Copyright Entries);
  Copyright registration records; Copyright
  renewal records, researching
Copyright owner's name. See Owner of
 copyright
Copyright registration, 25
 to cure omission of notice, 352
 of musical arrangements, 101
Copyright registration certificate, 388
Copyright registration number, 388
Copyright registration records
 of architectural plans, 198
 of artworks or reproductions, 128–129
 country of publication in, 274
 cured omission of notice and, 352, 353
 date of publication in, 323, 344
 of films, 168
 licensing of a work and, 350

of new versions of films, 178

obtaining copy of certificate, 388

of photo or work it is in, 153

researching, 387–388

of sheet music, 89, 92

of unpublished works registered before 1978,
326–327

Copyright renewal

with different title, 380

of films, 170–171, 174, 178, 380

foreign works and, 374–375

low renewal rates, 373–374

made automatic in 1992, 322

of music in films, 175

republished works and, 323, 376, 380–381

of software, 191

stated in copyright notice, 323

time span of concern for, 317, 319–321, 323,
337, 372–373

See also Copyright restoration

Copyright renewal records, researching,
375–386

hiring a private search firm, 377

hiring Copyright Office, 376–377

Internet resources for, 383, 384–386

methods for, 375

preliminary information for, 375–376

republished works and, 376, 380–381

researching them yourself, 377–386

Copyright restoration, 272, 321

ASCAP listing of restored music, 92

in European Union countries, 289

finding country where first published,
274–275

of foreign films, 171–172, 176

GATT Agreement and, 272–273

infringement of restored works, 278–282

lack of valid copyright notice and, 345

number of works restored, 275–276

ownership of restored works, 278

requirements for, 273, 275, 276, 374

rule of thumb on, 275

works not restored, 276–278, 328–329,
374–375

Copyright symbol

C surrounded by circle, 338

P for sound recordings, 338

Copyright terms

in Canada, 290–291, 296, 297, 298

chart for works first published in U.S., 320

in China, 292

in European Union, 287–289, 313

four rules to determine expiration, 317

in Germany, 296–297

in Japan, 292–293

online duration calculator, 320

running until end of year, 316

in Russia, 293–294

for sound recordings, 113–114, 115, 331–333

in United Kingdom, 297, 298

for unpublished works, 324–327

for works first published in U.S., 316–323

for works first published outside U.S., 327–331

See also Expiration of copyright

Copyright traps, 63–64. *See also* Compilations;
Derivative works

Copy shops, requiring permission, 36–37

Country of publication

of architectural plans, 199

of art, 127–129

of film, 168

finding out, 274–275

of photograph, 153

of sheet music, 91–93

of written works, 61, 62

See also Foreign copyright laws

Court decisions, 51, 53, 240, 302

CPA Act (Classics Protection and Access Act), 113–115, 332

Craftsmanship, artistic, 121, 133–134

Creative Commons, 305–306
  CC0 license of, 5, 59, 117, 157, 158, 305
  licenses of, 305–306
  photographs and, 157
  Public Domain Mark of, 10
  search engine of, 157, 305
  software and, 188
  sound recordings and, 117
  videos and, 183

Creativity. *See* Minimal creativity

Credit. *See* Attribution

Criticism. *See* Opinions; Parody; Reviews

Currency and coins of U.S.
  anticounterfeiting rules and, 50
  art on, 137

D

Dance. *See* Choreography

Dastar decision, 366–367

Databases
  aggressive assertion of ownership in, 222
  basic features of, 73, 222–223
  collections of hyperlinks, 312
  copyrightable pricing data in, 224
  creativity required for copyright, 223, 225–227
  encryption of, 234–235
  expiration of copyright, 230
  on Internet, 302
  lack of copyright notice and, 231
  license restrictions on, 229, 231–233
  limited copyright protection for, 223
  protected authorship added to, 227

  publication for copyright purposes, 230
  raw facts not protected by copyright, 223–225
  of state and local governments, 230
  thin copyright of, 223
  as trade secrets, 233–234
  of U.S. government, 228–229
  uses of, 221

Date of publication
  of architectural plans, 198–199
  of art, 127–129
  on copyright notice, 61, 323, 338, 339–340
  determining, 323, 344–345
  of film, 167–168
  of photograph, 152–153
  of sheet music, 89–91
  of written works, 61–62

Dedication to public domain. *See* Public domain, works dedicated to

De minimis compilations, 227, 239

Derivative works
  copyright notices for, 340, 346–347
  copyright owner's right to create, 4
  copyright renewal searches for, 379–380
  created from architectural plans, 200
  created from public domain art, 123
  created from restored work, 279–280
  Creative Commons licenses and, 306
  misuse of copyright notices in, 74, 77–78
  photos of copyrighted works, 159–160
  using titles of public domain works, 247–248
  See also New works

Derivative works, musical, 94–95
  digital copies of sound recordings, 116
  See also Arrangements of music

Derivative works from written works, 38, 64–65
  avoiding problems with, 72–73
  changes not meriting copyright protection, 67–68

digital copies of public domain writings and, 69–70

extent of copyright protection for, 67

films, 173–175

microfilms of public domain works and, 70–71

in public domain though original is not, 71–72

scholarly editions, 68–69

types of, 65–66

Design patents, 21, 139–140

for architectural designs and structures, 206

for typefaces, 136

for useful articles, 133

Digital copies

copyright claims for, 308

of court decisions, 53

of photos of public domain artworks, 146

placed on Internet, 303, 308

of public domain photos, 156, 308, 311

of public domain writings, 37, 69–70, 75–77, 308

of sound recordings, 116

See also Internet content

Digital Millennium Copyright Act (DMCA), 234–235

Digital Public Library of America, 77

Disclaimers

to avoid confusion of titles, 248–249

foreign copyright on Internet content and, 313–314

Display rights, 4

Distribution rights, 4

Documenting public domain status, 17

Domain names, 312

Dramatizations, 66

Dynamic markings on music, 104–105

E

E-book versions of public domain books, 34

Editorial revisions and elaborations, 65

Educational uses

of copyrighted music, 83

fair use and, 26, 35

photocopying for classroom use, 395

of public domain music, 85

Encryption of databases, 234–235

Encyclopedias. *See* Collections (collective works)

European Union (EU)

copyright terms in, 287–289, 313

Internet content and, 313

restoration of public domain works, 289

Exclusive rights of copyright owner, 4, 22

limited by fair use, 394

Expiration of copyright, 62–63

in architectural plans, 199

in art, 129

in art reproductions, 142

in choreography, 216

in a collection, 239

in computer software, 191–192

in a database, 230

in films, 168–175

four rules for determining, 317

legislatively frozen from 1998 to 2018, 31, 319

major cutoff of 95 years, 318

in maps, 208

in music, 93

in musical arrangements, 97

in photographs, 154

in television programs, 180–181

in written works, 62–63

See also Copyright terms

F

Fabric designs, 134–135
Fact compilations. *See* Databases
Facts
    attribution of, 253
    author's interpretation of, 266
    author's research on, 265–266
    in databases, 222, 223–225
    in factual settings of fictional works, 261
    "fictional," 257–258
    merger doctrine and, 56, 258–260
    not protected by copyright, 26, 223–225,
        256–257
    vs. opinions, 224
    selection and arrangement of, 269
    trade secret laws and, 257
Factual works
    fair use and, 397
    ideas in nonfiction and, 253
    public domain elements in, 265–269
Fair dealing, 393
Fair use, 26, 35–36, 393–403
    amount of material and, 398, 400
    brief appearance of artwork in a film and, 178
    brief appearance of artwork on TV and, 183
    doing your own analysis of, 399–401
    factors determining, 394–401
    factual vs. imaginative works and, 397
    importance of material and, 398–399, 400
    only in United States, 393
    parody and, 123, 395, 401–403
    potential market and, 399, 400–401
    purpose of, 393–394, 400
    as risky option, 393
    unpublished works and, 397–398, 399, 400
Fair Use Index, 394

Fictional characters, 253, 262–264
    as trademarks, 363, 365–366
Fictional elements in factual works, 268–269
Fictional "facts," 257–258
Fictionalizations, 65
Fictional works
    fair use and, 397
    ideas underlying, 252–253
    maps created as, 211
    novels in public domain, 40–41
    public domain elements in, 261–265
    right of publicity and, 358
    standard situations in, 264–265
Films, 165–179
    for advertising or other commercial purposes,
        179
    artworks in, 178
    based on a preexisting work, 173–175
    Canadian copyright terms, 290
    changed versions of public domain films,
        177–178
    Chinese copyright terms, 292
    colorized, 177, 286
    copies of public domain films, 177–178
    created for U.S. government, 176–177
    crowd shots in, 360
    of dances, 215, 216
    determining publication status of, 166–168
    distribution methods for, 166–167
    European Union copyright terms, 288
    expiration of copyright, 168–175
    foreign, 171–172, 176
    Japanese copyright terms, 292
    lack of copyright notice and, 176
    licenses for access to copies of, 177
    music in, 84–85, 175–176, 177–178

published in U.S. before 1964 and not
   renewed, 169–176
published in U.S. over 95 years ago, 168–169
renewal of copyright, 170–171, 174, 178, 380
right of publicity and, 179, 216, 357, 360
sources of public domain films, 184
title registration in private system, 246
trademarks and, 179, 364, 366–367
types in public domain, 165
unpublished, 170
uses of public domain films, 165
See also Screenplays
The Film Superlist, 171
Fingering suggestions, 103–104
First Amendment
   fair use and, 396
   right of publicity and, 356, 358
   trademark issues and, 356, 367
   uses of titles and, 249
Fixation required for copyright, 23
   of choreography, 214–215
   of musical compositions, 81
   of quotations, 268
   state copyright laws and, 268
Font software, 135–136
Foreign copyright laws
   copyright duration in, 287–294
   country where work will be used and, 284
   differences between U.S. laws and, 284–287,
      313
   Internet content and, 313–314
   lawsuit under, for works in U.S. public
      domain, 287, 313
   moral rights and, 285–286
   researching, 297–298
   rule of the shorter term and, 285, 294–297, 375

U.S. government materials claimed under, 229
   See also Copyright terms
Foreign governments
   Internet content created by, 301
   without copyright relations with U.S., 332–333
   written works of, 49
Foreign works
   copyright renewal in U.S. and, 374–375
   copyright terms in U.S. for, 327–331
   films, 171–172, 176
   music, 92
   published over 95 years ago, 317
   sound recordings, 332–333
   See also Copyright restoration
Forms. *See* Blank forms
Fraternal groups, copyrighted music used by, 83
Fraternity events, copyrighted music used at, 83
Freedom of Information Act, 48
Free shows, copyrighted music used in, 83
Free software, 188–189

G

GATT Agreement, 272–273
Genealogies, 227
Generic words and symbols, 368
Germany, copyright terms in, 296–297
Getty Images, 12, 308, 311
Google Book Search, 76
Google Books website, 11
Government
   quasi-official legal documents used by, 54
   three levels of, 45
   See also Foreign governments; Local
      governments; State governments; U.S.
      government
Gray areas in public domain, 12–15

H

Harmonies, original, 103
Harry Fox Agency, 105
HathiTrust Digital Library, 77
Hot news, unfair competition using, 258
HTML (Hypertext Markup Language), 302–303
Huckleberry Finn (Twain), 327
Hyperlinks, collections of, 312

I

Ideas
  artistic, 131, 144
  attribution of, 253
  merger doctrine and, 56, 258–260
  musical, 110
  patent law and, 256
  selection and arrangement of, 261
  state contract law and, 254
  three kinds of, 252–253
  trade secret law and, 254–255
  two-dimensional depictions of, 132
Independent contractors. *See* U.S. government contractors, works of
Insurance, and public domain status, 17
Interior design as trademark, 206
Internet Archive, 76
  Copyright Office records on, 383
Internet content
  copyright claims in digital copies, 308
  copyright notices on, 300–301
  databases, 302
  foreign copyright laws and, 313–314
  hyperlinks, 312
  laws and court decisions, 53, 302
  licenses used to protect, 307, 310–311
  misuse of words "public domain" for, 300, 304, 307
  problems with using, 307–311
  public domain works on, 11, 301–304
  sound recordings, 116
  two preliminary rules on, 300–301
  See also Creative Commons; Digital copies; Websites
Inventions, patentable, 21, 256
Inventory lists, 227

J

Japan, copyright terms in, 292–293
Jewelry, 133–134
  copyright notice and, 130, 142, 339–340, 351

K

Keyboard reductions, 102–103

L

Laws and court decisions
  copyright issues in use of, 51–53, 302
  licenses for collections of, 53, 240, 302
  protecting works of authorship, 21
Lawsuit for copyright infringement, 4
  defense when lack of notice is excused, 352–353
  fair use as defense in, 393, 395, 399
  in foreign country, 287, 313
  in public domain gray area, 13–15
  registration required for, 25
  See also Copyright infringement
Lawsuit for trademark infringement, 362, 364, 365, 369
Lawsuit for violating license, 29
Lawsuit for violating right of publicity, 357

Lawyer experienced in copyright law, 16–17

Lawyer organizations that help artists, 17

Library of Congress card catalog, 89

   country of publication and, 274

   country of publication for art, 128

   date of publication and, 92

   date of publication for architectural plan, 198

   date of publication for art, 128

   date of publication for photo, 153

Library of Congress digitization projects, 75

Licenses, 28–31

   for access to public domain films, 177

   of art museums, 124

   click-wrap, 28, 30, 232, 310

   for collections, 240

   for computer software, 188–189, 192

   for continued use of restored work, 279–280

   for copyrighted model codes, 53

   of Creative Commons, 305–306

   for databases, 231–233

   for databases of U.S. government data, 229

   for font software, 136

   lack of valid copyright notice and, 347–350, 353

   lawsuit for violation of, 29

   nonexclusive, 307

   of organizations that publish art photos, 145

   to protect Internet content, 307, 310–311

   for public performance of music, 82

   of stock photo agencies, 12, 150, 308, 311

   for U.S. government to use contractor's work, 46

   for websites of laws and court decisions, 53, 240, 302

   See also CC0 license of Creative Commons

Limited publication of artwork, 127

Literary devices, 265

Local governments, 45

   collections compiled by, 239

   databases created by, 230

   Internet content created by, 301

   laws and court decisions of, 47

   maps created by employees of, 209

   model codes used by, 53

   quasi-official legal documents used by, 54

   written works by employees of, 47

Location release, 205

Logos, as trademarks, 138, 362, 363

M

Magazines. *See* Collections (collective works)

Maps

   with elements in public domain, 210–212

   expiration of copyright, 208

   fictional or humorous, 211

   lack of copyright notice and, 208–209

   originality and creativity required for copyright, 210

   publication for copyright purposes, 208

   sources of public domain maps, 212

   types of graphics included under, 208

   by U.S. government employees, 209–210

Mass book digitization projects, 75–77

Mechanical royalties, 82–83

Melodies, not copyrightable, 110–111

Merchandise

   using public domain images on, 356

   See also Advertising or other commercial purposes; Right of publicity; Trademarks

Merger doctrine, 258–260

   forms and, 56

Method books, musical, 111

Methods
    not protected by copyright, 253
    protected by patent law, 256
Microfilms of public domain works, 70–71
Minimal creativity, 24
    of artworks, 130–131
    of collections, 238–239
    of collections of hyperlinks, 312
    of databases, 223, 225–227
    of maps, 210
    merger doctrine and, 259
    of musical collective works, 107–108
    of websites, 309–310
Model codes, 53
Moral rights, 285–286
Movies. *See* Films
Multimedia works. *See* Audiovisual works
Museums, controlling access to art, 12,
    123–124, 129, 140, 145
Music
    European Union copyright, 288–289
    in films, 84–85, 175–176, 177–178
    information that is common property for, 111
    reference works on, 90–91
    See also Arrangements of music; Sheet music;
        Sound recordings

N

Name of copyright owner. *See* Owner of
    copyright
Names
    not protected by copyright, 54
    right of publicity and, 357
    See also Brand names; Right of publicity
National Archives and Records Administration
    (NARA), 75

National Gallery of Art, 157
New editions
    copyright notices for, 340
    of public domain music, 101–102
    renewal searches for, 379
    See also Republished works
Newspapers. *See* Collections (collective works)
Newsreels, 169, 177
News reporting
    fair use and, 26, 35, 395–396
    unfair competition involving, 258
New works, from public domain materials, 6–7.
    See also Derivative works
Nondisclosure agreement, 234, 255
Nonexclusive licenses, 307
Nonprofit performance of music, 83
Notice of Intent to Enforce Copyright, 279, 280,
    281–282
Novels in public domain, 40–41

O

Open source software, 189
Opinions
    collection based on, 239
    in a database, 224, 226
    vs. facts, 224
    See also First Amendment
Originality, 23
    of architectural plans, 200
    of arrangements or adaptations of music,
        100–101
    of art reproductions, 142–146
    of constructed buildings, 204
    of maps, 210
    merger doctrine and, 259
    of photographs, 155–156
    of reconstructed quotations, 267

Orphan works, 391
  sound recordings, 114–115
Out-of-print works, 321
  fair use and, 398
Owner of copyright
  on copyright notice, 340–342
  getting permission from, 391–392
  orphan recordings and, 114, 391
  of restored work, 278

P

Panned and scanned films, 177
Parody, and fair use, 123, 395, 401–403
Parts lists, 227
Patent law, 21, 256
  computer software and, 192
  See also Design patents
Patent notice, 140
Performance rights, 4
Performance rights societies, 82, 105
Performance royalties, 82, 105
Performances, musical
  European Union copyright, 288–289
  nonprofit or religious, 83
  sheet music copyright and, 82, 83, 87, 105
Performing public domain writings, 38
Periodicals. *See* Collections (collective works)
Permission fees, 392
  public domain works and, 9–10
  for your own arrangements, 105
Permission to use copyrighted works, 390–393
  fair use after denial of, 395
Photocopies
  of copyrighted architectural plans, 200–201
  of out-of-print works, 398
  of public domain artworks, 143–144

of public domain music, 85
of public domain photos, 156
of public domain writings, 36–37, 42
of sheet music, 84
by teachers for classroom use, 395
Photographs
  in advertisements, 150, 155, 160
  architectural, 159, 204–205
  of art still under copyright, 159
  of artworks in public domain, 144–146
  Canadian copyright terms, 290
  Chinese copyright terms, 292
  of choreographic works, 216
  of copyrighted works, 159–160
  country of publication, 153
  crowd shots used commercially, 360
  date of publication, 152–153
  dedicated to public domain, 157–158
  digital copies of, 146, 156, 308, 311
  eligibility for copyright, 155–157
  expiration of copyright, 154
  Japanese copyright terms, 292–293
  lacking human authorship, 157
  lack of copyright notice and, 154–155
  of natural objects, 158
  originality of, 155–156
  photocopies of, 156
  products included under, 150
  publication for copyright purposes, 150–153
  right of publicity and, 160, 216, 357, 360, 366
  sources of public domain photos, 150, 161
  stock photo agencies, 12, 150, 308, 311, 392
  trademarks in, 150, 159, 160, 364
  by U.S. government employees, 156–157
  used for commercial purposes, 150, 155, 160, 360

Phrases, and copyright, 54–55

Plagiarism, 36, 253

Plays, 37

Plots of fictional works, 253, 261–262

Postage stamp designs, 136–137

Posthumous works, and Canadian copyright, 291

Postmortem right of publicity, 360–361

Privity limitation, 232–233

Product names, 363, 365

Product packaging, 363, 365

Project Gutenberg, 76

Property release, 205

Pseudonym. *See* Anonymous or pseudonymous work

Publication for copyright purposes, 59–62, 316
  of architectural plans, 197–199
  of art, 125–129
  of art reproductions, 141
  of choreography, 215
  of collections, 239–240
  of databases, 230
  of films, 166–168
  of maps, 208
  of photographs, 150–153
  of sheet music, 86–93
  of software, 191–192
  of television programs, 180–181
  of written works, 59–62
  See also Country of publication; Date of publication

Public domain
  cheat sheet for what is in, 317
  confusion about meaning of, 187–188, 300, 304, 307
  copyright protection and, 4–5
  definition of, 4
  federal laws dramatically reducing, 31
  grassroots movement for preservation of, 30
  gray areas in, 12–15
  lack of copyright notice and, 336–337
  looting of, 26–31
  purpose of, 6
  ways a written work may enter, 38–39

Public domain, works dedicated to, 58–59
  art, 138
  art reproductions, 147
  computer software, 135, 186–188, 190
  double-checking status of, 304
  on Internet, 303–307
  photographs, 157–158
  sound recordings, 117
  videos, 182–183
  written works, 58–59
  See also CC0 license of Creative Commons

Public domain calculators, 320

"Public domain day," 318

Public domain elements in copyrighted writings, 252
  facts and, 256–260
  ideas and, 252–256, 258–260
  merger doctrine and, 258–260
  in works of fact, 265–269
  in works of fiction, 261–265

Public Domain Mark, 10

Public domain materials
  challenge to your claim of, 15–17
  determining public domain status of, 10–11
  documenting public domain status of, 17
  fees for access to, 11–12, 28
  finding, 11
  free or low-cost editions of, 7

reasons to be in public domain, 5
saving on permission fees, 9–10
uses of, 6–10
See also Copyright claims, spurious; Copyright notice, works in public domain due to lack of; Sources of public domain works
Publicity. *See* Right of publicity
Publicity releases, 361–362

Q

Quasi-governmental organizations, 49, 137, 157
Quasi-official legal documents, 54
Quotations, 35–36, 266–268, 395, 397

R

Recipes for food and drink, 24, 57–58
Recleffing of sheet music, 102
Recordings. *See* Sound recordings
Registration of copyright. *See* Copyright registration
Registration of trademarks. *See* Trademark registration
Reliance parties, 278–282
Religious services, copyrighted music used in, 83
Renewal of copyright. *See* Copyright renewal
Renewal term, 320–321, 372
Reprints. *See* Republished works
Reproduction rights, 4
Republished works
with new matter added, 42, 380–381
of public domain writing, 35, 42
registration record of, 388
renewal stated in copyright notice, 323, 376
secondary meaning of titles and, 247
of sheet music, 84
See also New editions

Research
facts discovered by author during, 265–266
fair use in, 394, 395
Restatement (Third) of Unfair Competition, 362
Restoration of copyright. *See* Copyright restoration
Reviews
artist's work distributed for, 127
book title used in, 249
quoting a work in, 395, 396
Revisions and elaborations, editorial, 65
Rhythms, 104
Right of publicity, 21, 357–362
crowd shots and, 360
for dead people, 360–361
defining characteristics of, 357
film or photograph of dance and, 216
films and, 179, 216, 357, 360
lawsuit for violation of, 357
limitations on, 357–360
model law on, 362
photographs and, 160, 216, 357, 360, 366
photo of actor in advertisement and, 366
publicity releases and, 361–362
in state, not federal, laws, 361
television programs and, 184
videos and, 357, 360
Rights given to copyright owner, 4, 22
limited by fair use, 394
Royalties
for digital uses of sheet music, 85
mechanical royalties, 82–83
performance royalties, 82, 105
for use of your own arrangements, 105
"Royalty free," 158
Rule of the shorter term, 285, 294–297, 375
Russia, copyright terms in, 293–294

S

Satire, 401

Scanned images
  of public domain artworks, 146
  of public domain photographs, 156, 308
  See also Digital copies

Scènes à faire, 264–265

Scholarly editions, 68–69

Scholarship
  attribution by authors and, 253
  fair use and, 35–36, 394, 395, 396
  public domain materials used in, 9

Screenplays
  copyright status of film and, 173
  public domain novels to use for, 40–41

Sculptures, 121
  structures or structural elements as, 202–203
  See also Art, original works

Search firms
  for copyright renewal searches, 377
  for trademark searches, 364

Secondary meaning of titles, 243
  derivative works and, 248
  disclaimer and, 248–249
  republishing a public domain work and, 247
  of series, 245, 246
  use in other media and, 246

Selection and arrangement
  of collection of hyperlinks, 312
  of facts in a database, 222, 223
  of material in factual works, 269
  of material on a website, 308–310
  plot of fictional work and, 261
  of public domain collections, 237, 238–239
  of sheet music collections, 106–107

Semifree software, 189

Service marks, 138, 363, 369

SESAC, and your own arrangements, 105

Shapes
  design patents on, 139
  not copyrightable, 130
  as trademarks, 139, 363

Shareware, 189

Sheet music
  adaptations of, 85–86, 95–96, 100
  in audiovisual works, 84–85
  Canadian copyright terms, 291
  collective works composed of, 95–96, 100, 106–109
  copyright notice on, 88, 89–90, 93–94
  derivative works and, 94–95
  in digital products, 85
  educational uses of, 83, 85
  with elements in public domain, 109–111
  expiration of copyright, 93
  foreign music with restored copyright, 92
  ideas underlying, 110
  lack of copyright notice and, 93
  new editions of, 101–102
  nonprofit or religious performance and, 83
  publication for copyright purposes, 86–93
  public performance and, 82, 83, 87, 105
  recording of, 82–84, 87–88
  reference works on, 90–91
  reproduction of, 84
  simplified versions of, 105
  sound recording copyright and, 81–82, 112–113
  sources of public domain music, 111–112
  on television programs, 84–85
  uses of public domain music, 82–86
  in videos, 84–85
  See also Arrangements of music; Music

Short phrases, and copyright, 54–55
Slogans
  not protected by copyright, 54–55
  as trademarks, 363
Smithsonian Institution, 49, 50, 137, 157
Software. *See* Computer software
Songs. *See* Sheet music
Song titles, 111
Sonny Bono Copyright Term Extension Act, 319
Sorority events, copyrighted music used at, 83
Sound recordings, 112–117
  Canadian copyright terms, 290–291
  Chinese copyright terms, 292
  copyright notices for, 115, 338, 339, 345
  copyright symbol for, 338
  copyright terms in U.S., 113–114, 115,
    331–333
  dedicated to the public domain, 117
  European Union copyright terms, 288–289
  fees for your own arrangements, 105
  of foreign works in U.S., 332–333
  on the Internet, 116
  Japanese copyright terms, 293
  noncommercial use of orphan works, 114–115
  nonprofit or religious performance and, 83
  of sheet music, 82–84, 87–88
  sheet music copyright and, 81–82, 112–113
  of spoken words, 66, 116
  state laws and, 113, 115, 331, 345
  by U.S. government, 116
  See also Music
Sources of public domain works
  architectural plans, 202
  art, 140
  art reproductions, 148

computer software, 193
films, 184
maps, 212
photographs, 150, 161
sheet music, 111–112
television programs, 184
written works, 75–78
Standard Reference Data Program, 49, 229
State contract law
  protecting ideas, 254
  suit for violating a license and, 29
State copyright law, 22, 24
  choreography and, 215
  quotations and, 268
  sound recordings and, 113, 115, 331, 345
State governments
  collections compiled by, 239
  components of, 45
  databases created by, 230
  Internet content created by, 301
  laws and court decisions of, 47, 52
  maps created by employees of, 209
  model codes used by, 53
  quasi-official legal documents used by, 54
  written works by employees of, 47
State laws. *See* Right of publicity; State contract
  law; State copyright law; Trademarks; Trade
  secrets; Unfair competition laws
State trademark registration, 363–364
Stock characters, 253, 262–264
Stock photos, license fees for, 12, 150, 308, 311,
  392
Streaming of recorded music, 83
Styles, artistic, 131

Symbols
    generic, 368
    on maps, 212
    not copyrightable, 130, 131
    as trademarks, 138, 362
Synchronization licenses, 84–85
Syndication of TV programs, 180–181

T

Television programs, 179–184
    Chinese copyright terms, 292
    copyrighted visual art in, 183
    expiration of copyright, 180–181
    Japanese copyright terms, 293
    lack of copyright notice and, 182
    publication for copyright purposes, 180–181
    right of publicity and, 184
    sheet music copyright and, 84–85
    sources of public domain programs, 184
    syndication of, 180–181
    trademarks appearing in, 183–184, 367
    by U.S. government employees, 182
    used for advertising or other commercial
        purposes, 183–184
Terms and Conditions, 310–311
Themes in fiction, 253, 261
Thin copyright
    of collections, 237, 238–239
    of collections of sheet music, 106, 107, 108
    of databases, 223
3D printing of artworks, 146
Title availability search, 243
Titles, 242–249
    of copyrighted works, 242–246, 248
    disclaimers to avoid confusion, 248–249

to identify goods and services, 249
    informational or editorial uses of, 249
    movie title private registration, 246
    of public domain works, 246–249
    renewal of copyright under different title, 380
    of series of works, 245, 246
    of songs, 111
    as trademarks, 242–246, 248, 249, 363
    unfair competition laws and, 242–245, 246,
        248, 249
    See also Secondary meaning of titles
Trade dress, 138, 363
Trademark dilution, 244–245
Trademark infringement, 362, 364, 365, 369
Trademark registration, 363–364
    of series titles, 245
    symbol of, 139, 160, 245, 369
    of titles used on merchandise, 249
Trademarks, 21, 362–369
    abandonment of, 368
    architectural photographs used as, 159
    artworks used as, 133, 138–139
    buildings used as, 159, 204–206
    clothing designs and, 135
    computer software and, 192
    definition of, 362
    determining whether something is, 363–364
    domain names and, 312
    fictional characters and, 363, 365–366
    films and, 179, 364, 366–367
    generic words or symbols and, 368
    informational or editorial uses of, 367
    interior design used as, 206
    limits on protection by, 366–368
    names of fonts and, 136

photographs containing, 150, 159, 160, 364

public domain materials and, 364–367

television programs containing, 183–184, 367

titles used as, 242–246, 248, 249, 363

types of, 363

Trademark searches, 245, 363–364

to determine whether abandoned, 368

professional search firms and, 364

Trade secrets, 21

collections as, 240

computer software and, 192

databases as, 233–234

facts protected as, 257

ideas protected as, 254–255

legal status of, 233

Transformative uses of copyrighted material, 395–396, 399, 400

Translations into new language, 66

copyright renewal and, 379

Translations into new medium, 66

copyright renewal and, 379

Transposition of music, 102

Tweets, 55

Typeface designs, 135–136

countries with copyright of, 285

Typography

Chinese copyright of, 292

countries with copyright of, 285

U

Unfair competition laws

protecting hot news, 258

titles and, 242–245, 246, 248, 249

United Kingdom

copyright coverage in, 285

copyright terms in, 297, 298

counterpart to fair use in, 393

United Nations, works prepared by, 49

Unpublished works

before and after 1978, 24–25

by authors dead more than 70 years, 324–325

copyright notice not required on, 343

copyright terms for, 324–327

fair use and, 397–398, 399, 400

films, 170

made for hire more than 120 years ago, 325–326

published outside U.S. before 1978, 329–330

registered before 1978, 326–327

registration of copyright, 25

state copyright law and, 22, 24

state or local government documents, 47

See also Publication for copyright purposes

U.S. currency and coins, art on, 137

U.S. Department of Commerce, reference data, 49, 229

U.S. Geological Survey (USGS), maps by, 209–210

U.S. government

agency logos and insignias, 137, 157

branches and agencies, 45

making copyright claims in foreign countries, 229

quasi-official legal documents used by, 54

U.S. government contractors, works of

databases, 228

films, 177

software, 190

sound recordings, 116

written works, 45–47

See also Works made for hire

U.S. government employees, works of
architectural plans, 199–200
art, 136–137
art reproductions, 136
collections, 239
created outside of official duties, 43–44
databases, 228, 229
films, 176–177
Internet content, 301
maps, 209–210
photographs, 156–157
quotations, 267
software, 189, 190
sound recordings, 116
television programs, 182
writings, 42–44, 48, 49–50
See also U.S. government written works
U.S. government written works
anticounterfeiting rules and, 49–50
classified, 48
copyrighted works containing materials of, 44
by independent contractors, 45–47
not publicly available, 48
by officers or employees, 42–44, 48, 49–50
U.S. Patent and Trademark Office (PTO)
patent law and, 256
registration of series titles, 245
registration of trademarks, 363–364, 369
Useful articles
copyrightable design features of, 132–133
copyrightable representations of, 132
copyright notices for, 339–340
patent and trademark protection, 133

V

Veterans' organizations, copyrighted music used by, 83
Video games, and sheet music copyright, 85
Videogram licenses, 84–85
Videos
Canadian copyright terms, 290
crowd shots in, 360
dedicated to public domain, 182–183
pirated copies on YouTube, 184
right of publicity and, 357, 360
sheet music copyright and, 84–85

W

Websites
as collective works, 70, 308–310
copyright notice on, 70
format and layout, 302
hyperlinks and, 312
republishing sheet music on, 84
See also Internet content
Wikipedia, license used by, 306
Words
generic, 368
never protected by copyright, 54
as trademarks, 362
Works made for hire
defining criteria of, 326
published without copyright notice, 349
term if published after 1977, 322
term if unpublished, 325–327
for U.S. government, 45–46
See also U.S. government contractors, works of

Works of authorship, 4, 22

Written works

blank forms, 55–57

categories never protected by copyright, 39, 42

choreographic notation in, 215

compilations, 73–74

dedicated to public domain, 58–59

expiration of copyright, 62–63

foreign government works, 49

information that is common property in, 57

lack of copyright notice and, 63

laws and court decisions, 51–53

misuse of copyright notices on, 74, 77–78

pathways to public domain, 38–39

publication for copyright purposes, 59–62

of quasi-governmental organizations, 49, 137, 157

quasi-official legal documents, 54

recipes, 24, 57–58

reprints of public domain works, 35, 42

sources of public domain works, 75–77, 78

state and local government works, 47

U.S. government works, 42–47, 48, 49–51

uses of public domain works, 34–38

words and phrases, 54–55

See also Compilations; Derivative works from written works; Public domain elements in copyrighted writings

Y

YouTube videos, 184

On Nolo.com you'll also find:

Books & Software

Nolo publishes hundreds of great books and software programs for consumers and
business owners. Order a copy, or download an ebook version instantly, at Nolo.com.

Online Forms

You can quickly and easily make a will or living trust, form an LLC or corporation,
apply for a provisional patent, or make hundreds of other forms—online.

Free Legal Information

Thousands of articles answer common questions about everyday legal issues,
including wills, bankruptcy, small business formation, divorce, patents,
employment, and much more.

Plain-English Legal Dictionary

Stumped by jargon? Look it up in America's most up-to-date source for
definitions of legal terms, free at Nolo.com.

Lawyer Directory

Nolo's consumer-friendly lawyer directory provides in-depth profiles of lawyers all
over America. You'll find information you need to choose the right lawyer.

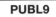